Computer Architecture and Organization

Shuangbao Paul Wang

Computer Architecture and Organization

Fundamentals and Architecture Security

 Springer

Shuangbao Paul Wang
Department of Computer Science
Morgan State University
Baltimore, MD, USA

ISBN 978-981-16-5661-3   ISBN 978-981-16-5662-0   (eBook)
https://doi.org/10.1007/978-981-16-5662-0

Jointly published with Higher Education Press
The print edition is not for sale in China (Mainland). Customers from China (Mainland) please order the print book from: Higher Education Press

This Springer imprint is published by the registered company Springer Nature Singapore Pte Ltd.
The registered company address is: 152 Beach Road, #21-01/04 Gateway East, Singapore 189721, Singapore

To my father who educated thousands of students, including his sons. To my 93-year-old mother who cares me throughout my journey. To my wife, Ruming, and daughters, Jennifer and Jane, for their love and endless support.

Preface

This book introduces a new realm of computing architecture that incorporates computer architecture, computer organization, and the science of security into trusted computer and chip design.

The book covers a spectrum of topics in cache and nonvolatile memory, instructional set architecture (ISA), reduced instruction set computer (RISC-V), hyper-threading, virtualization, trusted computing modules (TPMs), field-programmable gate arrays (FPGAs), graph and queue theories, cryptographic hardware, and instruction-level parallelism. In addition, the book also discusses quantum computing architecture, quantum random number generator (QRNG), quantum key distribution (QKD), and post-quantum cryptography (PQC).

The book is essential for computer science, computer engineering, and cybersecurity professionals to thrive in today's digital age and survive in the workplace. It features an innovative design approach with practical skills to modern computer architecture and organization from author's cutting-edge research in architecture security and quantum leap.

Traditionally, computers and microcomputing chips were designed mainly for speed and performance. Security has been a weak point for most CPUs and computers on the market. As a result, attackers are able to use sophisticated techniques to penetrate into cache memory in modern CPUs, therefore, to break the isolation principle of virtualization, which causes vulnerabilities in cloud computing systems. This book integrates security in every aspect of computer architecture and system design, aiming to design and develop next-generation computers that have less vulnerabilities and are immune from attacks. In this book, the author illustrates theoretical concepts with easy-to-understand examples to explain the perception and practical implementations.

This book is intended for undergraduate and graduate students, engineers, cybersecurity professionals, and researchers who are interested in design and develop trusted computer architecture and systems. The book can also be used as a gateway for career-changing individuals who want to enter computer and cybersecurity field but their educational background was not in computer science and information technology related fields.

The book comes with a website that provides slides, further readings, and updates for students and lecture notes for instructors. *Computer Architecture and Organization* provides readers with not only the sections that the traditional textbooks contain but also the latest development of computing architecture, security, and quantum computing technologies.

Acknowledgments

The author would like to acknowledge Dr. Robert S. Ledley, who was the inventor of body CT scanner, a doctoral adviser, mentor, and supervisor for his vision in computing and being a coauthor of the first "Computer Architecture and Security" book published in 2013.

The author would like to thank IBM for the initial training at the Yorktown research center and providing the quantum computing resources. MIT's quantum computing certificate program provides cutting-edge theoretical and practical knowledge, especially the lectures taught by the renowned Professor Dr. Peter Shor.

The author would also like to extend gratitude to Ms. Ying Feng for her incredible help in preparing this manuscript.

Contents

About the Author

Dr. Shuangbao Paul Wang is a Professor and Chair of Computer Science at the Morgan State University. He is a LINK Fellow in Advanced Simulation and Training. Paul has held positions as TSYS Endowed Chair in Cybersecurity by a $5 million endorsement, Director of Center for Security Studies with more than 3000 cyber students, and Chief Information and Technology Officer (CIO/CTO) of the National Biomedical Research Foundation (NBRF). He has been a consultant to many companies and serving on multiple boards and government and private sector technology committees. Paul was directly involved in drafting of the National Initiatives of Cybersecurity Education (NICE) framework. His research areas are secure architecture, quantum algorithms, AI/ML IoT/CPS, cryptology, and video indexing.

In addition to books, referred publications, conference speakers, and numerous grant activities, including recent grants from the NSF, NSA, Apple, and Microsoft, Paul has four patents; three of them had been licensed to the industry. In teaching, one of his students appeared in *Time* magazine for doing his class project, which he commercialized. One of his published papers ranked the first place in ScienceDirect's TOP25 Hottest Articles. His research was awarded the Best Invention Award in Entrepreneurship Week USA. Paul was feathered in ACM and a number of news outlets.

Paul received his Ph.D. under Dr. Robert S. Ledley, the inventor of body CT scanner, a member of the National Academy of Sciences, a recipient of the National Medal of Technology, and an inductee of the National Inventors Hall of Fame. Paul received his post-doc certificates in Quantum Computing from the MIT following a renowned scholar Dr. Peter Shor and in Data Science from the University of Cambridge.

During 1994–1999, Paul was the Director of the Institute of Information Science and Technology at Qingdao (ISTIQ), where he oversaw more than 120 faculty and staff, acquired 12 grants, received 18 academic awards, and was the PI for over 15 grants and projects. Paul is credited for setting up the first city-wide Internet Service Provider (ISP) in 1995 and for inventing flash memory as early as 1985, three years before the first commercial flash memory came down to earth.

Chapter 1
Introduction to Computer Architecture and Organization

A computer is composed of a number of difference components: hardware, software, network, data, and the interactions between those elements for executing instructions to solve problems that can be computed. Turing machine sets up the theoretical foundation for computer science in modeling hardware, algorithms, and computation.

The modern concept of hardware can be either physical or virtual. Virtual hardware is actually a piece of software that emulates the functionalities of specific computer hardware. Software can be divided into two categories: data and programs. Programs are collection of instructions for manipulating data and yield results.

Computer architecture is the study of designing computer systems. It includes the central processing unit (CPU), instructions, computer memory and storage, input and output devices (I/O), and network components.

Computer organization involves studying the level of abstractions above the digital logic level, but below the operating system level. It refers to the operational units and their interconnections that realize or recognize the specifications of computer architecture.

All computer systems have vulnerabilities that could be compromised. Many attack-preventing mechanisms are based on passive techniques. They only work after attacks have taken place.

Figure 1.1 shows a conceptual model of general computing systems. In addition to Neuman model, a network component is added for data flow in and out of the computer systems.

Figure 1.2 shows a conceptual model of a secure computer system. Note that it has a sandbox that "separates" the computer system from the outside world. In this book, we call it a virtual semi-conductor or semi-"network conductor." It allows the computer operator to control information and data access so that hackers are no longer able to steal data from the computer system. We will discuss this in more detail in the following chapters.

© The Author(s), under exclusive license to Springer Nature Singapore Pte Ltd. 2021
S. P. Wang, *Computer Architecture and Organization*,
https://doi.org/10.1007/978-981-16-5662-0_1

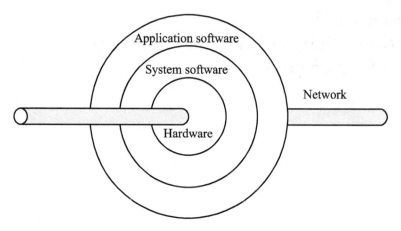

Fig. 1.1 A conceptual diagram of a common computer system

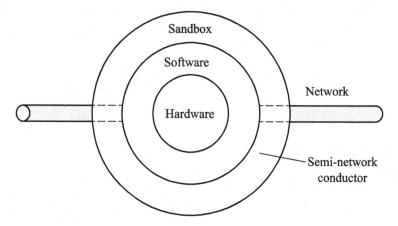

Fig. 1.2 A conceptual diagram of a secured computer system

Computer Architecture and Organization introduces fundamentals of computer systems, examines security of computer components, presents cutting-edge topics in computing, and teaches you how to design next-generation computer systems that can be trusted and free of vulnerabilities.

1.1   History of Computer Systems

Computers originally mean to compute or to calculate. The Electronic Numerical Integrator and Calculator (ENIAC) was used to calculate bomb trajectories and to develop hydrogen bombs during WWII. John von Neumann, professor of Princeton University, developed a stored-program electronic computer in 1945. It is generally accepted as the first digital computer. The von Neumann architecture has been the foundation of modern computers.

Early computers were made of vacuum tubes. Solid-state transistors were used in the mid-1960s to the early 1970s. Then integrated circuits (IC) were used on Minicomputer PDP-11 in 1970, supercomputer CDC (Cray), and mainframe IBM 360. Intel 8080 and Zilog Z80 are 8-bit processors made of large-scale IC. Later, Intel's 8086 (16-bit), 80286 (16-bit), and Motorola's 68000 (16/32-bit) made of very large-scale IC (VLSI) opened the era of so-called microcomputers.

The uses of microcomputers were greatly increased by the software development. UNIX/Linux and MS-DOS which later became Windows are still being used as operating systems today. FORTRAN, C, Java, Python, and many other computer languages assist software developers to program new software applications.

Now computers have grown from single-chip single-core processor to multiple processors each with multiple cores. Smart phones and pads have the ability to handle information and data for most people. Microcontrollers such as Raspberry Pi and Arduino have shown advantages in Internet of things (IoT) applications.

1.1.1 Timeline of Computer History

The timeline of computer history covers the most important advancements in computer research and development during the 1939 to 1988 period. During that period, Hewlett-Packard (HP), ENIAC computer, Harvard Mark I, EDVAC, IBM System/360, CDC 6600, PIP-11, Intel's 8080, Apple I, Cray I, TRS-80, DEC's VAX 11/780, Microsoft's MS-DOS Operating System, IBM-PC/XT, Motorola 68000, and Apple Macintosh are the milestones (Computer history 2019).

Innovation and commercialization are the main characteristics during these 50 years of period. After that, DEC announced the 64-bit RISC-based Alpha chip architecture in 1992. The same year, IBM manufactured a prototype of SSD module using non-violate memory. The IBM Deep Blue supercomputer defeated world chess champion Garry Kasparov. In 2006, Amazon launched cloud-based services. Infrastructure as a Service (IaaS) and Platform as a Service (PaaS) made it possible to use "virtual hardware" for computing. A UK company released a credit card size single-board computer, Raspberry Pi, for $25–$35 in 2010. In 2017, IBM unveiled its 17-qubit quantum computer. Recently, IBM announced the birth of its 65-qubit quantum computer. A 1000-qubit quantum computer is expected by 2023.

1.1.2 Timeline of Internet History

The timeline of Internet history covers the most important advancements in Internet research and development from the year 1962 to 1995. During that period, ASCII code, ARPANET, FTP, the symbol for address Telnet, Vint Cerf and Bob Kahn's "internetting" demonstration, TCP/IP, ISO OSI, Novell, DNS, routers, Netscape, WWW, and the Mosaic browser were discovered.

In about 40 years, the Internet has become a vital part of our daily life. Technology innovation speeds fast. On the other hand, computer and network security emerged as the result of worms, viruses, and malicious attacks.

It is worth mentioning that the author of this book launched the first city-level Internet Service Provider in the country in 1995. The backbone was based on a satellite communication link. The Cisco gateway cost some $50,000. He then established an Internet Society in Qingdao, a city with more than eight million people back then, and later became the founding President. The institution he worked as Director made a profit by offering training for people to learn how to navigate the Internet.

1.1.3 Timeline of Computer Security History

Since the 1990s, attacks on computers and networks have become common. The situation is getting worse in recent years. The attacks shut down the oil pipelines, steal sensitive data, and slow down or stop servers and network communication.

The notable events in the last 20 years are $10 million hack from Citibank by Russian hackers, a 15-year-old who penetrated the US Air Force base in Guam, the logic bomb planted in Yahoo, the $1.46 billion computer security initiative announced by then Present Bill Clinton, the formation of the hacker group: Anonymous, the US Office of Personnel Management (OPM) attack which had 22 million federal employee's data exposed to adversaries, and RSA Security which had 40 million employee records stolen. Recent research has revealed that newer CPUs are vulnerable to Spectre and Meltdown exploits that are caused by CPU architecture. Cache memory hierarchy, pipelines, conditional branches, and exceptions, technologies used to speed up CPUs, could expose security risks. This book aims to address these problems and provide solutions in designing secure architecture and computer systems.

1.2 John von Neumann Computer Architecture

The Neumann architecture was the first design of a modern computer based on the stored program concept (Dumas 2006). Figure 1.3 shows a block diagram of the Neumann architecture. The arithmetic and logic units are where calculations take place. The control unit interprets the instructions and coordinates the operations. Memory (MEM) is used to store instructions and data as well as intermediate results. Input and output (I/O) interfaces are used to read data and write results.

Neumann defines a computer as a "very high speed automatic digital computing system, and in particular with its logical control" (Foster and Iberall 1985).

Fig. 1.3 Neumann computer
architecture

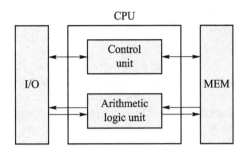

As a computing device, it will have to perform elementary arithmetic operations including addition, subtraction, multiplication, and division. It may be extended to include such operations as square roots, logarithmic, and triangulation (sin, cos, arcsin, arccos, etc.). This part is the central arithmetical (CA) component which later is considered as the central arithmetic and logic unit (ALU).

The logic control component is to efficiently sequence its operations carried out by a central control (CC) component. A considerable memory is needed to carry out a multiplication or a division and remember a series of intermediate results. At any rate the total memory constitutes the specific part of a computer system: M.

The three specific parts CA, CC (together C which is now named the central processing unit), and M correspond to the associate neurons in the human nervous system. There are input and output components equivalent to those of the motor or efferent neurons.

In summary, Neumann architecture depicts a computer as a machine with a central processing unit (CPU), internal memory (M) and external storage (S), input/output devices (I/O), and circuits which when linked together are called a bus.

Nowadays, computers still stick on this architecture. When we purchase a computer, we usually consider how fast the CPU, how large the memory and hard drive, and how well the I/O, such as the video card, screen resolution, and multimedia features.

RISC, or reduced instruction set computer, is another type of computer architecture that utilizes a small, highly optimized set of instructions, rather than a more specialized set of instructions. RISC processors have a CPI (clock per instruction) of one cycle (Shiva 2000). This is due to the optimization of each instruction on the CPU and a technique called pipelining. Pipelining allows for simultaneous execution of instructions to speed up the execution speed. RISC also uses large number of registers to prevent large amounts of interactions with memory.

RISC-V is an open instruction set architecture that is originally developed at Berkeley. It starts to address the very expensive design costs by forming a large community working collaboratively. It has widespread industry support from chip and device makers and is designed to be freely extensible and customizable to fit in any market.

Parallel processing architecture uses multiple processors to form a supercomputer to solve very large problems. The task is often broken into small ones and distributed across the multiple processors or machines and solved concurrently.

From security point of view, both RISC architecture and parallel processing architecture still fall into the Neumann architecture category. RISC uses one cycle execution time to improve the efficiency in pipelining. The change is mostly within the processors. The other system components (memory, I/O, storage) still the same as Neumann's. Parallel processing, on the other hand, contains multiple processors or computers. Each one is a Neumann architecture computer.

1.3   Memory and Storage

As Neumann has described, memory is used to carry out arithmetic operations and remember intermediate results. There are two factors to the memory that affect a computer speed the most: the size and the speed. More memory can bring in less intermediate results storage and less operations therefore improve computer speed. High speed memory can reduce the delays during each operation. A complex problem requires tremendous amount of computation. Thus, the delay would be significant if a low speed memory is used.

The ideal memory can be characterized as zero or less delay in read and write access, large scale or high density in size, reliable and durable, less expensive, and low power. That is why memory is now divided into different categories. Memory closer to the CPU is usually faster and more expensive, so it is usually small in capacity. Memory further away from the CPU is usually slower and less expensive, so it is usually large in capacity. We often refer to memory that attaches to the motherboard through a bus or network as storage. USB flash drives and hard drives are examples of external memories or storage.

The read and write property makes memory convenient to store data. On the other hand, it also is easy to be altered if a computer is compromised. So, memory needs to be defined into regions where program and data are separated. In addition, some policies and security measures need to be implemented.

A computer memory is organized into hierarchies centered with the CPU. Registers are the fastest memory. They are specially wired to guarantee the maximum speed. Cache memory is the next fast memory. The idea to use cache is to reduce the time for CPU to read/write data directly from the main memory, as this may cause longer delay. Cache memory, which usually uses static RAM or SRAM, is accessed by blocks and is often divided into two or three levels. The main memory has a much larger capacity to store applications and data. It usually uses dynamic RAM or DRAM, a type of memory that is cheaper and can be highly integrated but with a little bit less speed than SRAM.

Hard drives are external memory or storage that has the vast amount of capacity. Solid-state drive (SSD) is a newer type of storage that acts as normal hard drives but without mechanical movements, so they are more reliable and faster. With technology advancement, SSDs are becoming cheaper and more affordable.

Virtual memory emerges as a result of applications which utilize more and more memory. Virtual memory by its name is virtual. There is no physical memory associated with it. In computers, virtual memory uses a region of external memory to store programs and data.

The main memory is usually divided into different segments: program, data, data buffers, and so on. If a segment, for example, the data buffer, is extended beyond the limit reserved for that segment, then overflow may affect the other segments. If data overflow to the program segment, then programs may execute with unexpected results. If the overflow is set by an attacker, then it may direct program execution to some preset areas where malicious programs reside, the attacker may take control of the computer system and do even more damage to the computer systems across the network. This is called a buffer overflow attack.

1.4 Input, Output, and Network Interface

Computer systems typically have several I/O devices. The I/O interface is used to receive data in or write data out with devices such as a keyboard, a mouse, displays, and printers.

Comparing with the speed of CPU and memory, a keyboard is a very slow device, so an input interface can store data temporally typed from a keyboard and send to memory when reaching the capacity (or buffer size).

A display with animation however requires high speed to refresh the screen data. So, the interface (video card) needs more speed and more buffer size (or video memory) to accommodate.

Sometimes, we need to send volume data from input devices to the computer memory without requiring any computation or vice versa. We do this by using an interface called direct memory access (DMA). The benefit for using a DMA is that data will not go through the CPU so a computer can handle other tasks, while block data are read in or write out (Randell 1982).

Now computers are interconnected through network or the Internet. Most people tweet, stream, or check E-mails every hour, if not sooner. Vast information can be found on the Internet. So, a network interface card (NIC) has become an integral part of a computer system to handle data communication needs.

Computer networks did not exist in Neumann's age, so there was no network component on old computers. People usually consider a network component essentially belongs to input and output devices. When we look carefully at the differences between a general I/O and a network component, we can find out that a network by no means can be considered simply as a general I/O device.

With the widespread use of the Internet since the 1990s, data security has become a problem. Hackers are able to break into computers and servers to steal data, in many cases sensitive data. The loss caused by the data breach reached multiple billion dollars every year and is still on the increase. The damage is beyond money and threaten the national security. As a result, network security has become a big challenge in everyday computer and cloud operations.

I/O devices have slower speed compared with processors. Synchronous communication between them may cause problems. I/O devices will lose data if the CPU sends/receives data using processor cycles. On the other hand, considering the I/O device speed, the CPU would have to wait during each I/O operation. Thus, performance is downgraded. Interrupt is a signal that is used in collaborating communications between high-speed processors and low-speed I/O devices. When an I/O device has finished handling data received from the processor, it issues an interrupt request. When the CPU receives the request, it saves the current environment, sends/receives data, and then resumes the original tasks.

There are different interfaces to connect the processor and the I/O devices. Many I/O devices are equipped with the universal series bus (USB). USB unifies the interfaces with its easy to use, plug-and-play connectivity, and hot plug characteristics. In addition, the speed of the USB is considerably high that it can support most I/O devices. The new Super Speed USB 3.0 has the transfer speed of 5 Gb/s.

I/O security is also related with data security. Data stored on hard drives may be exposed to attackers especially insider attacks. Encrypting all data on hard drives is one solution, but it may result in performance or accessibility issues. USB storage devices can be used as bootable devices to start a computer. Unauthorized use can let attackers steal data on computer systems. In places where data security is a concern, USB booting should be disabled.

1.5   Single CPU and Multiple CPU Systems

Traditional computers contain one central processing unit. It is like a human brain that controls all activities and remembers all things around it. To solve a problem, an algorithm is programmed and executed as a serial stream of instructions. Only one instruction may be executed at a time.

A multiple CPU system on the other hand can process a computation task simultaneously by breaking the problem into independent parts (Hwang 1993). Each CPU then executes a portion of the problem. Such procedure is called parallel processing. Parallel processing systems contain multiple CPUs that are interconnected or manufactured together as multi-core processors.

Here is an example of a multiple CPU system compared with a single CPU system. Suppose we want to process a color picture. As we know, a color picture consists of three basic colors: red, green, and blue (RGB). If we process this picture using a computer with three CPUs, then each CPU can process on color. For a single CPU system, theoretically, it would have to take triple time to process this picture, first red, then green, and finally blue.

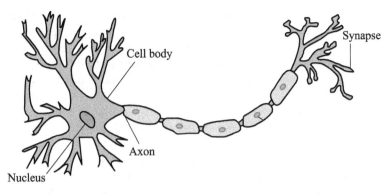

Fig. 1.4 Structure of a typical neuron (color)

People often refer to the CPU as the "brain" of a computer system. People in some parts of the world call a computer as an "electronic brain." For a multiple CPU computer system, how we correspond to a such match?

If you look inside the brain, there are about 100 billion (10^{11}) neurons. A neuron is a special type of cell that has a nucleus which contains genes and acts like the brain of the cell. It has electrical excitability and synapses used to transmit signals to other cells. Figure 1.4 shows the structure of a typical neuron.

There is a trend to add more CPUs into a computer. It by no means indicate there will be more "brains" in an identity (here is a computer). Instead people consider CPUs in parallel processing or multi-core computers as "neurons." A parallel processing computer has many CPUs, local memory, and interconnected networks. So, it does function like a neuron that contains synapses used to transmit and receive signals between neurons. This may be another explanation why no matter how many CPUs a computer has, its speed is no match with the human brain because no computer contains a million CPUs, not to mention 100 billion neurons in a human brain.

Processors were originally developed with only one core. More and more computers use multi-core processor where each core acts like an independent processor. The architecture of multi-core processor can be organized as each core contains a CPU and level 1 and 2 cache. A bus interface connects all cores and also provides with level 3 cache. All cores and interfaces are integrated on one circuit (one die).

More advanced parallel processing computer systems use multiple processors or an array of processors to form a supercomputer. The processors can be at a centralized location, or they can be at distributed locations.

In corporate businesses, more companies and organizations use services provided for them instead of buying a number of powerful computers (servers). This leads to the cloud computing concept. In the cloud computing model, some companies build the cloud which contains applications, platforms, and infrastructure. Other companies or organizations act as users to use these infrastructure, software, and platform as services. Since different organizations may share the same cloud, data separation and security are a common concern for running critical applications that contain sensitive data in a cloud. Since level 3 cache is shared by all cores or virtual processors, it may cause breaches in isolation in a cloud environment.

On the other hand, thin clients also have the momentum as the client is cheaper; consumes much less energy, therefore "greener"; and is easy to manage. Thin clients use computation power of a remote computer. The technology is perfect for situations where high-speed network is available and animation is not the main concern.

Distributed computing may have tremendous power to accomplish jobs that otherwise cannot be done with traditional computers. Pharmaceutical companies use hundreds of thousands of computers distributed across the country to simulate clinical tests. It can greatly shorten the time for a new drug test. Sophisticated computer hackers can also benefit from using the distributed computing platform. They were able to shut down VISA/Master card company's websites and other government websites. They launched the so-called distributed denial of service attackers, or DDoS attacks.

In a typical DDoS attack, the army of the attacker consists of master zombies and slave zombies. The hosts of both categories are compromised machines that have risen during the scanning process and are infected by malicious codes. The attacker coordinates and orders master zombies, and they, in turn, coordinate and trigger slave zombies. More specifically, the attacker sends an attack command to master zombies and activates all attack processes on those machines, which are in hibernation, waiting for the appropriate command to wake up and start attacking. Then, master zombies, through those processes, send attack commands to slave zombies, ordering them to mount a DDoS attack against the victim. In that way, the agent machines (slave zombies) begin to send a large volume of packets to the victim, flooding its system with useless load and exhausting its resources. Figure 1.5 shows this kind of DDoS attack.

1.6   Overview of Computer Security

Computer security relies on confidentiality, integrity, and availability, or in short CIA. A more comprehensive description includes:

- Authentication
- Authorization
- Confidentiality
- Integrity
- Availability
- Accountability
- Non-repudiation

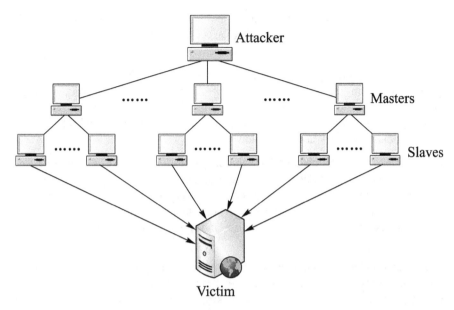

Fig. 1.5 A DDoS attack

Certified information systems security professional (CISSP) classifies information security into eight domains:

• Security and Risk Management
• Asset Security
• Security Architecture and Engineering
• Communications and Network Security
• Identity and Access Management
• Security Assessment and Testing
• Security Operations
• Software Development Security

1.6.1 Confidentiality

From an information security point of view, confidentiality is the concealment of information or resources. From the computer architecture perspective, confidentiality entails designing a computer system that is capable of protecting data and preventing intruders from stealing data in computer systems.

Access control mechanisms support confidentiality. A software solution to enforce access control mechanism is cryptography, which encrypts data to make it incomprehensible. A hardware solution is physical separation. Totally physical separation is impractical, so in many cases, we use the hybrid method which is partial physical separation plus (software) access control polices.

Below are two examples that further describe the concept of confidentiality.

Example 1.1 A company named GEE does not want competitors to be able to see exactly how many or which equipment its clients have been ordering from the company, because that may give them competitive information. So, GEE uses a secure protocol to encrypt all communication between its clients and the website. (More examples on this case will follow.)

Example 1.2 A newly proposed computer model enables a computer operator (owner) to control what data can go in and go out. Nobody can get data from this computer system without the permission of the computer operator. In this way, the confidentiality is guaranteed. Interested readers can read Appendix A for detailed technical description about how to design and implement such a secure computer system.

Information hiding is another important aspect of confidentiality. For example, a program can encrypt a secret message into a picture. Only people with the program (or key) can reveal the secret. Without the key, people can only view it as a normal image. An example of such encryption application programmed by the book author can be downloaded from the book website.

1.6.2   Integrity

Integrity refers to the trustworthiness of data. There are three aspects: data in motion, data at rest, and data in use. Data in motion usually refers to the transmissions of the data. Authentication is a way to assure data integrity of this kind. Data at rest means the content of the information itself. When stored in a computer, data need to be protected and non-altered.

Here is an example following the earlier example described in Sect. 1.6.1. Suppose that a client named Alice wants to order ten equipment from GEE, but an attacker wants to alter her order to zero equipment. If the attacker succeeds, then the client may eventually get frustrated with GEE and might decide to go to a competitor.

1.6.3   Availability

Availability refers to the ability to use the information or resources desired. For enterprise applications running on a server, availability is critical to the success of the business. Attempts to block availability, called denial of service (DoS) attacks, can be difficult to detect. A distributed DoS (DDoS) attack may even harder to be identified.

When designing a secured computer system, there is a trade-off between availability and confidentiality. We understand that both are important, but for a server, availability cannot be sacrificed, while for a personal computer, we may consider sacrificing the availability a little bit to enhance confidentiality and integrity. For example, many people would agree with sacrificing a millisecond (1/1000 s) to ensure their data will never be stolen.

1.6.4   Threats

A threat is a potential violation of security. The actions that the violation might occur are called attacks. Those who execute such actions are called attackers or hackers. Here are some common threats:

- Snooping   The unauthorized interception of data, such as wiretapping
- Alteration   An unauthorized change of data, such as man-in-the-middle attack
- Spoofing   An impersonation of an entity by another
- Phishing   An email scam that attempts to acquire sensitive information
- Delay or denial of service   An inhibition of a service

Computer security involves studying, detecting, preventing, and recovering from threats. For detection, applications include the intrusion detection system (IDS) and firewalls on the network or installed on a computer. Detection is like building a dam or levee to prevent flood. It is passive and has limited protection.

Computer Architecture and Organization helps you study how to design a secure computer system that can prevent threats and attacks. In other words, the goal of a secured computer system is immunity from attacks or to perform under attacks.

For recovery, most organizations have a disaster recovery plan, a part of the security policy. In the event the security is breached, the plan will help reduce loss of data and shorten mean time between failures (MTBF).

1.6.5   Firewalls

Firewalls are software or hardware implementations of a series of algorithms that detect and filter the transmission of information and data (usually be divided into small packets). A request to access of local resources from outside the firewall can be either granted or denied depending on the policies preset. On the other hand, a request to access remote resources from the inside can also be granted or denied. Correctly configured firewalls can protect computers or local area networks while still allowing legitimate packets going through. Sometimes, it is hard to tell whether the communication is an attack string or real data. So tightly configured firewalls may block legitimate traffic, and it is called false positive. Loosely configured firewalls, on the other hand, may let the attack string pass through without being detected. This is called false negative. False negative may cause severe damage to computer systems. In our daily life, these principles are also very useful. We remember the DC Metro train crash on June 22, 2009. If the Metrorail system had a policy to stop any trains in the event of any false alarms, the accident would not have happened.

Firewalls are used to block attacks just like levees are used to block flooded river. No matter how robust the levee system is, failure may still happen. Hurricane Katrina in New Orleans is a lesson in mind. Similarly, firewalls can only have limited protection to computer systems. Attackers may find vulnerabilities in firewall algorithms and bypass the firewall to gain access to the computer systems. Computer security should not only rely on passive detecting techniques, but it should also expend its scope to work actively to prevent attacks. The invention discussed in Appendix A is such a preventing technique.

1.6.6   Hacking and Attacks

Hacking means finding out weaknesses in an established system and exploiting them. A computer hacker is a person who finds out weaknesses in the computer and exploits it. Hackers may be motivated by a multitude of reasons, such as profit, protest, or challenge (Hacker 2019). The subculture that has evolved around hackers is often referred to as the computer underground, but it is now an open community.

A white hat hacker breaks security for non-malicious reasons, for instance, testing their own security system. This classification also includes individuals who perform penetration tests and vulnerability assessments within a contractual agreement. Often, this type of "white hat" hacker is called an ethical hacker.

A black hat hacker is a hacker who violates computer security for little reasons beyond maliciousness or for personal gain. Black hat hackers are the epitome of all that the public fears in a computer criminal. They break into secure networks to destroy data or make the network unusable for those who are authorized to use the network. The way black hat hackers choose the networks that they are going to break into is through a process that can be broken down into two parts: targeting and information gathering.

Bots are automated software tools, some freeware, available for the use of any type of hacker.

An attack is to compromise a computer system. A typical approach in an attack on Internet-connected system is:

- Network enumeration   Discovering information about the intended target
- Vulnerability analysis   Identifying potential ways of attack
- Exploitation   Attempting to compromise the system by employing the vulnerabilities found through the vulnerability analysis

In order to do so, there are several recurring tools of the trade and techniques used by computer criminals and security experts.

Some common attacking techniques often used by both black hat attackers and white hat attackers are listed on the book's website.

1.7   Security Problems in Neumann Architecture

In Neumann architecture, memory, storage, and I/O are connected through a bus to the CPU. A "system bus" representation of the Neumann model is shown in Fig. 1.6. It is equivalent to Fig. 1.2 with the introduction of DMA. This is just another view of the Neumann model, with the introduction of the concept of direct memory access (DMA). DMA enables data exchange directly between memory and I/O that otherwise cannot be done with the initial Neumann model.

Since the 1990s, computer networks especially the Internet have been widespread around the world. Computers are no longer only being used to compute as a stand-alone machine. The feature of information exchange through network becomes a vital component in today's computers. Unfortunately, John von Neumann was not able to foresee this change.

One can argue that we can consider a network as part of input/output devices which are already included in the Neumann model. However, the network interface is so important that it is not appropriate to classify it as a general I/O device. Furthermore, an I/O device in the Neumann model refers to those devices, such as a keyboard, a display, and a printer, which are used for direct interacting with the computers. Now, the way people use a computer is considerably different than that 70 years ago. So, an update of Neumann's computer architecture model is necessary to reflect this change.

Figure 1.7 shows the updated Neumann model. In Fig. 1.7, a network unit (interface) is added to the bus of a computer system. The I/O unit only deals with input and output devices such as keyboard, mouse, and display. The network interface is responsible for communicating with other computer and devices over the Internet. The separation of network unit from the general I/O devices offers great advantages in architecture security analysis.

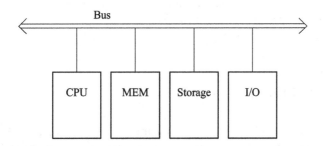

Fig. 1.6   A "system bus" representation of the Neumann model

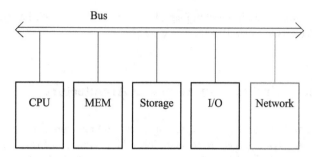

Fig. 1.7 The updated Neumann computer architecture model with network interface added and separated from the general I/O devices

The Neumann model is so dominant that no people ever dare to challenge it since its birth in 1945. However, if we look into the Neumann model from security perspective, we could find out that it does have some potential problems.

In the Neumann model, CPUs, memory, I/O, external storage, and network interface are all connected to one single bus that includes control bus, data bus, and address bus. Once intruders break into the system from any network locations, they can totally take over the computer system and do whatever they want.

For the Neumann model, the concept of CPU is a centralized control and arithmetic unit. Even though nowadays multi-processor or multi-core computer is very common, those processors are merely coordinated together by software to perform one task or a series of tasks. In other words, they share the same system bus. Intruders can still take over the whole system once they break into the system from any network port.

To solve this problem, numerous people have proposed different methods from securing CPU and memory to securing network interfaces by applying firewalls and intrusion detection systems. However, those solutions have not solved the information security problems thoroughly due to the limitation of the computer architecture they used. The author of this book has pointed out that there is a problem in the Neumann computer architecture model—the foundation of modern computer architecture. If this problem is not solved, information stored on a computer will hardly be secure. As a result, a modified Neumann architecture that is capable of securing data stored on a computer system is proposed. More information about the new secured architecture will be discussed in Appendix A.

1.8   Trusted Computing Base

Trusted computing (TC) is to guarantee the trustworthy of IT systems. It has shown promises in research, industrial projects, and military implementations. Practically, deploying a large system with trusted computing base (TCB) is still a challenge especially in IoT systems, where various protocols and legacy systems exist. Trusted computing entails building digital identities and increasing assurance of trust among devices that are connected to the network. It adds a level of security on top of what is provided by the operating systems and hardware. Trusted computing base adds a hardware device, which has non-volatile storage and cryptographic execution engines on each device.

A trusted computer system is a computer system that uses both hardware and software to ensure that security criteria are met. The security-relevant portion of the system, called the "trusted computing base," is made up of separate hardware and software components. It is the combination of these components that enforce the security requirements in a system. All programs and software outside the trusted computing base are considered untrusted.

1.9 Mobile Architecture

Modern cell phones are capable of doing basic computational works on their own or through the services in the cloud. The architecture of smart phones consists of three tiers: data, logic, and presentation.

At the data tier, information is stored and retrieved from a (light) database. The information is then passed to the logic tier for processing.

At the logic tier, a smart phone processes commands, makes logical decisions, and performs calculations. It then moves the process data to the presentation tier or data tier.

The presentation tier is the user interface that translates tasks to the logic layer and presents results to the user.

Android phones use Linux kernel. It includes a display driver, camera driver, flash memory driver, Wi-Fi driver, audio driver, power management, etc. On top, there are many software libraries including OpenGL, SQLite, SSL, Android runtime, etc. The top layer consists of applications: browser, phone, calendar, setup, maps, and a framework of resource managers.

Figure 1.8 is a typical mobile computing architecture diagram.

1.10 IoT Architecture

The Internet of things (IoT) is fed with billions of devices and trillions of sensors. IoT networks undergird critical infrastructure, such as electric grids, transportation hubs, and nuclear power plants. They also link to systems containing valuable and sensitive personal information, such as hospitals, schools, and government institutions. A failure in one of these systems or a cascade of such failures across systems, either in their operations or security, could lead to potentially catastrophic consequences for the population of that region, city, and beyond. Yet many of the hardware and software elements used to control, monitor, and connect these systems

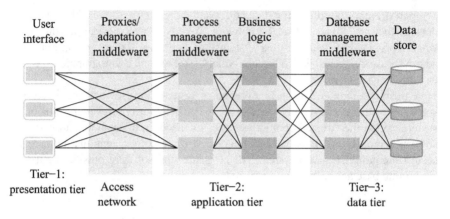

Fig. 1.8 Mobile computing architecture (color)

are not designed with built-in security, while others are outmoded and may not interface with newer technologies. For this reason, every IoT project must address the security and trust, and that can be hardened against tempering and compromise. The ideal IoT, Internet of Battlefield Things (IoBT), and Cyber Physical Systems (CPS) should be able to continue operating under attacks and provide guaranteed performance. Therefore, it is critical to secure edge devices and actuators and make IoT networks resilient in the face of cybersecurity threats.

Supervisory Control and Data Acquisition (SCADA) is a distributed Industrial Control System (ICS) which enables monitoring and control of processes distributed across remote sites. ICSs are typically used in industries such as clean water supply; water treatment plants; electric, oil, and gas; transportation; chemicals; and many other critical infrastructure sectors. SCADA systems are designed to collect data from the field, transfer it to a remote command and control center, perform data abstraction, and visualize the information to the operators and decision-makers in real time.

The paired firewall architecture uses a pair of firewalls positioned between the corporate and SCADA networks. Data servers are placed in the DMZ. The advantage of this architecture is the first firewall blocks the arbitrary packets coming to the SCADA network or servers in the DMZ. The second firewall prevents unwanted traffic from a compromised device from entering into the SCADA network, and it also prevents SCADA network traffic from impacting the shared servers in the DMZ. Figure 1.9 shows such architecture.

The defense-in-depth architecture using paired firewalls has three zones and contains one or more DMZs. It is a more secure, manageable, and segregated architecture for SCADA systems.

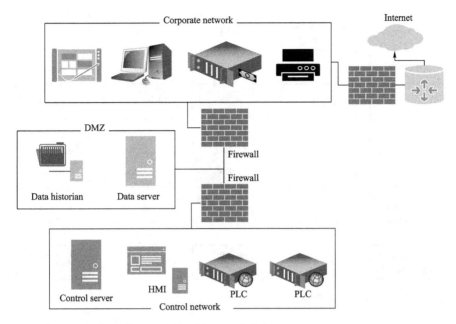

Fig. 1.9 A paired firewall secure IoT architecture (color)

1.11 Cloud Architecture

Cloud architecture refers to the various components of cloud platforms engineered to leverage the power of cloud resources from infrastructure, platforms, and software to solve business problems. Cloud architecture defines the components as well as the relationships between them.

IaaS is similar to the traditional IT infrastructure with pay-as-you-go cloud services such as storage, networking, and virtualization instead of establishing the infrastructure yourself.

PaaS contains virtual and hosted hardware and software tools available over the network. There is no need to make upgrades and updates from the client side. A user no longer "owns" the hardware and software.

SaaS is software as a service that's available via a third party over the network. On the user side, there is no need to develop, purchase, or install the software. Figure 1.10 shows the evolution from classical on premise, hosted, to cloud services.

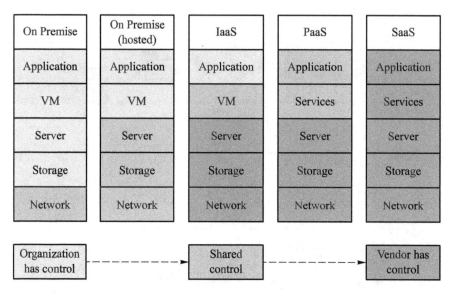

Fig. 1.10 Cloud computing architecture (color)

1.12   Summary

A computer is composed of hardware, software, network, and data. People have different views about a computer system. The level of abstraction from a computer designer and a general user is different.

Computer architecture involves the study of designing computer systems. *Computer architecture and organization* will teach you how to design secured computer systems. Moreover, this book explains how to secure computer architecture so that modern computers can be built on the new architecture that is free of data breaches.

The Neumann architecture was the first modern design for a computer based on the stored program concept. It is composed of an arithmetic and logic unit (ALU), a control unit (CU), memory (M), storage (S), and input/output (I/O) devices. With the introduction of the Internet, a network interface card (NIC) has become an integral part of a computer system.

Computer history reveals invention and innovation in early time followed by rapid network and Internet development. As technologies for both computers and networks are still growing, concerns about computer and network security are also increasing.

Computer security involves the study of confidentiality, integrity, and availability of a computer system. The Neumann system uses a single-bus architecture; therefore, it is vulnerable to attacks.

The modified Neumann architecture separates the network from other computer components. Experiments and tests have proofed that it is capable of securing data stored on a computer system.

Trusted computing guarantees the trustworthy of IT systems using Trusted Computing Base.

Mobile architecture consists of three tiers, data, logic, and presentation. The Access Network is a middleware between tier 1 presentation and tier 2 application.

Cloud architecture deals with infrastructure, platforms, and software to provide services such as IaaS, PaaS, and SaaS.

Projects

1.1 Study stories of Steve Jobs and Steve Wozniak's earlier innovation. How were they able to make the first-generation Apple computers in a garage? Write a brief report.
1.2 Many applications (such as E-mails, Word documents, and videos) run in a cloud environment. List three apps you wish to be added to the cloud service in the future.

Exercises

1.1 Describe the main components of a modern computer system.
1.2 Why is a network interface different from general I/O devices?
1.3 Traditionally, a user's view of a computer system is like an onion. Explain why this concept is outdated, and draw a new diagram based on the concept proposed in this book.
1.4 Computer firewalls are used to protect computer from data loss. Why can firewalls not guarantee data security?
1.5 What is a computer bus? Which types of data are carried on a computer bus?
1.6 What are the main advantages of the Neumann architecture compared with those of earlier computing devices?
1.7 Draw a diagram of the Neumann architecture and a single-bus diagram of the Neumann architecture.
1.8 Why is assembly language called low-level language?
1.9 Virtualization sometimes is called "computers on a computer." Describe how this works.
1.10 What are the differences between memory and storage?
1.11 Discover the NIC(s) on your computer? Is it wired or wireless?
1.12 Why is the Neumann architecture still considered the architecture for multiple CPU computers or multi-core computers?
1.13 Provide an example for each of the following security terms: authentication, authorization, confidentially, integrity, and availability.
1.14 What is cryptography? If you want to send a secret message to your friend using a computer, what is the best way to do it?

1.15 What does the term DoS attack stand for?

1.16 List some common threats to a computer system and network.

1.17 What are the problems existing in the Neumann architecture? How do you address those problems?

1.18 Trusted computing technologies now are deployed in enterprise systems, storage systems, networks, embedded systems, and mobile devices and can help secure cloud computing and virtualized systems. Describe how TPMs can secure your personal computers.

1.19 What are the differences in terms of computing between mobile devices and personal computers?

1.20 What are the main advantages using cloud services compared to the on-premise devices?

1.21 Conduct research on trusted computing architecture, and write a one-page report on recent developments on the topic.

References

Computer history. Computer history museum, Retrieved October 18, 2019.

Dumas, J. D. (2006). *Computer architecture: Fundamentals and principles of computer design.* Oxford: Taylor & Francis.

Foster, C. C., & Iberall, T. (1985). *Computer architecture* (3rd ed.). New York: van Nostrand Reinhold Company.

Hacker (computer security). Wikipedia. Retrieved February 2, 2019.

Hwang, K. (1993). *Advanced computer architecture: parallelism, scalability, programmability.* New York: McGraw-Hill, Inc.

Randell, B. (Ed.). (1982). *The designs of digital computers.* Berlin: Springer-Verlag.

Shiva, S. G. (2000). *Computer design and architecture* (3rd ed.). New York: Marcel Dekker, Inc.

Chapter 2
From Logic Circuit to Quantum Circuit

A computer consists of logic circuits that make the CPU and other components work. Logic gates are the fundamental parts inside CPUs and other circuits. After design and simulation, all circuits are taped out and sent to fabrication facility where microchips are manufactured. This chapter introduces logic gates, circuits, Boolean algebra, FPGA, and other VLSI design and case studies. Circuit level security will also be discussed.

Quantum computers follow the tradition of gates and circuits model, but quantum circuits have different meaning than digital circuits. The chapter ends with an introduction to quantum circuits.

2.1 Concept of a Logic Unit

A digital computer consists of different components. Every hardware component is made up of a large number of logic circuits. A logic circuit is an interconnection of several primitive logic components. It likes a "black box" that has one or more inputs and one or more outputs.

Input and output signals are restricted to one of the two states: on-off, one-zero, or represented as true-false. We know that the simple representation is sufficient to express all numbers we are using in daily life. We also know that the binary system is the foundation from basic logic components to computer systems.

A quantum computer uses quantum circuits that are beyond the binary systems. Details will be discussed in Chaps. 7 and 10.

Consider a logic circuit shown in Fig. 2.1. A binary system can only have value of 0 or 1; the four all possible combinations of those two inputs are listed in Fig. 2.2.

We can easily expand the pattern for three inputs. The combinations of three inputs are 8. In general, for N inputs, there will be 2^N possible combinations.

© The Author(s), under exclusive license to Springer Nature Singapore Pte Ltd. 2021   23
S. P. Wang, *Computer Architecture and Organization*,
https://doi.org/10.1007/978-981-16-5662-0_2

Fig. 2.1 A logic circuit with two inputs and one output

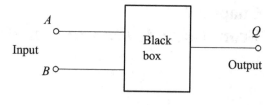

Fig. 2.2 Possible combinations of two binary inputs

A	B
0	0
0	1
1	0
1	1

Logic circuits are divided into two categories: an output which is a function of inputs at a particular time is called a combinational circuit; a circuit with "memory" is called a sequential circuit. The output of a sequential circuit is a function of not only inputs but also the state of the circuit at that time. The state of the circuit is dependent on what has happened to the circuit prior to that time. In other words, the current state of a sequential circuit is a function of previous inputs and states, so we say it has memory.

For small-scale logic, designers now use prefabricated logic gates from families of devices such as the TTL 7400 series by Texas Instruments and the CMOS 4000 series by RCA and their more recent descendants. Increasingly, these fixed-function logic gates are being replaced by programmable logic devices, which allow designers to pack a large number of mixed logic gates into a single integrated circuit. The field-programmable nature of programmable logic devices such as FPGAs has removed the "hard" property of hardware; it is now possible to change the logic design of a hardware system by reprogramming some of its components, thus allowing the features or function of a hardware implementation of a logic system to be changed.

2.2 Logic Functions and Truth Tables

Look at the input side of a black box (logic circuits) shown in Fig. 2.1. As we know, the output can only be 0 or 1. The question is how to design the logic circuit.

A	B	Q
0	0	0
0	1	0
1	0	0
1	1	1

Fig. 2.3 An example logic circuit inputs and output

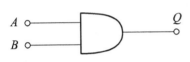

A	B	Q
0	0	0
0	1	0
1	0	0
1	1	1

Fig. 2.4 An AND gate with its truth table

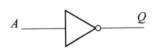

A	Q
0	1
1	0

Fig. 2.5 A NOT gate with its truth table

Example 2.1 Consider a black box with its inputs and output as shown in Fig. 2.3; what is the logic circuit inside the box?

Figure 2.3 clearly shows that the output is set to high if and only if (*iff*) both inputs are high. It is an "AND" relation. Such circuit is represented using symbol shown in Fig. 2.4. It is called an AND gate. The table (see Fig. 2.3) is called a truth table (Foster and Iberall 1985).

A NOT gate will reverse the input. It has only one input and one output. A NAND gate can be considered as a NOT gate with an AND gate. Figure 2.5 shows a NOT gate, and Fig. 2.6 shows a NAND gate.

A NAND gate functions like this way: if any of two inputs is low, then the output is set to high. On the other hand, the output is set to low *iff* both inputs are high.

Truth table is a very effective way in understanding logic circuits. It is also very useful in designing logic circuit and optimizing designs. A CMOS 4001 integrated

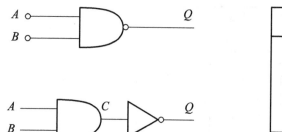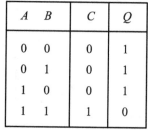

A	B	C	Q
0	0	0	1
0	1	0	1
1	0	0	1
1	1	1	0

Fig. 2.6 A NAND gate is equivalent to a NOT gate and an AND gate

circuit (IC) contains four 2-input NAND gates. You can get it online or at stores such as Micro Center or RadioShack in old times.

2.3 Boolean Algebra

The Boolean algebra is a symbolic notation to logic circuits with binary values of either true or false (Shiva 2000). We often refer to true as 1 or high (voltage) or false as 0 or low (ground). Like algebra we learned at elementary, Boolean algebra has theory to govern and theorems to define. This book will not study that part. Interested readers can find it in many computer science books. Unlike algebra, Boolean algebra only studies number 1 and 0 (true and false).

Let us look at the primitives, the building blocks of logic circuits: AND, OR, and NOT. For an AND gate with two input A and B and one output Q, its Boolean algebra expression is

$$Q(A, B) = A \cdot B \tag{2.1}$$

Figure 2.7 lists some common gates. Note that the exclusive OR (XOR) is a very useful operation in cryptography. It has a special property that can be used using one key for both encryption and decryption.

Suppose we want to reverse engineering (RE) a general combinational circuit (like a black box) with M inputs and N outputs. We can apply all the 2^M possible combinations to the inputs and measure the outputs. The results can be put in a truth table for further analysis based on the Boolean algebra. Once we have the function of inputs corresponding to the outputs, we can then design a logic circuit to replace the black box.

On the other hand, when we design a logic circuit, we can use Boolean algebra to calculate the outputs and put the results in a truth table. Comparing with building the circuit directly and testing the truthfulness, the mathematical method saves time and money. It also avoids building the circuit again should the first one fail to operate.

Fig. 2.7 Gates and Boolean algebra expression

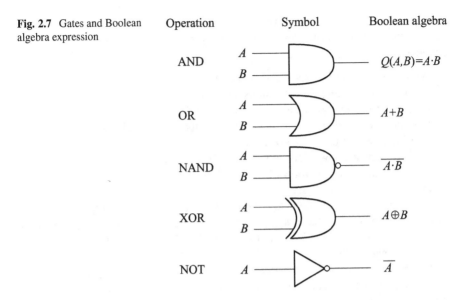

Operation	Symbol	Boolean algebra

AND — $Q(A,B)=A \cdot B$

OR — $A+B$

NAND — $\overline{A \cdot B}$

XOR — $A \oplus B$

NOT — $\overline{A}$

Such a device is very common nowadays. We call it a simulator. It can be a real device such as hardware or software running on a computer, or both.

Autodesk's Tinkercad is one of the popular free online tools for creating simple designs. Besides the basic modeling, it comes with a digital circuit design tool that users can quickly put together a breadboard style circuit. In addition, users can simulate the project without worrying about breaking the circuit.

efabless is an open electronic design automation (EDA) platform that can be used for design and prototype and published to the marketplace for tapeout and production.

2.4   Logic Circuit Design Process

A computer can be built with standard ICs, in many cases VLSIs. It seems that there is no need to build a circuit from the ground up. If we look at a new Sony PlayStation or even a USB key that enables your computer or server to run certain programs, we can easily draw the conclusion that circuit design is very important. Without circuit design personnel and their skills, an IC (not to mention VLSIs) cannot be manufactured.

Designing a logic circuit usually involves the following steps: feasibility study, circuit design, circuit simulation, and optimization. A well-designed circuit is then manufactured either using printed circuit board (PCB) with ICs on it or is packed into a special purpose IC. The tools can choose from *efabless* or other commercial EDA tools.

Example 2.2 Design a home alarm system. All six windows and two doors should be monitored. In the event when a person is trying to break in, the alarm should be sounded.

We are now following the design steps to build the circuit. There is no doubt about the feasibility that we can build such a system. A standard CMOS IC 4068, a NOR gate with eight inputs and one output, would serve the purpose.

We can get eight electric switches, similar as the light switches but much smaller in size. We then connect each switch to one input pin of the CD 4078 and wire the switches on the windows and doors. After that, we adjust the switches such that they are in "stable on" position when the windows and doors are closed. Then, we connect a buzzer and a battery.

At a normal state, all inputs to the CD 4078 are high and the output is low. The buzzer does not alarm. When one or more of the windows or doors are opened while the alarm system is on, the low input(s) of the CD 4078 will set the output to high. The buzzer will alarm.

Figure 2.8 provides the CD 4078 circuit and the home alarm system circuit. If we replace the mechanical switches with Hall switches, small contact-less switches which rely on magnetic field, there will be no mechanical contact no matter if the windows or doors are closed or open.

Next, the components need to be connected. This is usually done using a breadboard or printed circuit board (PCB). All connections need to be checked several times, making sure they are correct before connecting the power. This working process is generally for very small and new hardware designers only. More

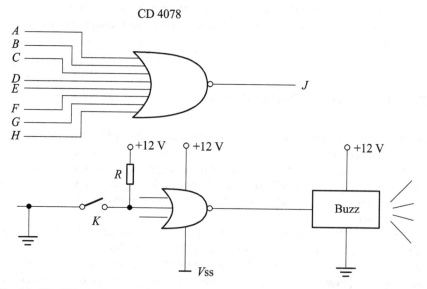

Fig. 2.8 CD 4078 pin diagram, logic circuit, and circuit of a simple home alarm system

complex projects usually start with designing the circuit and then performing the simulation.

Experienced hardware engineers may add other circuits to assist the main circuit such as anti-vibrating circuit and LED coupler. Mechanical switches may vibrate during switching process. This may cause malfunction for the circuit as a string of 01010101 may occur instead of a clean 1 or 0. A LED coupler can separate the digital circuit with high voltage or current circuits to reduce the interference.

2.5   Gates and Flip-Flops

From the previous section, we know that logic gates process signals which represent true (1, high) or false (0, low). Normally the positive supply voltage $+V_{cc}$ represents true and 0 V (GND) represents false. Gates are identified by their function: NOT, AND, NAND, OR, NOR, and XOR. Capital letters are normally used in text to make it clear that the term refers to a logic gate.

Logic gates are available on special ICs which usually contain several gates of the same type. For example, a CD 4001 IC contains four 2-input NOR gates. There are several families of logic ICs, and they can be categorized into two groups: 4000 series and 74 series. The 4000 and 74HC families are the best for battery-powered projects because they work with a wide range of supply voltages (usually 3–15 V) and they consume little power.

The logic circuits we have examined so far are all combinational logic, meaning any past states will not affect the current output. The output is only determined by the current inputs. There is another group of logic circuit that an output is determined by not only the current input states but also the previous states. We call these circuits as sequential circuits. Since the past states of the circuit affect the current and future output, the sequential circuit has memory.

Flip-flops are a very common type of sequential circuit (Dumas 2006). It can be constructed easily by using two NOR gates and by cross-couple connecting one input of the two circuits as shown in Fig. 2.9. Two inputs are named S (set) and R (reset), while the output is marked Q.

The initial state S and R are both low. When S changes from low to high and R keeps low, then Q is set to high. When S changes back from high to low, then the

Fig. 2.9 A flip-flop constructed with two NOR circuits

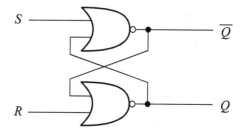

Fig. 2.10 State table of a SR
flip-flop

S	R	State
0	0	Keep state (memory mode)
0	1	$Q=0$
1	0	$Q=1$
1	1	Unstable/race condition

output ($Q = 1$) will not be affected, means the circuit state remains or the circuit is in memory mode. When R changes from low to high while S keeps low, then Q is set to low. When R changes back from high to low, then the output ($Q = 0$) will not be affected, which means again that the circuit is in memory mode. Figure 2.10 shows a partial truth table, and we call it a state table (Randell 1982) for the SR flip-flop.

In Boolean algebra expression, a SR flip-flop can be represented as

$$Q_{next} = S + \overline{R} \cdot Q \tag{2.2}$$

where Q is the current state and Q_{next} is the next state where change usually takes place by a synchronized clock. Formula (2.2) tells us that S can set the flip-flop to high and it will keep the state (data) even when S goes off, in condition that R keeps low. When S is low and the output Q is high, input R can reset the flip-flop, and it will keep low even input R is cleared, in condition that S keeps low. By observing Formula (2.2), we can come to a conclusion that a flip-flop's output is determined by both inputs and the previous output. Most importantly, a flip-flop can store either 1 or 0, and it remembers the data unless the condition changes. The property makes it a perfect candidate to build a computer memory.

Chapter 3 provides more in-depth discussion about computer memory.

2.6   Hardware Security

Generally speaking, hardware security protects hardware applications from being attacked, misused, or reverse engineered by unauthorized users. For a computer system, hardware security involves storing passwords on a chip, restricting unauthorized remote access, and replacing vulnerable software with secure hardware, etc. It also means securing the computer components such as secure memory and storage, secure CPU, secure I/O devices, and secure network devices on a computer system.

It is easy to understand why we need to secure computer hardware, but the reason as to why we need to secure a logic circuit is not obvious. Suppose you build a new computer with standard ICs (this was true in earlier times how a computer was built);

it is not difficult for other people to duplicate one by measuring the pins and making a PCB with the same circuit and plug on the standard ICs that can be purchased anywhere in the world.

TV manufacturers original equipment manufacturer (OEM) their products in developing countries where most countries have copyright issues. How do they get cheap labor while their intellectual property is still being protected?

In earlier times, Japanese companies use a counter to calculate the total TV sets the production line had manufactured. The counter was claimed unbreakable by adding hardware security mechanism to their products. However, it is not difficult to build a TV set outside their product line or play tricks on the counters.

Since the 1990s, TV companies have enhanced hardware security by putting the core technology and algorithms into an IC. They control the production by selling the special IC to the OEMs. Without this custom designed IC, the TV set cannot be built.

To counter reverse engineering, TV industries now use FPGA, a microprocessor with memory and interfaces, to replace the custom-designed IC. One benefit of using FPGA is that hardware security is enhanced. It prevents reverse engineering and destroys itself should the number of attempts exceed the preset value (e.g., three).

More hardware security-related topics regarding computer components will be discussed in the following chapters including memory access security, buses security, I/O devices security, CPU security, architecture security, and network security, etc.

2.7   FPGA and VLSI

FPGA stands for field-programmable gate array. It usually is a very large-scale integrated circuit (VLSI). A modern FPGA functions like a microcomputer; even technically, we call it a microprocessor. Theoretically, it can be used to implement any logic circuits. So, it can replace most of the logic circuits designed with standard IC like gates, flip-flops and registers, etc.

The fundamental blocks of FPGA architecture are hierarchical, integrated into different building blocks such as combinational and sequential logic circuits, arithmetic logic unit, clocks, input/output, delay locked loop (DLL), and memory (Hwang 1993). It is also integrated with routing feature that can be used to interconnect with other FPGAs or computers.

Figure 2.11 is a security system with fingerprint and other biometric inputs. The use of two series of FPGAs has made the system simpler and easy for quick development (Suhaili and Watanabe 2017). The biometric-based security system had a configurable interface and processing power and the ability to communicate with larger security networks.

Here:

uC: Micro-Controller

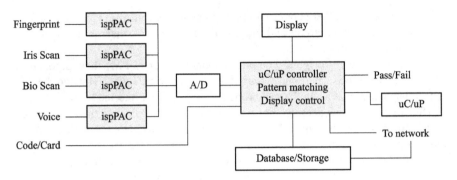

Fig. 2.11 A biometric security system with Lattice FPGAs

uP: Micro-Processor
A/D: Analog to Digital converter
ispPAC and uC/uP: Lattice FPGAs

We can see how easily a security system can be built with the FPGAs. FPGAs can not only help us build a security system, but they also have the advantages of securing themselves. Many FPGAs have control bits that can be programmed. Once the control bits are set, it will prevent the flash and SRAM memory from being read. An optional 64-bit flash lock key is required for erasure, and programming prevents accidental or unauthorized reprogramming. The one-time programmable (OTP) mode blocks any further erasure or reprogramming, therefore providing the ultimate assurance that the FPGA content have not been tampered with.

2.8 RFID and NFC

Some integrated circuits have the processing power and memory built-in. They may not need to be powered all the time as they can pick electromagnetic energy and convert them to power the chips on the fly.

2.8.1 A RIFD Student Attendance System

Radio-frequency identification (RFID) is the use of a wireless non-contact system that uses radio-frequency electromagnetic fields to transfer data from a tag attached to an object, for the purposes of automatic identification and tracking. Some tags require no battery and are powered by the electromagnetic fields used to read them (Thrasher 2018). Others use a local power source and emit radio waves (electromagnetic radiation at radio frequencies). The tag contains electronically stored information which can be read from up to several meters (yards) away. Unlike

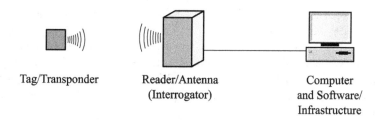

Tag/Transponder   Reader/Antenna   Computer
                         (Interrogator)   and Software/
                                                 Infrastructure

Fig. 2.12 A basic RFID system

a bar code, the tag does not need to be within the line of sight of the reader and may be embedded in the tracked object.

A basic RFID system consists of three components:

- An antenna or coil. The antenna emits radio signals to activate the tag and to read and write data to it.
- A transceiver (with decoder) and a transponder (RF tag) electronically programmed with unique information.
- The reader emits radio waves in ranges of anywhere from 1 inch to 100 feet or more, depending upon its power output and the radio frequency used. When an RFID tag passes through the electromagnetic zone, it detects the reader's activation signal.

The reader decodes the data encoded in the tag's integrated circuit (silicon chip), and the data is passed to the host computer for processing. Figure 2.12 shows such a system.

The purpose of an RFID system is to enable data to be transmitted by a portable device, called a tag, which is read by the RFID reader and processed according to the needs of a particular application. The data transmitted by the tag may provide identification or location information, or specifics about the product tagged, such as price, color, and date of purchase. RFID technology has been used by thousands of companies for a decade or more. RFID quickly gained attention because of its ability to track moving objects. As the technology is refined, more pervasive—and invasive—uses for RFID tags are in the works.

A typical RFID tag consists of a microchip attached to a radio antenna mounted on a substrate. The chip can store kilobytes of data, or even more.

To retrieve data stored on an RFID tag, you need a reader. A typical RFID reader is a device that has one or more antennas that emit radio waves and receive signals back from the tag. The reader then passes the information in digital form to a computer system.

RFID tags are used in many industries. An RFID attached to an automobile during production can be used to track its progress through the assembly line. Pharmaceuticals can be tracked through warehouses. Livestock and pets may have tags injected, allowing positive identification of the animal. RFID identity cards can give employees access to locked areas of a building, and RF transponders mounted in automobiles can be used to bill motorists for access to toll roads or parking.

A radio-frequency identification system uses tags, or labels attached to the objects to be identified. Two-way radio transmitter-receivers called interrogators or readers send a signal to the tag and read its response. The readers generally transmit their observations to a computer system running RFID software or RFID middleware.

The tag's information is stored electronically in a non-volatile memory. The RFID tag includes a small RF transmitter and receiver. An RFID reader transmits an encoded radio signal to interrogate the tag. The tag receives the message and responds with its identification information. This may be only a unique tag serial number or may be product-related information such as a stock number, lot or batch number, production date, or other specific information.

RFID tags can be either passive, active, or battery-assisted passive. An active tag has an on-board battery that periodically transmits its ID signal. A battery-assisted passive (BAP) has a small battery on-board that is activated when in the presence of a RFID reader. A passive tag is cheaper and smaller because it has no battery. Instead, the tag uses the radio energy transmitted by the reader as its energy source. The interrogator must be close for RF field to be strong enough to transfer sufficient power to the tag. Since tags have individual serial numbers, the RFID system design can discriminate several tags that might be within the range of the RFID reader and read them simultaneously.

Tags may either be read-only, having a factory-assigned serial number that is used as a key into a database, or may be read/write, where object-specific data can be written into the tag by the system user. Field programmable tags may be write-once, read-multiple; "blank" tags may be written with an electronic product code by the user.

RFID tags contain at least two parts: an integrated circuit for storing and processing information, modulating and demodulating a radio-frequency (RF) signal, collecting DC power from the incident reader signal, and other specialized functions and an antenna for receiving and transmitting the signal. Figure 2.13 shows such a RFID tag.

Fig. 2.13 A RFID tag

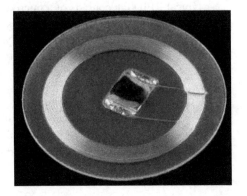

Fig. 2.14 A solid-state RFID reader

Fixed readers are set up to create a specific interrogation zone which can be tightly controlled. This allows a highly defined reading area for when tags go in and out of the interrogation zone. Figure 2.14 shows such a reader. Mobile readers may be handheld or mounted on carts or vehicles.

Example 2.3 Student attendance system. The student attendance system we are trying to build is a biometrics and RFID-based attendance management system for schools. It provides robust, secure, and automatic attendance management system for students. The system has an built-in facility of sending automatic SMS and E-mail alerts to Parents/Guardians of students.

The advantages of the student attendance system are:

- More efficient student attendance—System automates the student attendance, hence reducing irregularities in the attendance process arising due to human error.
- Time-saving—Important administrative and educational resources could be freed up by utilizing the system.
- Environment-friendly—Reduces paper and other resource requirements. System with its extremely small carbon footprint is a greener option.
- Better parent/guardian information system—Parents/guardians are better informed about their children's whereabouts with automatic SMS and E-mail facilities in the system.
- Improved parent/guardian-school relationship—The system brings the two principal stakeholders in a student's education closer, considerably improving the parent/guardian-school rapport, leading to an atmosphere of comfort and trust.

The system consists of the following technology elements as shown in the Fig. 2.15.

- Biometric attendance devices
- Biometric mobile devices
- Radio-frequency ID (RFID) tags
- A cloud server
- Client interface

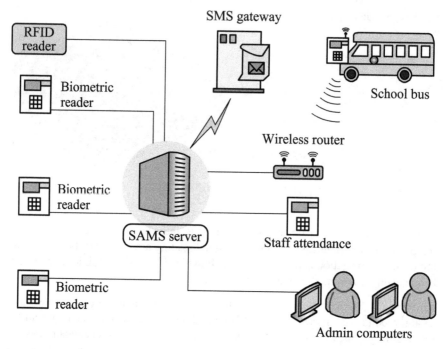

Fig. 2.15 Student attendance system diagram

- Management software
- Bulk SMS facility
- Automatic E-mail alerts

In a typical system setup, there is a RFID reader installed at each entrance of the school. These readers are connected with a server housed in the school or a virtual server in a cloud. A typical RFID reader that can be connected to computer system via USB is shown in Fig. 2.16.

Each day, students register their attendance with the RFID device. The server will download the attendance data at a preset time. It will process the attendance and send a SMS message to parents/guardians of the absentee student via SMS gateway server. The message template can be set by the school authorities to their liking.

The system also allows school authorities to send SMS alerts to parents/guardians regarding special events and emergencies.

The system also has a module which can monitor the students who use the school bus, and this data can be transferred to the school's server via Wi-Fi or GPRS.

The system can be built on a robust client-server or cloud architecture and supports multiple simultaneous clients which enable admin staff to perform their function with utmost ease.

Fig. 2.16 A RFID USB reader that can be connected to a computer system via the USB interface

The student attendance system also has fully integrated Time Manager Software which provides various employee attendance and HR-related functionalities, e.g., shift scheduling, attendance summary, and leave management. The time manager module can also be integrated with leading payroll processing software.

The features of the attendance system include:

- Accurate student attendance
- Automatic attendance collection
- Daily absentee report
- Automatic SMS alert to parent/guardian of absentee student
- Daily attendance register
- Monthly attendance register
- Yearly attendance report
- Bulk SMS facility for special events and announcements
- RFID options for young kids
- Mobile attendance data collection and reporting
- Robust employee attendance system

Figure 2.17 shows the work flow of the student attendance system. When a student walks through a school entrance, the RFID reader sends a signal to the RFID tag and powers the tag. The RFID tag then sends out its unique ID number (stored in built-in memory). The reader receives the data and sends the data to a computer. Data received by the computer is decoded to the corresponding student name. Final information such as student name and current time are stored in the database.

Figure 2.18 shows the algorithm in C# for a computer to receive data from a USB port. In the program, the RFID tag data is received in ASCII format and also converted into hexadecimal (HEX) format. For testing purposes, two names are

Fig. 2.17 Work flow of a RFID student attendance system

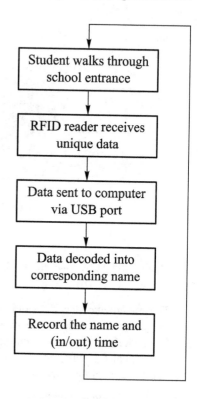

defined as string. If the data match to the person, then the name and the date/time information is displayed.

There are a few lines in the beginning (shaded in light yellow) to handle the data correctly. Due to the buffer limitation, each data string is received in two parts. The program puts them together before sending out to display. Otherwise, there will be a duplicate data entry every time a student walks in.

In the system, all data are stored into a database for archiving and further analysis. When a parent wants to check the child, she/he can either call the school or check online herself/himself. The system also has a web interface that interacts with school administrators and parents. The mobile app makes it possible for parents to check their kids anytime at anywhere.

2.8.2 Near Field Communication

Near field communication (NFC) is a technology that generally replaces the standard practice of typing in a username and/or password; multifactor authentication using NFC can be used in conjunction with either or both. The normal data exchange range of NFC is about 10 cm, which makes NFC a more secure way to transfer high-speed data. Meanwhile, NFC usually uses much less energy than Bluetooth Low Energy. Even though the NFC reader utilizes power, the NFC tag does not.

```
1    // Read all the data waiting in the buffer
2    string data = comport.ReadExisting();
3    string data1;
4
5    byte[] data_hex;
6    data_hex = System.Text.Encoding.ASCII.GetBytes(data);
7    data1 = ByteArrayToHexString(data_hex);
8
9    if (data.IndexOf('\n\) == = -1')
10   {
11       data2 = data1;
12   }
13   else
14   {
15       data3 = data1;
16   }
17   data1 = data2 + data3;
18
19   string Jane = "02 34 43 30 30 32 30 43 36 38 46 32 35 0D 0A 03";
20   string Paul = "02 34 43 30 30 32 30 45036 30 43 38 36 0D 0A 03";
21
22   if (data1 -- Jane)
23   {
24       data = "Jane: " + DateTime.Now + "\r\n"; //Jane!
25   }
26   else if (data1 == Paul)
27   {
28       data = "Paul: " + DateTime.Now + "\r\n"; //Paul!
29   }
30   else
31   {
32       data = "";
33   }
34
35   //Display the text to the user in the terminal
36   Log(LogMsgType.Incoming, data);
```

Fig. 2.18 Data receiving algorithm (color)

This allows each NFC tag to create its own power when in the presence of an NFC-enabled smartphone (BLE 2018).

There are several different NFC tags. A passive tag can give information but does not read the information itself. An active tag can read and be read. An example of an active NFC device is a mobile device, and an example of a passive NFC device is an NFC tag. Compared with RFID, NFC has a much closer contactless distance, so it is more secure.

The author of this book has mentored students to work on an NFC-based multifactor authentication application (Hufstetler et al. 2017; NFC 2018; Sucipto et al. 2017; Wolff 2018). Details can be found on the book's website.

2.9 Trusted Platform Module

Trusted computing (TC) guarantees the trustworthy of IT systems. It has shown promises in research, industrial projects, and military implementations.

The trusted platform module (TPM) is a robust chip that is integrated into the system providing hardware security and establishing trust within devices such as computers, weapons, vehicles, robots, wearables, actuators, and storage. TPM-enabled server, gateways, and sensors extend secure authentication and integrity by a TPM chip on each device. Mutual authentication of devices is required at session start, and signing and decipher are performed on the device.

TPMs provide a set of primitives that offer a high degree of security. A TPM chip can be embedded with a unique RSA key pair whose private key never leaves the physical perimeter of a TPM chip. As a result, TPMs can be used to identify a unique device's identity. Such as key can act as a globally unique machine identity, which is imperative within a cloud environment. In addition, TPMs can prevent malicious software over air updates and rollbacks. TPM is the building block in a various of security systems.

Trusted computing builds digital identities and increases assurance of trust among devices that are connected to the network. It adds a level of security on top of what is provided by the operating systems and hardware. TCB adds a hardware device (TPM), which has non-volatile storage and cryptographic execution engines on each device.

Practically, deploying a large system with trusted computing base (TCB) is still a challenge especially in CPS/IoT systems, where various protocols and legacy systems exist.

Though TPM can provide a good level of security, abusing remote validation by manufacturers may be able to decide what software would be allowed to run. In addition, the user's actions may be recorded in a proprietary database without the user actually knowing. This has happened in smart TVs, smart toys, and other voice-activated devices. As a result, privacy becomes an issue.

2.10 Physical Unclonable Function

The current best practice for providing such a secure memory or authentication source in such a mobile system is to place a secret key in a non-volatile electrically erasable programmable read-only memory (EEPROM) or battery-backed static random access memory (SRAM) and use hardware cryptographic operations such as digital signatures or encryption. This approach is expensive both in terms of design area and power consumption. In addition, such non-volatile memory is often vulnerable to invasive attack mechanisms.

Physical unclonable functions (PUFs) are a promising innovative primitive that are used for authentication and secret key storage without the requirement of secure

EEPROMs and other expensive hardware described above. This is possible, because instead of storing secrets in digital memory, PUFs derive a secret from the physical characteristics of the integrated circuit (IC). Here are the advantages of using PUF:

- PUF hardware uses simple digital circuits that are easy to fabricate and consume less power and area than EEPROM/RAM solutions with anti-tamper circuitry. In addition, simple PUF applications do not require expensive cryptographic hardware such as the secure hash algorithm (SHA) or a public/private key encryption algorithm.
- Since the "secret" is derived from physical characteristics of the IC, the chip must be powered on for the secret to reside in digital memory. Any physical attack attempting to extract digital information from the chip, therefore, must do so while the chip is powered on.
- Invasive attacks are more difficult to execute without modifying the physical characteristics from which the secret is derived. Therefore, continually powered active anti-tamper mechanisms are not required to secure the PUF.
- Non-volatile memory is more expensive to manufacture. EEPROMs require additional mask layers, and battery-backed RAMs require an external always-on power source.

2.11   Quantum Circuit

A quantum circuit consists of a sequence of quantum gates that carry out transformations on qubits. It is a model of problem-solving in quantum computation. Unlike traditional concept about circuits, which means hardware, a quantum circuit is the set of instructions, or an algorithm, to a quantum computer. Figure 2.19 is a quantum circuit to calculate $1 + 1$. Figure 2.20 shows a quantum circuit the book

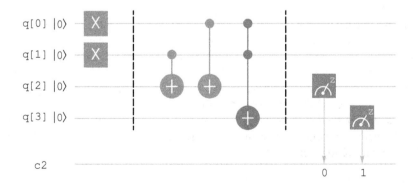

Fig. 2.19   A quantum circuit to calculate $1 + 1$ (color)

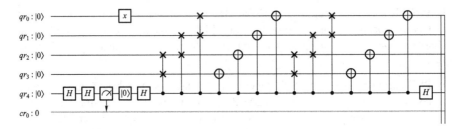

Fig. 2.20   An example of a quantum circuit

author "designed" using a Python program with Jupiter Notebook on an Ubuntu 18.10 Cosmic 64-bit virtual machine. This circuit can factor number 15 (into two prime numbers) with polynomial time, comparing an exponential time needed in a general case. A quantum circuit is essentially more like an algorithm than a logic circuit. More information about quantum circuits can be found in later chapters of this book.

2.12   Summary

Logic circuits are the building blocks for modern computers. Computers use binary number system as it is easy to be implemented with logic gates that have two stable states: on/off, true/false, or 1/0. A truth table provides all possible values of a combinational circuit's output corresponding to all inputs. A flip-flop's output is determined by not only the inputs of that moment but also the previous states of the circuit. So, it can remember, and it is the prototype of one-bit memory.

Computer system security includes three aspects: hardware, software, and management. Circuit security enables designers to prevent the circuit being reverse engineered. FPGAs can be implemented to replace a complex digital circuit. In addition, it has built-in security features and processing powers.

RFID tags have the advantage of using power provided by the reader wirelessly. They are commonly used in daily life such as EZPass, department stores, and animal monitoring. The student attendance system discussed here is another example.

TPMs provide a set of primitives that offer a high degree of security. Trusted computing builds digital identities and increases assurance of trust among devices that are connected to the network, often use TPMs.

A quantum circuit consists of a sequence of quantum gates that carry out transformations on qubits. A quantum circuit is essentially more like an algorithm than a hardware logic circuit.

Projects

2.1 Autodesk Tinkercad is a circuit simulation tool. Download the free tool, get familiar with the functionalities, and design the home alarm system described in the book.

2.2 Using the example from the book, design a RFID student attendance system.

2.3 Using the example from the book, design an FPGA biometric security system using *efabless*.

Exercises

2.1 A D flip-flop assumes the state of the D input. $Q(t+1) = 1$ if $D(t) = 1$, and $Q(t+1) = 0$ if $D(t) = 0$. Using a RS flip-flop, construct a D flip-flop.

2.2 Given the characteristic table shown in Fig. 2.10, determine which type of flip-flop it is?

2.3 Provide the truth table for the NAND gate.

2.4 A CD 4001 IC contains four 2-input NAND. How does one use it to make two AND gates?

2.5 Build an experimental home alarm system with standard IC that monitors ten windows and two doors. Draw the logic circuit.

2.6 Logic circuits built with standard ICs are easy to be duplicated. How can people secure the circuits such that they cannot be reverse engineered?

2.7 If we want to monitor temperature inside and outside the home, what kind of circuit do we need?

2.8 What are the purposes of using a flash lock key and one-time programmable mode in an FPGA?

2.9 Provide the truth table for an XOR gate.

2.10 Some RFID tags contain no battery or any other power connector. How will the tags send out data to the readers?

2.11 Study on trusted computing and describe the architecture of TPMs.

2.12 In the book, the author mentioned "A quantum circuit is essentially more like an algorithm than a hardware logic circuit." Why?

References

BLE vs. NFC: The future of mobile consumer engagement now (2014, January 31). Retrieved July 20, 2018.

Dumas, J. D. (2006). *Computer architecture: Fundamentals and principles of computer design*. Oxford: Taylor & Francis.

Foster, C. C., & Iberall, T. (1985). *Computer architecture* (3rd ed.). New York: Wan Nostrand Reinhold Company.

Hufstetler, W. A., Ramos, M. J. H., & Shuangbao, W. (2017). NFC unlock: secure two-factor computer authentication using NFC. In *IEEE 14th International Conference on Mobile Ad Hoc and Sensor Systems (MASS)* (pp. 507–510)

Hwang, K. (1993). *Advanced computer architecture: Parallelism, scalability, programmability.* New York: McGraw-Hill, Inc.

NFC UID. Retrieved July 15, 2018, from https://help.gototags.com/article/nfc-uid/.

Randell, B. (Ed.). (1982). *The designs of digital computers*. Berlin: Springer.

Shiva, S. G. (2000). *Computer design and architecture* (3rd ed.). New York: Marcel Dekker, Inc.

Sucipto, K., Chatzopoulos, D., Kosta, S., & Hui, P. (2017). Keep your nice friends close, but your rich friends closer–computation offloading using NFC. In *IEEE Conference on Computer Communications* (pp. 1–9).

Suhaili, S. B., & Watanabe, T. (2017). Design of high-throughput SHA-256 hash function based on FPGA. In *2017 6th International Conference on Electrical Engineering and Informatics (ICEEI)* (pp. 1–6).

Thrasher, J. RFID versus NFC: What's the difference between NFC and RFID? Retrieved July 6, 2018.

Wolff, D. Pgina/pgina. Retrieved July 09, 2018.

Chapter 3
Computer Memory and Storage

In this chapter, we introduce memory hierarchy starting from one-bit memory to large memory modules and study how memory is organized and connected. We then discuss different types of memory including volatile memory, non-volatile memory, networked memory, cloud memory and storage, and memory access security.

The amount of memory affects the speed of computer systems. The most important characteristics of memory are the speed and cost. For internal memory close to the CPU, we use the fastest memory circuits with a considerable number of control circuits. This is associated with high cost, so those memory (such as registers) are usually very limited. For main memory, regular RAM is used to reduce the cost but with great capacity and good speed. Data that are not immediately used are stored in external memory or storage. External memory includes USB drives, SSD drives, network drives, and storage in the cloud.

3.1 A One-Bit Memory Circuit

People use flash memory to store photos and documents. However, fewer people have asked how data on the flash memory are stored, what a single memory unit looks like, and why it can hold data without battery?

First let us look at the computer memory. A memory is a device that data can be written in and read out. Moreover, data need to be kept (stored) even after the writing/reading action is completed.

Figure 3.1 shows one of Edison's great inventions, a light bulb. When we turn on the switch K, the light is on and will stay on. When we turn off the switch, the light is off and will stay off until it is turned on again next time. Now we see, the bulb and switch device can remember.

We would not use this device to build a computer since every action (write) needs human interaction. A transistor can be used as an electronic switch. Figure 3.2

© The Author(s), under exclusive license to Springer Nature Singapore Pte Ltd. 2021   45
S. P. Wang, *Computer Architecture and Organization*,
https://doi.org/10.1007/978-981-16-5662-0_3

Fig. 3.1 A light bulb and a
switch

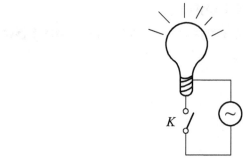

Fig. 3.2 An electronic
switch made of a transistor
and resistors

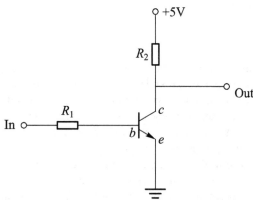

shows a circuit that uses a transistor as an electronic switch. When the input is
low (0 V), there will be no electric current from b to e. The "switch" c to e is shut
off (disconnected) and the output is high (+5 V). When a high (+5 V) voltage is
applied to the input, there will be current from b to e. The switch is on (c and e are
connected); therefore, output is low (0.2 V).

The traditional transistor-based electronic switch uses electric current to drive
the component. So, it is called current-based component. Current-based component
consumes much power, has heat problems, and therefore cannot be made in large
scale. The next step is to use metal-oxide-semiconductor (MOS), later replaced by
complementary metal-oxide-semiconductor (CMOS) component. Figure 3.3 shows
a simple MOS switch.

Among other advantages, a CMOS component theoretically consumes no current. It is a voltage-based component. With CMOS technology, a large number of
circuits can be integrated into one circuit, thus making large-scale integrated circuit
(LSI) and very-large-scale integrated circuit (VLSI) possible. Now most processors
are manufactured with VLSI technology.

Figure 3.4 shows an individual memory cell. It is one-bit memory corresponding
to the light bulb and switch. It is a circuit that connects two NOR gates together.
This circuit is called a flip-flop or a RS trigger. The set (S) and reset (R) are inputs,
the Q is the output, and the $\overline{Q}$ is the complement output.

Fig. 3.3 An electronic
switch made of MOS
component

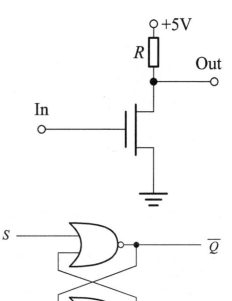

Fig. 3.4 A one-bit memory
cell constructed by a flip-flop

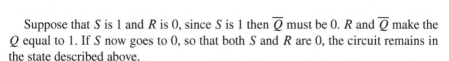

Suppose that S is 1 and R is 0, since S is 1 then $\overline{Q}$ must be 0. R and $\overline{Q}$ make the Q equal to 1. If S now goes to 0, so that both S and R are 0, the circuit remains in the state described above.

If R now becomes a 1, that will force Q to 0, but now both inputs S and Q to the upper NOR gate are zero so that $\overline{Q}$ becomes a 1. This state will also persist.

Here we see this flip-flop "remembers" the states of this two input signals, R and S. It functions like the light bulb and switch circuit, but all its components are electronic including the control signal. This is the brick of a computer memory system. Computer memory is composed of billions of this type of memory units with other circuits signaling with the processor.

3.2   Memory Hierarchy

There is a special type of memory that is used to hold a binary value temporarily for basic calculations and storage. It is wired within the CPU to perform a specific role. We call this special memory registers (Dumas 2016). Unlike memory, each register services a particular purpose based on the way it is wired. In terms of speed, register is the fastest memory possible in a computer system working directly with the CPU.

Registers are used in many different ways in a computer. One can be used to hold the address of current instruction being executed. It is called a program

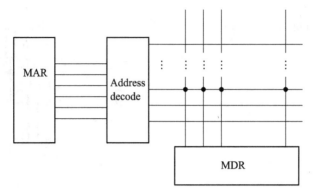

Fig. 3.5 The relationship between the MAR, MDR, and memory

counter register (PC). The instruction register (IR) holds the actual instruction being executed currently by the computer. The status register holds several one-bit registers that each one keeps track of special conditions of the CPU. The flags contain information such as arithmetic carry, negative sign, overflow, and other critical information that is monitored by the control unit.

Memory, or random-access memory (RAM), can be individually accessed in a random manner. Computer memory system usually contains billions of single one-bit memory unit. To access those memory units, a processor uses two registers: memory address register (MAR) and memory data register (MDR) (Foster and Iberall 1985). Sometimes, a memory data register is referred to a memory buffer register as it holds the data that is being stored or retrieved from the memory location currently addressed by the memory address register.

Figure 3.5 shows the relationship between the MAR, MDR, and memory. An address decoder is used to reduce the number of address required for a large number of memory units. For example, a 32-bit address bus can address $2^{32} = 4\,Gb$ memory.

In MAR, the highest bit is called most significant bit (MSB) and the lowest bit the least significant bit (LSB) (Randell 1982). In MDR, the number of bits that can be accessed at the same time is determined by the width of the register which is connected to the processor. For a 32-bit data bus, one instruction can process 32-bit data, while a 64-bit data can be processed within one instruction for a 64-bit data bus. So generally speaking, a 64-bit computer is faster.

The interaction between the CPU and the memory registers takes place as follows: to store data at a particular memory location, the CPU loads the address to the memory address register and data to the memory data register. The address is interpreted in the decoder such that only one output is activated according to the address in MAR. The CPU then sends a signal to the memory enabling the write line. Data is then transferred from MDR to the memory being selected.

To read data from a particular location, the CPU sends the address to MAR. The address is decoded, and that address is being selected. The CPU then issues a read command, and data is then read from selected memory location to MDR.

Here we see the MDR is a two-way register with both in and out, while MAR is a one-way register that always sends the signal out.

We know that a 32-bit computer can have as much as 4 gigabytes memory. In general, for a computer with k bits address in width, the total number of memory address is

$$M = 2^k$$

M here is also the total possible memory in a computer system. For an 8-bit processor such as Intel 8080 or Z80, the total possible memory is $2^8 = 256$. A 16-bit computer may have $2^{16} = 65536$ (64 k) memory. Again a 32-bit computer can have

$$2^{32} = 2^2 \times 2^{10} \times 2^{10} \times 2^{10}$$

unique memory address, which is roughly

$$4 \times 10^3 \times 10^3 \times 10^3 = 4 \times 10^9$$

As one gigabyte (G) approximately equals to 10^9 bytes, the total memory amounts to 4 G for a 32-bit computer.

For a 64-bit computer, the CPU usually contains 40 to 52 physical address bits, supporting from 1 TB to 4 PB of RAM. For a 64-bit CPU with 52 physical address bits

$$2^{52} = 2^2 \times 2^{10} \times 2^{10} \text{ GB} = 2^2 \times 2^{10} \text{ TB} = 4 \text{ PB}$$

Modern computers usually use random access memory (RAM) as the main memory. Dynamic RAM (DRAM) is mostly often seen on personal computers as it is cheaper and can be highly integrated due to its less power consumption. DRAM needs to be refreshed periodically to avoid data loss. Static RAM (SRAM) is faster than DRAM but with less integration rate. It is also more expensive, so it is commonly seen on servers or special fast computers.

3.3 Cache Memory

We know registers are a special type of memory that offer the fastest speed but with very limited numbers. On the other hand, memory (RAM) is much cheaper compared with registers and can be integrated with large quantity with easy access. But its speed is slower. To fill the gap, there is another type of memory called cache memory. A memory hierarchy of computer systems is shown in Fig. 3.6.

The cache is a small amount of fast memory that sits between the processor and memory to bridge the speed gap between the CPU and main memory (Hwang 1993).

Fig. 3.6 A memory hierarchy of computer systems

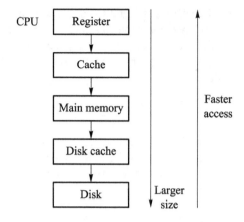

Cache is much smaller than the main memory. The working mechanism for the cache memory is to prefetch the data from the main memory and make them handy when the processor needs them. If the prediction is accurate, then the processor can get the data directly from the fast cache memory without requiring accessing the main memory.

It is not surprising that people would ask why cache memory works and how to predict the data needed before executing the program? Let us look at the "block" idea. Suppose we want to add two matrices with M row and N column together; we need to add $M \times N$ times. If the data are all in cache, we call it a read hit, and then it would save much time getting data from the cache than sending address to the address buffer (MAR) and waiting for data from the data buffers (MDR) with every add operation.

If the data that the processor is requesting are not in the cache, we call it a read miss; then the address and data buffers are enabled, and data are read directly from the main memory. The predicting algorithm will move more adjacent locations into cache foreseeing that there might be immediate need for those data as well. Statistics shows that the block data moving from main memory to cache whenever there is a read miss reduces the overall access time, therefore improving the machine speed.

With the "wholesale" concept, now we see the data transfer between cache memory and main memory is block based, while data transfer between cache memory and register is word based depending on the actual length of the instruction and data.

Some processors have two-level caches, primary and secondary. Newer processors have three level caches labeled L_1, L_2, and L_3. A processor first attempts to access L_1 cache for the requested data; if a miss occurs, then go to level 2 cache. If an L_2 cache miss occurs, then the data must be retrieved from the main memory. The selected block from the main memory is also written into both caches. A two-level cache system is shown in Fig. 3.7.

Cache memory improves the performance of computer systems. By using blocks and predicting and moving those blocks from main memory to cache memory, the memory access time is greatly improved.

Fig. 3.7 Two-level cache memory and data transfer

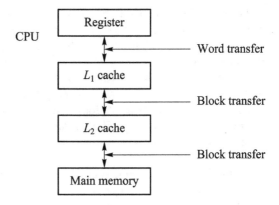

3.4 Virtual Memory

We understand the importance of the amount of main memory corresponding to the computer speed. It is very common that programs run simultaneously. That is why we add large amount of memory. No matter how large the main memory is, it may still not satisfy the amount of memory needed for running programs. Virtual memory gives programs a larger memory space than its physical memory. It occupies part of the much slower disk storage. Like cache memory, virtual memory is a transition between main memory and the disk storage. Unlike cache memory, virtual memory does not exist itself. It directly uses part of the disk storage. Figure 3.8 shows the concept of virtual memory in computer memory systems.

The key here is how to map a much larger virtual memory address space to the physical memory address place. To implement virtual memory, the virtual memory address is divided into segments or pages. The operating system translates a virtual page number to a physical page number (Shiva 2000).

Fig. 3.8 Computer memory, virtual memory, and disk storage

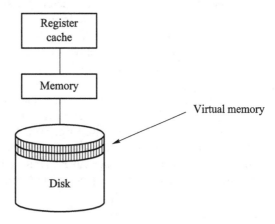

For example, to map a 32-bit virtual address space to a 24-bit physical address space, we can reserve the 12 least significant bits (LSB) for one page. So, the page size is $2^{12} = 4$ KB. The rest bits can be used as a pointer (page number) pointing to the page. In this case we need to map 2^{20} virtual pages to 2^{12} physical pages.

If the main memory is full, then the system will replace the current page with another one based on the mapping function in the operating system. The operating system is responsible for managing translation of virtual memory address to physical memory address. If a virtual page is to be replaced, the system always replaces the oldest one with the current one. Such mechanism is called a first-in-first-out (FIFO) policy.

Virtual memory shares the similarities with cache memory for increasing accessing speed. In addition, it virtually increases the main memory so that programs are able to run on a computer concurrently without worrying about memory limitations.

3.4.1 Paged Virtual Memory*

Nearly[1] all implementations of virtual memory divide a virtual address space into pages and blocks of contiguous virtual memory addresses. Pages are usually at least 4 KB in size; systems with large virtual address ranges or amounts of real memory generally use larger page sizes.

Page tables are used to translate the virtual addresses seen by the application into physical addresses used by the hardware to process instructions; such hardware that handles this specific translation is often known as the memory management unit. Each entry in the page table holds a flag indicating whether the corresponding page is in real memory or not. If it is in real memory, the page table entry will contain the real memory address at which the page is stored. When a reference is made to a page by the hardware, if the page table entry for the page indicates that it is not currently in real memory, the hardware raises a page fault exception, invoking the paging supervisor component of the operating system.

Systems can have one-page table for the whole system, separate page tables for each application and segment, a tree of page tables for large segments, or some combination of these. If there is only one-page table, different applications running at the same time use different parts of a single range of virtual addresses. If there are multiple page or segment tables, there are multiple virtual address spaces, and concurrent applications with separate page tables redirect to different real addresses.

Paging supervisor is a part of the operating system which creates and manages page tables. If the hardware raises a page fault exception, the paging supervisor accesses secondary storage, returns the page that has the virtual address that resulted in the page fault, updates the page tables to reflect the physical location of the virtual address, and tells the translation mechanism to restart the request.

---

[1] The mark * denotes the advanced topic.

When all physical memory is already in use, the paging supervisor must free a page in primary storage to hold the swapped-in page. The supervisor uses one of a variety of page replacement algorithms such as least recently used to determine which page to free.

3.4.2 Segmented Virtual Memory*

Some systems use segmentation instead of paging, dividing virtual address spaces into variable-length segments. A virtual address here consists of a segment number and an offset within the segment. The Intel 80286 supports a similar segmentation scheme as an option, but it is rarely used. Segmentation and paging can be used together by dividing each segment into pages; systems with this memory structure, such as Multics and IBM System/38, are usually paging-predominant, segmentation providing memory protection.

In the Intel 80386 and later IA-32 processors, the segments reside in a 32-bit linear, paged address space. Segments can be moved in and out of that space; pages there can "page" in and out of main memory, providing two levels of virtual memory; few if any operating systems do so, instead using only paging. Early non-hardware-assisted x86 virtualization solutions combined paging and segmentation because x86 paging offers only two protection domains, whereas a VMM/guest OS/guest application stack needs three. The difference between paging and segmentation systems is not only about memory division; segmentation is visible to user processes, as part of memory model semantics. Hence, instead of memory that looks like a single large vector, it is structured into multiple spaces.

This difference has important consequences; a segment is not a page with variable length or a simple way to lengthen the address space. Segmentation that can provide a single-level memory model in which there is no differentiation between process memory and file system consists of only a list of segments (files) mapped into the process's potential address space.

This is not the same as the mechanisms provided by calls such as mmap and Win32's MapViewOfFile, because inter-file pointers do not work when mapping files into semi-arbitrary places. In Multics, a file (or a segment from a multi-segment file) is mapped into a segment in the address space, so files are always mapped at a segment boundary. A file's linkage section can contain pointers for which an attempt to load the pointer into register or make an indirect reference through it causes a trap. The unresolved pointer contains an indication of the name of the segment to which the pointer refers and an offset within the segment; the handler for the trap maps the segment into the address space, puts the segment number into the pointer, changes the tag field in the pointer so that it no longer causes a trap, and returns to the code where the trap occurred, re-executing the instruction that caused the trap. This eliminates the need for a linker completely and works when different processes map the same file into different places in their private address spaces.

3.5   Non-volatile Memory

Most computers use random access memory (RAM) as the main memory. RAM is a type of read-write memory which has fast access speed and can be easily integrated in large scale. On the other hand, RAM is volatile, meaning it will lose data once power is removed.

3.5.1   The Concept of Computer Memory Before 1985

Contrast to storage, computer memory by default is a type of volatile RAM. Modern RAMs are made of semi-conductor silicon. It is understandable that if the power is disconnected, the data will be lost. This is true for both SRAM and DRAM. The latter needs to be refreshed in order to keep the data. This is inconvenient in some cases where data need to be kept even when the power is off. For example, for the intermediate data of a train in motion, one solution to this is to add a battery to the memory. But a battery cannot last long or work in extreme conditions. Another solution is to store data on an Erasable Electrically Programmable ROM (E^2PROM). The issue is when erasing, you have to erase all data. So, it does not provide random access (read/write).

3.5.2   The Wide Use of Flash Memory Since the Twenty-First Century

Non-volatile memory keeps data even when power is removed. Flash memory and E^2PROM are non-volatile memories.

The author of this book, an engineer in a research institution, invented a flash memory card in 1987, 1 year earlier than the first commercial flash chip was manufactured by Intel Corporation in 1988. The flash memory card was integrated on a standard bus (STD bus) circuit board with digital circuits designed by the author (Non-Volatile Memory 1988). The technology was tested at a well-known computer corporation and applied to the anti-skip/anti-slide system (now called ABS) for rail trains, a key science and technology project from 1985 to 1989 in the nation. A photo of the non-volatile memory card is shown in Fig. 3.9.

Read-only memory (ROM) is non-volatile, but it cannot be re-written. Programmable ROM (PROM) can only be written once with special device. Erasable PROM (EPROM) has a window on the chip. Data can be erased by ultraviolet light lasting 20–30 min. So, it is not capable of random read/write. Electrically erasable PROM (EEPROM or E^2PROM) is the father of modern flash memory. In earlier E^2PROMs, data can be electrically erased, but after erasing, the entire chip is set to blank.

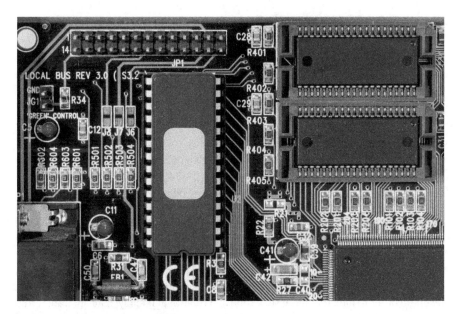

Fig. 3.9 A non-volatile memory card invented in 1987

The USB flash drive and memory cards for digital cameras are a new type of non-volatile memory based on E^2PROM technology with the speed between main memory and hard disk drives.

3.6 External Memory

External memory, or secondary memory, is a high capacity data storage. The external memory is usually much larger than the main memory. The most often seen external memory is computer hard drives. USB flash drives, backup drives, and network storage are all external memory. In many cases, we refer to external memory as storage.

Some external memory such as hard drives is connected directly to the CPU via the system bus. Some others such as USB flash drives are connected via serial interface. It takes time to put together the address and data that is required to communicate with the CPU. So, it is usually slower than direct connection.

With technology advances, solid-state drives (SSD) are common in the market. SSD has the advantage of being more reliable because it does not contain mechanical parts and is faster and more compact. It is projected that in the not so far future, the price of SSD will break even with hard disk drives (HDD).

Cloud computing brings another storage model, that is, storage in the cloud. As network has become one of the four key components (hardware, software, network, and data) in a computer system, storing data across the network is very common. Cloud storage adds another dimension to the computer memory system and has become more and more popular.

3.6.1 Hard Disk Drives and Solid-State Drives

In modern computers, hard disk drive is usually used as secondary storage. The time taken to access a given byte of information stored on a hard disk is typically a few thousandths of a second, or milliseconds. By contrast, the time taken to access a given byte of information stored in random access memory is measured in billionths of a second, or nanoseconds. This illustrates a significant access-time difference which distinguishes solid-state memory from rotating magnetic storage devices: hard disks are typically about a million times slower than memory. Rotating optical storage devices, such as CD and DVD drives, have even longer access times. With disk drives, once the disk read/write head reaches the proper placement and the data of interest rotates under it, subsequent data on the track are very fast to access. As a result, in order to hide the initial seek time and rotational latency, data are transferred to and from disks in large contiguous blocks.

When data reside on disk, block access to hide latency offers a ray of hope in designing efficient external memory algorithms. Sequential or block access on disks is orders of magnitude faster than random access, and many sophisticated paradigms have been developed to design efficient algorithms based upon sequential and block access. Another way to reduce the I/O bottleneck is to use multiple disks in parallel in order to increase the bandwidth between primary and secondary memory.

Some other examples of secondary storage technologies are flash memory (e.g., USB flash drives or keys), floppy disks, magnetic tape, paper tape, punched cards, stand-alone RAM disks, and Iomega Zip drives.

The secondary storage is often formatted according to a file system format, which provides the abstraction necessary to organize data into files and directories, providing also additional information (called metadata) describing the owner of a certain file, the access time, the access permissions, and other information.

Most computer operating systems use the concept of virtual memory, allowing utilization of more primary storage capacity than is physically available in the system. As the primary memory fills up, the system moves the least-used chunks (pages) to secondary storage devices (to a swap file or page file), retrieving them later when they are needed. As more of these retrievals from slower secondary storage are necessary, the more the overall system performance is degraded.

Now more and more computers use solid-state drive as the mail external storage. Not only does it have less noise due to no mechanical movements, but it also runs faster.

3.6.2 Tertiary Storage and Offline Storage*

Tertiary storage, or tertiary memory, provides a third level of storage. Typically, it involves a robotic mechanism which will mount (insert) and dismount removable mass storage media into a storage device according to the system's demands; these data are often copied to secondary storage before use. It is primarily used for archiving rarely accessed information since it is much slower than secondary storage (e.g., 5–60 s vs. 1–10 ms). This is primarily useful for extraordinarily large data stores, accessed without human operators. Typical examples include tape libraries and optical jukeboxes.

When a computer needs to read information from the tertiary storage, it will first consult a catalog database to determine which tape or disc contains the information. Next, the computer will instruct a robotic arm to fetch the medium and place it in a drive. When the computer has finished reading the information, the robotic arm will return the medium to its place in the library.

Offline storage is a computer data storage on a medium or a device that is not under the control of a processing unit. The medium is recorded, usually in a secondary or tertiary storage device and then physically removed or disconnected. It must be inserted or connected by a human operator before a computer can access it again. Unlike tertiary storage, it cannot be accessed without human interaction.

Offline storage is used to transfer information, since the detached medium can be easily physically transported. Additionally, in case a disaster, for example, a fire, destroys the original data, a medium in a remote location will probably be unaffected, enabling disaster recovery. Offline storage increases general information security, since it is physically inaccessible from a computer, and data confidentiality or integrity cannot be affected by computer-based attack techniques. Also, if the information stored for archival purposes is rarely accessed, offline storage is less expensive than tertiary storage.

In modern personal computers, most secondary and tertiary storage media are also used for offline storage. Optical discs and flash memory devices are most popular and to a much lesser extent removable hard disk drives. In enterprise uses, magnetic tape is predominant. Older examples are floppy disks, Zip disks, or punched cards.

3.6.3 Serial Advanced Technology Attachment

Serial advanced technology attachment or serial ATA (SATA) is a computer bus interface for connecting host bus adapters to mass storage devices such as hard disk drives and optical drives. Serial ATA was designed to replace the older parallel ATA (PATA) standard (often called by the old name IDE), offering several advantages over the older interface: reduced cable size and cost (7 conductors instead of 40), native hot swapping, faster data transfer through higher signaling rates, and more efficient transfer through an (optional) I/O queuing protocol.

SATA host adapters and devices communicate via a high-speed serial cable over two pairs of conductors. In contrast, parallel ATA (the redesign for the legacy ATA specifications) used a 16-bit-wide data bus with many additional support and control signals, all operating at much lower frequency. To ensure backward compatibility with legacy ATA software and applications, SATA uses the same basic ATA and ATAPI command set as legacy ATA devices.

As of 2009, SATA has replaced parallel ATA in most shipping consumer desktop and laptop computers and is expected to eventually replace PATA in embedded applications where space and cost are important factors. SATA's market share in the desktop PC market was 99% in 2008. PATA remains widely used in industrial and embedded applications that use CompactFlash storage, though even there, the next CFast storage standard will be based on SATA.

Serial ATA industry compatibility specifications originate from The Serial ATA International Organization (aka SATA-IO, serialata.org). The SATA-IO group collaboratively creates, reviews, ratifies, and publishes the interoperability specifications, the test cases, and plug-fests. As with many other industry compatibility standards, the SATA content ownership is transferred to other industry bodies: primarily the INCITS T13 subcommittee ATA, the INCITS T10 subcommittee (SCSI), a subgroup of T10 responsible for Serial Attached SCSI (SAS). The remainder of this chapter will try to use the terminology and specifications of SATA-IO.

3.6.4 Small Computer System Interface

Small computer system interface (SCSI) is a set of standards for physically connecting and transferring data between computers and peripheral devices. The SCSI standards define commands, protocols, and electrical and optical interfaces. SCSI is most commonly used for hard disks and tape drives, but it can connect a wide range of other devices, including scanners and CD drives, although not all controllers can handle all devices. The SCSI standard defines command sets for specific peripheral device types; the presence of "unknown" as one of these types means that in theory it can be used as an interface to almost any device, but the standard is highly pragmatic and addressed toward commercial requirements.

SCSI is an intelligent, peripheral, buffered, peer-to-peer interface. It hides the complexity of physical format. Every device attaches to the SCSI bus in a similar manner. Up to 8 or 16 devices can be attached to a single bus. There can be any number of hosts and peripheral devices, but there should be at least one host. SCSI uses handshake signals between devices; SCSI-1 and SCSI-2 have the option of parity error checking. Starting with SCSI-U160 (part of SCSI-3), all commands and data are error checked by a CRC32 checksum. The SCSI protocol defines communication from host to host, host to a peripheral device, and peripheral device to a peripheral device. However, most peripheral devices are exclusively SCSI targets, incapable of acting as SCSI initiators—unable to initiate SCSI transactions themselves. Therefore, peripheral-to-peripheral communications are uncommon, but possible in most SCSI applications. The Symbios Logic 53C810 chip is an example of a PCI host interface that can act as a SCSI target.

SCSI is available in a variety of interfaces. The first, still very common, was parallel SCSI (now also called SPI), which uses a parallel electrical bus design. As of 2008, SPI is being replaced by Serial Attached SCSI (SAS), which uses a serial design but retains other aspects of technology. Many other interfaces which do not rely on complete SCSI standards still implement the SCSI command protocol; others (such as iSCSI) drop physical implementation entirely while retaining the SCSI architectural model. iSCSI, for example, uses TCP/IP as a transport mechanism.

SCSI interfaces have often been included on computers from various manufacturers for use under Microsoft Windows, macOS, Unix, Commodore Amiga, and Linux operating systems, either implemented on the motherboard or by means of plug-in adaptors. With the advent of SAS and SATA drives, provision for SCSI on motherboards is being discontinued. A few companies still market SCSI interfaces for motherboards supporting PCIe and PCI-X.

3.6.5 Serial Attached SCSI

Serial attached SCSI (SAS) is a communication protocol used to move data to and from computer storage devices such as hard drives and tape drives. SAS is a point-to-point serial protocol that replaces the parallel SCSI bus technology which first appeared in the mid-1980s in data centers and workstations, and it uses the standard SCSI command set. SAS offers backward compatibility with second-generation SATA drives. SATA 3 Gbit/s drives may be connected to SAS backplanes, but SAS drives may not be connected to SATA backplanes.

The T10 technical committee of the International Committee for Information Technology Standards (INCITS) develops and maintains the SAS protocol; the SCSI Trade Association (SCSITA) promotes the technology.

A typical serial attached SCSI system consists of the following basic components:

- An Initiator: a device that originates device service and task management requests for processing by a target device and receives responses for the same requests from other target devices. Initiators may be provided as an on-board component on the motherboard (as is the case with many server-oriented motherboards) or as an add-on host bus adapter.
- A Target: a device containing logical units and target ports that receives device service and task management requests for processing and sends responses for the same requests to initiator devices. A target device could be a hard disk or a disk array system.

- A Service Delivery Subsystem: the part of an I/O system that transmits information between an initiator and a target. Typically, cables connecting an initiator and target with or without expanders and backplanes constitute a service delivery subsystem.
- Expanders: devices that form part of a service delivery subsystem and facilitate communication between SAS devices. Expanders facilitate the connection of multiple SAS End devices to a single initiator port.

A SAS Domain is the SAS version of a SCSI domain—it consists of a set of SAS devices that communicate with one another by means of a service delivery subsystem. Each SAS port in a SAS domain has a SCSI port identifier that identifies the port uniquely within the SAS domain. It is assigned by the device manufacturer, like an Ethernet device's MAC address, and is typically worldwide unique as well. SAS devices use these port identifiers to address communications to each other.

In addition, every SAS device has a SCSI device name, which identifies the SAS device uniquely in the world. One doesn't often see these device names because the port identifiers tend to identify the device sufficiently.

For comparison, in parallel SCSI, the SCSI ID is the port identifier and device name. In fiber channel, the port identifier is a WWPN, and the device name is a WWNN.

In SAS, both SCSI port identifiers and SCSI device names take the form of a SAS address, which is a 64-bit value, normally in the NAA IEEE Registered format. People sometimes call a SAS address a World Wide Name or WWN, because it is essentially the same thing as a WWN in fiber channel.

Below are the comparison of SAS with parallel SCSI:

- The SAS bus operates point-to-point, while the SCSI bus is multidrop. Each SAS device is connected by a dedicated link to the initiator, unless an expander is used. If one initiator is connected to one target, there is no opportunity for contention; with parallel SCSI, even this situation could cause contention.
- SAS has no termination issues and does not require terminator packs like parallel SCSI.
- SAS eliminates clock skew.
- SAS allows up to 65,535 devices through the use of expanders, while Parallel SCSI has a limit of 8 or 16 devices on a single channel.
- SAS allows a higher transfer speed (3 or 6 Gb/s) than most parallel SCSI standards. SAS achieves these speeds on each initiator-target connection, hence getting higher throughput, whereas parallel SCSI shares the speed across the entire multidrop bus.
- SAS controllers may connect to SATA devices, either directly connected using native SATA protocol or through SAS expanders using SATA Tunneled Protocol (STP).
- Both SAS and parallel SCSI use the SCSI command set.

3.7 Networked Memory

Common types of networked memory are network-attached storage, storage area network, and cloud storage.

3.7.1 Network-Attached Storage*

A network-attached storage (NAS) is a file-level computer data storage connected to a computer network providing data access to heterogeneous clients. NAS not only operates as a file server but is specialized for this task either by its hardware, software, or configuration of those elements. NAS is often made as a computer appliance—a specialized computer built from the ground up for storing and serving files—rather than simply a general-purpose computer being used for the role.

As of 2010, NAS devices are gaining popularity, as a convenient method of sharing files among multiple computers. Potential benefits of network-attached storage, compared to file servers, include faster data access, easier administration, and simple configuration.

NAS systems are networked appliances which contain one or more hard drives, often arranged into logical, redundant storage containers or RAID arrays. Network-attached storage removes the responsibility of file serving from other servers on the network. They typically provide access to files using network file sharing protocols such as NFS, SMB/CIFS, or AFP.

A network-attached storage (NAS) unit is a computer connected to a network that only provides file-based data storage services to other devices on the network. Although it may technically be possible to run other software on a NAS unit, it is not designed to be a general-purpose server. For example, NAS units usually do not have a keyboard or display and are controlled and configured over the network, often using a browser.

A fully featured operating system is not needed on a NAS device, so often a stripped-down operating system is used. For example, FreeNAS, an open-source NAS solution designed for commodity PC hardware, is implemented as a stripped-down version of FreeBSD.

NAS systems contain one or more hard disks, often arranged into logical, redundant storage containers or RAID arrays.

NAS uses file-based protocols such as NFS (popular on UNIX systems), SMB/CIFS (Server Message Block/Common Internet File System) (used with MS Windows systems), or AFP (used with Apple Macintosh computers). NAS units rarely limit clients to a single protocol.

3.7.2   Storage Area Network*

A storage area network (SAN) is a dedicated network that provides access to consolidated, block-level data storage. SANs are primarily used to make storage devices, such as disk arrays, tape libraries, and optical jukeboxes, accessible to servers so that devices appear like locally attached devices to the operating system. A SAN typically has its own network of storage devices that are generally not accessible through the local area network by other devices. The cost and complexity of SANs dropped in the early 2000s to levels allowing wider adoption across both enterprise and small-to-medium-sized business environments.

A SAN does not provide file abstraction, only block-level operations. However, file systems built on top of SANs do provide file-level access and are known as SAN file systems or shared disk file systems.

Historically, data centers first created "islands" of SCSI disk arrays as direct-attached storage (DAS), each dedicated to an application and visible as a number of "virtual hard drives" (i.e., LUNs). Essentially, a SAN consolidates such storage islands together using a high-speed network.

Operating systems maintain their own file systems on their own dedicated, non-shared LUNs, as though they were local to themselves. If multiple systems were simply to attempt to share a LUN, these would interfere with each other and quickly corrupt the data. Any planned sharing of data on different computers within a LUN requires advanced solutions, such as SAN file systems or clustered computing.

Despite such issues, SANs help increase storage capacity utilization, since multiple servers consolidate their private storage space onto the disk arrays.

Common uses of a SAN include provision of transactionally accessed data that require high-speed block-level access to hard drives such as E-mail servers, databases, and high-usage file servers.

NAS provides both storage and a file system. This is often contrasted with SAN (Storage Area Network), which provides only block-based storage and leaves file system concerns on the "client" side. SAN protocols are SCSI, Fiber Channel, iSCSI, ATA over Ethernet (AoE), or HyperSCSI.

One way to loosely conceptualize the difference between a NAS and a SAN is that a NAS appears to the client OS (operating system) as a file server (the client can map network drives to shares on that server), whereas a disk available through a SAN still appears to the client OS as a disk, visible in disk and volume management utilities (along with client's local disks), and available to be formatted with a file system and mounted.

Despite their differences, SAN and NAS are not mutually exclusive, and may be combined as a SAN-NAS hybrid, offering both file-level protocols (NAS) and block-level protocols (SAN) from the same system. An example of this is Openfiler, a free software product running on Linux-based systems.

Sharing storage usually simplifies storage administration and adds flexibility since cables and storage devices do not have to be physically moved to shift storage from one server to another.

Other benefits include the ability to allow servers to boot from the SAN itself. This allows for a quick and easy replacement of faulty servers since the SAN can be reconfigured so that a replacement server can use the LUN of the faulty server. While this area of technology is still new, many views it as being the future of the enterprise datacenter.

SANs also tend to enable more effective disaster recovery processes. A SAN could span a distant location containing a secondary storage array. This enables storage replication either implemented by disk array controllers, by server software, or by specialized SAN devices. Since IP WANs are often the least costly method of long-distance transport, the Fiber Channel over IP (FCIP) and iSCSI protocols have been developed to allow SAN extension over IP networks. The traditional physical SCSI layer could only support a few meters of distance—not nearly enough to ensure business continuance in a disaster.

3.8   Cloud Storage

Cloud storage is a model of networked online storage where data is stored in virtualized pools of storage which are generally hosted by third parties. Hosting companies operate large data centers, and people who require their data to be hosted buy or lease storage capacity from them. The data center operators, in the background, virtualize the resources according to the requirements of the customer and expose them as storage pools, which the customers can themselves use to store files or data objects. Physically, the resource may span across multiple servers.

Cloud storage services may be accessed through a web service application programming interface (API) or through a web-based user interface.

Cloud storage has the same characteristics as cloud computing in terms of agility, scalability, elasticity, and multi-tenancy. It is believed to have been invented by Joseph Carl Robnett Licklider in the 1960s. Since then, cloud computing has developed along a number of lines, with Web 2.0 being the most recent evolution. However, since the Internet only started to offer significant bandwidth in the 1990s, cloud computing for the masses has been something of a late developer.

One of the first milestones for cloud computing was the arrival of Salesforce.com in 1999, which pioneered the concept of delivering enterprise applications via a simple website. The services' firm paved the way for both specialist and mainstream software firms to deliver applications over the Internet. FilesAnywhere also helped pioneer cloud-based storage services that also enable users to securely share files online. Both of these companies continue to offer those services today.

It is difficult to pin down a canonical definition of cloud storage architecture, but object storage is reasonably analogous. Cloud storage services like Amazon S3, cloud storage products like EMC Atmos, and distributed storage research projects like OceanStore are all examples of object storage and infer the following guidelines.

Cloud storage is:

- made up of many distributed resources, but still acts as one.
- highly fault tolerant through redundancy and distribution of data.
- highly durable through the creation of versioned copies.
- typically consistent with regard to data replicas.

The advantages of cloud storage include:

- Companies need only pay for the storage they actually use as it is also possible for companies by utilizing actual virtual storage features like thin provisioning.
- Companies do not need to install physical storage devices in their own data center or offices, but the fact that storage has to be placed anywhere stays the same (maybe localization costs are lower in offshore locations).
- Storage maintenance tasks, such as backup, data replication, and purchasing additional storage devices, are offloaded to the responsibility of a service provider, allowing organizations to focus on their core business, but the fact stays the same that someone has to pay for the administrative effort for these tasks.
- Cloud storage provides users with immediate access to a broad range of resources and applications hosted in the infrastructure of another organization via a web service interface.

There is a number of security issues associated with the cloud storage for using public cloud services. Three general areas that people concern the most: security, privacy, compliance, and legal or contractual issues.

3.8.1   Amazon S3

Amazon Simple Storage Service is storage for the Internet. It is designed to make web-scale computing easier for developers.

Amazon S3 has a simple web services interface that you can use to store and retrieve any amount of data, at any time, from anywhere on the web. It gives any developer access to the same highly scalable, reliable, fast, inexpensive data storage infrastructure that Amazon uses to run its own global network of web sites. The service aims to maximize benefits of scale and to pass those benefits on to developers.

The core concepts of Amazon S3 are buckets and objects and how to work with these resources using the Amazon S3 application programming interface (API).

A bucket is a container for objects stored in Amazon S3. Every object is contained in a bucket. For example, if the object named photos/puppy.jpg is stored in the johnsmith bucket, then it is addressable using the URL http://johnsmith.s3.amazonaws.com/photos/puppy.jpg.

Buckets serve several purposes:

- Organize the Amazon S3 namespace at the highest level.

- Identify the account responsible for storage and data transfer charges.
- Play a role in access control.
- Serve as the unit of aggregation for usage reporting.

Objects are the fundamental entities stored in Amazon S3. Objects consist of object data and metadata. The data portion is opaque to Amazon S3. The metadata is a set of name-value pairs that describe the object. These include some default metadata, such as the date last modified, and standard HTTP metadata, such as Content-Type. You can also specify custom metadata at the time the object is stored.

A key is the unique identifier for an object within a bucket. Every object in a bucket has exactly one key. The combination of a bucket, key, and version ID uniquely identify each object.

3.8.2 OneDrive, Dropbox, and iCloud

There are many cloud storage services we use today, including Google drive, Microsoft OneDrive, Dropbox, and Apple iCloud.

Dropbox is a cloud storage service. It keeps a local copy so people can work even offline. When network resumes, local copy will merge with remote cloud copy, so changes made can be updated. The sync feature is especially useful as Dropbox will sync data across all devices.

iCloud has the same feature as Dropbox. In addition, people find it helpful to sync Apple device data in case a recovery or device upgrade is needed.

3.9 Memory Access Security

Executable space protection is the making of memory regions as non-executable, such that an attempt to execute machine code in these regions will cause an exception. It makes use of hardware features such as the NX (non-executable) bit.

If an operating system can mark some or all writable regions of memory as non-executable, it may be able to prevent the stack and heap memory areas from being executed. This helps prevent certain buffer overflow exploits from succeeding, particularly those that inject and execute code, such as the Sasser and Blaster worms. These attacks rely on some part of memory, usually the stack, being both writable and executable; if it is not, the attack fails.

As we know, dynamic random access memory (DRAM) stores data in separate capacitors within an integrated circuit. It needs to be refreshed, e.g., every 64 ms, to avoid data loss. In reality the memory cell capacitors will often retain their values for significantly long, particularly at low temperatures. In many cases, most of the data in DRAM can be recovered even if the DRAM has not been refreshed for several minutes.

This long-lasting capacitor property can be used by hackers to recover data kept in memory by quickly rebooting the computer and dumping the contents of the RAM or by cooling the chips and transferring them to a different computer.

USB flash drives are convenient external memory to store data or even sensitive data. The main disadvantage is the physical security. It is easy to be lost or stolen. To ensure data security, people usually use hardware solutions or software solutions, or both, to protect data.

A software solution to protect data is to use encryption. There are programs that can encrypt data on a USB drive automatically and transparently. A hardware solution is to embed hardware encryption. Hardware solution may offer additional feature by overwriting the data on the drive if a wrong password is entered more than a certain number of times.

Segmentation is another technique to provide not only more virtual address but also protection of the data stored in the segments. Stacks and some arrays use dynamic data structure. A growing data structure might bump into the next one. If operating systems allocate the addresses linearly or in other words use single address space, it may overwrite each other.

The memory being overwritten may cause system to crash or a breach of system security. A carefully planned memory that is overwritten may let hackers take control of a computer system, stop services, and steal data. It is commonly seen as buffer overflow attacks.

A buffer is an area of memory that can be used to store user input, for example. Buffers often have some fixed maximum size. If the user provides more input than it can fit into the buffer, the extra input might end up in unexpected places in memory, and the buffer is said to overflow.

An execution stack is to keep track of what function programs are running at any particular time and what function they need to return to after finishing the current function.

Figure 3.10a shows a single memory address space. As the stack grows up, it may overwrite the program. In Fig. 3.10b, program, data, and stack are stored in separate segments. We can make the program segment execute only and make the data segment non-executable. This will address the memory overwritten and some buffer overflow problems.

Let us look at another example as shown in Fig. 3.11. The main program checks the password; if the password is correct, then ATM is opened (Buffer overflow 2019). Here the password is supposed to be 16 characters long.

If the user enters a password that is more than 16 characters, the extra characters will overwrite the return address (back to the main program). A hacker can construct the 17th to 20th characters in a way that they are exactly the same as the address of open ATM subroutine. Now even if the password is entered incorrectly, the ATM may still be opened! The crafted 17th to 20th characters are called attack string.

It is common for corporations to use cloud services for E-mail and some non-critical applications. Storing sensitive data such as financial and marketing data in the cloud is less common. The main skeptical issue is data security. Now many

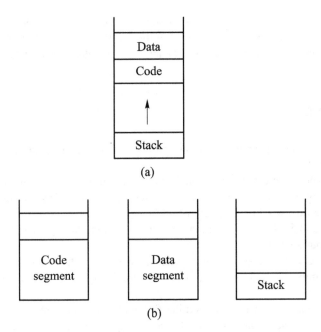

Fig. 3.10 Memory segmentation and memory access security. (**a**) Single address space. (**b**) Memory space segmentation

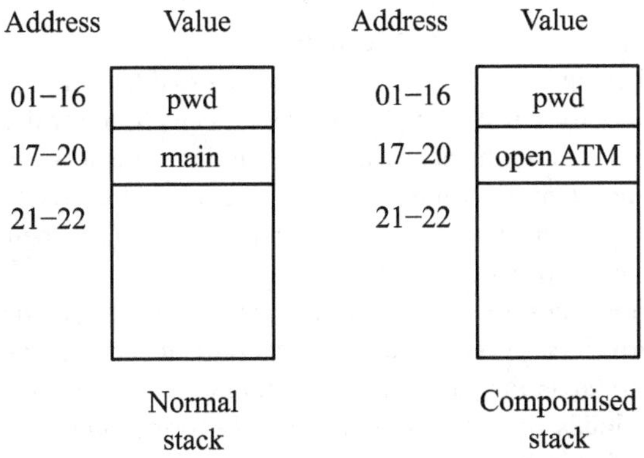

Fig. 3.11 Buffer overflow attack

organizations use Virtual Private Clouds (VPCs) for accessing corporate data. Cloud data security is an important and ongoing topic that needs to be solved.

Cache are faster memory that can improve the overall speed of computer systems. It is assessed by blocks and divided by two to three levels. As most of the enterprise computers are now cloud based, this means they provide large numbers of services through virtualization technology, a technology that "turns" one computer into many "independent" computers.

Ideally all virtual machines (hosts) should be isolated, so there is no data access from one host to another. Spectre and Meltdown, attacks that can access data across virtual machines, add another layer of concern to the data security in the cloud.

3.10 Summary

We have discussed different memories and how a basic memory unit is constructed using a flip-flop.

A computer memory system contains vast amount of memory units. To access each memory unit, we use the matrix style method by decoding the address using MAR and store a word of data with MDR.

DRAM and SRAM are common memory in a computer system. They provide fast speed but are volatile.

Cache memory is faster memory than main memory but small in quantity. It provides handy data access to the CPU by predicting and pre-fetching the data blocks.

Virtual memory shares some similarities with the cache memory to increase memory address space and increase the accessing speed. With the help of virtual memory, programs are able to run concurrently without worrying about the memory limitations.

Non-volatile memory includes ROM, PROM, EPRPM, and EEPROM. USB flash drives are built based on EEPROM technology.

Hard drives belong to external memory. They provide vast amount of memory, but the speed is usually slower than flash drives and much slower than main memory.

Many computer security breaches are the result from memory violations. Protecting memory is important to ensure computer security. Buffer overflow is a common problem in security. Executable space protection can protect memory from being executed by malicious programs.

Data encryption can protect unauthorized data access stored on computers and flash drives. Hardware encryption and protection can remove data in the event a hacker is trying to break the password for certain times. Cloud storage has become popular. Public clouds provide infrastructure, platforms, and software as services for customers. Before moving sensitive data in a cloud, studies should be conducted to guarantee data security.

Projects

3.1 Use Tinkercad design and simulation one-bit memory circuit.

3.2 Amazon S3. Set up a free AWS account, and store some files on the S3.

Exercises

3.1 Design a one-bit memory circuit and provide a state table and state diagram for the circuit.

3.2 MDR is used to decode address signals from the CPU. For a 16-bit address bus, how much memory can be attached to the system directly?

3.3 RAM is volatile; why not use non-volatile memory in main memory?

3.4 We know registers are faster than cache memory and cache memory is faster than main memory. Why not replace all main memory with cache memory?

3.5 Now some computers use flash memory-based solid disk to replace hard drives. In addition to be noise-less, what are other advantages?

3.6 A 32-bit processor can address 4 G memory. How can one build a 32-bit computer with more than 4 G memory?

3.7 What are the similarities between cache memory and virtual memory?

3.8 What are the difference between cache memory and virtual memory?

3.9 A computer uses virtual memory to increase the memory space. How do you translate a virtual address to a physical address?

3.10 What are the benefits of using memory segmentation technique?

3.11 How can "executable space protection" enhance memory access security?

3.12 How to secure memory to prevent buffer overflow attacks?

3.13 Visit a computer store such as Micro Center or online, and discover USB flash drives that provide best security features to protect data.

3.14 DRAM keeps data after power went off. (T/F)

3.15 A 32-bit CPU usually contains 32-bit physical address lines, same as that for 16-bit and 8-bit CPUs. Explain why a 64-bit CPU usually contains 40 to 52 physical address lines, less than 64-bit as the architecture implies.

3.16 Cloud service providers offer a large number of private virtual clouds to many users. At the server side, data from all users are loaded to cache memory. Study the potential vulnerabilities of cloud platforms, and write a 300-word summary with countermeasures.

References

Buffer overflow. Wikipedia. Retrieved February 29, 2019.

Dumas, J. D. (2016). *Computer architecture: Fundamentals and principles of computer design*. Abingdon: Taylor & Francis.

Foster, C. C., & Iberall, T. (1985). *Computer architecture* (3rd ed.). New York: van Nostrand Reinhold Company.

Hwang, K. (1993). *Advanced computer architecture: Parallelism, scalability, programmability*. New York: McGraw-Hill, Inc.

Non-Volatile Memory – featured Shuangbao Wang for his invention of flash memory. Qingdao Daily. Dec. 19, 1988.

Randell, B. (Ed.). (1982). *The designs of digital computers*. Berlin: Springer-Verlag.

Shiva, S. G. (2000). *Computer design and architecture* (3rd ed.). New York: Marcel Dekker Inc.

Chapter 4
Bus and Interconnection

Computer architecture is the study of building robust and secure CPUs, memory, and other key components and the connection between those components. Computer buses consist of three types of signals: address, data, and control. In (Neumann) single-bus architecture, all bus signals are usually integrated together according to a certain standard which can be easily connected to the CPU, memory, video, network, and other general devices.

Earlier computers use one motherboard to integrate the CPU, memory, and internal buses. Other I/O cards such as video and network can be inserted later if they comply with the bus standard of the motherboard.

Laptop computers and all-in-one computers are usually designed to integrate all circuits including the CPU, memory, video, sound, and network cards into one circuit board. In these systems, the system bus is not obviously to be seen, but it still exists as the traditional computers.

4.1 System Bus

A system bus, or in other term an internal bus, is usually referred to as all signals that connect to a processor. A system bus consists of three sub-bus systems, an address bus, a data bus, and a control bus. Figure 4.1 shows the Neumann architecture and the three buses.

The address bus is used for addressing a specific memory unit or a specific I/O device.

The width (the number of address lines) determines the CPU's addressing ability. For an 8-bit processor, the addressing space is 256. For a 32-bit processor, the addressing space is 4 G.

The data bus is used for accessing data with the main memory. The wider it is (more data bus lines), the more access to data the processor will be able to have at

© The Author(s), under exclusive license to Springer Nature Singapore Pte Ltd. 2021
S. P. Wang, *Computer Architecture and Organization*,
https://doi.org/10.1007/978-981-16-5662-0_4

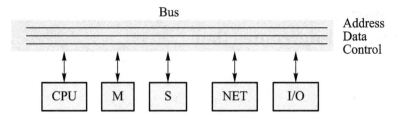

Fig. 4.1 A system bus consists of an address bus, a data bus, and a control bus

one time. For an 8-bit data bus, data can be read/write 8 bits at one time. If the data contains 30 bits, then it requires four reading times to get the data. While for a 32-bit data bus, it only requires one read instruction to get all the 30-bit data.

The control bus is a collection of control signals from the CPU. Here are some control signals in the control bus:

- **Clock** The clock signal (usually represented as φ) is used to synchronize memory and other devices with the processor. Some instructions only need one cycle (such as shift, logical bit operations), while others may require more cycles to perform the instruction. For a processor with the clock frequency f, the cycle $T = 1/f$.
- **Reset** Reset signal will initialize the processor. It is usually referred to as warm reboot. Many computers come with a reset button. In the event the system is frozen, a warm start usually can solve the problem.
- **Read/Write** The R/W signal is used to communicate with the memory or I/O devices to send or receive data to or from the CPU.
- **Interrupt** The interrupt signal is used to indicate if there is a device requesting data exchange with the CPU. There is also an acknowledgement (ACK) signal that tells the device if the request has been granted.

4.1.1 Address Bus

An address bus is a computer bus (a series of lines connecting two or more devices) that is used to specify a physical address. When a processor or DMA-enabled device needs to read or write to a memory location, it specifies that memory location on the address bus (the value to be read or written is sent on the data bus). The width of the address bus determines the amount of memory a system can address (Dumas 2006). For example, a system with a 32-bit address bus can address 2^{32} (4,294,967,296) memory locations. If each memory address holds 1 byte, the addressable memory space is 4 GB.

Early processors used one wire for each bit of the address. For example, a 16-bit address bus has 16 physical wires making up the bus. As the buses became wider, this approach became expensive in terms of the number of chip pins and board traces. Beginning with the Mostek 4096 DRAM, multiplexed addressing became common. In a multiplexed address scheme, the address is sent in two equal parts. This half the number of address bus signals required to connect to the memory. For example, a 32-bit address bus can be implemented by using 16 wires and sending the first half of the memory address, immediately followed by the second half.

A 64-bit register can store $2^{64} = 18,446,744,073,709,551,616$ different values, a number in excess of 18 quintillion. Hence, a processor with 64-bit memory addresses can theoretically directly access 2^{64} bytes of byte-addressable memory.

Without further qualification, a 64-bit computer architecture generally has integer and addressing registers that are 64 bits wide, allowing direct support for 64-bit data types and addresses. However, a CPU might have external data buses or address buses with different sizes from the registers, even larger or smaller (the 32-bit Pentium had a 64-bit data bus, for instance). The term may also refer to the size of low-level data types, such as 64-bit floating-point numbers.

Some computers have direct connections from the address bus of the processor and other system devices to the main memory. Many peripheral controllers can share system memory with the processor using a technique called Direct Memory Access (DMA). A network, hard disk, or graphics controller may be a DMA-enabled device (Foster and Iberall 1985). This allows the controller to transfer data to and from the system faster than sending it through the processor one piece at a time.

Regardless of whether the physical address comes from the processor or a DMA device, it is latched onto the address bus. This action alerts the memory that a read or write request for that memory address is about to be made. If a write operation is pending, the data to be written is latched onto the data bus, and a memory write signal is triggered. A read operation can be performed by triggering the memory read signal and reading the data bus.

Most personal computer (PC)-compatible servers and desktops use a memory controller chip which is separate from the main processor. This controller communicates with the main system memory over the memory bus. This bus includes the address bus, data bus, and many control signals. The memory controller is located in the northbridge device and interfaces with the main processor using the front-side bus (FSB).

The northbridge memory controller and the FSB can create a bottleneck in some systems, slowing the processor's memory access. For this reason, a system's high-speed cache memory uses an entirely separate and wider cache bus. The cache is directly connected to the processor through this bus, bypassing the FSB and the northbridge completely. The cache bus, also known as the back-side bus (BSB), functions as an address bus, data bus, and control bus for the cache memory exclusively.

Some PC-compatible processors include a memory controller in the main processor itself. This controller accesses the main system memory directly, without using the FSB or the northbridge device. With these bottlenecks removed, the processor spends less time waiting on main system memory accesses. Cache memory is often included in these processors as well, and any external cache is accessed through the cache bus.

4.1.2 Data Bus

A data bus is a computer subsystem that allows for the transfer of data from one component to another on a motherboard or system board, or between two computers. This can include transferring data to and from the memory, or from the central processing unit to other components. Each one is designed to handle many bits of data at a time. The amount of data in which a data bus can handle for a certain period of time is called bandwidth.

A typical data bus is 32-bit or 64-bit wide. This means that up to 32 bits or 64 bits of data can travel through a data bus every cycle.

In the early days of the personal computer, manufacturers created motherboards with data buses that were directly connected to the computer's memory and peripherals. These electrical buses were designed to run parallel to each other and had multiple connections. This direct connection was problematic for a number of reasons, but especially because all devices were forced to run at the same speed.

To eliminate this problem, developers used a bus controller to separate the CPU and memory from the peripheral devices, allowing CPU speed to be increased without requiring the same increase in peripheral speeds. This system also allowed expansion cards to speak to each other without going through the CPU, leading to quicker data transfer. All devices still must speak to each other at the same speed; however, low bus speeds may slow an entire computer system.

Modern computers use both parallel and serial data buses. Parallel data buses carry data on many wires simultaneously. Each wire, or path, as they are sometimes called, carries one bit of data. The common parallel buses found in computers are the ATA, which stands for Advanced Technology Attachment; the PC card, which stands for personal computer and is used in laptops; and the SCSI, or Small Computer System Interface. A serial data bus has one wire or path and carries all the bits, one after the other. The most common serial data buses include the USB, also known as the universal serial bus, FireWire, Serial ATA, and Serial Attached SCSI.

Nearly every computer contains internal and external data buses. The internal data bus, also known as a local bus, connects all components on the motherboard, like the CPU and memory. The external data bus connects all peripheral devices to the motherboard. A variety of different external data buses are available, and the appropriate type of data bus depends on the peripheral being attached to the computer. Nowadays, the USB is de facto a standard for peripherals.

4.1.3 Control Bus

A control bus is what a computer's central processing unit (CPU) uses to communicate with other devices inside the machine over a set of physical connections like cables or printed circuits. It is a diverse collection of signals, including read, write, and interrupt, which allow the CPU to direct and monitor what the different parts of the computer are doing. This is one of the three types of buses that make up the system or computer bus. Its exact composition varies among processors.

In general, the purpose of any bus is to decrease the number of pathways necessary for communication between computer components. A bus allows communication between components over one data channel and is characterized by how much information it can transmit at once. The amount of data is expressed in bits and corresponds to the number of physical lines over which the information is sent. For example, a ribbon cable with 32 wires can send 32 bits in parallel.

Each computer usually has an internal and an expansion bus. The internal or front-side bus facilitates communication between the CPU and the central memory, while the expansion or input/output bus links the motherboard components like hard drives and ports. Most system buses are typically composed of between 50 and 100 separate physical lines for communication. These lines are subdivided into three sub-assemblies or types of buses: the address or memory bus, the data bus, and the command or control bus.

The control bus is bidirectional; it transmits command signals from the CPU and response signals from the hardware. It helps the CPU synchronize its command signals to the computer's components and slower external devices. As a result, the control bus consists of control lines that each send a specific signal, like read, write, and interrupt. The control lines that make up a control bus differ between processors, but most include system clock lines, status lines, and byte-enable lines.

For example, a CPU uses the data bus to transmit information to and from the central memory. The control bus allows the CPU to determine whether and when the system sends or receives the data, because a control bus has a control line for read and one for write that determine the direction the information flows (memory to CPU or CPU to memory). If the CPU needs to write some data to the central memory, it will send a signal on (assert) the control bus's write control line. Sending a signal on the read control line allows the CPU to receive data from memory.

The other types of buses that make up a system bus are the data and address buses. The data bus moves instructions and information between all the functional computer components. It is bidirectional and can transmit in only one direction at a time. The data bus transmits information between the CPU and memory and also between memory and the input/output section.

The address bus is unidirectional and functions like a map for the memory. When the computer system needs to access a particular memory location or input/output device, it asserts the appropriate address on the address bus. This address is recognized by the appropriate circuitry that then instructs the corresponding memory or device to read or send data on the data bus. Only the device or memory location that corresponds to the address on the address bus will respond.

4.2   Parallel Bus and Serial Bus

Buses on motherboard are mostly parallel buses. A word of data can be read from memory at one time with one instruction. The industry standard bus (ISA) and peripheral component interconnect (PCI), mini PCI, and STD-bus are parallel buses.

PCI express is a high-speed serial system bus that has 1–32-bit bus width. It is commonly used for disk array controllers, gigabit Ethernet, and Wi-Fi to supersede accelerated graphics post (AGP) and PCI buses.

The universal serial bus (USB) is the most common serial bus we are using right now. It can connect with most computer peripherals such as keyboard, mouse, printers, and external hard drives.

A standard USB connector has four pins, two reserved for data and two for the power (Shiva 2000). Figure 4.2 shows the cable wiring for USB 1.0/2.0. To reduce the interferences, the two data lines are pairs and twisted.

USB 2.0 is able to transmit at the speed up to 480 Mb/s. It is generally considered sufficient for a variety of devices. However, with today's ever-increasing demands on high-definition video content and terabyte storage devices, this speed is not really fast enough.

USB 3.0, or super speed USB, offers higher transfer rate up to 5 Gb/s (Universal serial bus 2019). It is backward compatible with USB 2.0. In addition, it provides better power management features.

4.2.1   Parallel Buses and Parallel Communication

In telecommunication and computer science, parallel communication is a method of sending several data signals simultaneously over several parallel channels. It contrasts with serial communication; this distinction is one way of characterizing a communications link.

PIN	Name	Des	Color
1	V_{CC}	+5 V	Red
2	D−	Data−	White
3	D+	Data+	Green
4	GND	Ground	Black

Fig. 4.2   USB pinout and cable wiring diagram

The basic difference between a parallel and a serial communication channel is the number of distinct wires or strands at the physical layer used for simultaneous transmission from a device. Parallel communication implies more than one such wire/strand, in addition to a ground connection. An 8-bit parallel channel transmits eight bits (or a byte) simultaneously. A serial channel would transmit those bits one at a time. If both operated at the same clock speed, the parallel channel would be eight times faster. A parallel channel will generally have additional control signals such as a clock, to indicate that the data is valid, and possibly other signals for handshaking and directional control of data transmission.

Examples of parallel communication include peripheral buses such as ISA, ATA, SCSI PCI, and IEEE-1284 (printer port).

Before the development of high-speed serial technologies, the choice of parallel links over serial links was driven by these factors:

- Speed   Superficially, the speed of a parallel data link is equal to the number of bits sent at one time times the bit rate of each individual path; doubling the number of bits sent at once doubles the data rate. In practice, clock skew reduces the speed of every link to the slowest of all of the links.
- Cable length   Crosstalk creates interference between the parallel lines, and the effect worsens with the length of the communication link. This places an upper limit on the length of a parallel data connection that is usually shorter than a serial connection.
- Complexity   Parallel data links are easily implemented in hardware, making them a logical choice. Creating a parallel port in a computer system is relatively simple, requiring only a latch to copy data onto a data bus. In contrast, most serial communication must be converted back into parallel form by a universal asynchronous receiver/transmitter (UART) before they may be directly connected to a data bus.

The decreasing cost of integrated circuits, combined with greater consumer demand for speed and cable length, has led to parallel communication links becoming deprecated in favor of serial links, for example, IEEE 1284 printer ports vs. USB, Parallel ATA vs. Serial ATA, and SCSI vs. FireWire.

On the other hand, there has been a resurgence of parallel data links in RF communication. Rather than transmitting one bit at a time (as in Morse code and BPSK), well-known techniques such as PSM, PAM, and multiple-input multiple-output communication send a few bits in parallel (each such group of bits is called a "symbol"). Such techniques can be extended to send an entire byte at once (256-QAM). More recently techniques such as OFDM have been used in asymmetric digital subscriber line (ADSL) to transmit over 224 bits in parallel and in DVB-T to transmit over 6048 bits in parallel.

4.2.2 Serial Bus and Serial Communication

In telecommunication and computer science, serial communication is the process of sending data one bit at a time, sequentially, over a communication channel or computer bus. This is in contrast to parallel communication, where several bits are sent as a whole, on a link with several parallel channels. Serial communication is used for all long-haul communication and most computer networks, where the cost of cable and synchronization difficulties make parallel communication impractical. Serial computer buses are becoming more common even at shorter distances, as improved signal integrity and transmission speeds in newer serial technologies have begun to outweigh the parallel bus's advantage of simplicity (no need for serializer and de-serializer, or SerDes) and to outstrip its disadvantages (clock skew, interconnect density). The migration from PCI to PCI Express is an example.

Integrated circuits are more expensive when they have more pins. To reduce the number of pins in a package, many ICs use a serial bus to transfer data when speed is not important. Some examples of such low-cost serial buses include SPI, I^{2}C, UNI/O, and 1-Wire.

The communication links across which computers—or parts of computers—talk to one another may be either serial or parallel. A parallel link transmits several streams of data simultaneously along multiple channels (e.g., wires, printed circuit tracks, or optical fibers), while a serial link transmits a single stream of data.

Although a serial link may seem inferior to a parallel one, since it can transmit less data per clock cycle, it is often the case that serial links can be clocked considerably faster than parallel links in order to achieve a higher data rate. A number of factors allow serial to be clocked at a higher rate:

- Clock skew between different channels is not an issue (for unclocked asynchronous serial communication links).
- A serial connection requires fewer interconnecting cables (e.g., wires/fibers) and hence occupies less space. The extra space allows for better isolation of the channel from its surroundings.
- Crosstalk is less of an issue, because there are fewer conductors in proximity.

In many cases, serial is a better option because it is cheaper to implement. Many ICs have serial interfaces, as opposed to parallel ones, so that they have fewer pins and are therefore less expensive.

Examples of serial communication architecture include Morse code, RS-232, Ethernet, MIDI, USB, Serial Attached SCSI (SAS), Serial ATA (SATA), PCI Express, SONET, etc.

4.2.2.1 RS-232

In telecommunications, RS-232 is the traditional name for a series of standards for serial binary single-ended data and control signals connecting between a data

Fig. 4.3 25-pin RS-232
connector

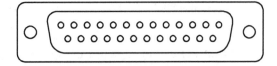

terminal equipment (DTE) and a data circuit-terminating equipment (DCE) (Randell 1982). It is commonly used in computer serial ports. The standard defines the electrical characteristics and timing of signals, the meaning of signals, and the physical size and pin out of connectors. The current version of the standard is TIA-232-F interface between data terminal equipment and data circuit-terminating equipment employing serial binary data interchange, issued in 1997.

An RS-232 port (as shown in Fig. 4.3) was once a standard feature of a personal computer for connections to modems, printers, mice, data storage, un-interruptible power supplies, and other peripheral devices. However, the limited transmission speed, relatively large voltage swing, and large standard connectors motivated development of the universal serial bus which has displaced RS-232 from most of its peripheral interface roles. Many modern personal computers have no RS-232 ports and must use an external converter to connect to older peripherals. Some RS-232 devices are still found especially in industrial machines or scientific instruments.

In the book PC 97 Hardware Design Guide, Microsoft deprecated support for the RS-232-compatible serial port of the original IBM PC design. Today, RS-232 has mostly been replaced in personal computers by USB for local communications. Compared with RS-232, USB is faster, uses lower voltages, and has connectors that are simpler to connect and use. However, USB is limited by standard to no more than 5 m of cable, thus favoring RS-232 when longer distances are needed. Both standards have software support in popular operating systems. USB is designed to make it easy for device drivers to communicate with hardware. However, there is no direct analog to the terminal programs used to let users communicate directly with serial ports. USB is more complex than the RS-232 standard because it includes a protocol for transferring data to devices. This requires more software to support the protocol used. RS-232 only standardizes the voltage of signals and the functions of the physical interface pins. Serial ports of personal computers are also sometimes used to directly control various hardware devices, such as relays or lamps, since the control lines of the interface can be easily manipulated by software. This is not feasible with USB, which requires some form of receiver to decode the serial data.

As an alternative, USB docking ports are available which can provide connectors for a keyboard, mouse, one or more serial ports, and one or more parallel ports. Corresponding device drivers are required for each USB-connected device to allow programs to access these USB-connected devices as if they were the original directly connected peripherals. Devices that convert USB to RS-232 may not work with all software on all personal computers and may cause a reduction in bandwidth along with higher latency.

Personal computers may use a serial port to interface to devices such as uninterruptible power supplies. In some cases, serial data is not exchanged, but the control lines are used to signal conditions such as loss of power or low-battery alarms.

Many fields (e.g., laboratory automation, surveying) provide a continued demand for RS-232 I/O due to sustained use of very expensive but aging equipment. It is often far cheaper to continue using RS-232 than to replace the equipment. Additionally, modern industrial automation equipment, such as PLCs, VFDs, servo drives, and CNC equipment, are programmable via RS-232. Some manufacturers have responded to this demand: Toshiba re-introduced the DE-9M connector on the Tecra laptop.

Serial ports with RS-232 are also commonly used to communicate to headless systems such as servers, where no monitor or keyboard is installed, during boot when operating system is not running yet, and therefore no network connection is possible. An RS-232 serial port can communicate to some embedded systems such as routers as an alternative to network mode of monitoring.

4.2.3   Ethernet

Ethernet is a family of computer networking technologies for local area networks (LANs) commercially introduced in 1980. Standardized in IEEE 802.3, Ethernet has largely replaced competing wired LAN technologies.

Systems communicating over Ethernet divide a stream of data into individual packets called frames. Each frame contains source and destination addresses and error-checking data so that damaged data can be detected and re-transmitted.

The standards define several wirings and signaling variants. The original 10BASE5 Ethernet used coaxial cable as a shared medium. Later the coaxial cables were replaced by twisted pair and fiber-optic links in conjunction with hubs or switches. Data rates were periodically increased from the original 10 megabits per second to 100 gigabits per second.

Since its commercial release, Ethernet has retained a good degree of compatibility. Features such as the 48-bit MAC address and Ethernet frame format have influenced other networking protocols. Figure 4.4 shows a RJ-45 jack.

Ethernet evolved to include higher bandwidth, improved media access control methods, and different physical media. The coaxial cable was replaced with point-to-point links connected by Ethernet repeaters or switches to reduce installation costs, increase reliability, and improve management and troubleshooting. Many variants of Ethernet remain in common use.

Ethernet stations communicate by sending each other data packets, blocks of data individually sent and delivered. As with other IEEE 802 LANs, each Ethernet station is given a 48-bit MAC address. The MAC addresses are used to specify both the destination and the source of each data packet. Ethernet establishes link-level connections, which can be defined using both the destination and source addresses. On reception of a transmission, the receiver uses the destination address to determine whether the transmission is relevant to the station or should be ignored.

Fig. 4.4 RJ-45 jack

Network interfaces normally do not accept packets addressed to other Ethernet stations. Adapters come programmed with a globally unique address. An Ether-type field in each frame is used by the operating system on the receiving station to select the appropriate protocol module (i.e., the Internet protocol module). Ethernet frames are said to be self-identifying, because of the frame type. Self-identifying frames make it possible to intermix multiple protocols on the same physical network and allow a single computer to use multiple protocols together. Despite the evolution of Ethernet technology, all generations of Ethernet (excluding early experimental versions) use the same frame formats (and hence the same interface for higher layers) and can be readily interconnected through bridging.

Due to the ubiquity of Ethernet, the ever-decreasing cost of the hardware needed to support it, and the reduced panel space needed by twisted pair Ethernet, most manufacturers now build Ethernet interfaces directly into PC motherboards, eliminating the need for installation of a separate network card.

For signal degradation and timing reasons, coaxial Ethernet segments had a restricted size. Somewhat larger networks could be built by using an Ethernet repeater. Early repeaters had only two ports, allowing, at most, a doubling of network size. Once repeaters with 4, 6, 8, and more ports became available, it was possible to wire the network in a star topology. Early experiments with star topologies (called "Fibernet") using optical fiber were published by 1978.

In 1989, the networking company Kalpana introduced their EtherSwitch, the first Ethernet switch. This worked somewhat differently from an Ethernet bridge, in that only the header of the incoming packet would be examined before it was either dropped or forwarded to another segment. This greatly reduced the forwarding latency and the processing load on the network device. The Ethernet physical layer evolved over a considerable time span and encompasses quite a few physical media interfaces and several magnitudes of speed. The most common forms used are 10BASE-T, 100BASE-TX, and 1000BASE-T. All three utilize twisted pair cables and 8P8C modular connectors. They run at 10 Mb/s, 100 Mb/s, and 1 Gb/s, respectively. Fiber-optic variants of Ethernet offer high performance, electrical isolation, and distance (tens of kilometers with some versions). In general, network protocol stack software will work similarly on all varieties.

4.2.4   MIDI*

Musical instrument digital interface (MIDI) is an electronic musical instrument industry specification that enables a wide variety of digital musical instruments, computers, and other related devices to connect and communicate seamlessly with one another.

The primary functions of MIDI include communicating event messages about musical notation, pitch, velocity, control signals for parameters such as volume, vibrato, audio panning, cues, and clock signals (to set and synchronize tempo) between multiple devices; these complete a signal chain and produce audible sound from a sound source. For users, MIDI enables a single player to sound as though they are playing two or more instruments simultaneously. As an electronic protocol, it is notable for its widespread adoption throughout the music industry.

Establishment of the MIDI standard occurred in the early 1980s, yielding a number of significant benefits to musicians, recording artists, and hobbyists.

- Common language and syntax   Electronic keyboards, drum machines, computers, music sequencers, and other specialty instruments designed to work with MIDI indiscriminately communicate with one another.
- Simplified connectivity   Decreased the complexity (and volume) of connection cables required between devices.
- Fewer contributors required   Beginning in the 1980s, musical acts can perform live with as few as one or two members who operate multiple MIDI-enabled devices simultaneously and successfully deliver a performance which sounds similar to that of a much larger group of live musicians.
- Increased accessibility   Enabled users to create, edit, layer, and build high-quality digital music recordings with less expense; professional musicians can now do this using a home recording space (or any other environment) without the need for renting a professional recording studio and staff. It has also enabled hobbyists, with little or no musical training, to produce high-quality recordings with the powerful capabilities of MIDI music editing software.
- Portability of electronic music gear   Greatly reduced the amount and variety of equipment (as well as wired connections) that performing musicians needed to travel around with, haul, pack and unpack, set up, and connect, in order to produce a variety of sounds.

Standard applications that use MIDI:

- Electronic keyboards   Synthesizers and samplers which feature a built-in keyboard, MIDI keyboards (also referred to as MIDI controllers), or hardware music workstations.
- Personal computers   Equipped with an internal MIDI-capable sound card.

- MIDI interfaces   Used to connect MIDI devices to devices without built-in MIDI capability. A common usage scenario is enabling MIDI support on a computer via an external sound card, which connects via USB or FireWire. Other applications include interconnectivity with analog (non-digital) audio outputs, microphone inputs, and optical audio cables.
- Audio control surfaces   Often resembling a mixing console in appearance, enable a level of hands-on control for changing parameters such as sound levels and effects applied to individual tracks of a multitrack recording or live performance output.
- Digital effects units   Apply audio effects such as reverb, delay, and chorus to simulate the sound of the music being played in a large hall, or in a canyon, or with multiple voices all playing at once, respectively.
- Digital percussion devices   Trigger percussive or other relatively short sounds, usually via specifying a pattern or order in which the sounds should be played, on a drum machine or rhythm machine (also referred to as simply "beat boxes").
- Other musical instruments   Non-traditional and DIY devices custom built to accept MIDI input, or devices adapted with additional hardware to provide MIDI-compatible signals. The MIDI guitar and MIDI violin are two such instruments.

In popular parlance, piano-style musical keyboards are called "keyboards," regardless of their functions or type. Among MIDI enthusiasts, however, keyboards and other devices used to trigger musical sounds are called "controllers," because with most MIDI setups, the keyboard or other device does not make any sounds by itself. MIDI controllers need to be connected to a voice bank or sound module in order to produce musical tones or sounds; the keyboard or other device is "controlling" the voice bank or sound module by acting as a trigger. The most common MIDI controller is the piano-style keyboard, either with weighted or semi-weighted keys or with unweighted synth-style keys. Keyboard-style MIDI controllers are sold with as few as 25 keys (2 octaves), with larger models such as 49 keys, 61 keys, or even the full 88 keys being available. Different models have different feature sets, the simplest being only keys, while the more extravagant have sliders, knobs, and wheels to provide more controlling options. These include a variety of parameters that can be programmed within the controller or sent to a computer to control software.

MIDI controllers are also available in a range of other forms, such as electronic drum triggers, pedal keyboards that are played with the feet (e.g., with an organ), wind controllers for performing saxophone-style music, and MIDI guitar synthesizer controllers. A wind controller is designed for performers who want to play the saxophone, clarinet, oboe, bassoon, and other wind instrument sounds with a synthesizer module. When wind instruments are played using a MIDI keyboard, it is hard to reproduce the expressive control found on wind instruments that can be generated with the wind pressure and embouchure. A typical wind controller has an air pressure level sensor and (usually) a bite sensor in the mouthpiece and touch sensors or keys (commonly approximating saxophone key arrangement) arrayed along the body. Additionally, controls such as buttons, touch sensors, and pitch wheels for generating additional MIDI messages or changing the way the controller behaves (e.g., note sustain or octave shifts) are typically located in positions where they can, more or less easily, be accessed while playing. A less common type of wind controller mimics the mechanics of valve brass instruments.

Pad controllers are used by musicians and DJs who make music through the use of sampled sounds or short samples of music. Pad controllers often have banks of assignable pads and assignable faders and knobs for transmitting MIDI data or changes; the better-quality models are velocity-sensitive. More rarely, some performers use more specialized MIDI controllers, such as triggers that are affixed to their clothing or stage items (e.g., magicians Penn and Teller's stage show).

A MIDI foot controller is a pedalboard-style device with rows of switches that control banks of presets and MIDI program change commands and send MIDI note numbers (some also do MIDI merges). Another specialized type of controller is the drawbar controller; it is designed for Hammond organ players who have MIDI-equipped organ voice modules. The drawbar controller provides the keyboard player with many of the controls which are found on a vintage 1940s or 1950s Hammond organ, including harmonic drawbars, a rotating speaker speed control switch, vibrato and chorus knobs, and percussion and overdrive controls. As with all controllers, the drawbar controller does not produce any sounds by itself; it only controls a voice module or software sound device.

While most controllers do not produce sounds, there are some exceptions. Some controller keyboards called "performance controllers" have MIDI-assignable keys, sliders, and knobs, which allow the controller to be used with a range of software synthesizers or voice modules. Yet, at the same time, the controller also has an internal voice module which supplies keyboard instrument sounds (piano, electric piano, clavichord), sampled or synthesized voices (strings, woodwinds), and Digital Signal Processing (distortion, compression, flanging, etc.). These controller keyboards are designed to allow the performer to choose between the internal voices or external modules.

MIDI composition and arrangement typically takes place using either MIDI sequencing/editing software on PC-type computers or using specialized hardware music workstations. Some composers may take advantage of MIDI 1.0 and General MIDI (GM) technology to allow musical data files to be shared among various electronic instruments by using a standard, portable set of commands and parameters. On the other hand, composers of complex, detailed works to be distributed as produced audio typically use MIDI to control the performance of high-quality digital audio samples and/or external hardware or software synthesizers.

Digital audio workstations (DAW) are becoming one of the most centric and common tools in the studio, and many are specifically designed to work with MIDI as an integral component. Through the use of MIDI mapping, various MIDI controllers can be used to command the program. MIDI piano rolls have been developed in many DAWs so that the recorded MIDI messages can be extensively modified. Virtual instruments created by third-party companies in one of a number of commonly used formats (e.g., VST or RTAS) may be loaded as plug-ins thus providing a virtually limitless supply of sounds for a musician and are designed to be commanded by MIDI controllers, especially in the DAW environment.

MIDI data files are much smaller than recorded audio waveforms. Many computer-sequencing programs allow manipulation of the musical data such that composing for an entire orchestra of sounds is possible. This ability to manipulate musical data has also introduced the concept of surrogate orchestras, providing a combination of half-sequenced MIDI recordings and half musicians to make up an entire orchestral arrangement; however, scholars believe surrogate orchestras have the possibility of affecting future live musical performances in which the use of live musicians in orchestral arrangements may cease entirely because the composition of music via MIDI recordings proves to be more efficient and less expensive. Further, the data composed via the sequenced MIDI recordings can then be saved as a standard MIDI file (SMF), digitally distributed, and reproduced by any computer or electronic instrument that also adheres to the same MIDI, GM, and SMF standards.

Although not a wave audio file format, the SMF was, due to its much smaller file size, attractive to computer users as a substitute before broadband Internet became widespread. Later, the advent of high-quality audio compression such as the MP3 format has decreased the size advantages of MIDI-encoded music to some degree, though MP3 is still much larger than SMF.

A standard for MIDI over USB was developed in 1999 as a joint effort between IBM, Microsoft, Altec Lansing, Roland Corporation, and Philips. To transmit MIDI over USB, a Cable Number and Cable Index are added to the message, and the result is encapsulated in a USB packet. The resulting USB message can double the size of the native MIDI message. Since USB is over 15,000 times faster than MIDI (480,000 kb/s vs 31.25 kb/s,), the USB has the potential to be much faster. However, due to the nature of the USB, there is more latency and jitter introduced that is usually in the range of 2 to 10 ms, or about 2 to 10 MIDI commands. Some comparisons done in the early part of the 2000s showed USB to be slightly slower with higher latency, and this is still the case today. Despite the latency and jitter disadvantages, MIDI over USB is increasingly common on musical instruments.

4.3   Synchronous Bus and Asynchronous Bus

Synchronous buses use system clock to provide time information for all signals on the buses. A signal is considered invalid unless it is synchronized by the falling edge (or raising edge) of the clock. On the other hand, signals should be in stable state before the clock edge to avoid competition that may cause the circuit or system to be in an unstable state.

When the CPU wants to read data from memory, the address signals are first enabled, and then the read commend is issued. The data will not be read until the next clock edge is reached. So, at the time the "read" action takes place, all data are already stored in MDR and in stable condition. The whole procedure is shown in Fig. 4.5.

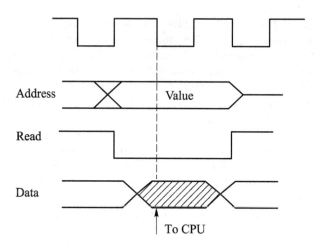

Fig. 4.5 A process of synchronous read

Direct memory access (DMA) uses synchronous method to transfer data. Once the initial negotiation process is succeeded, a block of data will be transferred between the device and memory synchronized by the clock.

Unlike synchronous bus which uses clock to coordinate transactions, asynchronous bus uses handshakes to conduct bus communication. Handshaking enables low-speed devices to communicate with high-speed CPU easily.

As technology advances, most computers use synchronous bus. The clock frequency is an important factor for a computer bus. If the devices have different speeds, we have to set the bus speed to the speed of the slowest devices in the system. For example, the conventional PCI bus uses 33 MHz or 66 MHz. The capacity is up to 266 MB/s for a 32-bit computer. The capacity of PCI Express bus can reach up to 8 GB/s for a version 2.0 with 16 lane slots.

To connect I/O devices to the processor, asynchronous operations are more efficient. Asynchronous buses have the advantage of matching devices communicating with the processor with various speeds.

Synchronous systems negotiate the communication parameters at the data link layer before communication begins. Basic synchronous systems will synchronize the signal clocks on both sides before transmission begins, reset their numeric counters, and take other steps. More advanced systems may negotiate things like error correction and compression.

It is possible to have both sides try to synchronize the connection at the same time. Usually, there is a process to decide which end should be in control. Both sides in synchronous communication can go through a lengthy negotiation cycle where they exchange communications parameters and status information. With a lengthy connection establishment process, a synchronous system using an unreliable physical connection will spend a great deal of time in negotiating, but not in actual data transfer. Once a connection is established, the transmitter sends out a signal, and the receiver sends back data regarding that transmission, and what it received. This connection negotiation process takes longer on low error-rate lines but is highly efficient in systems where the transmission medium itself (an electric wire, radio signal, or laser beam) is not particularly reliable.

Asynchronous communication utilizes a transmitter, a receiver, and a wire without coordination about the timing of individual bits. There is no coordination between the two end points on just how long the transmitter leaves the signal at a certain level to represent a single digital bit. Each device uses a clock to measure out the "length" of a bit. The transmitting device simply transmits. The receiving device has to look at the incoming signal and figure out what it is receiving and coordinate and retime its clock to match the incoming signal.

Sending data encoded into your signal requires that the sender and receiver are both using the same encoding/decoding method and know where to look in the signal to find data. Asynchronous systems do not send separate information to indicate the encoding or clocking information. The receiver must decide the clocking of the signal on its own. This means that the receiver must decide where to look in the signal stream to find ones and zeroes and decide for itself where each individual bit stops and starts. This information is not in the data in the signal sent from transmitting unit.

When the receiver of a signal carrying information has to derive how that signal is organized without consulting the transmitting device, it is called asynchronous communication. In short, the two ends do not always negotiate or work out the connection parameters before communicating. Asynchronous communication is more efficient when there is low loss and low error rates over the transmission medium because data is not retransmitted and no time is spent setting negotiating the connection parameters at the beginning of transmission. Asynchronous systems just transmit and let the far end station figure it out. Asynchronous is sometimes called "best effort" transmission because one side simply transmits, while the other does its best to receive, and any lost data is recovered by a higher-level protocol.

4.4 Single Bus and Multiple Buses

A bus is usually referred to as address, data, and control signals that connect to a processor. An actual computer may have more buses than just only one single bus. For example, a PCI bus can be used to connect CPU, LAN, and on-board graphics, an AGP bus to connect newer graphic cards or graphic processing units (GPUs), a memory bus to connect memory, and a USB bus to connect keyboard, mouse, and other I/O devices. In addition, a SATA bus connects hard drives and CD-ROMs. Figure 4.6 is a diagram of a computer with abovementioned buses.

Moreover, many recent computers come with multiple cores (processors) that were manufactured together on one chip. Some others use multiple independent processors as we often see on server computers. For those computers, exchange data and coordinate operations between processors are important. The interconnection

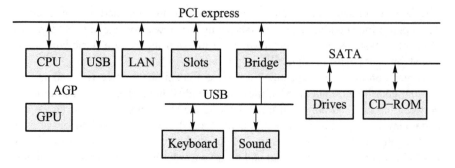

Fig. 4.6 A computer with PCI, AGP, SATA, and USB buses

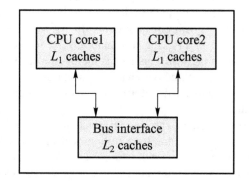

Fig. 4.7 Diagram of a dual-core processor

buses are designed for this purpose. We will discuss interconnection buses in detail in the next section.

Now let us look into the single process and multi-core (dual or quad) computers. Figure 4.6 shows that there are many buses in a computer system. If we look into it, we can see that it is essentially a single-bus system. In addition to the PCI bus, the AGP is merely a graphics accelerator. It goes through a bridge that bridges AGP and PCI together. Similarly, SATA and USB also go through a bridge that exchange signals between SATA and USB with PCI. So, it is essentially a single-bus system with some variations.

As a multi-core (quad-core or more) computer contains two or more processors integrated on one chip, people would think this is a multi-bus system. If we look at the architecture (diagram shown in Fig. 4.7), we can see that both processors are connected to a bus interface. This tells us that it uses one bus to connect to the outside "world." Two or more processors (cores) just add up the computation power. It should still be classified as a single-bus system.

For a computer with multiple independent CPUs (not multiple cores), they can each have their own memory or share common memory modules. To do this, we need an interconnection network (bus) to connect each CPU with the resources.

4.5   Interconnection Buses

Computers with multiple processors located in a central location or distributed locations are generally considered as a parallel processing system (Hwang 1993). Here multiple processors mean multiple processing units. It is different from multi-core computers that we have just discussed.

In parallel processing, instructions and data have four combinations to connect them together:

- Single Instruction stream, Single Data stream (SISD)
- Single Instruction stream, Multiple Data stream (SIMD)
- Multiple Instruction stream, Single Data stream (MISD)
- Multiple Instruction stream, Multiple Data stream (MIMD)

A SISD computer is a Neumann machine built with a single processor.

For a MIMD system, each processor has its own cache memory. They also share the main memory, storage, and I/O devices in order to share data among the processors.

Figure 4.8 shows a typical MIMD architecture where P stands for processors, M for main memory, and D for disks (storage).

In Fig. 4.6, processors are interconnected through the interconnection bus that connects not only the processors but also the main memory and I/O devices.

A distributed MIMD system is illustrated in Fig. 4.9.

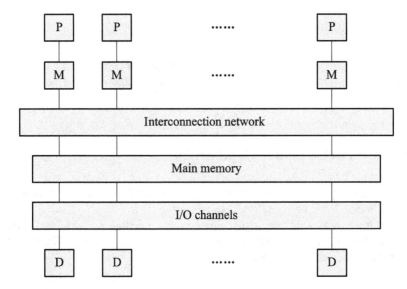

Fig. 4.8 A typical MIMD architecture

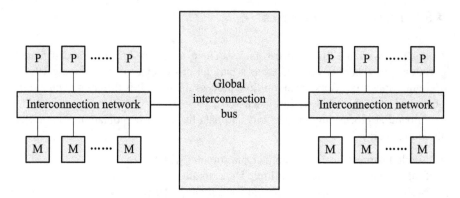

Fig. 4.9 A diagram of a distributed MIMD system

4.6   Front-Side Bus and Northbridge

Front-side bus (FSB) functions as the processor bus, memory bus, or system bus that connects the CPU with the main memory and L2 cache. FSB can range from 133 MHz to 400 MHz and up. In most cases, it is configurable via BIOS.

Northbridge is a core logic chipset architecture that connects directly to the CPU via the FSB.

4.7   Internal Bus

An internal bus is a type of data bus that only operates internally in a CPU, mostly between Northbridge and Southbridge. It carries data and operations similar to the FSB.

4.8   Low Pin Count and Southbridge

Unlike FSB that provides fast connections with CPU, low pin count (LPC) connects slower devices. It can be considered as a substitute for ISA bus.

Southbridge is another core logic chipset architecture that is not connected to the CPU directly. Instead, it connects I/O and other lower-speed devices. Figure 4.10 is a diagram of the bridge architecture.

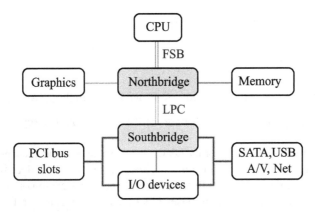

Fig. 4.10 Northbridge and southbridge (color)

4.9 Security Considerations for Computer Buses

Fewer people have studied the vulnerabilities of computer buses to attackers. A computer system can be taken over from devices that are attached to the buses. The data stored on the computer can also be exposed to the programs or virtual machines that were booted from a USB memory attached to a computer USB port.

In single-bus system, CPU, memory and I/O devices are all connected to the system bus. A compromised device can issue attacks on this computer system through interruptions to stop processors from executing normal tasks.

On the other hand, attackers may divert the program handling the interruptions to a predefined location where malicious program is stored. The malicious program then can steal data or stop the services.

USB-booting attack is another type of attack that is launched from a universal serial bus. Most recent computers are able to be booted from a flash drive that is connected to the USB port. An attacker can insert a USB flash drive and boot a virtual service or virtual machine on top of the current operating system. The virtual service or virtual machine then may be able to access the local hard drives to get the data.

The challenge for distributed interconnection buses is even bigger. MIMD computers share common memory. If one local area is compromised, the problem could spread out to the entire system.

To stop USB-booting attack, people can either physically block the access to the USB ports or disable the ports by default. On the other hand, people can disable the USB boot feature so that no program can be executed from USB devices.

4.10   A Dual-Bus Interface Design

A dual-bus interface is a circuit that:

• connects one device to two buses
• enables the device to be accessed simultaneously from those two buses.

Being able to access from both buses at the same time is a key for a dual bus interface.

Here is an example: an external DVD may have two or more buses (USB and 1394) that can be connected. This does not necessarily mean it is dual-bus enabled. We can choose to use either USB or 1394 to connect to a computer system. Since normally we cannot connect both buses to a computer system, therefore it is not a dual-bus device.

4.10.1   Dual-Channel Architecture*

Dual-channel-enabled memory controllers in a PC system architecture utilize two 64-bit data channels. Dual channel should not be confused with double data rate (DDR), in which data exchange happens twice per DRAM clock. The two technologies are independent of each other, and many motherboards use both, by using DDR memory in a dual-channel configuration.

Dual-channel architecture requires a dual-channel-capable motherboard and two or more DDR, DDR2 SDRAM, or DDR3 SDRAM memory modules. The memory modules are installed into matching banks, which are usually color coded on the motherboard. These separate channels allow each memory module access to the memory controller, increasing throughput bandwidth. It is not required that identical modules be used (if motherboard supports it), but this is often recommended for best dual-channel operation. It is possible to use a single-sided module of 512 MB and a double-sided module of 512 MB in a dual-channel configuration, but how fast and stable it depends on the memory controller.

If the motherboard has two pairs of differently colored DIMM sockets (the colors indicate which bank they belong to, bank 0 or bank 1), then one can place a matched pair of memory modules in bank 0, but a different capacity pair of modules in bank 1, as long as they are of the same speed. Using this scheme, a pair of 1 GB memory modules in bank 0 and a pair of matched 512 MB modules in bank 1 would be acceptable for a dual-channel operation.

Modules rated at different speeds can be run in dual-channel mode, although the motherboard will then run all memory modules at the speed of the slowest module. Some motherboards, however, have compatibility issues with certain brands or models of memory when used in dual-channel mode. For this reason, it is generally advised to use identical pairs of memory modules, which is why most memory manufacturers now sell "kits" of matched-pair DIMMs. Several motherboard manufacturers only support configurations where a "matched pair" of modules is used. A matching pair needs to match in:

- Capacity (e.g., 1024 MB). Certain Intel chipsets support different capacity chips in what they call Flex Mode: the capacity that can be matched is run in dual channel, while the remainder runs in single channel.
- Speed (e.g., PC 5300). If speed is not the same, the lower speed of the two modules will be used. Likewise, the higher latency of the two modules will be used.
- Number of chips and sides (e.g., two sides with four chips on each side).
- Matching size of rows and columns.

Dual-channel architecture is a technology implemented on motherboards by the motherboard manufacturer and does not apply to memory modules. Theoretically any matched pair of memory modules may be used in either single-channel or dual-channel operation, provided the motherboard supports this architecture.

Dual-channel technology was created to address the issue of bottlenecks. Increased processor speed and performance require other, less prominent components to keep pace. In the case of dual-channel design, the intended target is the memory controller, which regulates data flow between the CPU and system memory (RAM). The memory controller determines the types and speeds of RAM as well as the maximum size of each individual memory module and the overall memory capacity of the system. However, when the memory is unable to keep up with the processor, a bottleneck occurs, leaving the CPU with nothing to process. Under the single-channel architecture, any CPU with a bus speed greater than the memory speed would be susceptible to this bottleneck effect.

The dual-channel configuration alleviates the problem by doubling the amount of available memory bandwidth. Instead of a single memory channel, a second parallel channel is added. With two channels working simultaneously, the bottleneck is reduced. Rather than wait for memory technology to improve, dual-channel architecture simply takes the existing RAM technology and improves the method in which it is handled. While the actual implementation differs between Intel and AMD motherboards, the basic theory stands.

There have been varying reports as to the performance increase of dual-channel configurations, with some tests citing significant performance gains, while others suggest almost no gain.

Tom's Hardware found little significant difference between single-channel and dual-channel configurations in synthetic and gaming benchmarks (using a "modern" system setup). In its tests, dual channel gave at best a 5% speed increase in memory-intensive tasks. Another comparison by laptoplogic.com resulted in a similar conclusion for integrated graphics. The test results published by Tom's Hardware had a discrete graphics comparison.

The difference can be far more significant in applications that manipulate large amounts of data in memory. A comparison by *TechConnect Magazine* demonstrated considerable gains for dual-channel in tasks using block sizes greater than 4 MB, and during stream processing by the CPU.

4.10.2   Triple-Channel Architecture*

DDR3 triple-channel architecture is used in the Intel Core i7-900 series (the Intel Core i7-800 series only support up to dual channel) and the LGA 1366 platform (e.g., Intel X58). AMD Socket AM3 processors do not use the DDR3 triple-channel architecture but instead use dual-channel DDR3 memory. The same applies to the Intel Core i3, Core i5, and Core i7-800 series, which are used on the LGA 1156 platforms (e.g., Intel P55). According to Intel, a Core i7 with DDR3 operating at 1 066 MHz will offer peak data transfer rates of 25.6 GB/s when operating in triple-channel interleaved mode. This, Intel claims, leads to faster system performance as well as higher performance per watt.

When operating in triple-channel mode, memory latency is reduced due to interleaving, meaning that each module is accessed sequentially for smaller bits of data rather than completely filling up one module before accessing the next one. Data is spread among the modules in an alternating pattern, potentially tripling available memory bandwidth for the same amount of data, as opposed to storing it all on one module.

The architecture can only be used when all three, or a multiple of three, memory modules are identical in capacity and speed and are placed in three-channel slots. When two memory modules are installed, the architecture will operate in dual-channel mode.

DDR3 quadruple-channel architecture is used in the AMD G34 platform and the Intel LGA 2011 platform (e.g., Intel X79). AMD processors which are used on the C32 platform instead use dual-channel DDR3 memory. Intel processors which are used on the LGA 1155 platform (e.g., Intel Z68) instead use dual-channel DDR3 memory.

The architecture can only be used when all four, or a multiple of four, memory modules are identical in capacity and speed and are placed in quad-channel slots. When two memory modules are installed, the architecture will operate in dual-channel mode. When three memory modules are installed, the architecture will operate in triple-channel mode.

4.10.3   A Dual-Bus Memory Interface

Figure 4.11 shows a diagram of a dual-bus interface. Here control signal EN is used to enable or disable the communication between a bus and the storage S.

Motorola's MPC 8260 is a chip that contains a 64-bit PowerPC microprocessor and a versatile communications processor module (CPM). The MP 8260 is used in a wide array of applications, especially those in the communications and networking markets. Examples include remote access servers, regional office routers, cellular base stations, and SONET transmission controllers.

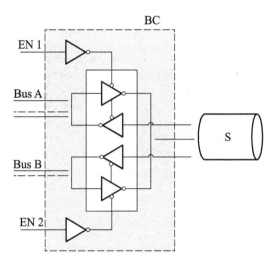

Fig. 4.11 A dual-bus interface diagram

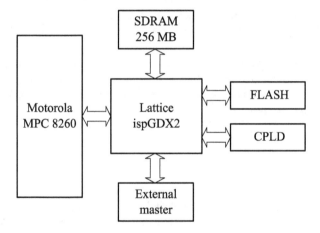

Fig. 4.12 Diagram of ispGDX2 multiport interface

A Lattice's ispGDX2™ Generic Digital Crosspoint Switch is used as a multiport interface. The ispGDX2 device can interface the MPC 8260 with an external master and a number of slaves including SDRAM and FLASH. The control logic for the SDRAM and FLASH is built in a CPLD which is used to interface the MPC 8260 to the ispGDX2 device and to control the read/write to the memory. This function can be implemented in Lattice CPLDs. Figure 4.12 shows the diagram using MPC 8260 with the multiport interface (Wang et al. 2007).

4.11   Summary

In this chapter, we discussed various computer buses and the connections between different computer components. A system bus consists of an address bus, a data bus, and a control bus. The address bus determines the addressing space of a computer system. In other words, it specifies how much memory can be attached onto a computer system. The data bus determines how much data can be read or written between CPU and memory or I/O devices at a time. A wider data bus will reduce the read/write times and therefore will increase the system speed.

Computer buses can be categorized as parallel buses and serial buses. A parallel bus enables high throughput, so it is most commonly seen in motherboard and interfaces that require best speed performances. A serial bus, on the other hand, is small in size and easy to build. With the technology advancement, the speed carried on by serial buses is considerable high. So serial buses have wide applications. USB 3.0 is able to transfer data at the speed up to 5 Gb/s (625 MB/s) with only four data signals. Parallel computers usually have many processors each with its own memory and also share the common memory. They also have shared I/O devices that are connected through the interconnection buses. Due to technology advancement, some parallel buses are replaced with serial buses such as SATA for IDE and SAS for SCSI.

Computer buses are also vulnerable to attacks. USB-booting attacks can be prevented by physical blocking the USB ports or disabling the booting feature from the operating system. Attacks launched from compromised devices can be addressed in the following chapters.

Projects

4.1 Parallel buses allow all data to send/receive at the same time, while serial buses send/receive data one bit at a time. Conduct research on SCSI vs. SAS and IDE vs. SATA to see which is faster, serial buses or parallel buses. Why?
4.2 Dual-port memory buses. Use Tinkercad to simulate the dual-bus interface discussed in the book.

Exercises

4.1 What is a system bus? What is a system bus composed of?
4.2 A processor has 8-bit data bus width. How many times does it need to read a 28-bit data into the processor? What if the processor has a 32-bit data bus?
4.3 What is a parallel bus? What is a serial bus?
4.4 USB is the most common serial bus; it can connect many computer peripherals. Is it possible to be used as the video interface, and why?

4.5 Why does DMA transfer data efficiently than handshakes mode?

4.6 If we need to contact low-speed devices to a processor, what considerations should we take?

4.7 A computer has an AGP bus that connects to the graphic card. It has a PCI bus that connects SCSI. It also has a USB that connects keyboard and mouse. In addition, it has a SATA bus that connects an SSD and CD-ROM. Why is this multiple-bus computer still considered as a single-bus Neumann architecture?

4.8 People consider a dual-core or quad-core computer as a single-bus Neumann architecture. Do you agree or disagree, and why?

4.9 What does SISD, SIMD, MISD, and MIMD mean? What are used to connect the processors in those systems?

4.10 How does a USB-booting attack work? How to prevent such attacks?

4.11 An external hard drive has two interfaces: USB 2.0 and IEEE 1393. Do you think it is a dual-port interface device or not?

References

Dumas, J. D. (2006). *Computer architecture: Fundamentals and principles of computer design.* Abingdon: Taylor & Francis.

Foster, C. C., & Iberall, T. (1985). *Computer architecture* (3rd ed.). New York: Van Nostrand Reinhold Company.

Hwang, K. (1993). *Advanced computer architecture: Parallelism, scalability, programmability.* New York: McGraw-Hill Inc.

Randell, B. (Ed.). (1982). *The designs of digital computers.* Berlin: Springer-Verlag.

Shiva, S. G. (2000). *Computer design and architecture* (3rd ed.). New York: Marcel Dekker Inc.

Universal serial bus. Wikipedia. Retrieved February 29, 2019.

Wang, S., & Ledley, R. (2007). Modified Neumann architecture with micro-OS for security. In Proceedings of CIICT (pp. 303–310).

Chapter 5
I/O and Network Interface

People use computers to solve problems. An input device takes the tasks and data to pass to the central processing unit. The CPU executes the algorithms and produces results. The results are then sent out to an output device. In case data being used by CPUs are not local, they will be transmitted over the network using networking protocols through a network interface card or device.

I/O devices contain internal registers. The registers are used to receive command and data from the process. On the other hand, I/O devices carry data differently. Some data are at high speed, while some others are at very low speed. The registers are used as a buffer to match the different speeds usually via interrupts. A general I/O diagram is shown in Fig. 5.1.

Animated video images on the other hand are quite different. For every second, a CPU needs to send out at least 60 frames. Each frame may contain millions of pixels, and each pixel contains a 32-bit color depth. If we add a double buffer and stereo feature, for example, a 3D movie, the overall bit rate would exceed 10^9 b/s or even higher if the refresh rate is higher.

Data transmitted through I/O devices could be very few, or it could be very large. For a large data transfer, like a hard drive, in order to save CPU time, we usually use a specialized interface named DMA.

5.1 Direct Memory Access

If we move large trunk of data from I/O devices to main memory, the overhead for each move has to be considered. Traditionally, data are read into registers and then write to the memory from the CPU. It requires two steps.

With a DMA controller, data can be read/write directly from/to memory without requiring interactions with the CPU during transmission (Dumas 2006).

© The Author(s), under exclusive license to Springer Nature Singapore Pte Ltd. 2021   99
S. P. Wang, *Computer Architecture and Organization*,
https://doi.org/10.1007/978-981-16-5662-0_5

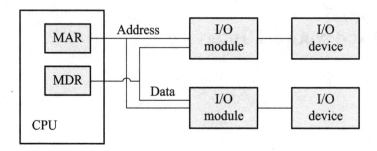

Fig. 5.1   A general I/O interface diagram

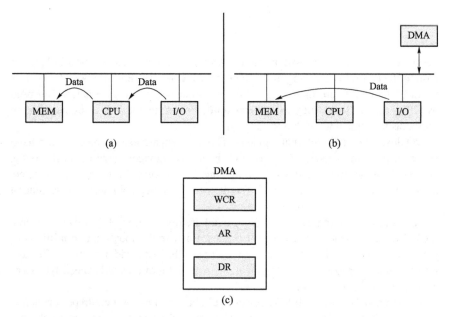

Fig. 5.2   I/O diagrams. (**a**) Architecture diagram of a DMA. (**b**) I/O data exchange with DMA. (**c**) DMA architecture

The DMA controller is controlled by the CPU. It receives data transfer instructions from the processor. Usually the CPU sends out I/O device numbers, memory start address, and number of bytes to the DMA controller. Once this is done, the DMA controller will do the rest. It will initiate the transmission until the data are all read. The writing process from memory to I/O is the same except data are moved in a reverse direction.

Once the DMA controller completes the transmission, it will send an interrupt signal to notify the CPU.

A DMA device usually contains a word-count register (WCR), an address register (AR), and a data register/buffer (DR). Figure 5.2 shows different I/O diagrams.

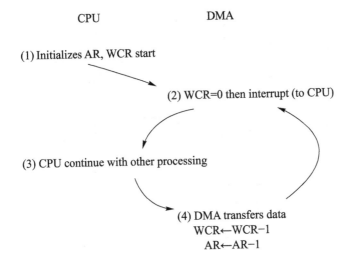

CPU   DMA

(1) Initializes AR, WCR start

(2) WCR=0 then interrupt (to CPU)

(3) CPU continue with other processing

(4) DMA transfers data
WCR←WCR−1
AR←AR−1

Fig. 5.3 DMA handshake process

DMA data transfers include a handshaking process. First the CPU initializes the AR and WCR on the DMA side, and it first checks whether WCR=0. If yes, it means the transfer is complete, and DMA will send an interrupt signal to the CPU.

If WCR≠0, then the DMA starts data transfer. At each iteration, the work-count register reduces by one, and the address register increases by one. WCR ← WCR-1, AR ← AR+1. The data continue transferring until WCR=0. Figure 5.3 shows a DMA handshake process.

5.2 Interrupts

A processor normally executes programs with no interrupts. In some situations, the processor may be interrupted by external condition to handle some emergency tasks (Foster and Iberall 1985). Here are some special conditions:

- A system reset
- Power failure
- Buffer overflow or underflow
- Illegal instruction code
- Completion of DMA data transfer
- Software requests

In each of these conditions, the processor must stop the current process to handle the event. After handling the interruptions, the processor will resume the current operation. Figure 5.4 shows a diagram how the CPU handles an interrupt.

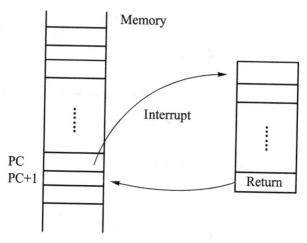

Fig. 5.4 Interrupt handling

The interrupts handling process first saves the current program counter+1 to a stack and then jumps to the interruption service procedure.

The interruption service routine usually performs the following functions:

- Save the processor status
- Handle the interrupt
- Return from the interrupt
- Pop the stack and get the returning address: PC+1
- Jump to PC+1

During the process of saving the processor status, the processor may disable further interrupts in order to prevent status change (Randell 1982).

Interrupts can be prioritized in program or in hardware. With flip-flops, interrupt requests can be groups into multi-priority. At any time, a higher-priority device can always interrupt a lower-priority device, while a lower-priority device cannot interrupt a higher-priority device. Some CPUs use a mask register to enable/disable certain devices to interrupt.

5.3 Programmed I/O

Keyboards, mouses, displays, and printers are all standard I/O devices. The interfaces that connect to the registers in the CPU are designed for a single purpose, just like a keyboard and a mouse which cannot be misplaced on PS/2 interfaces.

In many cases, we want to have a general I/O module that can either be set to input or in some other time be set to output depending on the applications. The CPU first tells the I/O module what function the CPU wants it to be and then sends the

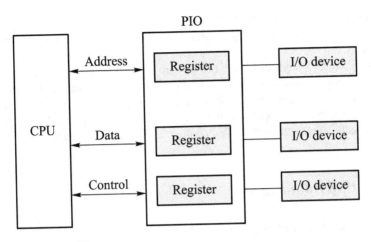

Fig. 5.5 Programmed I/O

data. I/O module whose functions can be set by instructions are called programmed I/O or in short PIO. Figure 5.5 shows a diagram of PIO connected to a CPU.

The input/output data and address registers work similarly to the memory address register (MAR) and memory data register (MDR). They share the same bus as the memory does.

There are two ways of mapping I/O ports: memory-mapped I/O and isolated I/O. Memory-mapped I/O maps I/O ports to reserved memory address space. In this method, processors write to an I/O port similar to writing to memory.

Isolated I/O mapping does not use any memory space. It used separate I/O address space. Most Intel processors support isolated mapping. In these systems, special I/O instructions are needed to access I/O devices.

Systems designed with processors that support the isolated I/O have the flexibility of using memory mapped I/O or isolated I/O. For example, a keyboard, a mouse, and a monitor (KVM) are usually mapped to I/O space, while a video card could be mapped to a block of memory address using the memory mapping interface.

5.4 USB and IEEE 1394

The universal serial bus was developed in 1995. The major goal of the USB was to define an external expansion bus that makes attaching peripherals to a computer as easy as hooking up a telephone to a jack.

Before the USB, computer users had many problems connecting peripherals. We have seen a normal PC may contain PS/2 for keyboard and mouse, parallel for printer, VGA for display, serial and modem for gaming and communication, etc. If people want to connect two printers, he needs a splitter to switch manually.

With the introduction of the USB, now people can connect a keyboard, a mouse, printers, external memory and hard drives, camera, and up to 127 devices through USB ports.

If we connect a keyboard and a printer through USB ports, the biggest question is how will a processor identify whether it is a keyboard or a printer? USB supports true plug-and-play connectivity. It avoids setting jumpers and configuring new devices. In addition, people can hot-plug the USB devices and the system will automatically detach the devices and configure it for immediate use.

5.4.1 USB Advantages

Here are some main advantages of the USB:

- Power distribution. The USB cable can provide +5 V power to the device. For small devices (100 ~ 500 mA), it helps avoid using an external power supply.
- Expandable USB provides expandability through USB hubs that are as small as an eraser, and it is very cheap. A four-port hub costs less than $10.
- Power conservation USB devices enter a suspend state if there are no activities on the bus for 3 ms. In the suspended state, devices draw only about 2.5 mA current.

5.4.2 USB Architecture

The host hardware consists of a USB host controller and a root hub. The host controller initiates transmissions over the USB, and the root hub provides the connection points. Figure 5.6 shows the diagram of USB architecture.

A host controller interface (HCI) is a register-level interface which allows host controller hardware to communicate with the operating system of a host computer. There are three types of USB host controller interfaces:

- Open host Controller Interface (OHCI)
- Universal HCI
- Enhanced HCI

With USB revision 1.0 and 1.1, there were two HCI specifications, OHCI and UHCI. With the introduction of USB revision 2.0, EHCI was developed. The single integrated EHCI specification eliminates many of the problems that existed because of competing OHCI and UHCI standards. EHCI is used by all USB 2.0 devices and is the only HCI that supports high-speed transfers.

USB encapsulates application data in several transactions. Each transaction consists of several packets. USB packets consist of the following fields:

- SYNC   All packets must start with a sync field. The sync field is 8 bits long at low and full speed or 32 bits long for high speed and is used to synchronize the

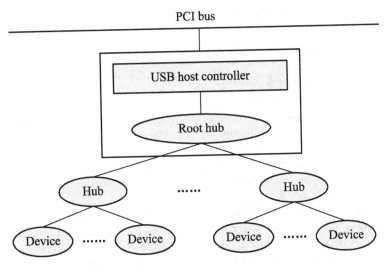

Fig. 5.6 USB architecture

SYNC	PID	ADDR	ENDP	CRC	EOP

Fig. 5.7 USB transmission packet format

clock of the receiver with that of the transmitter. The last two bits indicate where the PID fields start.

- **PID** PID stands for Packet ID. This field is used to identify the type of packet that is being sent. There are 4 bits to the PID; however, to ensure it is received correctly, the 4 bits are complemented and repeated, making an 8-bit PID in total. The resulting format is shown below.
- **ADDR** The address field specifies which device the packet is designated for. Being 7 bits in length allows for 127 devices to be supported. Address 0 is not valid, as any device which is not yet assigned an address must respond to packets sent to address 0.
- **ENDP** The endpoint field is made up of 4 bits, allowing 16 possible endpoints.
- **CRC** Cyclic redundancy checks are performed on the data within the packet payload. All token packets have a 5-bit CRC, while data packets have a 16-bit CRC.
- **EOP** End of packet. Signaled by a single-ended zero (SE0) for approximately 2-bit times followed by a J for 1-bit time.

The packet format is shown in Fig. 5.7.

A synchronization sequence is 00000001. Each packet consists of a packet ID, packet data, and a CRC field.

5.4.3   USB Version History

USB 1.0 was released in January 1996 with specified data rates of 1.5 Mb/s and 12 Mb/s.

USB 2.0 was released in April 2000 with the maximum bandwidth of 480 Mb/s (60 MB/s). It is also call Hi-Speed USB.

USB 3.0 was released in November 2008 with a maximum transmission speed of up to 5 Gb/s (625 MB/s), which is more than 10 times as fast as USB 2.0 (480 Mb/s, or 60 MB/s), although this speed is typically only achieved using powerful professional grade or developmental equipment. USB 3.0 reduces the time required for data transmission, reduces power consumption, and is backward compatible with USB 2.0.

The USB 3.0 Promoter Group announced on 17 November 2008 that the specification of version 3.0 had been completed and had made the transition to the USB Implementers Forum (USB-IF), the managing body of USB specifications. This move effectively opened the specification to hardware developers for implementation in future products. A new feature is the "SuperSpeed" bus, which provides a fourth transfer mode at 5.0 Gb/s. The raw throughput is 4 Gb/s (using 8 b/10 b encoding), and the specification considers it reasonable to achieve around 3.2 Gb/s (0.4 GB/s or 400 MB/s), increasing as hardware advances in the future take hold. Two-way communication is also possible.

In USB 3.0, full-duplex communications are done when using SuperSpeed (USB 3.0) transfer. In previous USB versions (i.e., 1.x or 2.0), all communication is half-duplex and directly controlled by the host.

5.4.4   USB Design and Architecture*

The design architecture of USB is asymmetrical in its topology, consisting of a host, a multitude of downstream USB ports, and multiple peripheral devices connected in a tiered-star topology. Additional USB hubs may be included in the tiers, allowing branching into a tree structure with up to five tier levels. A USB host may implement multiple host controllers, and each host controller may provide one or more USB ports. Up to 127 devices, including hub devices if present, may be connected to a single host controller.

USB devices are linked in series through hubs. One hub is known as the root hub which is built into the host controller.

A physical USB device may consist of several logical sub-devices that are referred to as device functions. A single device may provide several functions, for example, a webcam (video device function) with a built-in microphone (audio device function). This kind of device is called composite device. An alternative for this is compound device in which each logical device is assigned a distinctive address by the host and all logical devices are connected to a built-in hub to which the physical USB wire is connected.

USB device communication is based on pipes (logical channels). A pipe is a connection from the host controller to a logical entity, found on a device, and named an endpoint. Because pipes correspond 1-to-1 to endpoints, the terms are sometimes used interchangeably. A USB device can have up to 32 endpoints, 16 into the host controller and 16 out of the host controller. The USB standard reserves one endpoint of each type, leaving a theoretical maximum of 30 for normal use. USB devices seldom have this many endpoints.

There are two types of pipes: stream and message pipes depending on the type of data transfer.

- Isochronous transfers   At some guaranteed data rate (often, but not necessarily, as fast as possible) but with possible data loss (e.g., real-time audio or video).
- Interrupt transfers   Devices that need guaranteed quick responses (bounded latency) (e.g., pointing devices and keyboards).
- Bulk transfers   Large sporadic transfers using all remaining available bandwidth, but with no guarantee on bandwidth or latency (e.g., file transfers).
- Control transfers   Typically used for short, simple commands to the device and a status response, used, for example, by the bus control pipe number 0.

A stream pipe is a unidirectional pipe connected to a unidirectional endpoint that transfers data using an isochronous, interrupt, or bulk transfer. A message pipe is a bidirectional pipe connected to a bidirectional endpoint that is exclusively used for control data flow. An endpoint is built into the USB device by the manufacturer and therefore exists permanently. An endpoint of a pipe is addressable with a tuple (device_address, endpoint_number) as specified in a TOKEN packet that the host sends when it wants to start a data transfer session. If the direction of the data transfer is from the host to the endpoint, an OUT packet (a specialization of a TOKEN packet) having the desired device address and endpoint number is sent by the host. If the direction of the data transfer is from the device to the host, the host sends an IN packet instead. If the destination endpoint is a unidirectional endpoint whose manufacturer's designated direction does not match the TOKEN packet (e.g., the manufacturer's designated direction is IN while the TOKEN packet is an OUT packet), the TOKEN packet will be ignored. Otherwise, it will be accepted, and the data transaction can start. A bidirectional endpoint, on the other hand, accepts both IN and OUT packets.

Endpoints are grouped into interfaces, and each interface is associated with a single device function. An exception to this is endpoint zero, which is used for device configuration and which is not associated with any interface. A single device function composed of independently controlled interfaces is called a composite device. A composite device only has a single device address because the host only assigns a device address to a function.

When a USB device is first connected to a USB host, the USB device enumeration process is started. The enumeration starts by sending a reset signal to the USB device. The data rate of the USB device is determined during the reset signaling.

After reset, the USB device's information is read by the host, and the device is assigned a unique 7-bit address. If the device is supported by the host, the device drivers needed for communicating with the device are loaded, and the device is set to a configured state. If the USB host is restarted, the enumeration process is repeated for all connected devices.

The host controller directs traffic flow to devices, so no USB device can transfer any data on the bus without an explicit request from the host controller. In USB 2.0, the host controller polls the bus for traffic, usually in a round-robin fashion. The throughput of each USB port is determined by the slower speed of either the USB port or the USB device connected to the port.

High-speed USB 2.0 hubs contain devices called transaction translators that convert between high-speed USB 2.0 buses and full- and low-speed buses. When a high-speed USB 2.0 hub is plugged into a high-speed USB host or hub, it will operate in high-speed mode. The USB hub will then either use one transaction translator per hub to create a full-/low-speed bus that is routed to all full- and low-speed devices on the hub or will use one transaction translator per port to create an isolated full-/low-speed bus per port on the hub.

Because there are two separate controllers in each USB 3.0 host, USB 3.0 devices will transmit and receive at USB 3.0 data rates regardless of USB 2.0 or earlier devices connected to that host. Operating data rates for them will be set in the legacy manner.

5.4.5   USB Mass Storage

USB implements connections to storage devices using a set of standards called the USB mass storage device class (MSC or UMS). This was at first intended for traditional magnetic and optical drives but has been extended to support a wide variety of devices, particularly flash drives, because many systems can be controlled with the familiar metaphor of file manipulation within directories. The process of making a novel device look like a familiar device is also known as extension. The ability to boot a write-locked SD card with a USB adapter is particularly advantageous for maintaining the integrity and non-corruptible, pristine state of the booting medium.

Though most post-2005 computers are capable of booting from USB mass storage devices, the USB is not intended to be a primary bus for a computer's internal storage: buses such as Parallel ATA (PATA or IDE), Serial ATA (SATA), or SCSI fulfill that role in PC class computers. However, the USB has one important advantage in that it is possible to install and remove devices without rebooting the computer (hot-swapping), making it useful for mobile peripherals, including drives of various kinds. Originally conceived and still being used today for optical storage devices (CD-RW drives, DVD drives, and so on), several manufacturers offer external portable USB hard disk drives, or empty enclosures for disk drives, which offer performance comparable to internal drives, limited by the current number and type of attached USB devices and by the upper limit of the USB interface (in practice about 30 MB/s for USB 2.0 and potentially 400 MB/s or more or USB 3.0). These external drives have typically included a "translating device" that bridges between a drive's interface to a USB interface port. Functionally, the drive appears to the user much like an internal drive. Other competing standards for external drive connectivity include eSATA, ExpressCard, and FireWire (IEEE 1394).

Another use for USB mass storage devices is the portable execution of software applications (such as web browsers and VoIP clients) with no need to install them on the host computer.

Joysticks, keypads, tablets, and other human-interface devices (HID) are also progressively migrating from MIDI and PC game port connectors to USB. USB mouse and keyboards can usually be used with older computers that have PS/2 connectors with the aid of a small USB-to-PS/2 adapter. Such adaptors contain no logic circuitry: the hardware in the USB keyboard or mouse is designed to detect whether it is connected to a USB or PS/2 port and communicate using the appropriate protocol. Converters also exist to allow PS/2 keyboards and mouse (usually one of each) to be connected to a USB port. These devices present two HID endpoints to the system and use a microcontroller to perform bidirectional translation of data between the two standards.

5.4.6   USB Interface Connectors

The connectors specified by the USB committee are designed to support a number of USB's underlying goals and to reflect lessons learned from the menagerie of connectors which have been used in the computer industry. The connector mounted on the host or device is called the receptacle, and the connector attached to the cable is called the plug. In the case of an extension cable, the connector on one end is a receptacle. The official USB specification documents periodically define the term male to represent the plug and female to represent the receptacle. Figure 5.8 shows some common USB connectors.

By design, it is difficult to attach a USB connector incorrectly. Connectors cannot be plugged in upside down, and it is clear from the physical act of making a connection, when the plug and receptacle are correctly mated. The USB specification states that the required USB icon is to be "embossed" on the "topside" of the USB plug, which "provides easy user recognition and facilitates alignment during the mating process." The specification also shows that the "recommended" (optional) "Manufacturer's logo" ("engraved" on the diagram but not specified in the text) is on the opposite side of the USB Icon. The specification further states "the USB Icon is also located adjacent to each receptacle. Receptacles should be oriented to allow the icon on the plug to be visible during the mating process." However, the specification does not consider the height of the device compared to the eye level height of the user, so the side of the cable that is "visible" when mated to a computer on a desk can depend on whether the user is standing or kneeling.

Fig. 5.8 USB connectors

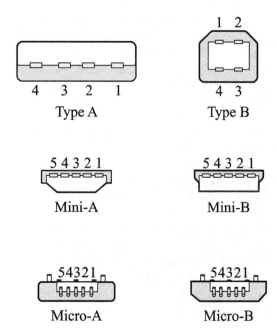

Only moderate insertion/removal force is needed. USB cables and small USB devices are held in place by the gripping force from the receptacle (without need of the screws, clips, or thumb-turns other connectors have required). The force needed to make or break a connection is modest, allowing connections to be made in awkward circumstances (i.e., behind a floor-mounted chassis, or from below) or by those with motor disabilities.

The standard connectors were deliberately intended to enforce the directed topology of a USB network: type A connectors on host devices that supply power and type B connectors on target devices that receive power. This prevents users from accidentally connecting two USB power supplies to each other, which could lead to dangerously high currents, circuit failures, or even fire. The USB does not support cyclical networks, and the standard connectors from incompatible USB devices are themselves incompatible. Unlike other communications systems (e.g., network cabling), gender changers make little sense with USB and are almost never used.

The standard connectors are designed to be robust. Many previous connector designs are fragile, specifying embedded component pins or other delicate parts which proved vulnerable to bending or breakage, even with the application of modest force. The electrical contacts in a USB connector are protected by an adjacent plastic tongue, and the entire connecting assembly is usually protected by an enclosing metal sheath.

The connector construction always ensures that the external sheath on the plug makes contact with its counterpart in the receptacle before any of the four connectors within make electrical contact. The external metallic sheath is typically connected to system ground, thus dissipating damaging static charges. This enclosure design also provides a degree of protection from electromagnetic interference to the USB signal while it travels through the mated connector pair (the only location when the otherwise twisted data pair travels in parallel). In addition, because of the required sizes of the power and common connections, they are made after the system ground but before the data connections. This type of staged make-break timing allows for electrically safe hot-swapping.

The newer micro-USB receptacles are designed for up to 10,000 cycles of insertion and removal between the receptacle and plug, compared to 1500 for the standard USB and 5000 for the Mini-USB receptacle. This is accomplished by adding a locking device and by moving the leaf-spring connector from the jack to the plug, so that the most-stressed part is on the cable side of the connection. This change was made so that the connector on the less expensive cable would bear the most wear instead of the more expensive micro-USB device.

The USB standard specifies relatively loose tolerances for compliant USB connectors to minimize physical incompatibilities in connectors from different vendors. To address a weakness present in some other connector standards, the USB specification also defines limits to the size of a connecting device in the area around its plug. This was done to prevent a device from blocking adjacent ports due to the size of the cable strain relief mechanism (usually molding integral with the cable outer insulation) at the connector. Compliant devices must either fit within the size restrictions or support a compliant extension cable which does.

In general, cables have only plugs (very few have a receptacle on one end, although extension cables with a standard A plug and jack are sold), and hosts and devices have only receptacles. Hosts almost universally have type-A receptacles and devices one or another type-B variety. Type-A plugs mate only with type-A receptacles and type-B with type-B; they are deliberately physically incompatible. However, an extension to USB standard specification called USB On-The-Go allows a single port to act as either a host or a device—chosen by which end of the cable plugs into the receptacle on the unit. Even after the cable is hooked up and the units are communicating, the two units may "swap" ends under program control. This capability is meant for units such as PDAs in which the USB link might connect to a PC's host port as a device in one instance, yet connect as a host itself to a keyboard and mouse device in another instance.

USB 3.0 receptacles are electrically compatible with USB Standard 2.0 device plugs if they physically match. USB 3.0 type-A plugs and receptacles are completely backward compatible, and USB 3.0 type-B receptacles will accept USB 2.0 and earlier plugs. However, USB 3.0 type-B plugs will not fit into USB 2.0 and earlier receptacles. eSATAp (eSATA/USB) port is also compatible with USB 2.0 devices.

5.4.7 USB Connector Types

There are several types of USB connectors, including some that have been added while the specification progressed. The original USB specification detailed Standard-A and Standard-B plugs and receptacles. The first engineering change notice to the USB 2.0 specification added Mini-B plugs and receptacles.

The data connectors in the Standard-A plug are actually recessed in the plug as compared to the outside power connectors. This permits the power to connect first which prevents data errors by allowing the device to power up first and then transfer the data. Some devices will operate in different modes depending on whether the data connection is made. This difference in connection can be exploited by inserting the connector only partially. For example, some battery-powered MP3 players switch into file transfer mode and cannot play MP3 files while a USB plug is fully inserted, but can be operated in MP3 playback mode using USB power by inserting the plug only part way so that the power slots make contact while the data slots do not. This enables those devices to be operated in MP3 playback mode while getting power from the cable.

To reliably enable a charge-only feature, modern USB accessory peripherals now include charging cables that provide power connections to the host port but no data connections, and both home and vehicle charging docks are available that supply power from a converter device and do not include a host device and data pins, allowing any capable USB device to be charged or operated from a standard USB cable.

The USB 2.0 Standard-A type of USB plug is a flattened rectangle which inserts into a "downstream-port" receptacle on the USB host, or a hub, and carries both power and data. This plug is frequently seen on cables that are permanently attached to a device, such as one connecting a keyboard or mouse to the computer via USB connection.

USB connections eventually wear out as the connection loosens through repeated plugging and unplugging. The lifetime of a USB-A male connector is approximately 1 500 connect/disconnect cycles.

A Standard-B plug—which has a square shape with beveled exterior corners—typically plugs into an "upstream receptacle" on a device that uses a removable cable, e.g., a printer. A Type B plug delivers power in addition to carrying data. On some devices, the Type B receptacle has no data connections, being used solely for accepting power from the upstream device. This two-connector-type scheme (A/B) prevents a user from accidentally creating an electrical loop. Figure 5.9 shows standard A/B connector.

Various mini- and micro-connectors have been used for smaller devices such as PDAs, mobile phones, or digital cameras. These include the now-deprecated (but standardized) Mini-A and the currently standard Mini-B, Micro-A, and Micro-B connectors.

The Mini-A and Mini-B plugs are approximately 3 by 7 mm. The micro-USB plugs have a similar width and approximately half the thickness, enabling their

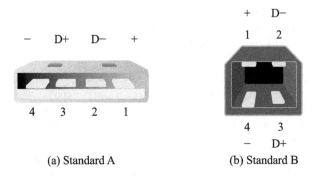

(a) Standard A　　　　　　(b) Standard B

Fig. 5.9 USB standard A/B connector

integration into thinner portable devices. The micro-A connector is 6.85 by 1.8 mm with a maximum overmold size of 11.7 by 8.5 mm. The micro-B connector is 6.85 by 1.8 mm with a maximum overmold size of 10.6 by 8.5 mm.

The micro-USB connector was announced by the USB-IF in January 2007. The Mini-A connector and the Mini-B receptacle connector were deprecated in May 2007. While many currently available devices and cables still use Mini plugs, the newer micro connectors are being widely adopted, and as of December 2010, they are the most widely used. The thinner micro connectors are intended to replace the Mini plugs in new devices including smartphones and personal digital assistants. The Micro plug design is rated for at least 10,000 connect-disconnect cycles which is significantly more than the Mini plug design. The Universal Serial Bus Micro-USB Cables and Connectors Specification details the mechanical characteristics of Micro-A plugs, Micro-AB receptacles, and Micro-B plugs and receptacles, along with a Standard-A receptacle to Micro-A plug adapter.

As of January 2009, micro-USB has been accepted and is being used by almost all cellphone manufacturers as the standard charging port (including Hewlett-Packard, HTC, LG, Motorola, Nokia, Research In Motion, Samsung, Sony Ericsson) in most of the world.

On 29 June 2009, following a request from the European Commission and in close co-operation with the Commission services, major producers of mobile phones have agreed in a Memorandum of Understanding (MoU) to harmonize chargers for data-enabled mobile phones sold in the European Union. Industry commits to provide charger compatibility on the basis of the micro-USB connector. Consumers will be able to purchase mobile phones without a charger, thus logically reducing their cost. Following a mandate from the European Commission, the European Standardization Bodies CEN-CENELEC and ETSI have now made available the harmonized standards needed for the manufacture of data-enabled mobile phones compatible with the new common External Power Supply (EPS) based on micro-USB.

In addition, in October 2009, the International Telecommunication Union (ITU) has also announced that they had embraced micro-USB as the Universal Charger

Solution its "energy-efficient one-charger-fits-all new mobile phone solution," and added: "Based on the Micro-USB interface, UCS chargers will also include a 4-star or higher efficiency rating—up to three times more energy-efficient than an unrated charger."

A USB On-The-Go device is required to have one and only one USB connector: A Mini-AB or Micro-AB receptacle. This receptacle is capable of accepting both Mini-A and Mini-B plugs and, alternatively, Micro-A and Micro-B plugs, attached to any of the legal cables and adapters as defined in Micro-USB1.01.

The OTG device with the A-plug inserted is called the A-device and is responsible for powering the USB interface when required and by default assumes the role of host. The OTG device with the B-plug inserted is called the B-device and by default assumes the role of peripheral. An OTG device with no plug inserted defaults to acting as a B-device. If an application on the B-device requires the role of host, then the HNP protocol is used to temporarily transfer the host role to the B-device.

OTG devices attached either to a peripheral-only B-device or a standard/embedded host will have their role fixed by the cable since in these scenarios it is only possible to attach the cable one way around.

5.4.8   USB Power and Charging

The USB 1.x and 2.0 specifications provide a 5 V supply on a single wire from which connected USB devices may draw power. The specification provides for no more than 5.25 V and no less than 4.75 V (5 V $\pm 5\%$) between the positive and negative bus power lines. For USB 3.0, the voltage supplied by low-powered hub ports is $4.45 \sim 5.25$ V.

A unit load is defined as 100 mA in USB 2.0 and 150 mA in USB 3.0. A device may draw a maximum of 5-unit loads (500 mA) from a port in USB 2.0 and 6-unit (900 mA) in USB 3.0. There are two types of devices: low power and high power. A low-power device draws at most 1-unit load, with minimum operating voltage of 4.4 V in USB 2.0 and 4 V in USB 3.0. A high-power device draws the maximum number of unit loads permitted by the standard. Every device functions initially as low power, but the device may request high power and will get it if the power is available on the providing bus.

Some devices, such as high-speed external disk drives, require more than 500 mA of current and therefore cannot be powered from one USB 2.0 port. Such devices usually come with Y-shaped cable that has two USB connectors to be plugged into a computer. With such a cable, a device can draw power from two USB ports simultaneously.

A bus-powered hub initializes itself at 1-unit load and transitions to maximum unit loads after it completes hub configuration. Any device connected to the hub will draw 1-unit load regardless of the current draw of devices connected to other ports of the hub (i.e., one device connected on a four-port hub will draw only 1-unit load despite the fact that more unit loads are being supplied to the hub).

A self-powered hub will supply maximum supported unit loads to any device connected to it. In addition, the VBUS will present 1-unit load upstream for communication if parts of the Hub are powered down.

The Battery Charging Specification of 2007 defines new types of USB ports, e.g., charging ports. As compared to standard downstream ports, where a portable device can only draw more than 100 mA current after digital negotiation with the host or hub, charging ports can supply currents above 0.5 A without digital negotiation. A charging port supplies up to 500 mA at 5 V, up to the rated current at 3.6 V or more, and drops its output voltage if the portable device attempts to draw more than the rated current. The charger port may shut down if the load is too high.

Charging ports exist in two flavors: charging downstream ports (CDP), supporting data transfers as well, and dedicated charging ports (DCP), without data support. A portable device can recognize the type of USB port from the way the D+ and D− pins are connected. For example, on a dedicated charging port, the D+ and D− pins are shorted. With charging downstream ports, current passing through the thin ground wire may interfere with high-speed data signals. Therefore, current draw may not exceed 900 mA during high-speed data transfer. A dedicated charge port may have a rated current between 0.5 A and 1.5 A. There is no upper limit for the rated current of a charging downstream port, as long as the connector can handle the current (standard USB 2.0 A-connectors are rated at 1.5 A).

Before the battery charging specification was defined, there was no standardized way for the portable device to inquire how much current was available. For example, Apple's iPod and iPhone chargers indicate the available current by voltages on the D− and D+ lines. When D+ = D− = 2 V, the device may pull up to 500 mA. When D+ = 2.0 V and D− = 2.8 V, the device may pull up to 1000 mA of current.

Dedicated charging ports can be found on USB power adapters that convert utility power or another power source—e.g., a car's electrical system—to run attached devices and battery packs. On a host (such as a laptop computer) with both standard and charging USB ports, the charging ports should be labeled as such.

To support simultaneous charge and sync, even if the communication port doesn't support charging a demanding device, so-called accessory charging adapters are introduced, where a charging port and a communication port can be combined into a single port.

The Battery Charging Specification 1.2 of 2010 makes clear that there are safety limits to the rated current at 5 A coming from USB 2.0. On the other hand, several changes are made, and limits are increasing including allowing 1.5 A on charging ports for unconfigured devices, allowing high-speed communication while having a current up to 1.5 A and allowing a maximum current of 5 A.

Sleep-and-charge USB ports can be used to charge electronic devices even when the computer is switched off. Normally, when a computer is powered off, the USB ports are powered down. This prevents phones and other devices from being able to charge unless the computer is powered on. Sleep-and-charge USB ports remain powered even when the computer is off. On laptops, charging devices from the USB port when it is not being powered from AC will drain the laptop battery faster.

Desktop machines need to remain plugged into AC power for sleep-and-charge to work.

On 22 October 2009, the International Telecommunication Union (ITU) announced that it had embraced the Universal Charger Solution as its "energy-efficient one-charger-fits-all new mobile phone solution" and added: "Based on the Micro-USB interface, UCS chargers will also include a 4-star or higher efficiency rating—up to three times more energy-efficient than an unrated charger."

Some USB devices require more power than is permitted by the specifications for a single port. This is common for external hard and optical disc drives and generally for devices with motors or lamps. Such devices can use an external power supply, which is allowed by the standard, or use a dual-input USB cable, one input of which is used for power and data transfer, the other solely for power, which makes the device a non-standard USB device. Some USB ports and external hubs can, in practice, supply more power to USB devices than required by the specification, but a standard-compliant device may not depend on this.

In addition to limiting the total average power used by the device, the USB specification limits the inrush current (i.e., that used to charge decoupling and filter capacitors) when the device is first connected. Otherwise, connecting a device could cause problems with the host's internal power. USB devices are also required to automatically enter ultralow-power suspend mode when the USB host is suspended. Nevertheless, many USB host interfaces do not cut off the power supply to USB devices when they are suspended.

Some non-standard USB devices use the 5 V power supply without participating in a proper USB network which negotiates power draws with the host interface. These are usually referred to as USB decorations. The typical example is a USB-powered keyboard light; fans, mug coolers and heaters, battery chargers, miniature vacuum cleaners, and even miniature lava lamps are available. In most cases, these items contain no digital circuitry, and thus are not standard compliant USB devices at all. This can theoretically cause problems with some computers, such as drawing too much current and damaging circuitry; prior to the Battery Charging Specification, the USB specification required that devices connect in a low-power mode (100 mA maximum) and communicate their current requirements to the host, which would then permit the device to switch into high-power mode.

Some devices, when plugged into charging ports, draw even more power (10 W or 2.1 A) than the Battery Charging Specification allows. The iPad and MiFi 2200 are two such devices. Barnes & Noble NOOK devices also require a special charger that runs at 1.9 A.

Powered USB uses standard USB signaling with the addition of extra power lines. It uses four additional pins to supply up to 6 A at either 5 V, 12 V, or 24 V (depending on keying) to peripheral devices. The wires and contacts on the USB portion have been upgraded to support higher current on the 5 V line, as well. This is commonly used in retail systems and provides enough power to operate stationary barcode scanners, printers, PIN pads, signature capture devices, etc. This modification of the USB interface is proprietary and was developed by IBM, NCR, and FCI/Berg. It is essentially two connectors stacked such that the bottom connector accepts a standard USB plug and the top connector takes a power connector.

5.4.9   IEEE 1394

Apple was among the earliest one to develop this high-speed peripheral interface. FireWire is another name (trademark) of Apple. Before USB 3.0 was introduced, FireWire was faster than USB. It can be seen in many earlier digital video products. Now USB 3.0 supersedes FireWire in speed.

Same as USB, IEEE 1394 can be hot attached or removed without requiring shutting down the computer.

The power distribution for a IEEE 1394 port is much higher than the USB. The voltage can range between $8 \sim 33$ V, and the current can be up to 1.5 A.

5.4.10   USB 3.0

USB 3.0 is SuperSpeed (SS) data transfer technology that can support up to 5 Gb/s. It comes with a dual-bus architecture that enables both USB 2.0 and USB 3.0 (SuperSpeed) to operate simultaneously. A standard USB 3.0 connector has 9 pins. The SuperSpeed bus is a layered architecture that has three elements.

The physical layer defines the physical connection between the upstream and the downstream. The SuperSpeed physical connection is a combination of two differential data pairs, the transmit path and the receive path.

The link layer connects the logical and physical ports.

The protocol layer defines the end-to-end communication rules between a device and a host.

5.5   Network Interface Card

A network interface card (NIC) is a computer hardware component that connects a computer to a computer network.

A NIC implements the electronic circuitry required to communicate using a specific physical layer and data link layer standard such as Ethernet or Wi-Fi. This provides a base for a full network protocol stack, allowing communication among small groups of computers on the same LAN and large-scale network communications through routable protocols, such as IP.

Although other network technologies exist, Ethernet has achieved near ubiquity since the mid-1990s.

Every Ethernet network controller has a unique 48-bit serial number called a MAC address, which is stored in read-only memory carried on the card for add-on cards. Every computer on an Ethernet network must have at least one controller. Each controller must have a unique MAC address. Normally, it is safe to assume that no two network controllers will share the same address, because controller vendors purchase blocks of addresses from the Institute of Electrical and Electronics Engineers (IEEE) and assign a unique address to each controller at the time of manufacture.

Ethernet network controllers typically support 10 Mb/s Ethernet, 100 Mb/s Ethernet, and 1000 Mb/s Ethernet varieties. Such controllers are designated 10/100/1000, and this means they can support a notional maximum transfer rate of 10,100 or 1000 megabits per second (Hwang 1993).

5.5.1   Basic NIC Architecture

The NIC allows computers to communicate over a computer network. It is both an OSI layer 1 (physical layer) and layer 2 (data link layer) device, as it provides physical access to a networking medium and provides a low-level addressing system through the use of MAC addresses. It allows users to connect to each other either by using cables or wirelessly. Figure 5.10 shows the block diagram of NIC architecture.

Most NICs have a DMA interface unit, a medium access control (MAC) unit, memory, and control logic. In the case of a programmable NIC, the control logic is one or more programmable processors that run compiled-code firmware. The DMA unit is directed by the onboard control logic to read and write data between the local NIC memory and the host's memory. The medium access unit interacts with the control logic to receive frames into local buffer storage and to send frames from

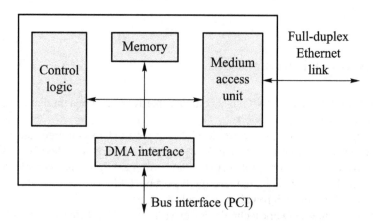

Fig. 5.10 NIC architecture block diagram

local buffer storage out onto the network. The memory is used for temporary storage of frames, buffer descriptors, and other control data.

5.5.2 Data Transmission

NICs facilitate the transmission and receipt of data (frames) between the network and host operating system. Sending and receiving frames happens in a series of steps completed by the host and NIC.

Typically, the host OS maintains a series of buffers, which are used for frame headers and contents. The OS also maintains a queue or ring of buffer descriptors. Each buffer descriptor indicates where in host memory the buffer resides and how big the buffer is.

5.5.2.1 Send

The steps of sending a single Ethernet frame are listed below. A NIC diagram of sending process is shown in Fig. 5.11.

1. The host operating system is informed that a frame is in host memory and is ready to be sent. The OS builds a buffer descriptor regarding this frame in host memory.

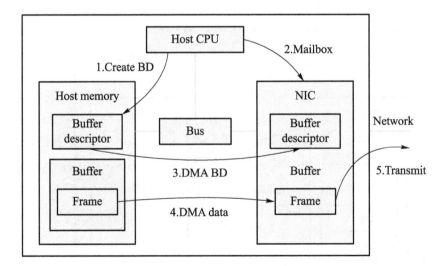

Fig. 5.11 NIC send (Color)

2. The OS notifies the NIC that a new buffer descriptor is in host memory and is ready to be fetched and processed. This is typically referred to as a "mailbox" event.
3. The NIC initiates a direct memory access (DMA) read of the pending buffer descriptor and processes it.
4. Having determined the host address of the pending frame, the NIC initiates a DMA read of the frame contents.
5. When all segments of the frame (which may use several buffer descriptors and buffers) have arrived, the NIC transmits the frame out onto the Ethernet.
6. Depending on how the OS has configured the NIC, the NIC may interrupt the host to indicate that the frame has completed.

5.5.2.2   Receive

The steps of receiving a single Ethernet frame are listed below. A diagram of the receiving process is shown in Fig. 5.12.

1. The NIC receives a frame from the network into its local receiving buffer.
2. Presuming there is enough host memory available for this received frame, the NIC initiates a DMA write of the frame contents into host memory. The NIC determines what the starting host address is by examining the next free buffer descriptor (which it has previously fetched).
3. The NIC modifies the previously fetched buffer descriptor regarding the space that the new frame now occupies and fills in the frame length and possibly

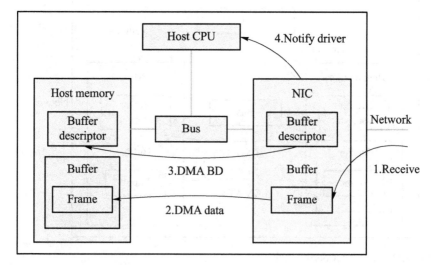

Fig. 5.12 NIC receive (Color)

checksum information. After modifying this buffer descriptor, the NIC initiates a DMA write of it to the host.

4. Depending on how the OS has configured the NIC, the NIC may interrupt the host to indicate that a frame has arrived.

5.6 Keyboard, Video, and Mouse Interfaces

A computer usually has a keyboard, a mouse, and one or more video displays. A keyboard and a mouse can be either connected directly to the computer, integrated into laptop computers, or connected to a computer wirelessly. Depending on the graphic card, a computer can attach one display, two displays, or even more. Usually laptops can connect an external display, and the resolution on the external display is higher. Due to the high transmission rate requirement, monitors cannot be wirelessly connected to a computer system.

5.6.1 Keyboards

A keyboard contains a keyboard controller that scans the keyboard and reports key depressions and releases. A scan code is assigned to each key with a unique number. It has nothing to do with the ASCII code of the character.

5.6.2 Video Graphic Cards

A video card is an expansion card that allows the computer to send graphical information to a video display device such as a monitor or projector.

Many modern computers do not have video expansion cards but instead have GPUs integrated directly onto the motherboard (Shiva 2000). This allows for a less expensive computer but also for a less powerful graphic system. This option is wise for the average business and home user not interested in advanced graphics capabilities or the latest games.

The digital visual interface (DVI) is a video interface standard covering the transmission of video between a computer and a display device. Most contemporary PCs, monitors, projectors, and televisions feature HDMI and DisplayPort interfaces.

More and more computers have graphic processing unit (GPU) that can not only handle graphics need but also perform actual computations.

5.6.3 Mouses

In computing, a mouse is a pointing device that functions by detecting two-dimensional motion relative to its supporting surface. Some mouses provide three-dimensional information. It is usually seen in computer gaming and other areas that require 3D coordinates. Physically, a mouse is an object held under one of the user's hands, with one or more buttons. It sometimes features other elements, such as "wheels," which allow the user to perform various system-dependent operations, or extra buttons or features that can add more control or dimensional input. The mouse's motion typically translates into the motion of a cursor on a display, which allows for fine control of a graphical user interface. Touchpads are common on laptops. They have similar features as mouses.

5.7 Virtual I/O

I/O virtualization is technology that uses software to logically abstract upper-layer protocols from physical connections. The technique takes a single physical component and presents it to devices as logically multiple components.

I/O virtualization allows a single IT resource to be shared among virtual machine. It sets up a virtual path between a physical server and nearby peripherals. The technique is commonly used in RAID controllers, Ethernet NICs, Fiber Channel host bus adaptor (HBA), graphic cards, and internal SSDs.

For example, when you install VirtualBox on your computer, a single network to the host can be shared by many guest virtual machines that each has unique virtual NICs.

In addition to NIC virtualization, there are other types of I/O virtualization technologies such as virtual SCSI, virtual MAC address, virtual HBA, and virtual I/O servers.

Intel virtualization technology for directed I/O (VT-d) extends Intel's visualization technology roadmap by providing hardware assists for virtualization solutions.

IT security mechanisms are based on the ability to create isolated execution environments that are less susceptible to attack. Intel VT and VT-d technology are instrumental in creating such trusted environments that can act in the case of malicious attack or hardware failure.

5.8 Software-Defined Networking

Software-defined networking (SDN) is getting more popular than traditional network in that the data, control, and management are no longer in separated planes, thus reducing the physical connections that could mess up with the wires.

Network controllers are separated from the physical infrastructure layer to allow the control layer to have a global view of the entire network. At the application layer, applications running on VMs only work with the control layer; therefore, programs do not interact a particular physical device. It all leaves to the network controller to do the tasks.

The new architecture model provides a way to configure the OpenFlow switches at runtime.

5.9 3D I/O Devices

More input and output devices stimulate the human visual, haptic, auditory, and tactile systems by providing 3D perspectives. Common 3D I/O devices include 3D scanners, 3D printers, volumetric displays, and autonomous eyes.

5.9.1 3D Scanners

3D scanners are three-dimensional measurement devices used to capture real-world objects or environments so that they can be remodeled or analyzed in the digital world. The latest generation of 3D scanners do not require contact with the physical object being captured.

5.9.2 3D Printers

3D printing is a process used to make three-dimensional objects. Additive manufacturing creates parts from the ground up by fusing together layers of material. Its counterpart, subtractive manufacturing, begins with material and removes excess until only the desired shape remains.

There are several methods of 3D printing. The most commonly recognized is called Fused Deposition Modeling (FDM). This method uses a single nozzle head to extrude melted material, typically plastic, layer by layer onto a build platform according to the 3D data that has been supplied to the printer. One of the most familiar printers in this space, the MakerBot, uses the FDM method. Other 3D printing processes, like Stereolithography (SLA), fuse together liquid material by curing it with a UV laser, while Binder Jetting fuses together powder material with a binding spray. Today, these methods are still more expensive and specialized than FDM.

The materials used in 3D printing are often dependent on the method. Binder Jetting, for instance, might use sandstone material, while SLA and FDM typically use plastic or resin. But what was once a small list of printable materials has been rapidly expanding. Plastics today include stronger substances like nylon, as well as biodegradable plastic. Paper, ceramics, and metals are growing in popularity and helping to expand applications for 3D printing. Most recently on the scene are food materials like chocolate, sugar, and even meat.

It's important to note that the process of 3D printing has many steps and is not as automated as some might think. From file preparation (e.g., creation, conversion), actual printing, to the finishing work post-print (e.g., sanding, coating, removing support material), the output of 3D printing takes time. However, open-source file sharing on sites like Thingiverse and GrabCAD is making it faster for designers to get started.

5.9.3   Autonomous Eyes

Advanced driver assistance systems (ADAS) are already a reality, with features like pedestrian detection, adaptive cruise control, collision avoidance, lane correction, and automated parking becoming increasingly commonplace. Autonomous eyes rely on not only sensor networks to "see" the road but also AI to process the data and to make decisions.

Full self-driving automation means vehicles can perform all driving functions and monitor roadway conditions for an entire trip and so may operate with occupants who cannot drive and without human occupants.

Human error is reportedly the cause of 90% of all accidents. Safety is the primary impetus behind the push to autonomous driving. Advocates believe the number of accidents, injuries, and fatalities could drop dramatically when the risk of human error is removed by networks of sensors, cameras, radar, lidar, GPS receivers, and sophisticated electronic control units (ECUs). Computers, it is reasoned, react more quickly than humans and make better judgments based on thousands of instantaneous calculations. Moreover, they don't get groggy behind the wheel, and their minds don't wander.

Autonomous eyes have been widely used in cars as well as in trains and planes. Advocates say it will save lives and reduce fuel consumption, emissions, and costs.

5.10   Input/Output Security

I/O security ranges from physical security, operation security, application security, etc. Security threats can affect all input and output devices. An unlocked keyboard is an example of physical security. An un-encrypted hard drive may expose sensitive data to unauthorized person.

5.10.1 Disable Certain Key Combinations

Keyboard should always be locked if not in use. For a server, you may want to disable the ctrl-alt-del combination. An attacker may shut down a server by pressing the combination keys if it is not properly protected.

5.10.2 Anti-Glare Displays

If you a frequent traveler, you may want to add an anti-glare screen filter so that nobody other than yourself can read the content on a computer display.

5.10.3 Adding Password to Printers

Printers can be protected by adding passwords so that only authorized users can print. Once the printing job is done, the documents should be collected immediately.

5.10.4 Bootable USB Ports

USB ports provide convenience to computer users. However, many USB flash drives contain a small operating system which is bootable. A bootable flash drive can start a virtual machine on top of the computer system. From the virtual machine, the attacker can easily read data stored on the host machine.

To prevent such attacks, all USB ports should be set not to bootable. Unused USB ports should be disabled.

5.10.5 Encrypting Hard Drives

Hard drives are also vulnerable to attackers. Sensitive data should be stored separately and encrypted. This will prevent any person to view the data by taking off the hard drive from the current computer and attach to another one.

For security related to network, there will be further discussions in later chapters.

5.11   Summary

In this chapter, we studied input and output devices and network interfaces. I/O devices contain several internal registers. The registers are used to receive command and data from the process. With DMA technology, data transmission between I/O devices and memory can be done directly without taking up CPU resources. To solve the low-speed problem which in some cases may slow down the CPU operations, we use interrupts so that an I/O device will not occupy the CPU until the I/O job is done or its buffer (I/O register) is full.

USB is a common I/O interface and is becoming a standard interface on many I/O devices. The USB 3.0 is capable of transmitting and receiving at the speed of 400 MB/s.

The network interface card is a special-type I/O device that manages network data communication. Every NIC comes with a MAC address, a unique address to identify the device on the Internet.

I/O virtualization allows a single IT resource to be shared among virtual machine. SDN reduces complexity by decoupling the control and data planes while making automation highly secure and scalable. 3D displays are able to present 3D images for people to view with or without special glasses.

Security problems for classical I/O devices may not be so hard to deal with. However, network-related security is a very broad topic that is usually hard to eliminate. Chapter 9 will discuss this topic in detail.

Projects

5.1   USB 3.0 speed test

USB Flash Benchmark is a simple tool that allows you to benchmark your USB flash drive speed, capacity, and overall performance.

Download the free tool, insert a USB 3.0 flash drive, and test the speed. What could be the reasons if the measured speed is lower than the marked speed on the drive?

5.2   Hide your computer with virtual MAC

A device's MAC address is assigned by the manufacturer, but it can be changed when you need to. Some people do so to conceal computers from the Internet. Conduct research on changing the MAC address of your computer.

Exercises

5.1   What is DMA? Why can DMA reduce CPU workload?

5.2   When an interrupt happens, the CPU will respond to the interrupt and execute the interrupt handling program. How does CPU know to resume current task?

5.3 A PC (=FE17) points to the top of the stack. The bottom of the stack is at address FFFF. After execute instructions, PUSH, PUSH and POP, what is the value in the PC?

5.4 A simple character printer could use programmed I/O reasonably well, since the printer speed is slow compared to the CPU. Yet most modern printers use DMA, why?

5.5 What is a USB root hub? How many USB devices can be connected to a root hub?

5.6 A mouse with illuminate light was attached to a lightweight laptop computer. However, the mouse does not function. When plugging the same mouse to a desktop computer, it works perfectly. What could be the reason that caused the problem?

5.7 A bootable USB flash drive can set up a virtual machine on top of the host computer. On the virtual machine, a user may be able to access the files and data on the host computer. This is a convenient feature, but sometimes it may cause threats to the security. Describe how to effectively address this problem?

5.8 A KVM device can allow two or more computers to share one display, one keyboard, and one mouse. With the earlier ones, people have to switch manually. The newer models allow you to switch with key combinations or mouse clicks. Draw a conceptual diagram of such design (hint: PIO).

5.9 Data on a hard drive are protected by a password that is managed by the operating system. Describe the flaws of this type of "protection" technique.

5.10 At least one MAC address exists on a NIC card. What is the MAC address used for?

5.11 Describe the sending and receiving processes of a NIC card.

5.12 USB is defac to the "standard" for I/O devices. It replaces old printer interfaces, keyboard and mouse interfaces, and many others. However, the mainstream for computer displays is either HDMI or display port. Conduct a research to see whether it is possible to replace HDMI or display port with USB. Explain why we can/cannot do it.

5.13 A holographic display can create a virtual 3D image of an object. The main advantage is it does not require any special glasses to view the image. Conduct research in this area, and explain how a holographic display can construct a 3D image.

5.14 DMA is a common controller that is connected to the CPU. When initiated, DMA will transmit data between memory and I/O devices without going through the CPU, therefore saving CPU time. Design a flowchart of the DMA handshake process.

References

Dumas, J. D. (2006). *Computer architecture: Fundamentals and principles of computer design.* Abingdon: Taylor & Francis.

Foster, C. C., & Iberall, T. (1985). *Computer architecture* (3rd ed.). New York: Van Nostrand Reinhold Company.

Hwang, K. (1993). *Advanced computer architecture: Parallelism, scalability, programmability.* New York: McGraw-Hill Inc.

Randell, B. (Ed.). (1982). *The designs of digital computers.* Berlin: Springer.

Shiva, S. G. (2000). *Computer design and architecture* (3rd ed.). New York: Marcel Dekker Inc.

Chapter 6
Central Processing Unit

The central processing unit (CPU) or general-purpose graphic processing unit (GPU) is the brain of a computer system. Some large-scale ICs may contain CPU, memory, I/O, and network components in one chip commonly known as system on a chip (SoC). Other than mainframes and personal computers, modern mobile phones are usually equipped with CPU/GPUs that can perform most jobs for ordinary people. SoC is very common now in many IoT devices.

Personal computers may only contain one CPU. Servers in data center running cloud applications usually contain many CPUs and GPUs. A CPU has a certain number of address, data, and control bus signals. The number of data bits that can be processed at one time is called a word. Unlike byte which is a fixed number of equal to 8 bits, size of a word differs from computers to computers. For example, a word for a 32-bit computer is $32/8 = 4$ B (byte), while a word for a 64-bit computer is $64/8 = 8$ B.

6.1 The Instruction Set

The instruction set provides an interface that allows users to take the full use of the processor. The selection of the instructions is determined by the application for which the processor is intended. For example, a computationally intensive computer may choose processors that are built with larger word size, more math functions, and lots of memory management features. On the other hand, a processor designed for embedded systems such as TV remote controls and air conditioners may only contain less or simple instructions, small word size, and easy addressing features.

© The Author(s), under exclusive license to Springer Nature Singapore Pte Ltd. 2021   129
S. P. Wang, *Computer Architecture and Organization*,
https://doi.org/10.1007/978-981-16-5662-0_6

6.1.1   Instruction Set Architecture

The Instruction Set Architecture (ISA) is the part of the processor that is visible to programmers. The ISA serves as the boundary between software and hardware.

Unlike common computers with instructions of varying length, a reduced instruction set computer (RISC) has instructions that all have exactly the same size. Thus, they can be prefetched and pipelined to improve the efficiency.

6.1.2   Instruction Classifications

Instructions usually contain two components, operation code (opcode) and operands. An instruction can have one opcode and zero or more operands. Some common instruction formats are shown in Fig. 6.1.

The operands are located either in registers (fast speed) or in a memory location. Table 6.1 lists some common classes of instructions

The logic instructions and arithmetic instructions are a subset of the memory and register reference instructions.

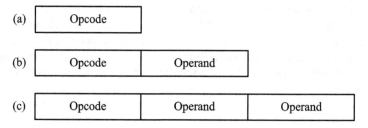

Fig. 6.1 Opcode and operands

Table 6.1 Common classes of instructions

Instruction type	Operations
Memory to memory instructions	Both operands are in memory
Memory to register instructions	One of the operands is in memory, another one is in register
Register reference instructions	The operation is performed on the contents of one or more registers
Memory reference instructions	The operation is performed on the contents of memory location
Control instructions	Branching, halt, pause, etc.
Input/output instructions	Input or output
Macroinstructions	A set of instructions

Fig. 6.2 Logical
operation—XOR

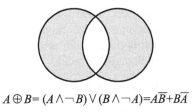

$$A \oplus B = (A \wedge \neg B) \vee (B \wedge \neg A) = A\overline{B} + B\overline{A}$$

6.1.3 Logic Instructions

All processors have logical operation instructions. The common logical operations are AND, OR, NOT, and Exclusive OR (*XOR*). AND needs both inputs equal to 1 in order to output 1. OR needs one or more one inputs in order to output 1. In other words, OR output 0 *iff* (if and only if) both inputs are 0. NOT operation inverts the input. *XOR* is just like adding both inputs and discarding the carry (if there is one). So, if two inputs are different then output 1, otherwise 0. Figure 6.2 shows the examples of the logical operation—*XOR*.

6.1.4 Arithmetic Instructions

Arithmetic instructions include ADD, SUB, MUL, DIV, etc.

The implementation of the arithmetic instructions varies from processor to processor. It mostly depends on the length of the instruction. Based on the number of operands, the instructions can be organized as follows:

- Three addresses (operands)
- Two addresses
- One address
- Zero address

For a three-address machine, there are the two operands, and the results are stored separately. Two-address machine will reuse one address as one of the operands and later holds the result. One-address machine usually uses the accumulator (ACC) with one address (commonly a register) to perform the execution.

The word "address" here may refer to a register, a memory unit, or both. Since registers are much faster than memory, instructions that use registers as operands are faster than those that use memory. Common processors use registers to perform arithmetic operations. Some embedded chips use memory to do so.

Here are some examples of instructions with different operands

- Three-address machine

    ADD A, B, C $C \leftarrow A + B$

Each of the instructions needs three registers or memory access during each execution. In practice, the majority of operations are based on two operands with the result occupying the position of one of the operand. Therefore, a two-address instruction may be good for such processors.

- Two-address machine

ADD A, B $A \leftarrow A + B$

Two-operand instructions are also common in processors. In addition to fetch-execution cycle, it adds a write back cycle to store the result to the location of one of the operands.

- One-address machine

ADD B $ACC \leftarrow ACC + B$

A one-address processor is similar to a two-address processor except it uses the accumulator (ACC), a register in the CPU, to be default.

The addressing modes for operands can be direct, indirect, or register. Direct addressing means the operand is a number. The indirect addressing means the operand is an address pointing to a memory location. The register addressing means the operand is stored in a register.

- Direct addressing: ADD $A, 3$ $A \leftarrow A + 3$
- Indirect addressing: ADD A, π $A \leftarrow A + \pi$

In indirect addressing, the operand Pi (π) is a label or pointer pointing to the memory location of the actual number.

6.1.5   Intel 64/32 Instructions*

The data transfer instructions move data between memory and the general-purpose and segment registers. They also perform specific operations such as conditional moves, stack access, and data conversion.

6.1.5.1   Move Instructions

The MOV (move) instructions transfer data between memory and registers or between registers.

The MOV instruction performs basic load data and store data operations between memory and the processor's registers and data movement operations between registers.

The MOV instruction cannot move data from one memory location to another or from one segment register to another segment register. Memory-to-memory moves are performed with the MOVS (string move) instruction.

6.1.5.2 Stack Manipulation Instructions

The PUSH, POP, PUSHA (push all registers), and POPA (pop all registers) instructions move data to and from the stack. The PUSH instruction decrements the stack pointer (contained in the ESP register) and then copies the source operand to the top of stack. It operates on memory operands, immediate operands, and register operands (including segment registers). The PUSH instruction is commonly used to place parameters on the stack before calling a procedure. It can also be used to reserve space on the stack for temporary variables.

The PUSHA instruction saves the contents of the eight general-purpose registers on the stack. This instruction simplifies procedure calls by reducing the number of instructions required to save the contents of the general-purpose registers.

The registers are pushed on the stack in the following order: EAX, ECX, EDX, EBX, the initial value of ESP before EAX was pushed, EBP, ESI, and EDI.

The POP instruction copies the word or doubleword at the current top of stack (indicated by the ESP register) to the location specified with the destination operand. It then increments the ESP register to point to the new top of stack.

The destination operand may specify a general-purpose register, a segment register, or a memory location.

The POPA instruction reverses the effect of the PUSHA instruction. It pops the top eight words or doublewords from the top of the stack into the general-purpose registers, except for the ESP register. If the operand-size attribute is 32 bits, the doublewords on the stack are transferred to the registers in the following order: EDI, ESI, EBP, ignore doubleword, EBX, EDX, ECX, and EAX. The ESP register is restored by the action of popping the stack. If the operand-size attribute is 16, the words on the stack are transferred to the registers in the following order: DI, SI, BP, ignore word, BX, DX, CX, and AX.

6.1.5.3 Shift Instructions

The SAL (shift arithmetic left), SHL (shift logical left), SAR (shift arithmetic right), and SHR (shift logical right) instructions perform an arithmetic or logical shift of the bits in a byte, word, or doubleword.

The SAL and SHL instructions perform the same operation. They shift the source operand left from 1 to 31 bit positions. Empty bit positions are cleared. The CF flag is loaded with the last bit shifted out of the operand.

The SHR instruction shifts the source operand right from 1 to 31 bit positions. As with the SHL/SAL instruction, the empty bit positions are cleared, and the CF flag is loaded with the last bit shifted out of the operand.

The SAR instruction shifts the source operand right from 1 to 31 bit. This instruction differs from the SHR instruction in that it preserves the sign of the source operand by clearing empty bit positions if the operand is positive or setting the empty bits if the operand is negative. Again, the CF flag is loaded with the last bit shifted out of the operand.

6.1.5.4   Rotate Instructions

The ROL (rotate left), ROR (rotate right), RCL (rotate through carry left), and RCR (rotate through carry right) instructions rotate the bits in the destination operand out of one end and back through the other end. Unlike a shift, no bits are lost during a rotation. The rotate count can range from 0 to 31.

The ROL instruction rotates the bits in the operand to the left (toward more significant bit locations). The ROR instruction rotates the operand right (toward less significant bit locations).

The RCL instruction rotates the bits in the operand to the left, through the CF flag. This instruction treats the CF flag as a one-bit extension on the upper end of the operand. Each bit that exits from the most significant bit location of the operand moves into the CF flag. At the same time, the bit in the CF flag enters the least significant bit location of the operand.

The RCR instruction rotates the bits in the operand to the right through the CF flag. For all the rotate instructions, the CF flag always contains the value of the last bit rotated out of the operand, even if the instruction does not use the CF flag as an extension of the operand. The value of this flag can then be tested by a conditional jump instruction (JC or JNC).

6.1.5.5   Control Transfer Instructions

The processor provides both conditional and unconditional control transfer instructions to direct the flow of program execution. Conditional transfers are taken only for specified states of the status flags in the EFLAGS register. Unconditional control transfers are always executed.

For the purpose of this discussion, these instructions are further divided into subordinate subgroups that process:

• Unconditional transfers
• Conditional transfers
• Software interrupts

The JMP, CALL, RET, INT, and IRET instructions transfer program control to another location (destination address) in the instruction stream. The destination can be within the same code segment (near transfer) or in a different code segment (far transfer).

Jump instruction—The JMP (jump) instruction unconditionally transfers program control to a destination instruction. The transfer is one way, that is, a return address is not saved. A destination operand specifies the address (the instruction pointer) of the destination instruction. The address can be a relative address or an absolute address.

A relative address is a displacement (offset) with respect to the address in the EIP register. The destination address (a near pointer) is formed by adding the displacement to the address in the EIP register. The displacement is specified with a signed integer, allowing jumps either forward or backward in the instruction stream.

An absolute address is an offset from address 0 of a segment. It can be specified in either of the following ways:

- An address in a general-purpose register   This address is treated as a near pointer, which is copied into the EIP register. Program execution then continues at the new address within the current code segment.
- An address specified using the standard addressing modes of the processor   Here, the address can be a near pointer or a far pointer. If the address is for a near pointer, the address is translated into an offset and copied into the EIP register. If the address is for a far pointer, the address is translated into a segment selector (which is copied into the CS register) and an offset (which is copied into the EIP register).

In protected mode, the JMP instruction also allows jumps to a call gate, a task gate, and a task-state segment.

6.1.5.6   Call and Return Instructions

The CALL (call procedure) and RET (return from procedure) instructions allow a jump from one procedure (or subroutine) to another and a subsequent jump back (return) to the calling procedure.

The CALL instruction transfers program control from the current (or calling procedure) to another procedure (the called procedure). To allow a subsequent return to the calling procedure, the CALL instruction saves the current contents of the EIP register on the stack before jumping to the called procedure. The EIP register (prior to transferring program control) contains the address of the instruction following the CALL instruction. When this address is pushed on the stack, it is referred to as the return instruction pointer or return address.

The address of the called procedure (the address of the first instruction in the procedure being jumped to) is specified in a CALL instruction the same way as in a JMP instruction. The address can be specified as a relative address or an absolute address. If an absolute address is specified, it can be either a near or a far pointer.

The RET instruction transfers program control from the procedure currently being executed (the called procedure) back to the procedure that called it (the calling procedure). Transfer of control is accomplished by copying the return instruction pointer from the stack into the EIP register. Program execution then continues with the instruction pointed to by the EIP register.

The RET instruction has an optional operand, the value of which is added to the contents of the ESP register as part of the return operation. This operand allows the stack pointer to be incremented to remove parameters from the stack that were pushed on the stack by the calling procedure.

6.1.5.7 Loop Instructions

The LOOP, LOOPE (loop while equal), LOOPZ (loop while zero), LOOPNE (loop while not equal), and LOOPNZ (loop while not zero) instructions are conditional jump instructions that use the value of the ECX register as a count for the number of times to execute a loop. All the loop instructions decrement the count in the ECX register each time they are executed and terminate a loop when zero is reached. The LOOPE, LOOPZ, LOOPNE, and LOOPNZ instructions also accept the ZF flag as a condition for terminating the loop before the count reaches zero.

The LOOP instruction decrements the contents of the ECX register (or the CX register, if the address-size attribute is 16) and then tests the register for the loop-termination condition. If the count in the ECX register is nonzero, program control is transferred to the instruction address specified by the destination operand. The destination operand is a relative address (i.e., an offset relative to the contents of the EIP register), and it generally points to the first instruction in the block of code that is to be executed in the loop. When the count in the ECX register reaches zero, program control is transferred to the instruction immediately following the LOOP instruction, which terminates the loop. If the count in the ECX register is zero when the LOOP instruction is first executed, the register is pre-decremented to FFFFFFFFH, causing the loop to be executed 2^{32} times.

The LOOPE and LOOPZ instructions perform the same operation (they are mnemonics for the same instruction). These instructions operate the same as the LOOP instruction, except that they also test the ZF flag.

If the count in the ECX register is not zero and the ZF flag is set, program control is transferred to the destination operand. When the count reaches zero or the ZF flag is clear, the loop is terminated by transferring program control to the instruction immediately following the LOOPE/LOOPZ instruction.

The LOOPNE and LOOPNZ instructions (mnemonics for the same instruction) operate the same as the LOOPE/LOOPPZ instructions, except that they terminate the loop if the ZF flag is set.

6.1.5.8 Random Number Generator Instruction

The RDRAND instruction returns a random number. All Intel processors that support the RDRAND instruction indicate the availability of the RDR- AND instruction via reporting CPUID.01H:ECX.RDRAND[bit 30]=1.

RDRAND returns random numbers that are supplied by a cryptographically secure, deterministic random bit generator DRBG. The DRBG is designed to meet the NIST SP 800-90 standard. The DRBG is re-seeded frequently from an on-chip non-deterministic entropy source to guarantee data returned by RDRAND is statistically uniform, non-periodic, and non-deterministic.

In order to meet its security goals for the hardware design, the random number generator continuously tests itself and the random data it is generating. Runtime failures in the random number generator circuitry or statistically anomalous data occurring by chance will be detected by the self-test hardware and flag the resulting data as being bad. In such extremely rare cases, the RDRAND instruction will return no data instead of bad data.

Under heavy load, with multiple cores executing RDRAND in parallel, it is possible, though unlikely, for the demand of random numbers by software processes/threads to exceed the rate at which the random number generator hardware can supply them. This will lead to the RDRAND instruction returning no data transitorily. The RDRAND instruction indicates the occurrence of this rare situation by clearing the CF flag.

The RDRAND instruction returns with the carry flag set (CF=1) to indicate valid data is returned. It is recommended that software using the RDRAND instruction to get random numbers retry for a limited number of iterations, while RDRAND returns CF=0 and complete when valid data is returned, indicated with CF=1. This will deal with transitory underflows. A retry limit should be employed to prevent a hard failure in the RNG (expected to be extremely rare) leading to a busy loop in software.

The intrinsic primitive for RDRAND is defined to address software's need for the common cases (CF=1) and the rare situations (CF=0). The intrinsic primitive returns a value that reflects the value of the carry flag returned by the underlying RDRAND instruction. The example below illustrates the recommended usage of an RDRAND intrinsic in a utility function, a loop to fetch a 64-bit random value with a retry count limit of 10. A C implementation might be written as follows:

```
# define SUCCESS 1
# define RETRY_LIMIT_EXCEEDED 0
# define RETRY_LIMIT 10

int get_random_64( unsigned __int 64 * arand)
{
       int i ;
       for ( i = 0; i < RETRY_LIMIT; i ++) {
       if(_rdrand64_step(arand) ) return SUCCESS;
       }
       return RETRY_LIMIT_EXCEEDED;
}
```

6.1.5.9 Program Environment Instructions

The programming environment for the general-purpose instructions consists of the set of registers and address space. The environment includes the following items:

- General-purpose registers   Eight 32-bit general-purpose registers are used in non-64-bit modes to address operands in memory. These registers are referenced by the names EAX, EBX, ECX, EDX, EBP, ESI EDI, and ESP.

- Segment registers   The six 16-bit segment registers contain segment pointers for use in accessing memory. These registers are referenced by the names CS, DS, SS, ES, FS, and GS.
- EFLAGS register   This 32-bit register is used to provide status and control for basic arithmetic, compare, and system operations.
- EIP register   This 32-bit register contains the current instruction pointer.

General-purpose instructions operate on the following data types. The width of valid data types is dependent on processor mode:

- Bytes, words, doublewords
- Signed and unsigned byte, word, doubleword integers
- Near and far pointers
- Bit fields
- BCD integers

6.2   Registers

Registers are designed for specific functions and are wired specifically for different purposes. A processor contains a number of registers to hold instruction and data. Some special registers are used to store the status of the current operation. Registers are the fastest memory in a computer system. The reason to use registers is to make computation and handling fast. By reducing the times to access internal and external memories, the RISC machines usually contain a large number of registers to improve the speed.

Processors usually assign special roles to certain registers, including these registers:

- An accumulator (ACC), which collects the result of computations [von Neumann, 2006].
- Address registers, which keep track of where a given instruction or piece of data is stored in memory. Each storage location in memory is identified by an address.
- Data registers, which temporarily hold data taken from or about to be sent to memory.
- Status registers, which are used to store current CPU status.
- Program counter (PC), which is used to point to the current instruction being executed.

Newly produced processors usually have more advanced control unit and dedicated control bits for security.

Intel Core i7-900 is based on 45 ns process technology. It contains an Execute Disable Bit that allows memory to be marked as executable or non-executable, when combined with a supporting operating system.

If code attempts to run in a non-executable memory, the processor raises an error to the operating system. This feature can prevent some classes of viruses or worms

Table 6.2 Some status registers

Term	Description
RO	Read Only. If a register bit is read only, the hardware sets its state. The bit may be read by software. Writes to this bit have no effect
WO	Write Only. The register bit is not implemented as a bit. The write causes some hardware event to take place
RW	Read/Write. A register bit with this attribute can be read and written by software
RWL	Read/Write/Lock. A register bit with this attribute can be read or written by software. Hardware or a configuration bit can lock the bit and prevent it from being updated
RRW	Read/Restricted Write. This bit can be read and written by software. However, only supported values will be written. Writes of non-supported values will have no effect
L	Lock. A register bit with this attribute becomes Read Only after a lock bit is set

that exploit buffer over run vulnerabilities and can thus help improve the overall security of the system (Daswani et al. 2007).

Table 6.2 shows some status registers on Intel Core i7. Those are only a small portion of registers used for enhancing system security.

RISC would always use registers for all operands for certain operations, e.g. ADD. This makes program running much faster. On the other hand, programmers have to load the value from memory to registers, thus making the program lengthy.

6.2.1 General-Purpose Registers

The IA-32 architecture provides 16 basic program execution registers for use in general system and application programming. These registers can be grouped into four categories:

- General-purpose registers. These eight registers are available for storing operands and pointers.
- Segment registers. These registers hold up to six segment selectors.
- EFLAGS (program status and control) register. The EFLAGS register reports on the status of the program being executed and allows limited (application program level) control of the processor.
- EIP (instruction pointer) register. The EIP register contains a 32-bit pointer to the next instruction to be executed.

The 32-bit general-purpose registers EAX, EBX, ECX, EDX, ESI, EDI, EBP, and ESP are provided for holding the following items:

- Operands for logical and arithmetic operations
- Operands for address calculations
- Memory pointers

Although all of these registers are available for general storage of operands, results, and pointers, caution should be used when referencing the ESP register. The ESP register holds the stack pointer and as a general rule should not be used for another purpose.

Many instructions assign specific registers to hold operands. For example, string instructions use the contents of the ECX, ESI, and EDI registers as operands. When using a segmented memory model, some instructions assume that pointers in certain registers are relative to specific segments. For instance, some instructions assume that a pointer in the EBX register points to a memory location in the DS segment.

The following is a summary of special uses of general-purpose registers:

- EAX   Accumulator for operands and results data
- EBX   Pointer to data in the DS segment
- ECX   Counter for string and loop operations
- EDX   I/O pointer
- ESI   Pointer to data in the segment pointed to by the DS register; source pointer for string operations
- EDI   Pointer to data (or destination) in the segment pointed to by the ES register; destination pointer for string operations
- ESP   Stack pointer (in the SS segment)
- EBP   Pointer to data on the stack (in the SS segment)

The lower 16 bits of the general-purpose registers map directly to the register set found in the 8086 and Intel 286 processors and can be referenced with the names AX, BX, CX, DX, BP, SI, DI, and SP. Each of the lower two bytes of the EAX, EBX, ECX, and EDX registers can be referenced by the names AH, BH, CH, and DH (high bytes) and AL, BL, CL, and DL (low bytes).

6.2.2   Segment Registers

The segment registers (CS, DS, SS, ES, FS, and GS) hold 16-bit segment selectors. A segment selector is a special pointer that identifies a segment in memory. To access a particular segment in memory, the segment selector for that segment must be present in the appropriate segment register.

When writing application code, programmers generally create segment selectors with assembler directives and symbols. The assembler and other tools then create the actual segment selector values associated with these directives and symbols. If writing system code, programmers may need to create segment selectors directly.

How segment registers are used depends on the type of memory management model that the operating system or executive is using. When using the flat (unsegmented) memory model, segment registers are loaded with segment selectors that point to overlapping segments, each of which begins at address 0 of the linear address space. These overlapping segments then comprise the linear address space for the program. Typically, two overlapping segments are defined: one for code and another for data and stacks. The CS segment register points to the code segment, and all the other segment registers point to the data and stack segment.

When using the segmented memory model, each segment register is ordinarily loaded with a different segment selector so that each segment register points to a different segment within the linear address space. At any time, a program can thus access up to six segments in the linear address space. To access a segment not pointed to by one of the segment registers, a program must firstly load the segment selector for the segment to be accessed into a segment register.

Each of the segment registers is associated with one of the three types of storage, code, data, or stack. For example, the CS register contains the segment selector for the code segment, where the instructions being executed are stored. The processor fetches instructions from the code segment, using a logical address that consists of the segment selector in the CS register and the contents of the EIP register. The EIP register contains the offset within the code segment of the next instruction to be executed. The CS register cannot be loaded explicitly by an application program. Instead, it is loaded implicitly by instructions or internal processor operations that change program control (such as procedure calls, interrupt handling, or task switching).

The DS, ES, FS, and GS registers point to four data segments. The availability of four data segments permits efficient and secure access to different types of data structures. For example, four separate data segments might be created: one for the data structures of the current module, another for the data exported from a higher-level module, a third for a dynamically created data structure, and a fourth for data shared with another program. To access additional data segments, the application program must load segment selectors for these segments into the DS, ES, FS, and GS registers, as needed.

The SS register contains the segment selector for the stack segment, where the procedure stack is stored for the program, task, or handler currently being executed. All stack operations use the SS register to find the stack segment. Unlike the CS register, the SS register can be loaded explicitly, which permits application programs to set up multiple stacks and switch among them.

6.2.3 EFLAGS Register

The 32-bit EFLAGS register contains a group of status flags, a control flag, and a group of system flags. Following initialization of the processor (by asserting either the RESET pin or the INIT pin), the state of the EFLAGS register is 00000002H. Bits 1, 3, 5, 15, and 22 through 31 of this register are reserved. Software should not use or depend on the states of any of these bits.

Some of the flags in the EFLAGS register can be modified directly, using special-purpose instructions (described in the following sections). There are no instructions that allow the whole register to be examined or modified directly.

The following instructions can be used to move groups of flags to and from the procedure stack or the EAX register: LAHF, SAHF, PUSHF, PUSHFD, POPF, and POPFD. After the contents of the EFLAGS register have been transferred to the procedure stack or EAX register, the flags can be examined and modified using the processor's bit manipulation instructions (BT, BTS, BTR, and BTC).

When suspending a task (using the processor's multitasking facilities), the processor automatically saves the state of the EFLAGS register in the task state segment (TSS) for the task being suspended. When binding itself to a new task, the processor loads the EFLAGS register with data from the new task's TSS.

When a call is made to an interrupt or exception handler procedure, the processor automatically saves the state of the EFLAGS registers on the procedure stack. When an interrupt or exception is handled with a task switch, the state of the EFLAGS register is saved in the TSS for the task being suspended.

The status flags (bits 0, 2, 4, 6, 7, and 11) of the EFLAGS register indicate the results of arithmetic instructions, such as the ADD, SUB, MUL, and DIV instructions. The status flag functions are:

- CF (bit 0) Carry flag   Set if an arithmetic operation generates a carry or a borrow out of the most significant bit of the result, cleared otherwise. This flag indicates an overflow condition for unsigned-integer arithmetic. It is also used in multiple-precision arithmetic.
- PF (bit 2) Parity flag   Set if the least significant byte of the result contains an even number of 1 bit, cleared otherwise.
- AF (bit 4) Adjust flag   Set if an arithmetic operation generates a carry or a borrow out of bit 3 of the result, cleared otherwise. This flag is used in binary-coded decimal (BCD) arithmetic.
- ZF (bit 6) Zero flag   Set if the result is zero, cleared otherwise.
- SF (bit 7) Sign flag   Set equal to the most significant bit of the result, which is the sign bit of a signed integer (0 indicates a positive value, and 1 indicates a negative value).
- OF (bit 11) Overflow flag   Set if the integer result is too large a positive number or too small a negative number (excluding the sign-bit) to fit in the destination operand, cleared otherwise. This flag indicates an overflow condition for signed-integer (two's complement) arithmetic.

Of these status flags, only the CF flag can be modified directly, using the STC, CLC, and CMC instructions. Also, the bit instructions (BT, BTS, BTR, and BTC) copy a specified bit into the CF flag.

The status flags allow a single arithmetic operation to produce results for three different data types: unsigned integers, signed integers, and BCD integers. If the result of an arithmetic operation is treated as an unsigned integer, the CF flag indicates an out-of-range condition (carry or a borrow); if treated as a signed integer (two's complement number), the OF flag indicates a carry or borrow; and if treated as a BCD digit, the AF flag indicates a carry or borrow. The SF flag indicates the sign of a signed integer. The ZF flag indicates either a signed- or an unsigned-integer zero.

When performing multiple-precision arithmetic on integers, the CF flag is used in conjunction with the add with carry (ADC) and subtract with borrow (SBB) instructions to propagate a carry or borrow from one computation to the next.

The condition instructions Jcc (jump on condition code cc), SETcc (byte set on condition code cc), LOOPcc, and CMOVcc (conditional move) use one or more of the status flags as condition codes and test them for branch, set-byte, or end-loop conditions.

6.3 The Program Counter and Flow Control

A program counter (PC) or instruction pointer is a special register to hold the current program execution location. The PC is incremented to point to the next instruction by adding one word after each instruction fetch (Hennessy and Patterson 2006).

$$PC \leftarrow PC + 1$$

Here the number 1 means the next instruction. For a 32-bit processor, the next instruction is placed at $PC + 4$. So, PC always points to the next instruction after the current instruction is fetched, interpreted, and executed.

A program may not always run linearly. It may stop at some point to handle works (interrupts) or jump to another instruction, here we call branching. There are two types of branches, conditional and unconditional.

The goto statement is a common way in implementing branches. However, there is a debate whether to use or not to use. Many computer languages support goto statement, but some others may not, like Java. The structured program theorem proved that the goto statement is not necessary to write programs (Knuth 1998). The goto statement often combines with If statement in the form of:

IF condition THEN goto label;

Dijkstra, a renowned computer scientist, published a paper *A Case against the GO TO Statement*. In the paper, he depreciates the goto statement and its effective replacement by structure language statement such as while loop statement (Dijkstra 1968).

Kruth, the author of the famous book series *The Art of Computer Programming*, wrote another paper *Structured Programming with go to Statements*; in the paper, he suggested that it is optimal to use goto statement (Kruth 1974).

6.3.1   Intel Instruction Pointer*

The instruction pointer (EIP) register on Intel processors contains the offset in the current code segment for the next instruction to be executed. It is advanced from one instruction boundary to the next in straight-line code, or it is moved ahead or backward by a number of instructions when executing JMP, Jcc, CALL, RET, and IRET instructions.

The EIP register cannot be accessed directly by software; it is controlled implicitly by control-transfer instructions (such as JMP, Jcc, CALL, and RET), interrupts, and exceptions. The only way to read the EIP register is to execute a CALL instruction and then read the value of the return instruction pointer from the procedure stack. The EIP register can be loaded indirectly by modifying the value of a return instruction pointer on the procedure stack and executing a return instruction (RET or IRET).

All IA-32 processors prefetch instructions. Because of instruction prefetching, an instruction address read from the bus during an instruction load does not match the value in the EIP register. Even though different processor generations use different prefetching mechanisms, the function of the EIP register to direct program flow remains fully compatible with all software written to run on IA-32 processors.

In 64-bit mode, the RIP register becomes the instruction pointer. This register holds the 64-bit offset of the next instruction to be executed. 64-bit mode also supports a technique called RIP-relative addressing. Using this technique, the effective address is determined by adding a displacement to the RIP of the next instruction.

6.3.2   Interrupt and Exception*

Interrupts and exceptions are events that indicate that a condition exists somewhere in the system or the processor or within the currently executing program or task that requires the attention of a processor. They typically result in a forced transfer of execution from the currently running program or task to a special software routine or task called an interrupt handler or an exception handler. The action taken by a processor in response to an interrupt or exception is referred to as servicing or handling the interrupt or exception.

Interrupts occur at random times during the execution of a program, in response to signals from hardware. System hardware uses interrupts to handle events external to the processor, such as requests to service peripheral devices. Software can also generate interrupts by executing the INT n instruction.

Exceptions occur when the processor detects an error condition while executing an instruction, such as division by zero. The processor detects a variety of error conditions including protection violations, page faults, and internal machine faults. The machine-check architecture of the Pentium 4, Intel Xeon, P6 family, and

Pentium processors also permits a machine-check exception to be generated when internal hardware errors and bus errors are detected.

When an interrupt is received or an exception is detected, the currently running procedure or task is suspended while the processor executes an interrupt or exception handler. When execution of the handler is complete, the processor resumes execution of the interrupted procedure or task. The resumption of the interrupted procedure or task happens without loss of program continuity, unless recovery from an exception was not possible or an interrupt caused the currently running program to be terminated.

6.3.2.1   Source of Interrupts

The sources of interrupts received by the processor are two types, external (hardware generated) interrupts and software-generated interrupts.

External interrupts are received through pins on the processor or through the local APIC. The primary interrupt pins on Pentium 4, Intel Xeon, P6 family, and Pentium processors are the LINT[1:0] pins, which are connected to the local.

When the local APIC is enabled, the LINT[1:0] pins can be programmed through the APIC's local vector table (LVT) to be associated with any of the processor's exception or interrupt vectors.

When the local APIC is global/hardware disabled, these pins are configured as INTR and NMI pins, respectively. Asserting the INTR pin signals the processor that an external interrupt has occurred. The processor reads from the system bus the interrupt vector number provided by an external interrupt controller, such as an 8259A.

The processor's local APIC is normally connected to a system-based I/O APIC. Here, external interrupts received at the I/O APIC's pins can be directed to the local APIC through the system bus (Pentium 4, Intel Core Duo, Intel Core 2, Intel® Atom™, and Intel Xeon processors) or the APIC serial bus (P6 family and Pentium processors).

The I/O APIC determines the vector number of the interrupt and sends this number to the local APIC. When a system contains multiple processors, processors can also send interrupts to one another by means of the system bus (Pentium 4, Intel Core Duo, Intel Core 2, Intel Atom, and Intel Xeon processors) or the APIC serial bus (P6 family and Pentium processors).

The LINT[1:0] pins are not available on the Intel486 processor and the earlier Pentium processors that do not contain an on-chip local APIC. These processors have dedicated NMI and INTR pins. With these processors, external interrupts are typically generated by a system-based interrupt controller (8259A), with the interrupts being signaled through the INTR pin.

Note that several other pins on the processor can cause a processor interrupt to occur. However, these interrupts are not handled by the interrupt and exception mechanism described in this chapter. These pins include the RESET#, FLUSH#, STPCLK#, SMI#, R/S#, and INIT# pins. Whether they are included on a particular processor is implementation dependent. Pin functions are described in the data books for the individual processors.

The INT *n* instruction permits interrupts to be generated from within software by supplying an interrupt vector number as an operand. For example, the INT 35 instruction forces an implicit call to the interrupt handler for interrupt 35.

Any of the interrupt vectors from 0 to 255 can be used as a parameter in this instruction. If the processor's predefined NMI vector is used, however, the response of the processor will not be the same as it would be from an NMI interrupt generated in the normal manner. If vector number 2 (the NMI vector) is used in this instruction, the NMI interrupt handler is called, but the processor's NMI-handling hardware is not activated.

Interrupts generated in software with the INT *n* instruction cannot be masked by the IF flag in the EFLAGS register.

6.3.2.2   Source of Exceptions

The processor receives exceptions from three sources:

- Processor-detected program-error exceptions
- Software-generated exceptions
- Machine-check exceptions

The processor generates one or more exceptions when it detects program errors during the execution in an application program or the operating system or executive. Intel 64 and IA-32 architectures define a vector number for each processor-detectable exception. Exceptions are classified as faults, traps, and aborts.

The INTO, INT 3, and BOUND instructions permit exceptions to be generated in software. These instructions allow checks for exception conditions to be performed at points in the instruction stream. For example, INT 3 causes a breakpoint exception to be generated.

The INT *n* instruction can be used to emulate exceptions in software, but there is a limitation. If INT *n* provides a vector for one of the architecturally defined exceptions, the processor generates an interrupt to the correct vector (to access the exception handler) but does not push an error code on the stack. This is true even if the associated hardware-generated exception normally produces an error code. The exception handler will still attempt to pop an error code from the stack while handling the exception. Because no error code was pushed, the handler will pop off and discard the EIP instead (in place of the missing error code). This sends the return to the wrong location.

The P6 family and Pentium processors provide both internal and external machine-check mechanisms for checking the operation of the internal chip hardware and bus transactions. These mechanisms are implementation dependent. When a machine-check error is detected, the processor signals a machine-check exception (vector 18) and returns an error code.

6.4   RISC Processors

A reduced instruction set computer (RISC) is a type of microprocessor that recognizes a relatively limited number of instructions. Until the mid-1980s, the tendency among computer manufacturers was to build increasingly complex CPUs that had ever larger sets of instructions. At that time, however, a number of computer manufacturers decided to reverse this trend by building CPUs capable of executing only a very limited set of instructions. One advantage of reduced instruction set computers is that they can execute their instructions very fast because the instructions are so simple. Another, perhaps more important advantage, is that RISC chips require fewer transistors, which makes them cheaper to design and produce. Since the emergence of RISC computers, conventional computers have been referred to as CISCs (complex instruction set computers).

6.4.1   History

The first RISC projects came from IBM, Stanford, and UC-Berkeley in the late 1970s and early 1980s. The IBM 801, Stanford MIPS, and Berkeley RISC 1 and 2 were all designed with a similar philosophy which has become known as RISC. Certain design features have been characteristic of most RISC processors:

- One cycle execution time   RISC processors have a CPI (clock per instruction) of one cycle. This is due to the optimization of each instruction on the CPU and a technique called pipelining.
- Pipelining   A technique that allows for simultaneous execution of parts, or stages, of instructions to more efficiently process instructions.
- Large number of registers   The RISC design philosophy generally incorporates a larger number of registers to prevent in large amounts of interactions with memory.

6.4.2   Architecture and Programming

The simplest way to examine the advantages and disadvantages of RISC architecture is by contrasting it with its predecessor: complex instruction set computers (CISC) architecture.

RISC processors only use simple instructions that can be executed within one clock cycle. Thus, the "MULT" (multiply) command has to be divided into three separate commands: "LOAD," which moves data from the memory bank to a register; "PROD," which finds the product of two operands located within the registers; and "STORE," which moves data from a register to the memory banks. Figure 6.3 shows a diagram of the multiply execution. In order to perform the exact

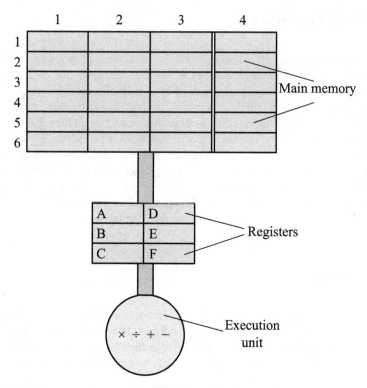

Fig. 6.3 MULT instruction executions in RISC architecture (Color)

series of steps described in the CISC approach, a programmer would need to code four lines of assembly:

```
LOAD A, 2:3 ;load data 1 from memory 2:3 to register A
LOAD B, 5:2 ;load data 2 from memory 5:2 to register B
PROD A, B ;multiply
STORE 2:3, A ;store result to memory 2:3
```

The primary goal of CISC architecture is to complete a task in as few lines of assembly as possible. A CISC processor would come prepared with a MULT instruction. When executed, this instruction loads the two values into separate registers, multiplies the operands in the execution unit, and then stores the product in the appropriate register. Thus, the entire task of multiplying two numbers can be completed with one instruction:

```
MULT 2:3, 5:2
```

6.4.3   Performance

The following equation is commonly used for expressing a computer's performance ability:

$$\frac{time}{program} = \frac{time}{cycle} \times \frac{cycle}{instruction} \times \frac{instruction}{program}$$

The CISC approach attempts to minimize the number of instructions per program, sacrificing the number of cycles per instruction. RISC does the opposite, reducing the cycles per instruction at the cost of the number of instructions per program.

6.4.4   Advantages and Disadvantages

There is still considerable controversy among experts about the ultimate value of RISC architectures. Its proponents argue that RISC machines are both cheaper and faster and are therefore the machines of the future. Skeptics note that by making the hardware simpler, RISC architectures put a greater burden on the software. They argue that this is not worth the trouble because conventional microprocessors are becoming increasingly fast and cheap anyway.

To some extent, the argument is becoming moot because CISC and RISC implementations are becoming more and more alike. Many of today's RISC chips support as many instructions as yesterday's CISC chips. And today's CISC chips use many techniques formerly associated with RISC chips.

6.4.5   Applications

RISC has not got the momentum on desktop computers and servers. However, its benefits in embedded and mobile devices have become the main reason to be used widely in these areas including iPhone, BlackBerry, Android, and some gaming devices.

Well-known RISC families include DEC Alpha, AMD 29k, MIPS, PA-RISC, ARM, PowerPC, SPARC, etc.

The hardware translation from x86 instructions into internal RISC-like micro-operations, which cost relatively little in microprocessors for desktops and servers, becomes significant in area and energy for mobile and embedded devices. Hence, ARM processors dominate cell phones and tablets today just as x86 processors dominate PCs. Atmel AVR is used in a variety of products ranging from Xbox handheld controllers to BMW cars.

6.5 Pipelining

Traditional pipelining is a standard feature in RISC processors that is much like an assembly line. Because the processor works on different steps of the instruction at the same time, more instructions can be executed in a shorter period of time.

6.5.1 Different Types of Pipelines

Computer-related pipelines include:

- Instruction pipelines   Instruction pipelining allows overlapping execution of multiple instructions with the same circuitry (Almasi and Gottlieb 1989). The circuitry is usually divided up into stages, including instruction decoding, arithmetic, and register fetching stages, wherein each stage processes one instruction at a time.
- Graphics pipelines   Graphics pipelining is found in most graphic cards, which consist of multiple arithmetic units, or complete CPUs, that implement the various stages of common rendering operations (perspective projection, window clipping, color and light calculation, rendering, etc.).
- Software pipelines   In software pipelining, commands can be written so that the output of one operation is automatically used as the input to the next, following operation. The Unix system called pipe is a classic example of this concept, although other operating systems do support pipes as well (Hockney et al. 1998).

6.5.2 Pipeline Performance Analysis

A useful method of demonstrating pipelining is the car manufacture analogy. Let's say that there are four steps to make a car, body, seats, tires, and painting. Suppose loading the body to the assembling line needs 20 min, installing seats needs 20 min,

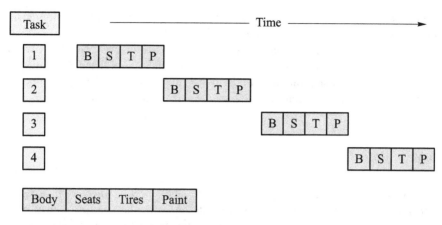

Fig. 6.4 Linear car manufacture process (Color)

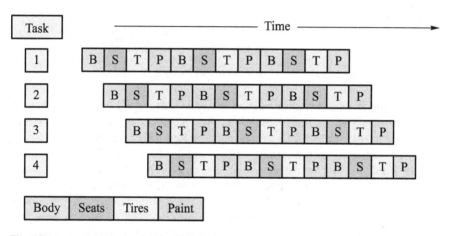

Fig. 6.5 A car manufacture pipeline (Color)

installing tires takes 20 min, and then painting takes 20 min. When the first car is manufactured, the process starts again from loading the body to finally painting.

Since each car needs 80 min to finish, this assembling line can manufacture 60 min × 8 h / 80 = 6 cars per day; that is equivalent to 180 cars a month. Figure 6.4 shows the linear car manufacture process.

However, a smarter approach to the problem would be to load the second car body after the first car moved to installing seats. When second car body is loaded, then start loading the third car body. The process is shown in Fig. 6.5.

Except the very beginning and the end of the pipeline, the number of cars manufactured increased approximately four times compared with the linear assembling line.

Generally, a car manufacture process can be divided into hundreds of steps. Let's take 80 steps as an example and assume each step takes the same time. Then on average the time needed to manufacture a car is 1 min! Without using pipelining, no one can imagine a car can be manufactured in 1 min!

In practice, each step is hardly to be divided exactly even. So, the overall performance of a pipeline may not reach the ideal result as predicted. On the other hand, if at a certain step the pipeline is stalled, then resuming the pipeline needs extra time and therefore decreases the pipeline performance (Blaise 2011).

6.5.3   Data Hazard

In pipeline, a data dependency (Culler et al. 1999) occurs when an instruction depends on the results of previous instructions. A particular instruction may need data in a register which has not yet been stored since the preceding instruction has not yet reached to the step in the pipeline.

For example:

$$R3 \leftarrow R1 + R2$$
$$R5 \leftarrow R3 + R4$$

In this example, the second instruction is to add $R3$ and $R4$ and store the result in $R5$. When the second instruction is in the second stage, the processor will be attempting to read $R3$ and $R4$ from the registers. Remember that the first instruction is just one step ahead of the second, so the contents of $R1$ and $R2$ are being added, but the result has not yet been written into register $R3$. The second instruction therefore cannot read from the register $R3$ because it hasn't been written yet and must wait until the data is ready. Consequently, the pipeline is stalled, and a number of empty instructions (known as bubbles) go into the pipeline. In this case, it is called RAW (read after write). Data dependency affects long pipelines more than shorter ones since it takes a longer period of time for an instruction to reach the final register-writing stage of a long pipeline.

6.6   Virtual CPU

Virtual machine can be simply considered as "computers on a computer." It is a tightly isolated software container that can run its own operating system and applications as if it were a physical computer. A virtual machine behaves exactly like a physical computer and contains its own virtual CPU, RAM, hard disk, and network interface card (NIC). Figure 6.6 shows a diagram of the VM architecture.

Virtual CPUs are logical processing units that are based on a physical processor or processors. The technology has been widely used in cloud computing and other virtualization-related fields.

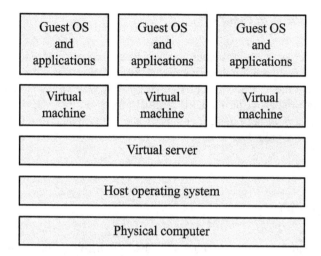

Fig. 6.6 VM architecture diagram

A virtual CPU is a software-based CPU that uses the resources of the host CPU and acts like a regular CPU (Englander 2010). An operating system can't tell the difference between a virtual CPU/machine and a physical CPU/machine, nor can applications or other computers on a network. Nevertheless, a virtual machine is composed entirely of software and contains no hardware components whatsoever. As a result, virtual machines offer a number of distinct advantages over physical hardware.

For system virtual machines, multiple OS environments can co-exist on the same computer, in strong isolation from each other. The virtual machine can provide an instruction set architecture (ISA) that is somewhat different from that of the real machine in application provisioning, maintenance, availability, and disaster recovery.

Here are the main characteristics of VMs.

- Run multiple operating systems on a single computer including Windows, Linux, and more.
- Reduce capital costs by increasing energy efficiency and requiring less hardware while increasing your server to admin ratio.
- Ensure enterprise applications perform with the highest availability and performance.
- Build up business continuity through improved disaster recovery solutions and deliver high availability throughout the datacenter.
- Improve enterprise desktop management and control with faster deployment of desktops and fewer support calls due to application conflicts.

Since virtual machines share the common resources with the host machine, it requires more memory and may have performance issues.

6.6.1   Virtual Processor

A virtual processor is a representation of a physical processor core to the operating system of a logical partition that uses shared processors.

vCPU is a time-dependent entity. A virtual processor is more likely amount of processing time spent on the CPU. Virtual processors are mapped to available logical processors in the physical computer and are scheduled by the Hypervisor software to allow processes to have more virtual processors than you have logical processors.

*6.6.2   Intel VT**

Intel virtualization technology (Intel VT) abstracts hardware that allows multiple workloads to share a common set of resources. On shared virtualized hardware, a variety of workloads can co-locate while maintaining full isolation from each other, freely migrate across infrastructures, and scale as needed.

Businesses tend to gain significant capital and operational efficiencies through virtualization because it leads to improved server utilization and consolidation, dynamic resource allocation and management, workload isolation, security, and automation. Virtualization makes on-demand self-provisioning of services and software-defined orchestration of resources possible, scaling anywhere in a hybrid cloud on-premise or off-premise per specific business needs.

Intel VT includes the following features:

1. CPU virtualization features enable faithful abstraction of the full prowess of Intel$^{®}$ CPU to a virtual machine. All software in the VM can run without any performance or compatibility hit, as if it was running natively on a dedicated CPU. Live migration from one Intel$^{®}$ CPU generation to another, as well as nested virtualization, is possible.
2. Memory virtualization features allow abstraction isolation and monitoring of memory on a per virtual machine basis. These features may also make live migration of VMs possible, add to fault tolerance, and enhance security. Example features include direct memory access remapping and extended page tables (EPT), including their extensions: accessed and dirty bits and fast switching of EPT contexts.
3. I/O virtualization features facilitate offloading of multi-core packet processing to network adapters as well as direct assignment of virtual machines to virtual functions, including disk I/O. Examples include Intel$^{®}$ virtualization technology for directed I/O (VT-d), virtual machine device queues (VMDQ), single root I/O virtualization (SR-IOV, a PCI-SIG standard), and Intel$^{®}$ data direct I/O technology (Intel$^{®}$ DDIO) enhancements.
4. Intel$^{®}$ graphics virtualization technology (Intel$^{®}$ GVT) allows VMs to have full and/or shared assignment of the graphics processing units (GPU) as well

as the video transcode accelerator engines integrated in Intel system-on-chip products. It enables usages such as workstation remoting, desktop-as-a-service, media streaming, and online gaming.

5. Virtualization of Security and Network functions enable transformation of traditional network and security workloads into compute. Virtual functions can be deployed on standard high-volume servers anywhere in the data center, network nodes, or cloud, and smartly co-located with business workloads. Examples of technologies making it happen include Intel® QuickAssist Technology (Intel® QAT) and the Data Plane Development Kit (DPDK).

6.6.3 Raspberry Pi Emulation with QEMU

QEMU is a generic and open-source machine emulator and virtualizer. When used as a machine emulator, QEMU can run OSes and programs made for one machine (e.g., an ARM board) on a different machine (e.g., your own PC). By using dynamic translation, it achieves very good performance.

For those who want to use Raspberry but do not want to get their "hands dirty," QEMU can emulate a Raspberry Pi locally on a personal computer. The main steps are as follows:

• Download and install QEMU kernel using git clone or sudo apt-get.
• Install Raspbian.
• Emulate Pi using QEMU kernel.
• Open terminal, and start the SSH service.
• On the host computer that launched the QEMU, you can SSH into the Pi system.

6.7 Mobile Processors

Mobile processors are microprocessors that are designed for mobile devices especially smart phones.

On the CPU front, most chips have a combination of larger cores that are more powerful and run faster and hotter and smaller cores that are more efficient. Typically, phones will use the smaller cores most of the time but for demanding tasks will switch to the higher-performance cores and use a combination of both cores and GPU and other cores to best manage performance needs and thermal considerations.

For graphics, there's more diversity, with some vendors choosing ARM's Mali line, others picking Imagination Technologies' PowerVR, and still others opting to design their own graphics cores. And there's even more diversity when it comes to things such as image processing, digital signal processing, and, as of late, AI functions.

Apple started pushing its AI capabilities in its fall phone announcements. The A11 Bionic is a six-core architecture, with two high-performance cores and four efficiency cores. Apple designs its own cores (under an ARM architecture license) and has traditionally pushed single-threaded performance. This is a step up from the four-core A10 Fusion, and Apple said the performance cores in the A11 are up to 25% faster than in the A10, while the four efficiency cores can be up to 70% faster than the A10 Fusion chip. It also said that the graphics processor is up to 30% faster.

Other companies including Qualcomm, Huawei, Samsung, MediaTek, Spredtrum, ARM, and Imagination Technologies all have their mobile processors that provide good speed, high DSP performance, and 5G technologies.

6.8 GPU

A central processing unit (CPU) is designed to handle complex tasks, such as time slicing, virtual machine emulation, complex control flows and branching, security, etc. In contrast, graphical processing units (GPUs) only do one thing well. They handle billions of repetitive low-level tasks.

Originally designed for the rendering of triangles in 3D graphics, they have thousands of arithmetic logic units (ALUs) compared with traditional CPUs that commonly have only 4 or 8. MPU architecture is shown in Fig. 6.7. Many types of scientific algorithms spend most of their time doing just what GPUs are good for: performing billions of repetitive arithmetic operations.

Computer scientists have been quick to harness the power of GPUs for computational science applications.

The reason behind the discrepancy in floating-point capability between the CPU and the GPU is that the GPU is specialized for compute-intensive, highly parallel

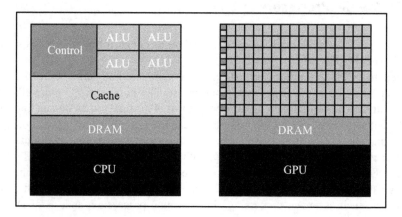

Fig. 6.7 MPU architecture (Color)

computation—exactly what graphics rendering is about—and therefore designed such that more transistors are devoted to data processing rather than data caching and flow control.

More specifically, the GPU is especially well suited to address problems that can be expressed as data-parallel computations—the same program is executed on many data elements in parallel—with a high ratio of arithmetic operations to memory operations.

Because the same program is executed for each data element, there is a lower requirement for sophisticated flow control, and because it is executed on many data elements and has high arithmetic intensity, the memory access latency can be hidden with calculations instead of big data caches.

A GPU program comprises two parts, a host part the runs on the CPU and one or more kernels that run on the GPU. Typically, the CPU portion of the program is used to set up the parameters and data for the computation, while the kernel portion performs the actual computation. In some cases, the CPU portion may comprise a parallel program that performs message passing operations using message passing interface (MPI).

With the right problem, a GPU can be thousands of times faster than a CPU.

6.9   TPU

Tensor processing units (TPUs) are Google's custom-developed application-specific integrated circuits (ASICs) used to accelerate machine learning workloads. TPUs are designed from the ground up with the benefit of Google's deep experience and leadership in machine learning.

Cloud TPU enables to run machine learning workloads on Google's TPU accelerator hardware using TensorFlow. Cloud TPU is designed for maximum performance and flexibility to help researchers, developers, and businesses build TensorFlow compute clusters that can leverage CPUs, GPUs, and TPUs. High-level Tensorflow APIs help you get models running on the Cloud TPU hardware.

6.10   CPU Security

Some tamper-resistant CPUs are packaged in a way that physical attempts to read or modify information inside the CPU cannot succeed easily. The CPU's tamper-resistant package protects its internal components, such as registers and cache, from hardware attacks. The CPU's internal cache is big enough (e.g., tens of megabytes) to contain a kernel and the working set of data for most programs, but not big enough to contain whole programs. Programs that require more memory use untrusted external memory. The CPU traps to a kernel when evicting or loading a cache line, so the kernel trap handler can protect data stored in external memory (Chen and Morris 2003).

Such CPU has a corresponding public-private key pair. The private key is hidden in the CPU and never revealed to anyone else (including software that runs on the CPU).

The CPU reveals the public key in a CPU certificate signed by the manufacturer. A user trusts a CPU if the CPU certificate is signed by a trusted manufacturer. A CPU uses the private key to sign and decrypt data, and users use the public key to verify signatures and encrypt data for the CPU.

At the software level, the system uses a kernel to create and schedule processes onto the CPU and to handle traps and interrupts. The kernel runs in privileged mode, and it can read or write all physical memory locations. Using page tables, the kernel partitions user-level processes into separate address spaces. The CPU applies conventional memory protection to prevent a program from issuing instructions that access or affect data in another address space. The page table of each address space is protected so only the kernel can change it. To prevent tampering of the kernel, the kernel text and some of its data reside in the secure CPU's cache and cannot be evicted. The secure CPU traps to the kernel when evicting data from its cache to external memory, or loading data from external memory into its cache. The kernel's trap handler decides, on a per-program basis, if and how the data should be protected. A program may ask the kernel to only authenticate or to both authenticate and copy-protect its instructions and data whenever they leave the secure CPU's internal cache. A secure processor diagram is shown in Fig. 6.8.

The overhead of taking a trap on every cache event depends on a program's memory access pattern and miss rate, the cost of cryptographic operations, and the level of security a program demands. It is to believe that an increase in the size of a CPU's cache and using hardware-assisted cryptographic operations decrease the overhead. Figure 6.8 shows what a system would look like. The kernel and some user-level servers that implement OS abstractions form a complete operating system. Users can also run virtualized operating systems in user space.

The computer system can also report the hardware and software configuration of a computer, so a user can decide if the hardware and software can be trusted to protect the user's program.

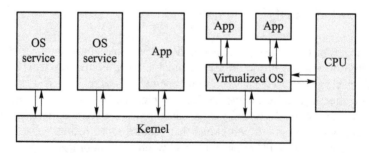

Fig. 6.8 A secure processor diagram

The CPU identifies each kernel by the content hash of the kernel's text and initialized data segment. If the kernel is modified before the system boots, its content hash would change. Because a kernel's text and data reside inside the tamper-resistant CPU, they cannot be changed (e.g., by a DMA device) after the system boots. Kernel's content hash is also referred to as the kernel signature.

A processor-secured computer boots in several stages. On a hardware reset, the CPU computes the content hash of the BIOS and jumps to the BIOS code. Next, the BIOS computes the content hash of the boot loader, stored in the first sector of the computer's master hard drive, and jumps to the boot loader code. Finally, the boot loader code computes the kernel signature and jumps into the corresponding kernel. Each stage uses a privileged CPU instruction to compute the content hash. The instruction stores the content hash in a register inside the CPU. The registers are protected so malicious programs cannot modify their content.

6.11 Summary

A CPU or GPU has a computing unit running instructions. An instruction has two components, opcode and operand. The addressing mode for operands can be direct or indirect.

Registers are the fastest memory in computer systems. Some important registers include the accumulator (ACC), address registers, data registers, status registers, and the program counter (PC). PC always points to the next instruction after the current instruction is fetched. Pipelining needs to perform prefetch that sometimes may cause problems when the intermediate results are not ready.

Reduced instruction set computers (RISC) have less instructions, and each instruction takes one cycle. The goal is to make instructions so simple that they could easily be pipelined, in order to achieve a single clock throughput at high frequencies. RISC processors are widely used in mobile electronics devices and mainframe computers, while traditional CISC processors are still leading personal computers and servers. RISC-V is an open standard ISA that has been widely adopted by academia and the industry.

To secure CPUs to prevent kernel to be tampered, one way is to use encryption by adding a public-private key pair or TPM.

Virtual CPUs are software-based CPUs that use the resources of the host CPU and act like regular CPUs. The virtual machine can provide an instruction set architecture (ISA) that functions like a regular machine. Since virtual machines share common resources with the host machine, it requires more memory and may have performance issues if not enough memory is attached.

Mobile processors are microprocessors designed for mobile devices especially smart phones. IoT devices often use SoC or RaspBerry Pi or Arduino microprocessors.

GPUs handle billions of repetitive low-level tasks. It is much faster than a CPU for certain tasks.

Projects

6.1 Little man computer (LMC)

Study LMC (https://www.101computing.net/category/lmc/), and write a program that adds two inputs together and output the result, and use the LMC Simulator to run your program.

6.2 CHERI

Capability hardware enhanced RISC instructions (CHERI) extends conventional hardware instruction-set architectures (ISAs) with new architectural features to enable fine-grained memory protection and highly scalable software compartmentalization. The CHERI memory protection features allow historically memory-unsafe programming languages such as C or C++ to be adapted to provide strong, compatible, and efficient protection against many currently widely exploited vulnerabilities.

Setup QEMU-CHERI on your computer. Follow the instruction at https://www.cl.cam.ac.uk/research/security/ctsrd/cheri/cheri-qemu.html.

Exercises

6.1 How much memory can a 32-bit CPU have?

6.2 List the algebraic expression and truth table for logical operation XOR.

6.3 Subtraction usually involves two operands. How to do subtraction on a one-address machine?

6.4 A 64-bit CPU has PC pointing to memory location 8000:1000. After fetching a one-word instruction, what is the value of the PC?

6.5 What is the performance of a CPU corresponding to the execution time?

6.6 Pipeline speed up can be expressed as

$$\text{Speedup} = \frac{\text{Pipeline depth}}{1 + \text{Pipeline stall CPI}} \times \frac{\text{Cycle Time}_{\text{unpipelined}}}{\text{Cycle Time}_{\text{pipelined}}}$$

where CPI stands for cycle per instruction.

Two RISC machines (CPI =1): Machine B has 1.05 times fast clock rate than machine A, and loads are 40% of instruction executed. Which machine is faster?

6.7 What is a virtual machine, and what is a host machine?

6.8 Two computers run two tasks. The rate is in the following table. Compute the average and relative throughputs, and specify which is faster.

	Rate	
System	Task 1	Task 2
A	10	20
B	20	10

6.9 Computer performance is usually expressed using the equation

$$\frac{\text{Time/s}}{\text{program}} = \frac{\text{Time/s}}{\text{cycle}} \times \frac{\text{cycle}}{\text{instruciton}} \times \frac{\text{instruction}}{\text{program}}$$

Suppose a program takes 1 billion instructions to execute on a processor running at 2 GHz. Also suppose that 50% of the instructions execute in 3 clock cycles, 30% execute in 4 block cycles, and 20% execute in 5 block cycles. What is the execution time for the program or task?

6.10 Conduct research and compare benchmarks between Apple A12, Intel Core i-9, and NVIDIA Quadro RTX 8000 processors.

References

Almasi, G. S., & Gottlieb, A. (1989) *Highly parallel computing.* Redwood City: Benjamin/Cummings.

Blaise, B. (2011). Introduction to parallel computing. In *Lawrence livermore national laboratory.* Retrieved November 12, 2011.

Chen, B., & Morris, R. (2003). Certifying program execution with secure processors. In *Proceeding of the 9th conference on Hot Topics in operating systems* (Vol. 9.23–9.29).

Culler, D. E., Singh, J. P., & Gupta, A. (1999). *Parallel computer architecture: A hardware/software approach.* San Francisco: Morgan Kaufmann Publishers.

Daswani, N., Kern, C., & Kesavan, A. (2007). *Foundations of security: What every programmer needs to know.* New York: Apress.

Dijkstra, E. W. (1968). A case against the GO TO statement. *ACM communication, 11,* 147–148.

Englander, I. (2010). *The architecture of computer hardware, systems software, and networking: An information technology approach.* Hoboken: John Wiley & Sons.

Hennessy, J. L., & Patterson, D. A. (2006). *Computer organization and design: The hardware/software interface.* San Francisco: Morgan Kaufmann Publishers.

Hockney, R. W., Jesshope, C. R., & Hockney, R, W. (1998) *Parallel computers 2: Architecture, programming, and algorithms.* Bristol: A. Hilger.

Knuth, D. E. (1998). *The art of computer programming* (3rd ed.). Boston: Addison-Wesley.

Kruth, D. E. (1974). Structured programming with GO TO statements. *Computing Burvey, 6,* 261–301.

Chapter 7
Advanced Computer Architecture

Advanced computer architecture includes study of instruction set design, parallel processing, bit, instruction, and data level parallelism, distributed computing, virtualization architecture, and cloud and mobile architecture. The chapter also introduces quantum computing architecture including quantum bits, quantum gates, quantum circuits and operations, and *Qiskit*, a toolkit for quantum computing programming and applications. Advanced architecture for AI/ML applications is also briefly discussed.

7.1 Multiprocessors

The central processor unit (CPU) was initially designed to include everything in a single chip. Over the years, more and more new processors have been developed with better speed and more functions. With the exponential growth for the need to further improve the performance of a computer system, the computer industry changes its approach from building faster chips to using multiple chips.

At first people started to explore the use of multiple microprocessors on the same motherboard. To do this, the hardware needs to support the manipulation of data so that the data can be sent to different central processing units. Later new architecture with multiple motherboards is used together with shared memory, storage, and interconnection networks.

7.1.1 Multiprocessing

Multiprocessing is a computer system that uses more than one CPU to handle data. The data needs to be broken into segments, and then each processor is given a task to

© The Author(s), under exclusive license to Springer Nature Singapore Pte Ltd. 2021
S. P. Wang, *Computer Architecture and Organization*,
https://doi.org/10.1007/978-981-16-5662-0_7

Fig. 7.1 A computer has two
processors, one CPU and one
math coprocessor

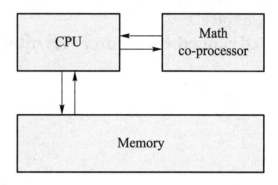

be performed. The division of work between the processors can be done in different ways. The idea of parallel central processing units was introduced in the 1970s. On the motherboard and the shared memory, each uses a CPU. Early on in the development, it was classified as a math coprocessor (as shown in Fig. 7.1). In this arrangement one of the central processing units has to be parent and the other is the child. The parent would break up the tasks and then assign a task to the child processor, and the results from the child would be passed back to the parent.

There were many problems to the first approach of multiprocessing units. The first approach had an overhead because the parent had to handle the flow of data and distribute it to the child. Both processors could not independently access the storage and make processing decisions. Though this was improvement to single central processing unit processor, it had still another overhead issue of the distance between the processors and the time to move between them. To solve the second problem, they moved the chip from its own socket on the motherboard and developed a stacked processor, with one chip on top of the other.

A multi-core processor is a single chip, or component, that contains two or more independent central processing units which can execute instructions independent of one another. The manufactures typically created integrated circuits that contained the central processing units, so that they were physically close together. They also gave the central processing units independent L_1 and L_2 caches.

7.1.2 Cache

A cache is a temporary memory device used by the central processing unit to store data that it could be working on. This type of memory is faster than main memory random access memory (RAM) because of how it is addressed and by its proximity to the central processing unit. The cache lessens the latency found when accessing the RAM. Most manufactures incorporated at least four independent caches to assist the processor so that it could function without sending requests down the bus to the main memory. One of these caches was the data cache which assists with the fetching of data stored in. L_1 and L_2 caches were pretty standard in the industry, but

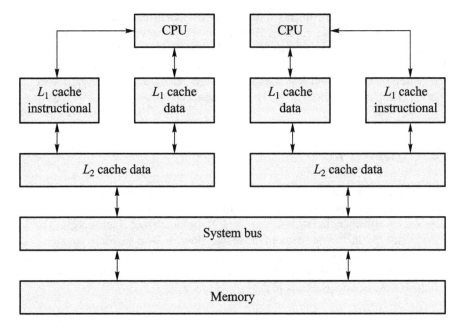

Fig. 7.2 Architecture of a dual-core CPU with two levels of caches

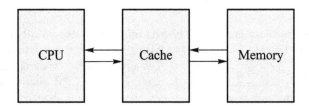

Fig. 7.3 Cache memory

some manufactures like IBM created an L_3 cache. Another cache was the Instruction Cache whose purpose was to decrease the time it takes to fetch the instruction set. Figure 7.2 shows such a type of architecture.

Cache read has two possibilities: one is HIT and another one is MISS. If CPU can ready data directly from cache, then it is a HIT. If the data is not in the cache, then a MISS happens. Data will need to be moved to cache from memory. Figure 7.3 shows a diagram of the interactions between CPU, cache, and memory. Cache is different than regular memory where individual data is accessed. Cache always moves in blocks. So, whenever a MISS happens, data will be moved by blocks.

Once the development of multi-core processing chips was adapted into the industry, it took the concept and started the move away from physically separated dual processors. The term core was introduced to refer to the number of central processing units in a chip. Intel and AMD started with the dual-core and moved to the quad-core which contains four core processors. The Hexa-core contains six cores and the Octal-core contains eight cores. The number of cores can scale up to 100. The limit is based mainly on how the data is transferred from the cores to the bus. Some manufactures have used switches in the cores to send data out of the central processing unit, and into another core other manufactures have used the mesh technique which links all of the cores data locations.

7.1.3 Hyper-Threading

Now that there is hardware that uses multiple central processing units, the industry had to adapt the operating systems to meet this new technology. The industry was led by Intel engineers, who created Hyper-threading Technology. This is the technology that is used to improve the flow of data to each processor. In order for each of the central processing units to be addressed by the Operation System efficiently, Intel created HTT. Hyper-threading Technology assists the parallelization of computations to the central processing unit.

7.1.4 Symmetric Multiprocessing

The computer industry created symmetric multiprocessing (SMP) which coordinates the use of two or more central processing units so that they can access a single shared memory (as shown in Fig. 7.4). The authors of this book created dual-port memory (DPM) that is essentially the same as SMP. DPM allows two CPUs to connect the main memory simultaneously without worrying about conflicts. Without proper "treatment," two CPUs cannot be connected to one memory unit as conflicts

Fig. 7.4 SMP diagram

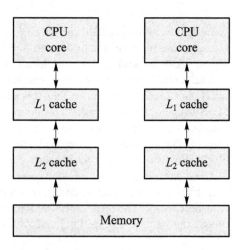

will occur if one CPU write 0 and another CPU write 1 to the memory at the same time.

Processor coupling is to stack the processors together such that they can be defined as tightly coupled SMP. The term loosely coupled multiprocessor systems is based on multiple standalone single or dual processors on the same motherboard that are physically separated. If power consumption is a design consideration, then the tightly coupled central processing unit is a more efficient approach.

A shared bus is where the CPUs share a path to the RAM. The CPUs can be interconnected to the bus in a number of ways including mesh, multiplexed memory, and crossbar switches.

7.1.5 Multiprocessing Operating Systems

One of the areas that slowed the development of a multiple processing chips was the operating system. Microsoft is one of the largest suppliers of operating system who was late to come to the development of multiple processing. In the late 1980s and 1990s, Microsoft was more focused on the user interface to achieve a large market share and was late in developing the multiple processor operating system. Early on, DOS and Windows did not have the ability to handle multiple CPUs. The operating system that did have the ability to handling multiple CPU was UNIX. The UNIX operating system, with its roots in the mainframe, had the ability to be modified and was developed to handle multiple central processing units.

Sun Microsystems Corporation was the manufacture that became the leader in this developmental race. Sun's approach to the computer market was to embrace the multiple processors and as such developed a computer that used this technology to stay on the cutting edge of computers. The Sun operating system is called Solaris and is a UNIX-based language. In early 1987, Sun introduced the scalable processor architecture (SPARC); it is a RISC instruction set (Dandamudi 2005). The system was based on their design and was initially a 32-bit structure, but in 1995 it went up to 64 bits.

7.1.6 The Future of Multiprocessing

Multipurpose processing development fell into the classic supply/demand model. From the inception of the processor, the demand for more processing power was always pushing the market and driving innovation. This was greatly enhanced by the Microsoft approach to the computer market and was defined by its effort to make the computer a tool that could be used by people with little computer experience.

The future will be based on enabling the central processing unit to the decision point. The industry has already done this by shifting the processing to a task. For example, the video of a computer was controlled by the CPU, but today the raw video data for video display is sent to the video card. This video card will have a CPU, and it will handle tasks that the main central processing units would have done in the past. A lot of programs require so much processing that multiple processors that were devoted to videos are now being sold on video cards directly.

Another example of domain/device specific computing is a solid-state drive (SSD), a device that is replacing the legacy of the mechanical hard drive. It has an onboard processor to take the data from the main central processing units and store on the SDD. The processor on the SDD handles the maintenance of storage and performs processes that run the SDD at its peak performance.

This concept has also been applied to networks. In the past, data went to the network, and the hub would just broadcast the traffic. Now we use a router which contains multiple processing units to handle the rerouting of the data. With the new security model, more and more central processing units are being deployed at the point of data exchange. With the implantation of DMZ and all new security devices, the industry is moving toward multiple central processing units at decision points. The evolution of the smartphone is another example of moving multiprocess closer to the decision point. Many smartphones have multiprocessors. So, we will continue to see the industry implement more multiprocessors at different levels of the network and user environment.

7.2   Parallel Processing

Parallel processing is the simultaneous usage of multiple machine resources. It often involves the breaking down a very large problem, involving many calculations, into smaller ones, distributing them across multiple machines, and solving them concurrently (Blaise 2011). An example of a problem involving many calculations would be finding the 1 trillionth digit of pi. A single computer calculating this problem would take a massive amount of time. However, if the calculations where spread among 1000 or 100,000 machines, the time would be considerably less. Parallel computing involves architecture that is capable of allowing multiple machines to work together. Flynn's taxonomy is representative of this architecture at many different levels: bit level, instruction level, data level, and task level. Several different hardware configurations have been developed to maximize the potential of using several machine's resources, more aptly referred to as distributed computing. In other words, distributed systems are groups of networked computers, which have the same goal for their work.

7.2.1   History of Parallel Processing

Traditionally, computers were designed for serial computing, a single-processor computer that executes one instruction after the other. This is in stark contrast with parallel computing. Serial computing must complete one execution prior to beginning another and is generally very slow. Conversely, parallel computing is capable of executing many instructions simultaneously (Almasi and Gottlieb 1989). This may seem very ordinary especially with today's technology, specifically processors with multiple cores. However, even with today's multi-core processors, an individual machine's ability to process many calculations is still limited to the amount of memory available to that operating system and motherboard. Below is a concept model created by Mozdzynski:

An IFS T2047L149 forecast model takes about 5000 s wall time for a 10-day forecast using 128 nodes of an IBM Power6 cluster. How long would this model take using a fast PC with sufficient memory (e.g., dual-core Dell desktop)? Answer: about 1 year. This PC would also need 2000 GB of memory.

The previous example shows that parallel processing saves time. In saving time, you also save money associated with executing a task. Additional economic advantages come from the cost and value associated with current technology. PC chipmaker Intel's current flagship CPU is the Intel Xeon X7560 Nehalem-EX processor rated at a speed of 2.26 GHz combined with eight individual processing cores. The cost for one of these is approximately $4000. However, Intel also has Core-i5 brand of processors, not nearly as robust, but has four individual processing cores, rated at a speed of 2.8 GHz for approximately $180. Roughly 22 Core-i7 CPUs may be purchased for the same price as one of their flagship CPUs giving you 11 times as many computational cores.

John von Neumann architecture is still the foundation of modern computers. It is important to note that parallel computers architecture remain Unchanged; however an increase in the number of computers creates the parallelism.

7.2.2 Flynn's Taxonomy

Flynn's taxonomy of computer systems has proved to be a useful tool for differentiating among uniprocessors (SISD), array and systolic machines (SIMD), and general multiprocessors (MIMD). Flynn classified programs and computers by whether they were operating using a single set or multiple sets of instructions (Hennessy and Patterson 1998; Hockney et al. 1998; Johnson 1988), whether or not those instructions were using a single or multiple set of data. SISD is the same as a system using sequential processing of a program's instructions. SIMD is repetitive processing of a program over a large amount of data. MISD is not a popular architecture. In practice, few actual examples of this class of parallelism have ever existed such that each processing unit operates on the data independently via separate instruction steams, and a single data stream is fed into multiple processing units. However, MIMD is the most popular, where many different calculations are carried out by many machines and used to calculate a very large amount of data. Figure 7.5 shows the Flynn's taxonomy.

Fig. 7.5 Flynn's taxonomy

Instruction stream

		Single	Multiple
Data stream	Single	SISD	MISD
	Multiple	SIMD	MIMD

7.2.3 Bit-Level Parallelism

Bit-level parallelism is a form of parallel computing based on increasing processor word size. It is done by performing the arithmetic on two numbers, bit by bit. The addition, for example, of two 32-bit numbers is performed in 32 machine cycles, by very simple circuitry capable only of adding one bit to another. Quite possibly the earliest use of parallelism in computers was to perform the operations on all bits simultaneously in parallel.

7.2.4 Instruction-Level Parallelism

Instruction-level parallelism performs many concurrent operations in a single computer program. For example:

1. $R3 \leftarrow R1 + R2$
2. $R6 \leftarrow R4 + R5$
3. $R7 \leftarrow R3 + R6$

The third operation is dependent on the prior two operations being completed. However, operations one and two are independent operations, so they can be calculated at the same time. The most efficient compiler and processor design would identify and take advantage of as much of this parallelism as possible. Ordinary programs are typically written under a sequential execution model where instructions execute one after the other and in the order specified by the programmer. Instruction level parallelism allows the compiler and the processor to overlap the execution of multiple instructions or even to change the order in which instructions are executed. Pipelining is an excellent example of this form of parallel processing. The idea of pipelining is that as each instruction completes a step, the following instruction moves into the stage just vacated. Thus, when the first instruction is completed, the next one is already one stage short of completion.

Data hazard occurs when processor fetches data $R3$ and $R6$. Since $R3$ and $R6$ have not been written back, the fetch may access to the wrong data (previously stored in $R3$ and $R6$, not the current ones). This is called "read after write" (RAW).

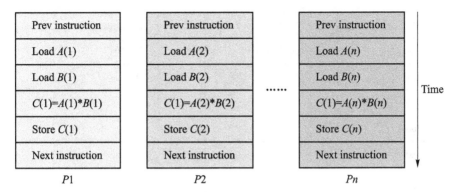

Fig. 7.6 Data-level parallelism

7.2.5 Data-Level Parallelism

Data-level parallelism is synonymous with Flynn's SIMD architecture—single instruction (all processing units perform identical instruction) and multiple data (each processing unit can operate on varying data elements). Data-level parallelism is accomplished when each processor performs the same task on different data inputs. In some circumstances, one thread may control operations on several different pieces of data (as shown in Fig. 7.6). In other situations, threads may control the operation, however executing the same code.

Data-level parallelism emphasizes the distributed (parallelized) nature of the data, as opposed to the processing (task parallelism) (Culler et al. 1999). Most modern computers, particularly those with graphics processor units (GPUs), employ SIMD instructions and execution units.

7.2.6 Task-Level Parallelism

Task-level parallelism in a multiprocessor system is synonymous with Flynn's MIMD architecture, which occurs when each CPU executes a different process on the same or different data. The varying threads can execute the same or completely different code. In any case, however, varying threads must communicate with one another as they work. Communication takes place usually to pass data from one thread to the next as part of a workflow. Figure 7.7 shows a diagram of task-level parallelism.

Task parallelism emphasizes the distributed (parallelized) nature of the processing (i.e., threads), as opposed to the data (data parallelism). Most real programs fall somewhere on a continuum between task parallelism and data parallelism. Most supercomputers fall into this category.

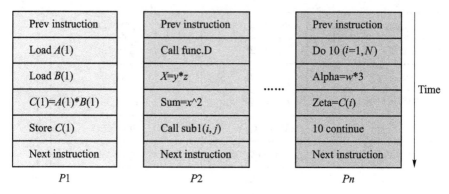

Fig. 7.7 Task-level parallelism

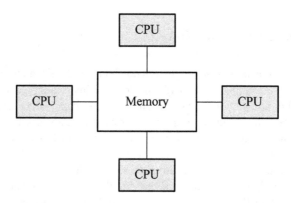

Fig. 7.8 UMA architecture

7.2.7   Memory in Parallel Processing

In regard to parallelism, memory can either be shared or distributed. Shared memory typically is comprised of one of the following two architectures, uniform memory access (or UMA) or non-uniform memory access (or NUMA). Regardless of the specific architecture, shared memory is generally accessible to all the processors in the system, and multiple processors may operate independently and continue to share the same memory.

Figure 7.8 illustrates UMA architecture. Multiple CPUs are capable of accessing one memory resource. This is also referred to as symmetric multiprocessor (or SMP). In contrast to this architecture is NUMA. NUMA is often made by physically linking two or more SMPs. One SMP is capable of directly accessing the memory of another SMP. An example of NUMA is pictured on the right.

Like shared memory systems, distributed memory systems (as shown in Fig. 7.9) vary widely but share a common characteristic. Distributed memory systems require a communication network to connect inter-processor memory. In this type of

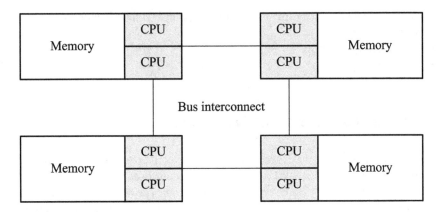

Fig. 7.9 Distributed memory system

architecture, processors have access to their own memory and do not share memory with another SMP. If a processor needs information from another data store, it has to communicate how and when it is to be accessed. This sharing generally comes about through a simple Ethernet connection. Hybrids of this technology have also been developed and are referred to as distributed-shared memory architecture. However, this type of architecture is generally used in supercomputers.

7.2.8 Specialized Parallel Computers

Within parallel computing, there are devices that provide a niche market because of its capabilities. As previously discussed, a system may have multiple cores, but may continue to be limited because of the amount of memory available to those cores. General-purpose computing on graphics processing units (GPGPU) is an inexpensive means of adding additional processing ability to a computer. A very beneficial and generous amount of memory is attached to video cards that are only accessible to its GPU. GPGPUs address the multiple cores and memory limitations as an add-on card to a single computer system (Boggan and Pressel 2007). As long as a motherboard has available PCI-Express x16 slot available, it will be capable of hosting a very powerful GPGPU.

The front runners of the GPGPU market belong to Nvidia and AMD. Their graphics cards are particularly useful because it is designed to compute massive amounts of graphics and operate linear algebra matrices. The table below provides a very brief glimpse at the applications of the areas where GPUs are being used in computing:

- Physical-based simulation and physics engines (usually based on Newtonian physics models).
- Weather forecasting.

- Global illumination-ray tracing, photon mapping, radiosity among others, sub-surface scattering.
- Fast Fourier transform.
- Medical imaging.

7.2.9 The Future of Parallel Processing

The exponential growth of the personal computers will continue as competition for business in the industry persists. Many computer enthusiasts compete for the titles of world's fastest or best for fame or simple recognition. The next hurdle for computer enthusiasts would be to break the exaflops (10^{18}) barrier. That is a supercomputer capable of achieving a million trillion calculations per second. In order to achieve this, massive parallel processing would need to be incorporated. Multiple computer nodes, with multiple processors, with multiple GPUs, attached to some form of dynamic RAM would accomplish this task.

With speed increases and increases in the number of cores present in a system, it may be possible for dedicated cores to ceaselessly navigate networks for intrusions and eliminate threats before they have a chance to propagate on a network. von Neumann's architecture has been around for so long; it's only a matter of time before a competing architecture becomes mainstream and capable of disrupting hackers and threats. With this in mind, many new types of parallelism will be in our future with regard to this new up-and-coming architecture (Wang 2021).

7.3 Grid and Distributed Computing

Grid computing is a term referring to the federation of computer resources from multiple administrative domains to reach a common goal. The grid can be thought of as a distributed system with non-interactive workloads that involve a large number of files. What distinguishes grid computing from conventional high-performance computing systems such as cluster computing is that grids tend to be more loosely coupled, heterogeneous, and geographically dispersed (Salchow 2011). Although a grid can be dedicated to a specialized application, it is more common that a single grid will be used for a variety of different purposes. Grids are often constructed with the aid of general-purpose grid software libraries known as middleware.

Grid size can vary by a considerable amount. Grids are a form of distributed computing, whereby a "super virtual computer" is composed of many networked loosely coupled computers acting together to perform very large tasks. For certain applications, "distributed" or "grid" computing can be seen as a special type of parallel computing that relies on complete computers (with onboard CPUs, storage, power supplies, network interfaces, etc.) connected to a network (private, public, or the Internet) by a conventional network interface, such as Ethernet. This is in contrast to the traditional notion of a supercomputer, which has many processors connected by a local high-speed computer bus.

Grid computing combines computers from multiple administrative domains to reach a common goal, to solve a single task, and may then disappear just as quickly.

7.3.1 Characteristics of Grid Computing

One of the main strategies of grid computing is to use middleware to divide and apportion pieces of a program among several computers, sometimes up to many thousands. Grid computing involves computation in a distributed fashion, which may also involve the aggregation of large-scale cluster computing-based systems. Figure 7.10 shows a diagram of grid computing.

The size of a grid may vary from small—confined to a network of computer workstations within a corporation, for example—to large, public collaborations across many companies and networks. "The notion of a confined grid may also be known as an intra-nodes cooperation whilst the notion of a larger, wider grid may thus refer to an inter-nodes cooperation."

Grids are a form of distributed computing, whereby a "super virtual computer" is composed of many networked loosely coupled computers acting together to perform very large tasks. This technology has been applied to computationally intensive scientific, mathematical, and academic problems through volunteer computing, and it is used in commercial enterprises for such diverse applications as drug discovery, economic forecasting, seismic analysis, and back office data processing in support for e-commerce and Web services.

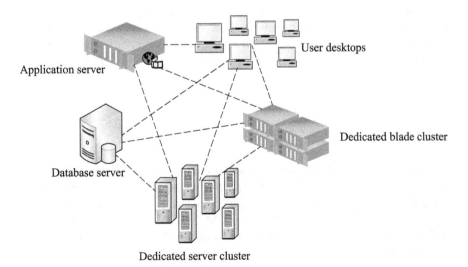

Fig. 7.10 Grid computing

"Distributed" or "grid" computing in general is a special type of parallel computing that relies on complete computers (with onboard CPUs, storage, power supplies, network interfaces, etc.) connected to a network (private, public, or the Internet) by a conventional network interface, such as Ethernet. This is in contrast to the traditional notion of a supercomputer, which has many processors connected by a local high-speed computer bus.

7.3.2   The Advantages and Disadvantages of Grid Computing

The primary advantage of distributed computing is that each node can be purchased as commodity hardware, which, when combined, can produce a similar computing resource as multiprocessor supercomputer, but at a lower cost. This is due to the economies of scale of producing commodity hardware, compared to the lower efficiency of designing and constructing a small number of custom supercomputers. The primary performance disadvantage is that the various processors and local storage areas do not have high-speed connections. This arrangement is thus well-suited to applications in which multiple parallel computations can take place independently, without the need to communicate intermediate results between processors. The high-end scalability of geographically dispersed grids is generally favorable, due to the low need for connectivity between nodes relative to the capacity of the public Internet.

There are also some differences in programming and deployment. It can be costly and difficult to write programs that can run in the environment of a supercomputer, which may have a custom operating system, or require the program to address concurrency issues. If a problem can be adequately parallelized, a "thin" layer of "grid" infrastructure can allow conventional, standalone programs, given a different part of the same problem, to run on multiple machines. This makes it possible to write and debug on a single conventional machine and eliminates complications due to multiple instances of the same program running in the same shared memory and storage space at the same time.

7.3.3   Distributed Computing

Distributed computing is a field of computer science that studies distributed systems. A distributed system consists of multiple autonomous computers that communicate through a computer network. The computers interact with each other in order to achieve a common goal. A computer program that runs in a distributed system is called a distributed program, and distributed programming is the process of writing such programs.

Distributed computing also refers to the use of distributed systems to solve computational problems. In distributed computing, a problem is divided into many tasks, each of which is solved by one or more computers.

The word distributed in terms such as "distributed system," "distributed programming," and "distributed algorithm" originally referred to computer networks where individual computers were physically distributed within some geographical area. The terms are nowadays used in a much wider sense, even referring to autonomous processes that run on the same physical computer and interact with each other by message passing.

7.3.4 Distributed Systems

While there is no single definition of a distributed system, the following defining properties are commonly used:

- There are several autonomous computational entities, each of which has its own local memory.
- The entities communicate with each other by message passing.
- Have a common goal, such as solving a large computational problem.
- Each computer may have its own user with individual needs, and the purpose of the distributed system is to coordinate the use of shared resources or provide communication services to the users.
- The system has to tolerate failures in individual computers.
- The structure of the system (network topology, network latency, number of computers) is not known in advance, the system may consist of different kinds of computers and network links, and the system may change during the execution of a distributed program.

7.3.5 Parallel and Distributed Computing

Distributed systems are groups of networked computers, which have the same goal for their work. The terms "concurrent computing," "parallel computing," and "distributed computing" have a lot of overlap, and no clear distinction exists between them. The same system may be characterized both as "parallel" and "distributed"; the processors in a typical distributed system run concurrently in parallel. Parallel computing may be seen as a particular tightly coupled form of distributed computing, and distributed computing may be seen as a loosely coupled form of parallel computing. Nevertheless, it is possible to roughly classify concurrent systems as "parallel" or "distributed" using the following criteria:

- In parallel computing, all processors have access to a shared memory. Shared memory can be used to exchange information between processors.

- In distributed computing, each processor has its own private memory (distributed memory). Information is exchanged by passing messages between the processors.

The situation is further complicated by the traditional uses of the terms parallel and distributed algorithm that do not quite match the above definitions of parallel and distributed systems; see the section Theoretical Foundations for more detailed discussion. Nevertheless, as a rule of thumb, high-performance parallel computation in a shared-memory multiprocessor uses parallel algorithms, while the coordination of a large-scale distributed system uses distributed algorithms.

7.3.6   *Distributed Computing Architectures*

Various hardware and software architectures are used for distributed computing. At a lower level, it is necessary to interconnect multiple CPUs with some sort of network, regardless of whether that network is printed onto a circuit board or made up of loosely coupled devices and cables. At a higher level, it is necessary to interconnect processes running on those CPUs with some sort of communication system. Figure 7.11 shows a diagram of distributed computing.

Distributed programming typically falls into one of several basic architectures or categories: client-server, 3-tier architecture, *n*-tier architecture, distributed objects, loose coupling, or tight coupling.

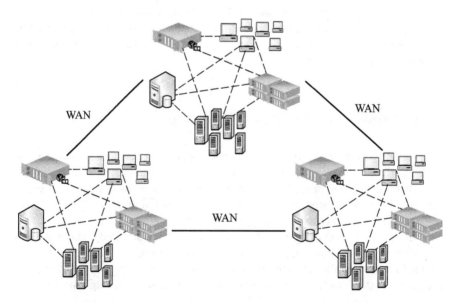

Fig. 7.11 Distributed computing (color)

- Client-server   Smart client code contacts the server for data then formats and displays it to the user. Input at the client is committed back to the server when it represents a permanent change.
- 3-tier architecture   Three tier systems move the client intelligence to a middle tier so that stateless clients can be used. This simplifies application deployment. Most web applications are 3-tier.
- N-tier architecture   *n*-tier refers typically to web applications which further forward their requests to other enterprise services. This type of application is the one most responsible for the success of application servers.
- Tightly coupled (clustered)   Refers typically to a cluster of machines that closely work together, running a shared process in parallel. The task is subdivided in parts that are made individually by each one and then put back together to make the final result.
- Peer-to-peer   An architecture where there is no special machine or machines that provide a service or manage the network resources. Instead all responsibilities are uniformly divided among all machines, known as peers. Peers can serve both as clients and servers.
- Space based   Refers to an infrastructure that creates the illusion (virtualization) of one single address-space. Data are transparently replicated according to application needs. Decoupling in time, space, and reference is achieved.

Another basic aspect of distributed computing architecture is the method of communicating and coordinating work among concurrent processes. Through various message passing protocols, processes may communicate directly with one another, typically in a master/slave relationship. Alternatively, a "database-centric" architecture can enable distributed computing to be done without any form of direct inter-process communication, by utilizing a shared database.

7.4   Ubiquitous and Internet Computing

Ubiquitous computing (ubicomp) is a post-desktop model of human-computer interaction in which information processing has been thoroughly integrated into everyday objects and activities. In the course of ordinary activities, someone "using" ubiquitous computing engages many computational devices and systems simultaneously and may not necessarily even be aware that they are doing so. This model is usually considered an advancement from the desktop paradigm. More formally, ubiquitous computing is defined as machines that fit the human environment instead of forcing humans to enter theirs. Figure 7.12 illustrates a diagram of ubicomp.

This paradigm is also described as pervasive computing, ambient intelligence, where each term emphasizes slightly different aspects. When primarily concerning the objects involved, it is also physical computing, the Internet of things, haptic computing, and things that think. Rather than propose a single definition for

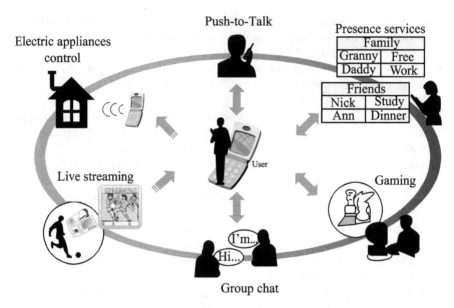

Fig. 7.12 Ubiquitous computing diagram (color)

ubiquitous computing and for these related terms, a taxonomy of properties for ubiquitous computing has been proposed, from which different kinds or flavors of ubiquitous systems and applications can be described.

7.4.1 Ubiquitous Computing Development

Intel's curiosity about how people use technology in cars is hardly surprising. Carmakers are keen to install extra computing power in their vehicles in order to impress customers with a taste for technology, and Intel hopes that this will translate into a big new market for its chips. Ford, for instance, has already developed a service called SYNC, based on a Microsoft operating system. SYNC allows drivers to make calls, play music, and do other things using voice commands. The car company has also created AppLink, a feature that lets people link their smartphones to a vehicle's voice-control system and operate their apps with it. For now, the system works with only a handful of apps, such as Pandora, an Internet-radio service, but Ford is hoping to expand that number rapidly.

Japan's Toyota has also been working on an in-car system, called Entune, to which drivers will be able to connect their smartphones via Bluetooth wireless links and other means. And it plans to make driving even more personal by helping people's cars "talk" to them. The firm has announced plans for a Twitter-like private social network, called Toyota Friend, which will be integrated into some electric and hybrid vehicles in Japan. Based on software from Salesforce.com and Microsoft, this will enable a car to send a tweet-like message to its owner telling him that, say, its battery is running low or a maintenance check is due. People foresee many more product social networks that will create more intimate relationships between people and the devices they own.

It is not just vehicles that are becoming more connected. So are homes, public places like sports stadiums, and even aircraft, where passengers are now sometimes offered in-flight Wi-Fi services for an extra charge. Cisco reckons that there could be almost 50 billion devices linked to the Internet in circulation by 2020, up from 7.5 billion in 2010. These will include everything from televisions and gaming consoles to coffee machines and cookers.

At their core, all models of ubiquitous computing share a vision of small, inexpensive, robust networked processing devices, distributed at all scales throughout everyday life and generally turned to distinctly commonplace ends. For example, a domestic ubiquitous computing environment might interconnect lighting and environmental controls with personal biometric monitors woven into clothing so that illumination and heating conditions in a room might be modulated, continuously and imperceptibly. Another common scenario posits refrigerators "aware" of their suitably tagged contents, able to both plan a variety of menus from the food actually on hand and warn users of stale or spoiled food.

7.4.2   Basic Forms of Ubiquitous Computing

Ubiquitous computing presents challenges across computer science: in systems design and engineering, in systems modeling, and in user interface design. Contemporary human-computer interaction models, whether command-line, menu-driven, or GUI-based, are inappropriate and inadequate to the ubiquitous case. This suggests that the "natural" interaction paradigm appropriate to a fully robust ubiquitous computing has yet to emerge, although there is also recognition in the field that in many ways we are already living in an ubicomp world. Contemporary devices that lend some support to this latter idea include mobile phones, digital audio players, radio-frequency identification tags, GPS, and interactive whiteboards.

Mark Weiser proposed three basic forms for ubiquitous system devices; see also smart device: tabs, pads, and boards.

- Tabs: wearable centimeter-sized devices.
- Pads: handheld decimeter-sized devices.
- Boards: meter-sized interactive display devices.

These three forms proposed by Weiser are characterized by being macro-sized, having a planar form and on incorporating visual output displays. If we relax each of these three characteristics, we can expand this range into a much more diverse and potentially more useful range of ubiquitous computing devices.

7.4.3   Augmented Reality

Ubiquitous computing is roughly the opposite of virtual reality. Where virtual reality puts people inside a computer-generated world, ubiquitous computing forces the computer to live out here in the world with people. Virtual reality is primarily a horse power problem; ubiquitous computing is a very difficult integration of human factors, computer science, engineering, and social sciences.

Augmented reality (AR) is a live, direct or indirect, view of a physical, real-world environment whose elements are augmented by computer-generated sensory input such as sound, video, graphics, or GPS data. It is related to a more general concept called mediated reality, in which a view of reality is modified (possibly even diminished rather than augmented) by a computer. As a result, the technology functions by enhancing one's current perception of reality. By contrast, virtual reality replaces the real world with a simulated one. An example of augmented reality is shown in Fig. 7.13.

Augmentation is conventionally in real time and in semantic context with environmental elements, such as sports scores on TV during a match. With the help of advanced AR technology (e.g., adding computer vision and object recognition), the information about the surrounding real world of the user becomes interactive and digitally manipulable. Artificial information about the environment and its objects can be overlaid on the real world. The term augmented reality is believed to have been coined in 1990 by Thomas Caudell, working at Boeing.

Research explores the application of computer-generated imagery in live video streams as a way to enhance the perception of the real world. AR technology includes head-mounted displays and virtual retinal displays for visualization purposes and construction of controlled environments containing sensors and actuators.

Fig. 7.13   Augmented reality (color)

7.4.4 Internet Computing Concept and Model

Internet computing can gain significant flexibility and agility with migrating sensitive data into remote, worldwide data centers. Integration of documents on web-based office suites can simplify processes and creates a more efficient way of doing business. It will allow for cost savings and easy access and streamline most daily activities. Internet computing powering can also support different aspect of businesses, which also utilized Internet computing with forms accessible by web application that electronically supports online collaboration in real time with other users. The information and communication systems used, whether networked or not, serves as a media to implement a business process. The objective of this section is to discuss the benefits of an Internet computing environment that improves agility, integrating modern-day technology (e.g., iPhone, iPad, web interface phone, etc.), and an example of Internet and computing online documents. It begins with an introduction of Internet computing by definition and its elements, referring to business benefits of utilizing of Internet computing, examples of Internet computing such as web base online office suites, and the integration of Internet computing and modern-day technology.

Internet computing is a model (De Leon 2011) similar to cloud computing model that enables convenient, on-demand network access to a shared pool of configurable computing resources (e.g., networks, servers, storage, application, and services) that can be rapidly provisioned and released with minimal management effort or service provider interaction. Figure 7.14 shows a diagram of Internet computing.

Internet computing model promotes availability and is composed of five essential characteristics, three service models, and four deployment models.

- The Hardware Layer (Client) consists of computer hardware that relies on Internet computing for application delivery and that is in essence useless without it. Examples include some computers, phones and other devices, operating systems, and browsers.
- The Virtualization Layer can be viewed as part of an overall trend in enterprise IT that includes autonomic computing, a scenario in which the IT environment will be able to manage itself based on perceived activity, and utility computing, in which computer processing power is seen as a utility that clients can pay for only as needed.
- The IaaS Layer extends the virtualization layer by providing the mechanisms to provision and control the virtual machines in a utility computing manner.
- The PaaS Layer (Platform) extends and abstracts the IaaS layer by removing the hassle of managing individual virtual machine instances.
- The SaaS Layer (Application) sometimes referred to as "on-demand software," is a software delivery model in which software and its associated data are hosted centrally (typically in the cloud) and are typically accessed by users using a thin client, normally using a web browser over the Internet.

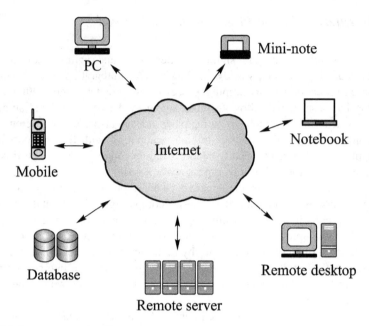

Fig. 7.14 Internet computing diagram

A critical issue in implementing cloud computing is taking virtual machines, which contain critical applications and sensitive data, to public and shared environments. Below are the four deployment models.

- Public describes computing in the traditional mainstream sense, whereby resources are dynamically provisioned to the general public on a fine-grained, self-service basis over the Internet, via web applications/web services, from an off-site third-party provider who bills on a fine-grained utility computing basis.
- Community shares infrastructure between several organizations from a specific community with common concerns (security, compliance, jurisdiction, etc.), whether managed internally or by a third-party and hosted internally or externally. The costs are spread over fewer users than a public cloud (but more than a private cloud), so only some of the benefits of cloud computing are realized.
- Hybrid is a composition of two or more clouds (private, community, or public) that remain unique entities but are bound together, offering the benefits of multiple deployment models. It can also be defined as multiple cloud systems that are connected in a way that allows programs and data to be moved easily from one deployment system to another.
- Private is infrastructure operated solely for a single organization, whether managed internally or by a third-party and hosted internally or externally. They have attracted criticism because users "still have to buy, build, and manage them" and thus do not benefit from lower up-front capital costs and less hands-on management, essentially lacking the economic model that makes cloud computing such an intriguing concept.

Each model comes with different options and different price. A critical issue in implementing Internet computing is taking virtual machines, which contain critical applications and sensitive data, to public and shared environments. Internet computing offers obvious advantages, such as co-locating data with computations and an economy of scale in hosting the services.

Figure 7.14 is an illustration of Internet computing components and shows a graphic depiction of how each element integrate with each other.

7.4.5 Benefit of Internet Computing for Businesses

Despite the fact that Internet computing is a relatively young concept with many questions still open, there is overwhelming consensus regarding the potential of this paradigm in advancing technology. New business solution, such as Akamai edge computing powered by WebSphere, will enable companies to supplement their existing IT infrastructure with virtualized Internet computing capacity on demand on a "pay-as-you-go" basis. A benefit of this business solution will allow data and programs to be swept up from desktop PCs and corporate server rooms and installed in the compute Internet cloud. Implementing Internet computing will allow the elimination of the responsibility of updating software with each new release and configuration of desktops on installs. Since applications run in the cloud and not on individual computers or desktops, you don't need hard drive space or processing power demanded by traditional desktop software. Corporations does not have to purchase high-powered personal computers (PC) and can purchase smaller hard disk, less memory, and more efficient processor. Files will essentially be stored in the cloud, as well as software programs, and this could assist in cutting overhead budget substantially. The "Internet computing" trend of replacing software traditionally installed on business computers with applications delivered via the Internet is driven by aims of reducing IT complexity and cost.

The ease of collaborating and updating documents is also a benefit of implementing. Regardless of the location of the person, you will be able to access and update files upon demand. This will give access regardless of location, from any device, the power to collaborate, compare, and clean Microsoft Office documents including Word, PowerPoint (including embedded objects), and Excel, as well as PDF files. The capabilities collaborating and sharing documents allow the same features as working on individual workstation. Some features are as the following:

- Compare all Microsoft Office and native PDF documents, including complex Microsoft Word, Excel, and PowerPoint documents with embedded objects and images.
- Compare Excel spreadsheets including both values and formulas.
- Remove metadata from all Microsoft Office and PDF documents to protect sensitive information and privacy.
- Convert Microsoft Office documents into a PDF file.

- Extract native PDF documents to Microsoft Word for editing or comparison and cleaning operations.
- Download resulting files online or have them sent to an E-mail account.

Businesses can also benefit from internet computing using:

- Infrastructure allows user to get the IT resources needed, only when needed. Pay only for what you use or additional storage.
- Flexibility adjust Internet computing-based resources up and down to meet real-time needs or offload onsite data to the cloud as needed to improve operational efficiencies. And since this online-demand access is an Internet-based, you can access these resources from anywhere, supporting remote work and continuity of operations.
- Collaboration gives the ability to effectively communicate and collaborate to improve business process. In many cases, the spark to use Internet computing will come from rank-and-file employees themselves seeking to have access at work to the cloud services that they use in their personal lives. With both the application and the data stored in the cloud, it becomes easy for multiple users—located anywhere in the world—to work together on the same project.
- Disaster recovery/continuity of operations with centralized data storage, management, and backups; data recovery in response to local business disruptions can be faster and easier.

Once an Internet protocol connection is established among several computers, it is possible to share services within any one of the aforementioned layers. Internet computing can completely transform business models and significantly improve a product, service or industry and in the process democratize them.

7.4.6   Examples of Internet Computing

Google App Engine enables you to build and host web apps on the same systems that power Google applications. App Engine offers fast development and deployment; simple administration, with no need to worry about hardware, patches, or backups; and effortless scalability. Google App Engine lets you run web applications on Google's infrastructure. App Engine applications are easy to build, easy to maintain, and easy to scale as your traffic and data storage needs grow. With App Engine, there are no servers to maintain: You just upload your application, and it's ready to serve your users.

App Engine includes the following feature:

- Dynamic web serving, with full support for common web technologies.
- Persistent storage with queries, sorting, and transactions.
- Automatic scaling and load balancing.
- APIs for authenticating users and sending E-mail using Google Accounts.
- A fully featured local development environment that simulates Google App Engine on your computer.

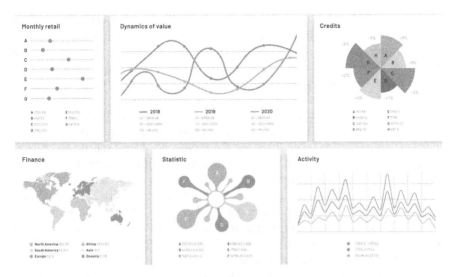

Fig. 7.15   An example of browser-based spreadsheet (color)

- Task queues for performing work outside of the scope of a web request.
- Scheduled tasks for triggering events at specified times and regular intervals.

Google Docs is a free, web-based office suite and data storage service offered by Google. It allows users to create and edit documents online while collaborating in real time with other users. Google Apps collection such as Gmail, Google Calendar, Docs, Spreadsheets, Presentations, and Drawings, with the latter four collectively referred to as Google Documents. An example of browser-based spreadsheet is shown on Fig. 7.15. Data storage of files up to 1 GB total in size was introduced on 13 January 2011, documents created inside Google Docs do not count towards this quota. Google Documents can store any type of file, up to 10 GB in size.

Google Docs is used simply as the G-Drive. Folders across multiple PCs and mobile devices just stay in sync automatically. Anything saved to these folders is automatically mirrored online and across all linked PCs. Below is an example of the Google documents spreadsheet and graph.

7.4.7   Migrating to Internet Computing

Internet computing also offers end users advantages in terms of mobility and collaboration. In the storage platform, all you need is a web browser and an Internet connection to view your data. Migrating Internet (cloud) computing and mobile technology has allowed the ability to access data, E-mails, or documents with just a push of button. Google App Engine, Google's cloud computing platform, and the iPhone, Apple's mobile platform, have developed an application that synchronizes its data from "The Cloud." No longer do you just browse the web, now you can fully interact with Internet solutions, and you can create a desktop client solution that consumes data hosted in an Internet cloud service that can then be accessed from your phone. This marriage allows individuals to have access to whatever they want anytime from anywhere.

Internet computing relies on sharing computing resources rather than having local servers or personal devices to handle applications. It consists of four deployment models, public, community, hybrid, and private cloud, and five layers, hardware, virtualization, IaaS, PaaS, and SaaS. Not only does it support an efficient and productive environment, it also supports a convenient environment. Individuals are able to access their documents as needed anywhere on campus or on the current network. Businesses are benefiting from replacing traditional software with applications available via the Internet and utilizing Internet computing. They are able to cut overhead cost by purchasing less software and upgrades. Cloud computing also support integration with web interface phones and other technology. The combination of Internet connected devices and Internet delivered services is the direction the industry is headed. It provides a platform that allows individuals to communicate from anywhere around the world. It's beneficial for working individual that are on the go or need to collaborate with teammates anywhere in the world. Overall, Internet computing 24 h access to needed documents and consistently involve into a mobile office. This gives way for businesses the ability to cut cost because they don't have to purchase as many desktops, hardware, and licenses for software. This gives the capability of investing funds in needed area, e.g., cutting-edge technology. Gone are the days that the corporation communities have to set foot in the office and convene in a stuffy building. You essentially can be anywhere in the world and participate in a virtual conference room which give you the entire world as your business platform. Despite all the latest innovations in the area of cloud computing, the reality remains that its current definition is somewhat limiting.

7.5 Virtualization

Virtualization is the creation of a virtual instance of an operating system, a server, a storage device, or network resources. If you have ever divided your hard drive into different partitions, then you have used the virtualization techniques. This is an early form of virtualization. A partition is the logical division of a hard disk drive to create, in effect, two separate hard drives.

Operating system virtualization is the use of software to allow computer hardware to run multiple operating system images at the same time. The technology got its start on mainframes decades ago, allowing administrators to avoid wasting expensive processing power. Figure 7.16 shows a diagram of virtualization.

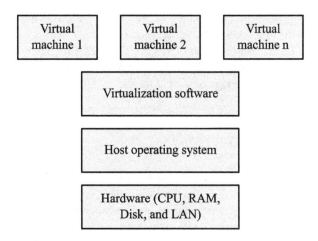

Fig. 7.16 A diagram of virtualization

7.5.1 Types of Virtualization

Hardware virtualization or platform virtualization refers to the creation of a virtual machine that acts like a real computer with an operating system. Software executed on these virtual machines is separated from the underlying hardware resources. For example, a computer that is running Microsoft Windows may host a virtual machine that looks like a computer with Ubuntu Linux operating system; Ubuntu-based software can be run on the virtual machine.

In hardware virtualization, the host machine is the actual machine on which the virtualization takes place, and the guest machine is the virtual machine. The words host and guest are used to distinguish the software that runs on the actual machine from the software that runs on the virtual machine. The software or firmware that creates a virtual machine on the host hardware is called a hypervisor or virtual machine monitor.

Virtualization software have been adopted faster than one imagined. There are three areas of IT where virtualization is making head roads, network virtualization, storage virtualization, and server virtualization.

- Network virtualization is a method of combining the available resources in a network by splitting up the available bandwidth into channels, each of which is independent from the others, and each of which can be assigned (or reassigned) to a particular server or device in real time. The idea is that virtualization disguises the true complexity of the network by separating it into manageable parts, much like your partitioned hard drive makes it easier to manage your files.
- Storage virtualization is the pooling of physical storage from multiple network storage devices into what appears to be a single storage device that is managed from a central console. Storage virtualization is commonly used in storage area networks (SANs).

- Server virtualization is the masking of server resources (including the number and identity of individual physical servers, processors, and operating systems) from server users. The intention is to spare the user from having to understand and manage complicated details of server resources while increasing resource sharing and utilization and maintaining the capacity to expand later.

7.5.2   History of Virtualization

In the mid-1960s, the IBM Watson Research Center was home to the M44/44X Project, the goal being to evaluate the then emerging time-sharing system concepts. The architecture was based on virtual machines: the main machine was an IBM 7044 (M44), and each virtual machine was an experimental image of the main machine (44X). The address space of a 44X was resident in the M44's memory hierarchy, implemented via virtual memory and multi-programming.

IBM had provided an IBM 704 computer, a series of upgrades (such as to the 709, 7090, and 7094), and access to some of its system engineers to MIT in the 1950s. It was on IBM machines that the compatible time sharing system (CTSS) was developed at MIT. The supervisor program of CTSS handled console I/O, scheduling of foreground and background (offline-initiated) jobs, temporary storage and recovery of programs during scheduled swapping, monitor of disk I/O, etc. The supervisor had direct control of all trap interrupts.

Around the same time, IBM was building the 360 family of computers. MIT's Project MAC, founded in the fall of 1963, was a large and well-funded organization that later morphed into the MIT Laboratory for Computer Science. Project MAC's goals included the design and implementation of a better time-sharing system based on ideas from CTSS. This research would lead to Multics, although IBM would lose the bid and General Electric's GE 645 would be used instead.

Regardless of this "loss," IBM has been perhaps the most important force in this area. A number of IBM-based virtual machine systems were developed: the CP-40 (developed for a modified version of IBM 360/40), the CP-67 (developed for the IBM 360/67), the famous VM/370, and many more. Typically, IBM's virtual machines were identical "copies" of the underlying hardware. A component called the virtual machine monitor (VMM) ran directly on "real" hardware. Multiple virtual machines could then be created via the VMM, and each instance could run its own operating system. IBM's VM offerings of today are very respected and robust computing platforms.

7.5.3   Virtualization Architecture

Generically speaking, in order to virtualize, you would use a layer of software that provides the illusion of a "real" machine to multiple instances of "virtual machines."

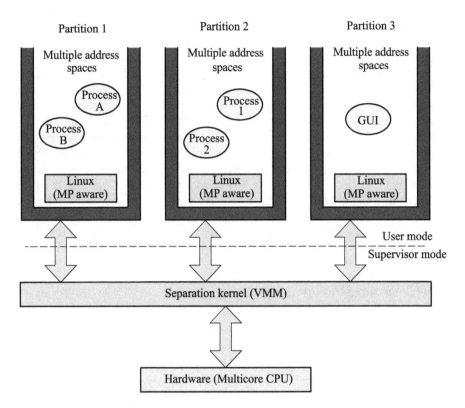

Fig. 7.17 Virtualization architecture (color)

This layer is traditionally called the virtual machine monitor (VMM). Figure 7.17 illustrates a such architecture.

There are many (often intertwined) high-level ways to think about a virtualization system's architecture. Consider some scenarios:

- A VMM could itself run directly on the real hardware without requiring a "host" operating system. In this case, the VMM is the (minimal) OS.
- A VMM could be hosted and would run entirely as an application on top of a host operating system. It would use the host OS API to do everything. Furthermore, depending on whether the host and the virtual machine's architectures are identical or not, instruction set emulation may be involved.

From the point of view of how (and where) instructions get executed: you can handle all instructions that execute on a virtual machine in software; you can execute most of the instructions (maybe even some privileged instructions) directly on the real processor, with certain instructions handled in software; you can handle all privileged instructions in software.

A different approach, with rather different goals, is that of complete machine simulation. SimOS and Simics, as discussed later, are examples of this approach.

Although architectures have been designed explicitly with virtualization in mind, a typical hardware platform and a typical operating system, both are not very conducive to virtualization.

As mentioned above, many architectures have privileged and non-privileged instructions. Assuming the programs you want to run on the various virtual machines on a system are all native to the architecture (in other words, it would not necessitate emulation of the instruction set). Thus, the virtual machine can be run in non-privileged mode. One would imagine that non-privileged instructions can be directly executed (without involving the VMM), and since the privileged instructions would cause a trap (since they are being executed in non-privileged mode), they can be "caught" by the VMM, and appropriate action can be taken (they can be simulated by the VMM in software, say). Problems arise from the fact that there may be instructions that are non-privileged, but their behavior depends on the processor mode; these instructions are sensitive, but they do not cause traps.

7.5.4   Virtual Machine Monitor

When a process on a guest system running on a (hosted) virtual machine invokes a system call, it should not be handled by the host. The host should notify the guest operating system. One solution is for the virtual machine monitor to use ptrace() to trace process execution and identify system call entry. The VMM can then nullify the system call (say, by "converting" it to getpid() or to an invalid system call), which is executed by the host. Upon system call exit, the VMM notifies the guest system kernel (through a signal, say), which can take appropriate action.

When a typical operating system kernel running on real hardware has nothing to do, it runs its idle thread, or loop. When the same kernel runs on a virtual machine, this behavior is undesirable, because the virtual machine is wasting its processor time. The virtual machine could have a mechanism to suspend itself, instead of running the idle loop. For example, the Denali isolation kernel uses a purely virtual instruction (idle-with-timeout) for this purpose.

7.5.5   Examples of Virtual Machines

VMware was founded in 1998. Its first product was VMware Workstation (1999). The GSX Server and ESX Server products were introduced in 2001.

VMware Workstation (as well as the GSX Server) has a hosted architecture; it needs a host operating system (such as Windows or Linux). In order to optimize the complex mix of performance, portability, ease of implementation, etc., the product acts both as a virtual machine monitor (talking directly to the hardware) and as an application that runs on top of the host operating system. The latter frees the VMM from having to deal with the large number of devices available on the PCs (otherwise the VMM would have to include device drivers for supported devices).

VMware Workstation's hosted architecture includes the following components: a user-level application (VMApp), a device driver (VMDriver) for the host system, and a virtual machine monitor (VMM) that is created by VMDriver as it loads. Thereafter, an execution context can be either native (i.e., the host's) or virtual (i.e., belonging to a virtual machine). The VMDriver is responsible for switching this context. I/O initiated by a guest system is trapped the VMM and forwarded to the VMApp, which executes in the host's context and performs the I/O using "regular" system calls. VMware uses numerous optimizations that reduce various virtualization overheads. GSX Server is also hosted, but is targeted for server deployments and server applications.

VMware ESX Server enables a physical computer to be available as a pool of secure virtual servers, on which operating systems can be run. This is an example of dynamic, logical partitioning. Moreover, ESX Server does not need a host operating system (like VMware workstation); it runs directly on hardware (in that sense, it is the host operating system). ESX Server was inspired by work on Disco and Cellular Disco, which virtualized shared memory multiprocessor servers to run multiple instances of IRIX. As mentioned earlier, the IA-32 architecture is not naturally virtualizable. Certain "sensitive" instructions must be handled by the VMM, and cannot be simply executed in non-privileged mode because they don't cause a General Protection exception. ESX Server solves this problem by dynamically rewriting portions of an operating system kernel's code to insert traps at appropriate places in order to catch such sensitive instructions. ESX Server can run multiple virtual CPUs per physical CPU. Multiple physical network interface cards can be logically grouped into a single, high-capacity, virtual network device.

Mac-on-Linux, or simply MOL, is a virtual machine implementation that runs under Linux on most PowerPC hardware and allows you to run Mac OS (7.5.2 to 9.2.2), Mac OS X, and Linux. Most of MOL's virtualization functionality is implemented as a kernel module. A user process takes care of I/O, etc. There's even an (very limited) Open Firmware implementation within MOL.

Virtualization and the server consolidation that it delivers will be the top priority for chief information officers in 2012, according to a survey by the research firm IDC. Savings from server consolidation will be invested in new IT initiatives such as cloud computing, mobility, data analytics, and use of social media for business purposes.

When CIOs were asked by IDC to name their top three IT priorities for this year, nearly 40% of them picked virtualization and server consolidation, more than any other area of IT. After virtualization, investment in cloud services came in second, followed by collaboration tools, business analytics, and the consolidation of application portfolios.

Enterprises made more of an investment in "big data" analytics from 2012 by IDC's report, to analyze the petabytes of data their businesses generate in order to make business decisions.

"The final bricks in the foundation for the intelligent enterprise were laid in 2012 in a number of key industries," IDC states, mentioning healthcare, utilities, and retail as industries making the most of analytics technology. Analytics jumped to number four on the list of CIO IT priorities for 2012, from ninth place in the previous survey.

IDC noted that the amount of data generated by enterprises was expected to grow by 48% and that 90% of it were unstructured data. In the new, all-digital issue of InformationWeek Government: as federal agencies close data centers, they must drive up utilization of their remaining systems. That requires a well-conceived virtualization strategy.

7.6 Cloud Computing Architecture

Cloud computing is an evolution from the notion of grid computing, which had come into vogue in the early 2000s, and involved the sharing of remote computing assets in a high-performance computing environment. However, while an evolutionary technology, cloud computing is a disruptive technology, meaning it has the ability to radically transform an accepted and time-tested business practice. The disruptive aspect of cloud computing will occur most dramatically at the enterprise level, where cloud computing will alter the premise that large enterprises purchase their own computer hardware, develop proprietary software, and build large private networks to facilitate access to its data. In order to succeed, cloud computing must address multiple concerns before widespread acceptance becomes a market reality, namely, issues surrounding access, security, data migration, resiliency, and regulatory. The cloud computing providers must also develop and refine their individual business models and promote transparency to address the many lingering concerns. Figure 7.18 illustrates a conceptual diagram of a cloud computing model.

7.6.1 Cloud Architecture

The National Institute of Standards and Technology (NIST), in an effort to classify the cloud computing industry, has defined the three service models within the cloud computing industry as I. infrastructure as a service (IaaS), which involves provisioning computer resources for customers on demand; II. software as a service (SaaS), involving access to applications running on a cloud platform; and III. platform as a service (PaaS), involving the ability to provision cloud infrastructure for a user's company/personal requirements (Mell and Grance 2010; Pocatilu et al. 2011). The key to cloud computing is utilizing virtualization to provide de facto increases in computing power.

- IaaS   This is the most basic of the cloud service models. Resources such as processing, storage, networks, and other fundamental computing can be

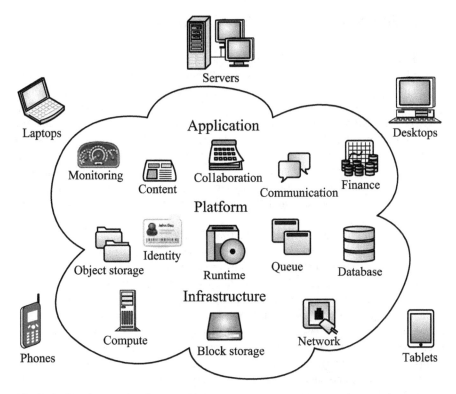

Fig. 7.18 Cloud computing diagram

provisioned by the consumer. The consumer would not have control of the cloud infrastructure but the use of the operating system or software applications.

- SaaS The highest layer in the cloud service model is SaaS. With the use of this model, the customer is purchasing the use of the provider's application which is already running on the cloud infrastructure. Some examples of this are NetSuite and SalesForce.com.
- PaaS The next layer PaaS is where the customer purchase or create an application that is fully functional to be placed on top of their infrastructure. Examples of this would be application stacks: Ruby on Rails, Java, or LAMP. Unlike IaaS, PaaS customers do not control or manage the cloud infrastructure, including network, servers, operating systems, or storage.

Utilizing the below cloud depiction, a "public cloud" is an example of SaaS, Amazon's Simple Storage Service (S3) is an example of PaaS, and the Amazon Elastic Compute Cloud would represent an example of IaaS. Of course, ceding one's control of a software service can be a dubious proposition for a firm, and factors such as technical feasibility, security, cloud resources, and transparency of the cloud service provider's (CSP) network policies and practices are paramount.

7.6.2   Technical Aspects of Cloud Computing

Cloud computing is a type of "parallel and distributed system," consisting of a collection of interconnected and virtualized computers that are dynamically provisioned and presented as one or more unified computing resource. The computing relationship is based on service-level agreements established through negotiation between the CSP and the user, be it an enterprise, a government, an individual, or some other type of user. The cloud infrastructure typically consists of commodity hardware, such as blade servers, and specialized programs for virtualization and resource management. Cloud computing utilizes a pay as you go (or pay what you use) business model and involves the dynamic provisioning of resources based on the requirements of the user and the capability of the system (Greengard 2010; Hayes 2008).

Cloud computing incorporates virtual machine (VM) to manage its resources. While a mainframe computer may share the same operating system (O/S), its processing is treated as if there were multiple central processing units (CPU) inside the same computer. In effect, that is what happens, but in fact, the computer's central resources, such as memory, CPU, and arithmetic/logic unit (ALU), are being shared.

IaaS is a growth field within the research and computing-intensive scientific community. The use of virtualization with scientific research illustrates one of the useful applications of IaaS. Scientific research, which may utilize high-throughput computing (HTC) workloads, often involves the use of great deals of computer processing power, and such infrastructure is very expensive. Cloud computing, via its virtualization and pay-as-you-go business model, presents a compelling case for such research. Virtualization permits encapsulating complex research applications found in scientific research and often, depending on CPU usage, will have little performance degradation. CSPs utilize a scheduler to manage work flows and resource requests from their client base. This scheduler, incorporating a series of algorithms to include service level agreements, job prioritization, CPU utilization, etc., will queue individual jobs.

7.6.3   Security Aspects of Cloud Computing

Cloud computing, by its very nature, introduces a host of security challenges, both for the cloud service provider and the users. At its core, the fundamental argument one might make is that an enterprise's data no longer resides on its servers within its domain, but rather on an amorphous platform, and is difficult, if not impossible, to know where the data actually resides. This implies an element of trust to the CSP that may or may not be warranted.

Ironically, cloud computing is often far more secure than traditional computing, because large cloud service providers, such as Google and Amazon, can attract and retain cyber security personnel of a higher quality than many companies or governmental agencies. Government employees commonly access cloud services such as Dropbox and Gmail in their personal lives. The use of such services by government employees on government computers may create a de facto security vulnerability; thus a case could be made that formally adopting such a service would be inherently more secure.

There are significant compliance aspects to the adoption of cloud computing, particularly for financial firms such as banks and insurance firms and healthcare providers such as hospitals. There are certain baseline principles applicable to enterprises that collect, use, store, or share customer information. It is the onus of the user entity to ensure its business practices, and control of data is compliant with the relevant regulatory bodies/acts and thus incumbent upon them to ensure their CSP likewise provides infrastructure, software, and security to ensure such compliance. However, CSPs may be reluctant to open up their infrastructure to those requiring access to conduct such information audits. An audit could be disruptive to a business model and could violate agreements with customers to carefully restrict access to the data hierarchy and lead to a denigration of service to other customers. Overall, this could impose a "brake" on the overall growth of the industry. At a minimum, customers will need to obtain industry standard certifications as to the adequacy of the internal controls of the provider and must insist on the ability of the regulators to conduct audits of the provider as may be required by such regulators.

In the European Union, the General Data Protection Regulation (GDPR) is a regulation that reshapes the way in which data is handled across every section. In banking, the payment card industry data security standard (PCI DSS) is a major consideration for those CSPs working within the financial sector. This obligation is usually contained within the merchant agreements executed by the company and the various payment card brands. If payment card information will be stored in the cloud, to remain PCI DSS compliant, a company will need to ensure that its service providers are PCI DSS compliant. For instance, the Gramm-Leach-Bliley Act (GLB Act) regulates the privacy and information security practices of financial institutions, including the obligation to disclose information on the means used to protect customer data. Similarly, the Health Insurance Portability and Accountability Act (HIPAA) similarly address compliance aspects of personal health information (Ryan 2011).

The physical location of sensitive personal data is of paramount importance. Different countries have different regulatory and privacy issues for the use and storage of personal information. For example, privacy issues are much more sensitive in European Union countries than in the United States; thus storage of information on European citizens on servers located in the United States would be potentially problematic. Cloud services may result in customer data being replicated and/or separated into small portions and stored on multiple servers. If data is sent across international boundaries, privacy and data security concerns related to such cross-border data can be triggered. It is important for a company to know where these servers are located and whether the cloud computing service provider offers the capability to limit the transfer of data across specific or all international boundaries.

7.6.4 Ongoing and Future Elements in Cloud Computing

Moore's law states that the number of transistors on a chip, or transistor density, doubles every 24 months. However, as transistor size decreases and transistor density and computing power increases, the heat generated by the chip becomes a major problem and multi-core processors become important. Consequently, the major chip manufacturers are now looking at doubling CPU performance by increasing the number of CPU cores (dual-core and quad-core processors), as against doubling the clock-speed of a single CPU. For applications to make effective use of these multiple cores, parallel programming code has to be written. Data centers housing cloud infrastructures are frequently made up of thousands of such multi-core CPUs. Thus, cloud access to parallel applications deployed in such multi-core machines will generally enhance users' experience and has potential to positively influence cloud adoption.

Cisco believes three areas are of paramount importance to ensure Cloud computing's acceptance: security, service level agreements, and interoperability. Isolating network traffic via partitioning would increase security, latency and quality of service (QoS) must be addressed in service level agreements, and different types of data and data access must be included in discussions about interoperability.

7.6.5 Adoption of Cloud Computing Industry Drivers

Cloud computing is at its infancy, and new applications for the use of cloud computing are discovered regularly. One consideration is to consolidate on new, offshore datacenters, which would be located where energy costs are low. Some US banks are looking seriously at rotating their heavy portfolio and risk calculations around the world, using grid computing to exploit cheaper and renewable sources of electricity, while other banks are considering locating server farms in places such as Iceland with renewable geothermal power. Such green initiatives are well suited to cloud computing, which potentially lends itself to reduced energy use and concomitant reduction in greenhouse emissions. Figure 1.10 shows the cloud architecture and adoptions. At enterprise level, PaaS is leading among the cloud services.

Green computing is environment-friendly computing, and one of its objectives is to make efficient use of electricity. Cloud computing infrastructures are generally deployed in very large data centers. For example, Google-designed data centers use about half the energy of a typical data center. People have increasingly become aware of the effects of computers on the environment, and this could be one of the key factors for broad acceptance of cloud computing. Other examples cite a European bank reduced its server count from 3100 to 1150 via virtualization, with a resultant 92% reduction in power usage. The Bank of Canada similarly virtualized 1500 small to mid-range servers, with a tremendous savings due to the consolidation, greater resilience, and performance. The bank still has far to go with over 8 000 servers in total, running Solaris, Linux, and SQL databases.

Currently, major chip manufacturers are now focused on dual-core and quad-core processors. Concurrent development of software programming code utilizing parallel processing, coupled with virtualization, would yield significant performance improvements. Indeed, manufacturers such as Intel look to double CPU performance by increasing the number of CPU cores. Data centers housing cloud infrastructures are frequently made up of thousands of such multi-core CPUs and has the potential to greatly enhance performance.

Initiatives to utilize low-cost computers for less-developed countries depend on cloud computing for storage and application resources. One such program is on being developed in India. In order to keep costs down, the LCACDs generally do not have in-built hard drives; data are stored in memory cards (much like the SD card used in smart phones) and/or inbuilt flash drives. Thus, the very configuration (this includes networking support, Internet browsing, media playing capabilities) of such devices makes it ideal for cloud usage. Applications such as Google docs can also be key to the effective utilization of such devices. Another example is the Massachusetts Institute of Technology Media La and its development of low-cost computing devices for developing countries. This work is based on the same principle, i.e., moving data onto the web and off of the laptop/desktop.

Service Level Agreements (SLA) are important documents between a cloud customer and cloud service providers.

Cloud computing has the potential to be a significant economic driver of business enterprise growth in the coming years. While there are significant obstacles to widespread adoption, the significant technology companies that have adopted cloud computing as a business model provide a significant opportunity for this initiative to succeed. While there are significant obstacles yet to overcome, namely, issues related to security, transparency, and interoperability, the industry is already well on its way to addressing those obstacles and producing tangible mechanisms to address those shortcomings. The momentum the industry has at present is likely to accelerate over the next several years, until such time that it becomes standard business practice throughout the large, computationally intensive industry sectors, and adoption proceeds down the scale to individual users and small entities.

7.7 Mobile Computing Architecture

The appearance of full-function laptop computers and wireless LANs in the early 1990s led researchers to confront the problems that arise in building a distributed system with mobile clients. The field of mobile computing was thus born. Although many basic principles of distributed system design continued to apply, four key constraints of mobility forced the development of specialized techniques. These constraints are unpredictable variation in network quality, lowered trust and

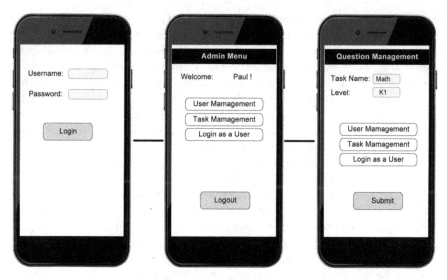

Fig. 7.19 A standalone app to collect behavioral data

robustness of mobile elements, limitations on local resources imposed by weight and size constraints, and concern for battery power consumption.

Figure 7.19 shows a data collection and analysis system that can collect frequency, duration, accuracy, and fluency data on the fly without requiring network connections. The system is able to run on different types of handheld devices including iPhone, iPad, Android, HP iPAQ, etc. It was from a Department of Education grant awarded to the author.

Mobile computing is still a very active and evolving field of research, whose body of knowledge awaits codification in textbooks. The results achieved so far can be grouped into the following broad areas:

- Mobile networking, including Mobile IP, ad hoc protocols, and techniques for improving TCP performance in wireless networks.
- Mobile information access, including disconnected operation, bandwidth-adaptive file access, and selective control of data consistency.
- Support for adaptive applications, including transcoding by proxies and adaptive resource management.
- System-level energy saving techniques, such as energy-aware adaptation, variable-speed processor scheduling, and energy-sensitive memory management.
- Location sensitivity, including location sensing and location-aware system behavior.

A future in which computers become pervasive, unobtrusive, and almost invisible is being brought a step closer. Recent development shows that demonstrator and prototype sensor networks that mark an important step forward in the cutting-edge field.

7.7.1 Mobile Apps

A mobile app is a software application developed specifically for use on handheld devices such as smartphones and tablets, rather than applications running on desktop or laptop computers. Mobile apps are categorized as native apps, which are created specifically for a given platform, web-based apps, or web apps, which are regular web applications that all computational works are done on the server side, or hybrid apps that combines both native and web apps. Mobile apps are generally referred as native apps. Apple iOS and Android are the most common mobile app platforms.

7.7.2 Android App Development

Android Studio is one of many app developments tools to create an Android app. After downloading and installation, one can create an Android app with the following steps:

- Create an Android project.
- Choose Java from the language drop-down menu.
- Add content to MainActivity.
- Generate manifest file.
- Build.

After that you will able to run either on a built-in emulator or on a real device. Note that the device (smartphone) needs to be connected to the development computer and has the USB debugging turned on under developer options.

So, it would probably take minutes to create a "Hello World" mobile app. To develop more advanced apps, you need to know Java and other features that come with the device.

7.7.3 Apple iOS App Development

Apple Inc. offers a free app develop tool Xcode; it includes everything needed to create apps and bring the apps to different Apple devices. The current all-new user interface framework SwiftUI is based on Swift syntax. It can simply build user interfaces across all Apple platforms. Here are the main steps to build an iOS app:

- Open Xcode choosing a template to create a new project.
- Select Swift for the language. Alternatively, you can choose Objective-C.
- Design the user interface using the Interface Builder.
- Add code to the ViewController.swift file.
- Connect user interface with code.
- Test the app on a simulator.

After that, developers can continue doing the simple exercises by changing the button color and replacing buttons with icons, etc.

To submit apps to the Apple app store, developers need to join the Apple developer program (for a $99 fee).

7.7.4 Mobile Computing in the Cloud

Some mobile apps need computational power beyond their own can handle. For example, a mobile app uses AI to identify people. In cases like this, apps need to send data back to the cloud letting AI services to identify the person and retrieve results from the cloud and display on the mobile device.

In general, mobile applications require cloud services for actions that can't be done directly on the device, such as offline data synchronization, storage, or data sharing across multiple users. People often have to configure, set up, and manage multiple services to power the backend. People also have to integrate each of those services into applications by writing multiple lines of code. However, as the number of application features grow, the code and release process become more complex, and managing the backend requires more time.

AWS services such as Amplify provisions and manages backends for mobile applications. One just selects the capabilities needed such as authentication, analytics, or offline data sync, and Amplify will automatically provision and manage the AWS service that powers each of the capabilities. One can then integrate those capabilities into applications through the Amplify libraries and UI components.

7.8 Biocomputers

Biocomputers use systems of biologically derived molecules, such as DNA and proteins, to perform computational calculations involving storing, retrieving, and processing data.

The development of biocomputers has been made possible by the expanding new science of nanobiotechnology. The term nanobiotechnology can be defined in multiple ways; in a more general sense, nanobiotechnology can be defined as any type of technology that uses both nano-scale materials, i.e., materials having characteristic dimensions of 1–100 nm, as well as biologically based materials. A more restrictive definition views nanobiotechnology more specifically as the design and engineering of proteins that can then be assembled into larger, functional structures., The implementation of nanobiotechnology, as defined in this narrower sense, provides scientists with the ability to engineer biomolecular systems specifically so that they interact in a fashion that can ultimately result in the computational functionality of a computer.

7.8.1 Biochemical Computers

Biochemical computers use the immense variety of feedback loops that are characteristic of biological chemical reactions in order to achieve computational functionality. Feedback loops in biological systems take many forms, and many different factors can provide both positive and negative feedback to a particular biochemical process, causing either an increase in chemical output or a decrease in chemical output, respectively. Such factors may include the quantity of catalytic enzymes present, the number of reactants present, the number of products present, and the presence of molecules that bind to and thus alter the chemical reactivity of any of the aforementioned factors. Given the nature of these biochemical systems to be regulated through many different mechanisms, one can engineer a chemical pathway comprising a set of molecular components that react to produce one particular product under one set of specific chemical conditions and another particular product under another set of conditions. The presence of the particular product that results from the pathway can serve as a signal, which can be interpreted, along with other chemical signals, as a computational output based upon the starting chemical conditions of the system, i.e., the input.

7.8.2 Biomechanical Computers

Biomechanical computers are similar to biochemical computers in that they both perform a specific output that can be interpreted as a functional computation based upon specific initial conditions which serve as input. They differ, however, in what exactly serves as the output signal. In biochemical computers, the presence or concentration of certain chemicals serves as the output signal. In biomechanical computers, however, the mechanical shape of a specific molecule or set of molecules under a set of initial conditions serves as the output. Biomechanical computers rely on the nature of specific molecules to adopt certain physical configurations under certain chemical conditions. The mechanical, three-dimensional structure of the product of the biomechanical computer is detected and interpreted appropriately as a calculated output.

7.8.3 Bioelectronic Computers

Bioelectronic computers can also be constructed to perform electronic computing. Again, like both biomechanical and biochemical computers, computations are performed by interpreting a specific output that is based upon an initial set of conditions that serve as input. In bioelectronic computers, the measured output is the nature of the electrical conductivity that is observed in the bioelectronic computer,

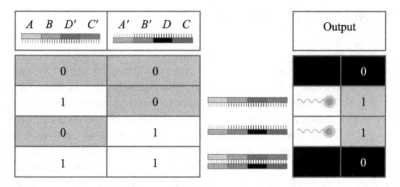

Fig. 7.20 A biochemical logic gate (color)

which comprises specifically designed biomolecules that conduct electricity in highly specific manners based upon the initial conditions that serve as the input of the bioelectronic system.

The new logic gates are formed from short strands of DNA and their complementary strands, which in conjunction with some simple molecular machinery mimic their electronic equivalent. Two strands act as the input: each represents a 1 when present or a 0 when absent. The response to their presence or absence represents the output, which can also be a 1 or 0.

Figure 7.20 is an "exclusive OR" or XOR logic gate. It produces an output when either of the two inputs is present but not when both are present or both are absent. To put the DNA version to the test, Willner and his team added molecules to both the complementary strands that caused them to fluoresce when each was present in isolation, representing a logical 1 as the output. But when both were present, the complementary strands combined and quenched the fluorescence, representing a 0 output. The inputs to an XOR logic gate are two complementary standards of DNA. If one or the other is present, the gate fluoresces, indicating an output of 1. If both are present, they bind together fluorescence, indicating an output of 0.

Currently, biocomputers exist with various functional capabilities that include operations of logic and mathematical calculations. Tom Knight of the MIT Artificial Intelligence Laboratory first suggested a biochemical computing scheme in which protein concentrations are used as binary signals that ultimately serve to perform logical operations. At or above a certain concentration of a particular biochemical product in a biocomputer chemical pathway indicates a signal that is either a 1 or a 0, and a concentration below this level indicates the other, remaining signal.

Many examples of simple biocomputers have been designed, but the capabilities of these biocomputers are still largely premature in comparison to commercially available non-biocomputers. However, there is definitely great potential in the capabilities that biocomputers may 1 day acquire. Evidence of the true potential of the computing capabilities of biocomputers exists in the most powerful, complex computational machine known to currently exist: the biocomputer that is the human brain. Certainly, there is plenty of room to improve in the realm of biocomputer computational ability; one may reasonably expect the science of biocomputers to advance greatly in the years to come.

7.9 Quantum Computing: IBM Q

A quantum computer is a machine that is able to manipulate quantum states following the rules of quantum mechanics through quantum bits, or qubits.

Quantum computing explore the implications of using quantum mechanics instead of classical mechanics to model information and its processing. The fundamental unit of computation is no longer the bit, but rather the quantum bit, or qubit.

7.9.1 Qubits

A qubit is the physical carrier of quantum information. It is the quantum version of a bit, and its quantum state can take values of $|0\rangle$, $|1\rangle$, or the linear combination of both, which is a phenomenon known as superposition.

A superposition is a weighted sum or difference of two or more states. For example, the state of the air when two or more musical tones sound at once. Ordinary, or "classical," superpositions commonly occur in macroscopic phenomena involving waves.

From quantum mechanics perspective, a qubit is a two-dimensional quantum-mechanical system with two energy levels $|0\rangle$ and $|1\rangle$

$$|0\rangle = \begin{bmatrix} 1 \\ 0 \end{bmatrix} \quad |1\rangle = \begin{bmatrix} 0 \\ 1 \end{bmatrix}$$

and a combination of two basis states, called a superposition state

$$|\psi\rangle = \alpha|0\rangle + \beta|1\rangle$$

where $|\alpha|^2 + |\beta|^2 = 1$.

A qubit or a system of qubits changes its state by going through a series of unitary transformations. A unitary transformation is described by a matrix U with complex entries. The matrix U is unitary if

$$U \cdot U^\dagger = U^\dagger \cdot U = I$$

A quantum algorithm can call a classical subroutine only if it is compiled into a sequence of reversible logical gates such as CNOT or Toffoli gate (in particular, the number of input and output wires in each gate must be the same).

7.9.2   Quantum Logic Gates

A quantum gate is an operation applied to a qubit to change its state. To generate entanglement, you must have at least a two-qubit gate equivalent to the CNOT.

Single quantum gates include X, H, Z, S, T, etc.

X gate is a bit flip gate that takes $|0\rangle$ to $|1\rangle$ or vice versa. It is similar to a classical NOT gate

$$X(|0\rangle) = |1\rangle$$

H gate is known as the Hadamard gate. When H gate apples to $|0\rangle$, we get $|+\rangle$ superposition state:

$$|+\rangle = \frac{1}{\sqrt{2}}(|0\rangle + |1\rangle)$$

Accordingly, if the H gate apples to $|1\rangle$, we get $|-\rangle$ superposition state:

$$|-\rangle = \frac{1}{\sqrt{2}}(|0\rangle - |1\rangle)$$

In above superposition states, the outcome has a 50% probability of 0 and 50% of 1 after measurement.

For multi-qubit gates, common gates include CNOT (controlled NOT) gate and Bell gate or entangled gates.

7.9.3   Operations

Entanglement is a property of quantum superpositions and does not occur in classical superpositions. In an entangled state, the whole system is in a definite state, even though the parts are not. Observing one of two entangled particles causes it to behave randomly, but tells the observer how the other particle would act if a similar observation was made on it. Because entanglement involves a correlation between individually random behaviors of the two particles, it cannot be used to send a message. Therefore, the term "instantaneous action at a distance," sometimes used to describe entanglement, is a misnomer. There is no action (in the sense of something that can be used to exert a controllable influence or send a message)—

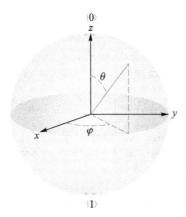

Fig. 7.21 Bloch sphere representation (color)

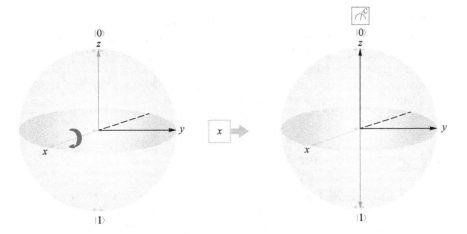

Fig. 7.22 X gate Bloch sphere representation (color)

only correlation, which, though uncannily perfect, can only be detected afterward
when the two observers compare notes. The ability of quantum computers to exist
in entangled states is responsible for much of their extra computing power, as well
as many other feats of quantum information processing that cannot be performed,
or even described, classically.

Quantum operations are commonly demonstrated with Bloch spheres (Figs. 7.21
and 7.22).

X (NOT) gate on Bloch sphere is to rotate π along x-axis.

H gate, known as Hadamard gate, on Bloch sphere is to a π rotation around $x + z$
axis: exchanges x and z.

G gate (Phase) is a π rotation around the z axis. The S gate is a rotation of $\pi/2$
(90°), and T gate is a $\pi/4$ rotation around z.

7.9.4 Qiskit

Qiskit is an open-source quantum computing framework for leveraging IBM quantum processors in research, education, and business. It consists of Terra, Aqua, Aer, and Ignis components.

Qiskit Terra provides a set of tools for composing quantum programs at the level of circuits and pulses.

Qiskit Aer provides a high-performance simulator framework for the Qiskit software stack. It contains optimized C++ simulator backends for executing circuits compiled in Qiskit Terra.

Qiskit Aqua contains a library of cross-domain quantum algorithms upon which applications for near-term quantum computing can be built. Currently there are chemistry, AI, optimization, and finance application on IBM Qiskit GitHub.

Qiskit Ignis is a framework for understanding and mitigating noise in quantum circuits and devices.

Qiskit is packaged with Conda, a dependency and environment management for any language including Python, R, Ruby, Java, JavaScript, and C/C++. The Qiskit community uses Jupyter notebooks to run and debug quantum algorithms, and the default language is Python.

Interested readers can find more information about Qiskit and Jupyter notebooks in Quantum Cryptography section in Chap. 10.

7.10 Architecture for AI Applications

A variety of emerging computer architecture come to the earth as the result of the advancement of AI. They include GPUs, ASICs, FPGAs, quantum computers, neuromorphic chips, nanomaterial-based chips, optical-based ICs, and biochemical architectures.

Graphics processing units (GPUs) have taken the computing world by storm in the last few years. Unlike CPUs, a GPU has a massively parallel architecture consisting of thousands of smaller, more efficient cores designed for handling multiple tasks simultaneously.

As deep learning requires high levels of computational power, neural network implementation on GPU-based systems accelerates the training process dramatically compared to traditional CPU architecture; this saves substantial time and money.

An application-specific integrated circuit (ASIC) is an IC customized for a particular use, rather than intended for general-purpose use. The advantage for AI is that an ASIC can be designed explicitly for fast processing speed and/or massive data analysis via deep learning.

A field-programmable gate array (FPGA) enables greater customization after manufacturing-ergo, field-programmable. The FPGA configuration is generally specified using a hardware description language (HDL), similar to that used for an application-specific integrated circuit (ASIC). FPGAs contain an array of programmable logic blocks, and a hierarchy of reconfigurable interconnects that allow the blocks to be "wired together," like many logic gates that can be inter-wired in different configurations.

As quantum computers become more capable with the addition of more qubits and customized software, we can expect more AI experts to seek out their unique capabilities. Several companies have developed advanced GPUs for deep learning and AI.

7.11 Summary

Advanced computer architecture including discussion of multiprocessors, multi-core processors, cache memory, parallel processing, multiprocessing, ubiquitous computing, mobile computing, grid computing, distributed computing, cloud computing, Internet computing, quantum computing, as well as other areas (such as vector computing, etc.) that are beyond the scope of this book.

Reader may find out that many areas may not fall exactly in the architecture domain, such as parallel processing, cloud computing, etc. However, those above-mentioned computing models are all supported by various architectures behind. Nowadays, hardware and software are gradually merging. To draw a line between them is almost important.

Cache is the fast memory next to registers. Using cache can improve the speed of a computer system. When a MISS happens, processors always move a block of data from memory to cache.

According to Flynn's taxonomy, parallel processing computer systems can be classified into four categories: SISD (uniprocessor as common personal computers), SIMD (multiple processors perform the same operation on multiple data simultaneously often being referred as data-level parallelism), MIMD (general multiprocessors and most common in parallel processing), and MISD (not popular).

Data dependency may occur for instruction-level parallelism when data being fetched currently have not been written back. This will affect the pipeline and reduce the overall performance. Read after write (RAW) is one type of data hazards that is attempting to read data before they are written back.

In parallel processing, memory can be all shared, all distributed, or both. A system with both shared memory and distributed memory is common.

Ubiquitous computing is to enable users to access applications anywhere, anytime, at any place, and with any computing devices such as handheld, pads, tabs, or boards. Augmented reality is the combination of virtual reality with real-time physical sensory. A solider able to "see through" the buildings in front of him using the "super X-ray machine" is an example of augmented reality. The solider wears a head-mounted device with one eye seeing the real world and the other eye seeing the virtual model inside the building. The virtual scene inside the building is generated by a supercomputer after gathering data from the sensor network inside the building. The thousands of sensors can be placed in the building by a bomb to collect the data and send back to the supercomputer.

Grid computing, distributed computing, cloud computing, and Internet computing are all something in common. They are not new inventions. Each one is a combination of infrastructure, software, and platform to provide various kinds of services to users.

In cloud computing, different organizations run applications (e.g., E-mail and calendar) on a same cloud. Security is the main concern even though there are different types of separations. Many originations still hesitate to move critical data (such as financial and marketing) into public cloud.

Virtual machine is to set up multiple computers on one physical computer. All virtual systems can share the resources with the host computer therefore providing the flexibilities to test new applications and to run multiple platform applications on a single server.

Internet computing is a very promising area. With Google doc and other apps, users are no longer needed to purchase commercial word processing software. This may also lead to the potential wide use of thin clients. A thin client is a very simple computer with very limited computation power and memory. It is small, cheaper, and fan-less, so there is no noise and "green." If more and more Internet-based applications come to earth, people can use thin clients to access all the applications easily without requiring purchasing new computers for every 2–3 years. A thin client can be built as simple as just to support a browser. In the near future, if you have a browser, you have a computer.

Cloud computing has defined as three service models: I. infrastructure as a service (IaaS), which involves provisioning computer resources for customers on demand; II. software as a service (SaaS), involving access to applications running on a cloud platform; and III. platform as a service (PaaS), involving the ability to provision cloud infrastructure for a user's company/personal requirements. The key to cloud computing is utilizing virtualization to provide services.

Mobile computing uses mobile apps running either natively, hybrid, or relying on the cloud to accomplish computational tasks.

A quantum computer is a machine that is able to manipulate quantum states following the rules of quantum mechanics through qubits.

Projects

7.1 Amazon EC2

Amazon Elastic Compute Cloud provides scalable computing capacity in the Amazon Web Services (AWS) cloud.

Using Amazon EC2 to launch a virtual server, configure security and networking, and manage storage.

7.2 Qiskit

Qiskit is an open-source quantum computing software development framework for leveraging today's quantum processors in research, education, and business. Download and install qiskit (find in qiskit website) on a VM of your computer and finish the "getting started with qiskit."

Exercises

7.1 What are the differences between multi-core processors and multiprocessors?

7.2 Why cache can improve the performance of a computer system?

7.3 Hit rate is defined by the fraction of accesses found in cache. A processor has the miss rate of 1%. What does the number mean?

7.4 For cache read, if a MISS happens, the processor usually read a block of data into the cache. What is the benefit for this?

7.5 According to Flynn's taxonomy, computer systems can be divided into four categories, SISD, MISD, SIMD, and MIMD. For each category, provide an example of the architecture.

7.6 Look at the operations below:

   a. $R3 \leftarrow R1 + R2$
   b. $R6 \leftarrow R4 + R5$
   c. $R7 \leftarrow R3 + R6$

When implementing instruction-level parallelism, data hazard occurs. How this impacts the performance of the pipeline and how to address them?

7.7 Computer A is n times faster than B means:
   [   ] Performance (A) / Performance (B) = n
   [   ] Execution_time (B) / Execution_time (A) = n
   [   ] Performance (A) / Performance (B) = $1/n$
   [   ] Execution_time (B) / Execution_time (A) = $1/n$

7.8 Give an example that augmented reality can help us in our daily life (hint: car technologies).

7.9 Some people use smartphones to replace computers. Discuss the advantages and disadvantages of such move.

7.10 Some countries charge different rates depending on the geographical locations of the websites you access. However when you access the Gmail, you are always considered as "local." Explain why this happens?

7.11 Map each term on the left to the corresponding facts on the right.
   IaaS   A cloud provides Windows and Linux.
   SaaS   Clients can choose which software to use.
   PaaS   Storage and other resources on a cloud.

7.12 A computer has 4 GB memory serving as a host. Each virtual machine requires 1 GB memory. How many virtual machines can resides on the host computer?

7.13 Virtualization usually involves a physical computer and a host operating system. The host computer supports the virtual machines through a layer called the virtual machine monitor (VMM). Can VMM replace the host operating system?

7.14 Conduct research on mobile computing in AWS. List the mobile services offered by AWS.

7.15 What are the differences between quantum computing and traditional computing?

References

Almasi, G. S., & Gottlieb, A. (1989). *Highly parallel computing*. Redwood City: Benjamin/Cummings.

Blaise, B. (2011). Introduction to parallel computing. In *Lawrence Livermore National Laboratory*.

Boggan, S. K,. & Pressel, D. M. (2007). *GPUs: an emerging platform for general-purpose computation*. Ft. Belvoir: Defense Technical Information Center.

Culler, D. E., Singh, J. P., & Gupta, A. (1999). *Parallel computer architecture: A hardware/software approach*. San Francisco: Morgan Kaufmann Publishers.

Dandamudi, S. (2005). *Guide to RISC processors: for programmers and engineers*. Berlin: Springer.

De Leon, E. The five layers within internet computing. Retrieved November 11, 2011.

Göhringer, D., Perschke, T., Hübner, M., & Becker, J. (2009). A taxonomy of reconfigurable single-/multiprocessor systems-on-chip. *International Journal of Reconfigurable Computing, 2009*, 395018, (p. 11). https://doi.org/10.1155/2009/395018.

Greengard, S. (2010). Cloud computing and developing nations. *Communications of the ACM, 53*(5), 18–20. https://doi.org/10.1145/1735223.1735232.

Hayes, B. (2008). Cloud computing. *Communication of ACM, 51*(7), 9–11.

Hennessy, J. L., & Patterson, D. A. (1998). *Computer organization and design: The hardware/software interface*. San Francisco: Morgan Kaufmann Publishers.

Hockney, R. W., Jesshope, C. R., & Hockney, R. W. (1998). *Parallel computers 2: Architecture, programming, and algorithms*. Bristol: A. Hilger.

Johnson, E. (1988). Completing an MIMD multiprocessor taxonomy.*ACM Sigarch Computer Architecture News, 16*(3), 44–47.

Mell, P., & Grance, T. (2010). The NIST definition of cloud computing. *Communications of the ACM, 53*(6), 50.

Pocatilu, P., Alecu, F., & Vetrici, M. Measuring the efficiency of cloud computing for E-learning systems. Retrieved November 12, 2011.

Ryan, M. (2011). Cloud computing privacy concerns on our doorstep. *Communications of the ACM, 54*(1), 36–38. https://doi.org/10.1145/1866739.1866751.

Salchow, K., Jr. (2011). Clustered multi-processing: changing the rules of the performance game [Article].

Shuangbao, P. W. (2021). Design high-confidence computers using trusted instructional set architecture and emulators. *High-Confidence Computing, 1*(2). https://doi.org/10.1016/j.hcc.2021.100009.

Chapter 8
Assembly Language and Operating Systems

Assembly language is the closest computer language to communicate with computers. It is the machine language (1s and 0s) that a CPU uses to operate in an easy to remember and understand format. Only assembly language can take the full advantages of the processor architecture, and it is hardware dependent. For example, Intel and AMD processors use different assembly languages. Even within the Intel processors, different CPUs have different assembly language instructions, even though many of them may be the same.

Programs written in machine languages have the highest efficiency. However, it is difficult to program therefore low productivity. This is the reason many high-level computer languages (C, Python, Java, etc.) are commonly used. To make computer language device independent, many high-level computer languages (C, Java, etc.) use compilers to compile the instructions or in other word to convert the instructions for that specific processor.

An operating system (OS) is a set of programs that manage computer hardware resources and provide common services for application software. An operating system is the most important type of system software in a computer system. In virtualization, the host can provide services without an OS. In this case, it uses (type 1) hypervisor, a critical piece of software that enables virtualization, to host the guests. A networked OS manages the networking of the whole network. OS security is one of the most important topics in cybersecurity nowadays. Software reverse engineering (SRE) has become the interest and challenge to many cyber professionals and nation states.

8.1 Assembly Language Basics

Programs written in assembly languages consist of different statements. Each statement will be translated into an instruction that can be executed in processors (Assembly language 2012). For study purpose, we will use Intel processors as exam-

© The Author(s), under exclusive license to Springer Nature Singapore Pte Ltd. 2021   213
S. P. Wang, *Computer Architecture and Organization*,
https://doi.org/10.1007/978-981-16-5662-0_8

ples throughout the chapter unless otherwise specified. For Intel processors, general-purpose (GP) instructions are a subset of the IA-32 instructions that represent the fundamental instruction set for the Intel IA-32 processors. These instructions are introduced into the IA-32 architecture with the first IA-32 processors (the Intel 8086 and 8088). Additional instructions are added to the general-purpose instruction set in subsequent families of IA-32 processors (the Intel 286, Intel 386, Intel 486, Pentium, Pentium Pro, and Pentium II processors).

Intel-64 architecture further extends the capability of most general-purpose instructions so that they are able to handle 64-bit data in 64-bit mode. A small number of general-purpose instructions (still supported in non-64-bit modes) are not supported in 64-bit mode.

General-purpose instructions perform basic data movement, memory addressing, arithmetic and logical, program flow control, input/output, and string operations on a set of integer, pointer, and BCD data types. This chapter provides an overview of the general-purpose instructions.

General-purpose instructions are divided into the following subgroups: data transfer, string, binary arithmetic, I/O, decimal arithmetic, enter and leave, logical, flag control, shift and rotate, segment register, bit and byte, miscellaneous, and control transfer.

Figure 8.1 shows the Intel IA-32 basic execution environment. The 64-bit mode execution environment is similar to the IA-32 with increased address space, upgraded registers from 32-bit to 64-bit, and increased number of registers.

8.1.1 Numbering Systems

Most modern computer systems do not represent numeric values using the decimal system. Instead, they typically use a binary or two's complement numbering system. To understand the limitations of computer arithmetic, you must understand how computers represent numbers.

People have been using the decimal (base 10) numbering system for so long that we probably take it for granted. When you see a number like "753," you don't think about the value 753; rather, you generate a mental image of how many items this value represents. In reality, however, the number 753 represents

$$7 \times 10^2 + 5 \times 10^1 + 3 \times 10^0 \text{ or}$$

$$700 + 50 + 3$$

Each digit appearing to the left of the decimal point represents a value between zero and nine times an increasing power of ten. Digits appearing to the right of the decimal point represent a value between zero and nine times an increasing negative

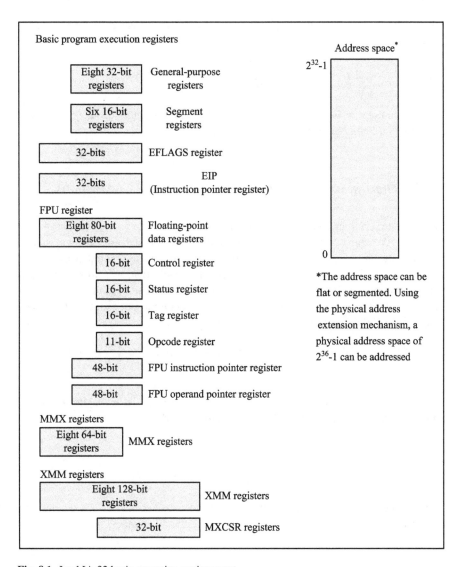

Fig. 8.1 Intel IA-32 basic execution environment

power of ten. For example, the value 246.359 means

$$2 \times 10^2 + 4 \times 10^1 + 6 \times 10^0 + 3 \times 10^{-1} + 5 \times 10^{-2} + 9 \times 10^{-3} \text{ or}$$
$$200 + 40 + 6 + 0.3 + 0.05 + 0.09$$

For any decimal number $m_{n-1}m_{n-2}m_{n-3}\cdots m_1m_0$, the value can be represented as

$$\sum_{i=0}^{n-1} m_i \times 10^i$$

here the number 10 is called a base. In base 10 (decimal) numbering system, there are ten unique numbers: 0, 1, 2, 3, 4, 5, 6, 7, 8, 9.

8.1.2   The Binary Numbering System and Base Conversions

Most modern computer systems operate in binary logic. Two voltage levels (usually 0 V and +5 V) correspond to the two digits used by the binary numbering system.

The binary numbering system works the same as the decimal numbering system, with two exceptions: binary is base 2 numbering system that only allows the digits 0 and 1 (rather than 0–9), and binary uses powers of two rather than powers of ten. Therefore, it is easy to convert a binary number to decimal. For example, the binary value 11001010 represents

$$1 \times 2^7 + 1 \times 2^6 + 0 \times 2^5 + 0 \times 2^4 + 1 \times 2^3 + 0 \times 2^2 + 1 \times 2^1 + 0 \times 2^0$$

that is, $128 + 64 + 8 + 2 = 202$ (base 10).

To convert a binary (base 2) number $m_{n-1}m_{n-2}m_{n-3}\cdots m_1m_0$ to a decimal number, here $m_i = \{0, 1\}$, the value can be represented as

$$\sum_{i=0}^{n-1} m_i \times 2^i$$

The most commonly seen base number in computer is 2, 8, and 16. To convert any base b number $m_{n-1}m_{n-2}m_{n-3}\cdots m_1m_0$ to a decimal number, the value can be represented as

$$\sum_{i=0}^{n-1} m_i \times b^i$$

8.1.3   The Hexadecimal Numbering System

A big problem with the binary system is verbosity. To represent the value 202 (decimal) requires eight binary digits. The decimal version requires only three decimal digits and, thus, represents numbers much more compactly than does the binary numbering system. When dealing with large values, binary numbers quickly become too unwieldy. Unfortunately, a digital computer thinks in binary, so most of the time, it is convenient to use the binary numbering system. Although we can convert between decimal and binary, the conversion is not a trivial task. The hexadecimal (base 16) numbering system solves these problems. Hexadecimal numbers (Hex) offer the two features we are looking for: they are very compact, and it's simple to convert them to binary and vice versa. Because of this, most binary computer systems use the hexadecimal numbering system. Since the radix (base) of a hexadecimal number is 16, each hexadecimal digit to the left of the hexadecimal point represents some value times a successive power of 16. For example, the number 1234 (hexadecimal) is equal to

$$1 \times 16^3 + 2 \times 16^2 + 3 \times 16^1 + 4 \times 16^0 \text{ or}$$

$$4096 + 512 + 48 + 4 = 4660 \text{ (decimal)}$$

Each hexadecimal digit can represent 1 of 16 values between 0 and 15. Since there are only ten decimal digits, we need to invent six additional digits to represent the values in the range 10 through 15. Rather than create new symbols for these digits, we'll use the letters A through F. The following are all examples of valid hexadecimal numbers

1234 DAD01 FEC0A BEEF 8A1DEAF

Table 8.1 provides the information to convert any hexadecimal number into a binary number or vice versa.

Table 8.1 Binary/Hex
adecimal conversion

Binary	Hexadecimal
0000	0
0001	1
0010	2
0011	3
0100	4
0101	5
0110	6
0111	7
1000	8
1001	9
1010	A
1011	B
1100	C
1101	D
1110	E
1111	F

To convert a hexadecimal number into a binary number, simply substitute the corresponding four bits for each hexadecimal digit in the number. For example, to convert FEC79A (Hex) into a binary value, simply convert each hexadecimal digit according to the table above

$$
\begin{array}{cccccc}
F & E & C & 7 & 9 & A \\
1111 & 1110 & 1100 & 0111 & 1001 & 1010
\end{array}
$$

To convert a binary number into hexadecimal format is almost as easy. The first step is to pad the binary number with zeros to make sure that there is a multiple of four bits in the number. For example, given the binary number 1011001010, the first step would be to add two bits to the left of the number so that it contains 12 bits. The converted binary value is 001011001010. The next step is to separate the binary value into groups of four bits, e.g., 0010 1100 1010. Finally, look up these binary values in the table above and substitute the appropriate hexadecimal digits, e.g., 2CA.

Since converting between hexadecimal and binary is an operation you will need to perform over and over again, you should take a few minutes and memorize the table above. Even if you have a calculator that will do the conversion for you, you'll find manual conversion to be a lot faster and more convenient when converting between binary and hexadecimal.

8.1.4   Signed and Unsigned Numbers

So far, we have treated binary numbers as unsigned values. The binary number 00000 represents zero, 00001 represents one, 00010 represents two, and so on toward infinity. What about negative numbers? Now we discuss how to represent negative numbers using the binary numbering system.

To represent signed numbers using the binary numbering system, we have to place a restriction on our numbers; they must have a finite and fixed number of bits. For our purposes, we are going to severely limit the number of bits to 8, 16, 32, or some other small number of bits.

With a fixed number of bits, we can only represent a certain number of objects. For example, with eight bits, we can only represent 256 different objects. Negative values are objects in their own right, just like positive numbers. Therefore, we'll have to use some of the 256 different values to represent negative numbers. In other words, we've got to use up some of the positive numbers to represent negative numbers. To make things fair, we'll assign half of the possible combinations to the negative values and half to the positive values. So, we can represent the negative values −128 to −1 and the positive values 0 to 127 with a single 8-bit byte. With a 16-bit word, we can represent values in the range −32,768 to +32,767. With a 32-bit double word, we can represent values in the range −2,147,483,648 to

+2,147,483,647. In general, with n bits, we can represent the signed values in the range -2^{n-1} to $+2^{n-1} - 1$.

In the two's complement system, the most significant bit (MSB) of a number is a sign bit. If the MSB is zero, the number is positive; if the MSB bit is one, the number is negative. Examples:

For 16-bit numbers

- 8000 Hex is negative because the MSB is one.
- 100 Hex is positive because the MSB is zero.
- 7FFF Hex is positive.
- 0FFFF Hex is negative.
- 0FFF Hex is positive.

If the MSB is zero, then the number is positive and is stored as a standard binary value. If the MSB is one, then the number is negative and is stored in the two's complement form. To convert a positive number to its negative, two's complement form, you use the following algorithm:

I. Invert all the bits in the number, i.e., apply the logical NOT function.
II. Add one to the inverted result.

For example, to compute the eight-bit equivalent of -5:

1. 00000101 Five (in binary).
2. 11111010 Invert all the bits.
3. 11111011 Add one to obtain result.

If we take minus five and perform the two's complement operation on it, we get our original value, 00000101, back again, just as we expect:

1. 11111011 Two's complement for -5.
2. 00000100 Invert all the bits.
3. 00000101 Add one to obtain result (+5).

The following examples provide some positive and negative 16-bit signed values:

- 7FFF: +32,767, the largest 16-bit positive number.
- 8000: $-32,768$, the smallest 16-bit negative number.
- 4000: +16,384.

To convert the numbers above to their negative counterpart (i.e., to negate them), do the following:

```
7FFF: 0111 1111 1111 1111    +32 767
      1000 0000 0000 0000    Invert all the bits (8000 Hex)
      1000 0000 0000 0001    Add one (8001 Hex or -32 767)
8000: 1000 0000 0000 0000    -32 768
      0111 1111 1111 1111    Invert all the bits (7FFF)
      1000 0000 0000 0000    Add one (8000 Hex or -32 768)
```

```
4000: 0100 0000 0000 0000     16 384
      1011 1111 1111 111      Invert all the bits (BFFFh)
      1100 0000 0000 0000     Add one (0C000 or -16 384)
```

8000h inverted becomes 7FFF. After adding one, we obtain 8000! Wait, what's going on here? $-(-32,768)$ is $-32,768$? Of course not. But the value $+32,768$ cannot be represented with a 16-bit signed number, so we cannot negate the smallest negative value. If you attempt this operation, then some processors may complain about signed arithmetic overflow.

Why bother with such a miserable numbering system? Why not use the MSB as a sign flag, storing the positive equivalent of the number in the remaining bits? The answer lies in the hardware. As it turns out, negating values is the only tedious job. With the two's complement system, most other operations are as easy as the binary system. For example, suppose you were to perform the addition $5 + (-5)$. The result is zero. Consider what happens when we add these two values in the two's complement system

$$\frac{\begin{array}{r} 00000101 \\ 11111011 \end{array}}{100000000}$$

The result ends up with a carry into the ninth bit and all other bits are zero. As it turns out, if we ignore the carry out of the MSB, adding two signed values always produces the correct result when using the two's complement numbering system. This means we can use the same hardware for signed and unsigned addition and subtraction. This wouldn't be the case with some other numbering systems.

It is worth mentioning that some large enterprise systems such as IBM Enterprise Systems Architecture/390 (ESA/390) use assembly language to control program at the byte or even bit level and to wrote subroutines for COBOL, FORTRAN, or PL/I.

8.2   Instructions

An opcode (operation code) is the portion of a machine language instruction that specifies the operation to be performed (Dumas 2006). Their specification and format are laid out in the instruction set architecture of the processor in question (which may be a general CPU or a more specialized processing unit). Apart from the opcode itself, an instruction normally also has one or more specifiers for operands (i.e., data) on which the operation should act, although some operations may have implicit operands, or none at all. There are instruction sets with nearly uniform fields for opcode and operand specifiers, as well as others (the x86 architecture for instance) with a more complicated, varied length structure.

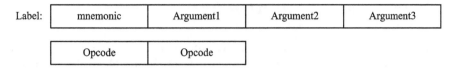

Fig. 8.2 Instruction format

Assembly language uses mnemonics (opcode), instructions, and operands to represent machine code (see Fig. 8.2). This enhances the readability while still giving precise control over the machine instructions.
where:

- A label is an identifier which is followed by a colon.
- A mnemonic is a reserved name for a class of instruction opcodes which have the same function.
- The operands argument1, argument2, and argument3 are optional. There may be from zero to three operands, depending on the opcode. When present, they take the form of either literals or identifiers for data items. Operand identifiers either are reserved names of registers or are assumed to be assigned to data items declared in another part of the program (which may not be shown in the example).

When two operands are present in an arithmetic or logical instruction, the right operand is the source and the left operand is the destination.

Depending on architecture, the operands may be register values, values in the stack, other memory values, I/O ports, etc., specified and accessed using more or less complex addressing modes. The types of operations include arithmetic, data copying, logical operations, and program control, as well as special instructions (such as CPUID and others).

Operands specify the data to be manipulated by the statement. The number of operands required depends on the specific statement. For example, executable statements may have zero, one, two, or three operands (Fig. 8.3).

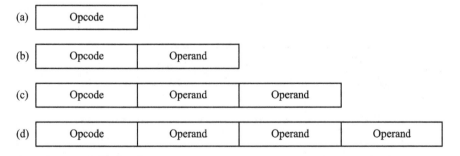

Fig. 8.3 Opcode and operands

8.3   Direct and Indirect Addressing

Some instructions use data encoded in the instruction itself as a source operand. These operands are called immediate operands (or simply immediate). For example, the following ADD instruction adds an immediate value of 14 to the contents of the EAX register:

ADD EAX, 14

All arithmetic instructions (except the DIV and IDIV instructions) allow the source operand to be an immediate value. The maximum value allowed for an immediate operand varies among instructions, but can never be greater than the maximum value of an unsigned double word integer (2^{32}).

Register operands is source, and destination operands can be any of the registers depending on the instruction being executed.

Some instructions (such as the DIV and MUL instructions) use quadword operands contained in a pair of 32-bit registers. Register pairs are represented with a colon separating them. For example, in the register pair EDX:EAX, EDX contains the high-order bits, and EAX contains the low order bits of a quadword operand.

Several instructions (such as the PUSHFD and POPFD instructions) are provided to load and store the contents of the EFLAGS register or to set or clear individual flags in this register. Other instructions use the state of the status flags in the EFLAGS register as condition codes for branching or other decision-making operations.

The processor contains a selection of system registers that are used to control memory management, interrupt and exception handling, task management, processor management, and debugging activities. Some of these system registers are accessible by an application program, the operating system, or the executive through a set of system instructions. When accessing a system register with a system instruction, the register is generally an implied operand of the instruction.

Memory operands means source and destination operands in memory are referenced by means of a segment selector and an offset (see Fig. 8.4). Segment selectors specify the segment containing the operand. Offsets specify the linear or effective address of the operand.

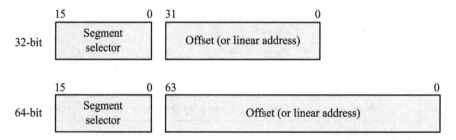

Fig. 8.4 Memory operand address (32-bit/64-bit)

Table 8.2 Default segment selection rules

Reference type	Register used	Segment used	Default selection rule
Instructions	CS	Code segment	All instruction fetches
Stack	SS	Stack segment	All stack pushes and pops
Local data	DS	Data segment	All data references
Destination string	ES	Data segment pointed to with the ES register	Destination of string instructions

Offsets can be 32-bit (represented by the notation m16:32) or 64-bit (represented by the notation m16:64).

The segment selector can be specified either implicitly or explicitly. The most common method of specifying a segment selector is to load it in a segment register and then allow the processor to select the register implicitly, depending on the type of operation being performed. The processor automatically chooses a segment according to the rules given in Table 8.2. When storing data in memory or loading data from memory, the DS segment default can be overridden to allow other segments to be accessed. Within an assembler, the segment override is generally handled with a colon ":" operator. For example, the following MOV instruction moves a value from register EAX into the segment pointed to by the ES register. The offset into the segment is contained in the EBX register:

```
MOV ES:[EBX], EAX;
```

8.4 Stack and Buffer Overflow

A stack is a memory segment that data can only be accessed from one side. The BOTTOM of a stack is fixed or cannot be changed. The TOP of a stack will be adjusted based on the operations PUSH or POP. An important property for stack is data is first-in-last-out (FILO) or last-in-first-out (LIFO).

The stack (see Fig. 8.5) is a contiguous array of memory locations (Shiva 2000). It is contained in a segment and identified by the segment selector in the SS register. When using the flat memory model, the stack can be located anywhere in the linear address space for the program. A stack can be up to 4 GB long, the maximum size of a segment.

Items are placed on the stack using the PUSH instruction and removed from the stack using the POP instruction. When an item is pushed onto the stack, the processor decrements the ESP register and then writes the item at the new top of stack. When an item is popped off the stack, the processor reads the item from the top of stack and then increments the ESP register. In this manner, the stack grows

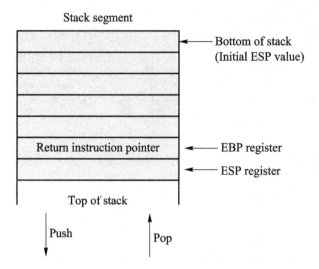

Fig. 8.5 Stack structure

down in memory (toward lesser addresses) when items are pushed on the stack and shrinks up (toward greater addresses) when the items are popped from the stack.

A program or operating system executive can set up many stacks. For example, in multitasking systems, each task can be given its own stack. The number of stacks in a system is limited by the maximum number of segments and the available physical memory.

Stack Manipulation Instructions—The PUSH, POP, PUSHA (push all registers), and POPA (pop all registers) instructions move data to and from the stack. The PUSH instruction decrements the stack pointer (contained in the ESP register) and then copies the source operand to the top of stack (see Fig. 8.6). It operates on memory operands, immediate operands, and register operands. The PUSH instruction is commonly used to place parameters on the stack before calling a procedure. It can also be used to reserve space on the stack for temporary variables.

If a stack has reached the maximum reserved memory and there is another PUSH operation, the TOP will overwrite the data in the other memory segment. This is called stack overflow. Or if the stack has reached the BOTTOM, and there is another POP operation; the data retrieved from the stack would be wrong. This is called stack underflow. If the POP operation is involved with an interrupt, then CPU may run into the unexpected program or data segment. If this was preset by a hacker, then it may launch a malicious program. This is called stack buffer overflow attack.

In software, stack buffer overflow occurs when a program writes to a memory address on the program's call stack outside of the intended data structure, usually a fixed length buffer. Stack buffer overflow bugs or attacks are caused when a program writes more data to a buffer located on the stack than there was actually allocated for that buffer. This almost always results in corruption of adjacent data on the stack and, in cases where the overflow was triggered by mistake, will often cause the

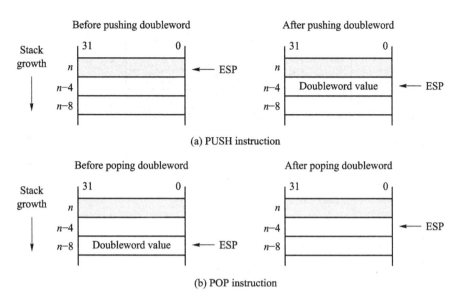

Fig. 8.6 Operation of PUSH/POP instructions

program to crash or operate incorrectly. This type of overflow is part of the more general class of programming bugs known as buffer overflows.

If the affected program is running with special privileges, or accepts data from untrusted network hosts (e.g., a webserver), then the bug is potential security vulnerability. If the stack buffer is filled with data supplied from an untrusted user, then that user can corrupt the stack in such a way as to inject executable code into the running program and take control of the process. This is one of the oldest and more reliable methods for hackers to gain unauthorized access to a computer.

8.4.1 Calling Procedures Using CALL and RET (return)

The CALL instruction allows control transfers to procedures within the current code segment (near call) and in a different code segment (far call). Near calls usually provide access to local procedures within the currently running program or task. Far calls are usually used to access operating system procedures or procedures in a different task.

The RET instruction also allows near and far returns to match the near and far versions of the CALL instruction. In addition, the RET instruction allows a program to increment the stack pointer on a return to release parameters from the stack.

When executing a near call, the processor does the following (see Fig. 8.7):

1. Pushes the current value of the EIP register on the stack.
2. Loads the offset of the called procedure in the EIP register.

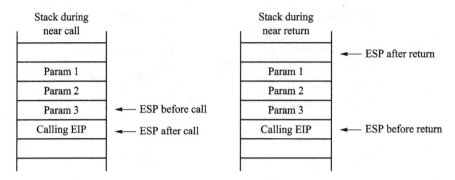

Fig. 8.7 Stack change using CALL and RET

3. Begins execution of the called procedure.

   When executing a near return, the processor performs these actions:

1. Pops the top-of-stack value (the return instruction pointer) into the EIP register.
2. If the RET instruction has an optional *n* argument, increments the stack pointer by the number of bytes specified with the *n* operand to release parameters from the stack.
3. Resumes execution of the calling procedure.

8.4.2   Exploiting Stack Buffer Overflows

The canonical method for exploiting a stack-based buffer overflow is to overwrite the function return address with a pointer to attacker-controlled data (usually on the stack itself). This is illustrated in the example below.

An example with strcpy

```
# include <string.h>
void foo (char *bar)
{
char c[12];
strcpy(c, bar); // no bounds checking...
}
int main (intargc, char **argv)
{
foo(argv[1]);
}
```

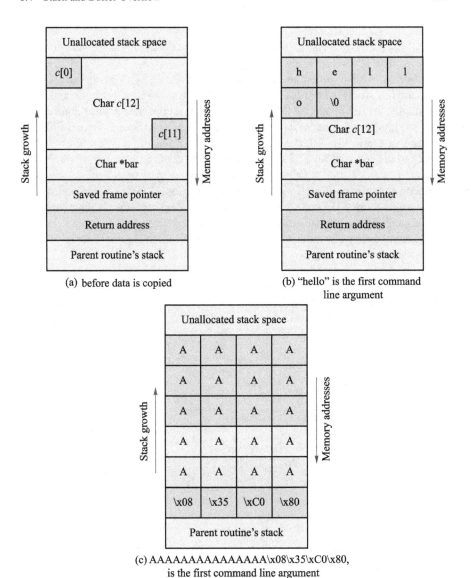

(a) before data is copied

(b) "hello" is the first command line argument

(c) AAAAAAAAAAAAAAAA\x08\x35\xC0\x80, is the first command line argument

Fig. 8.8 Program stack in foo() with various inputs (Color)

This code takes an argument from the command line and copies it to a local stack variable c. This works fine for command line arguments smaller than 12 characters (as you can see in Fig. 8.8b). Any arguments larger than 11 characters long will result in corruption of the stack. (The maximum number of characters that is safe is one less than the size of the buffer here because in the C programming language, strings are terminated by a zero-byte character. A 12-character input thus requires 13 bytes to store, the input followed by the sentinel zero byte. The zero byte then ends up overwriting a memory location that's one byte beyond the end of the buffer.)

Notice in Fig. 8.8, when an argument larger than 11 bytes is supplied on the command line, foo() overwrites local stack data, the saved frame pointer, and, most importantly, the return address. When foo() returns, it pops the return address off the stack and jumps to that address (i.e., starts executing instructions from that address). As you can see in Fig. 8.8, the attacker has overwritten the return address with a pointer to the stack buffer char c [12], which now contains attacker supplied data. In an actual stack buffer overflow exploit the string of "A"'s would be replaced with shellcode suitable to the platform and desired function. If this program had special privileges (e.g., the SUID bit set to run as the superuser), then the attacker could use this vulnerability to gain superuser privileges on the affected machine.

The attacker also can modify internal variables values to exploit some bugs. With same example:

```
# include <string.h>
# include <stdio.h>
void foo (char *bar)
{
float my_float = 10.5; // addr = 0x0023FF4C
char c[12]; // addr = 0x0023FF30
    // will print 10.500000
printf("my float value = %f\n", my_float);
    /* ~~~~~~~~~~~~~~~~~~~~~~~~~~~~~~~~~~~~
      memory map:
@ : c allocated memory
# :my_float allocated memory
    - : other memory

        *c                          *my_float
        0x0023FF30                  0x0023FF4C
        |                           |
        @@@@@@@@@@@@--------------#####
foo("my string is too long !!!!! XXXXX");
memcpy will put 0x1010C042 in my_float value.
    ~~~~~~~~~~~~~~~~~~~~~~~~~~~~~~~~~~~~~~~~~~~*/
memcpy(c, bar, strlen(bar)); // no bounds checking...
// Will print 96.031372
printf("my float value = %f\n", my_float);
}

int main (intargc, char **argv){
foo("my string is too long !!!!! \x10\x10\xC0\x42");
return 0;
}
```

8.4.3 Stack Protection

One approach to preventing stack buffer overflow exploitation is to enforce memory policy on stack memory region to disallow execution from the stack. This means that in order to execute shell code from the stack, an attacker must either find a way to disable the execution protection from memory or find a way to put her/his shell code payload in a non-protected region of memory. This method is becoming more popular now that hardware support for the no-execute flag is available in most desktop processors.

Intel uses a stack segment register (SS) to manage PUSH and POP operations. Any memory reference which uses ESP or EBP general purpose register as a base register.

8.5 FIFO and M/M/1 Problem

A queue is another important data structure in mathematics and computer science (Hwang 1993). A useful queuing model represents a real-life system with sufficient accuracy and is analytically tractable. A queuing model based on the Poisson process and its companion exponential probability distribution often meets these two requirements. A Poisson process models random events (such as a customer arrival, a request for action from a web server, or the completion of the actions requested of a web server) as emanating from a memoryless process. That is, the length of the time interval from the current time to the occurrence of the next event does not depend upon the time of occurrence of the last event. In the Poisson probability distribution, the observer records the number of events that occur in a time interval of fixed length. In the (negative) exponential probability distribution, the observer records the length of the time interval between consecutive events. In both scenarios, the underlying physical process is memoryless.

8.5.1 FIFO Data Structure

A queue is different than a stack as it has a FRONT and BACK. Data always move into queue from BACK and leave queue from FRONT. So it is a first-in-first-out (FIFO) data structure.

Queues are very common in our daily life. When people go through the checkpoint at the airport, they all follow the first-in-first-out (FIFO) model (if only one checkpoint is open at that time). If too many passengers arrived, then the line would be very long or the waiting time would be very long.

Queues provide services in computer science, transport, and operations research where various entities such as data, objects, persons, or events are stored and held to be processed later. In these contexts, the queue performs the function of a buffer.

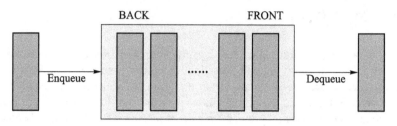

Fig. 8.9 A queue model is using the FIFO data structure

Queues are common in computer programs, where they are implemented as data structures coupled with access routines, as an abstract data structure or in object-oriented languages as classes. Common implementations are circular buffers and linked lists.

In Fig. 8.9, the customer or packet at the front of the line was the first one to enter, while at the end of the line is the last to have entered. Every time a customer finishes paying for their items, that object leaves the queue from the front. This represents the queue "dequeue" function. Every time another object or customer enters the line to wait, they join the end of the line and represent the "enqueue" function. The queue "size" function would return the length of the line, and the "empty" function would return true only if there was nothing in the line.

8.5.2   M/M/1 Model

In queuing theory, a discipline within the mathematical theory of probability, an M/M/1 queue represents the queue length in a system having a single server, where arrivals are determined by a Poisson process and job service times have an exponential distribution. The model name is written in Kendall's notation. Figure 8.10 shows a diagram of an M/M/1 model. The model is the most elementary of queuing models and an attractive object of study as closed-form expressions can be obtained for many metrics of interest in this model.

An M/M/1 queue is a stochastic process whose state space is the set $\{0, 1, 2, 3, \cdots, n\}$ where the value corresponds to the number of customers in the system, including any currently in service.

- Arrivals occur at rate λ according to a Poisson process and move the process from state i to $i + 1$.

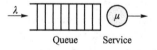

Fig. 8.10 M/M/1 model

Fig. 8.11 Markov chain

- Service times have an exponential distribution with parameter μ in the M/M/1 queue.
- A single server serves customers one at a time from the front of the queue. When the service is complete, the customer leaves the queue, and the number of customers in the system reduces by one.
- The buffer is of infinite size, so there is no limit on the number of customers it can contain.

This is the same continuous time Markov chain as in a birth-death process. The state space diagram for this chain is shown as Fig. 8.11.

The model is considered stable only if $\lambda < \mu$. If, on average, arrivals happen faster than service completions, the queue will grow indefinitely long, and the system will not have an equilibrium. Various performance measures can be computed explicitly for this model. We write $\rho = \lambda/\mu$ for the utilization of the buffer and require $\rho < 1$ for the queue to be stable; ρ represents the average proportion of time which the server is occupied.

It can be mathematically proved that the number of customers in the system is

$$\frac{\rho}{1 - \rho}$$

and the variance of number of customers in the system is $\rho/(1 - \rho)2$.

For customers who arrive and find the queue as a stationary process, the average time (the sum of both waiting time and service time) spent waiting is

$$\frac{1}{\mu - \lambda} - \frac{1}{\mu} = \frac{\rho}{\mu - \lambda}$$

8.6 Kernel, Drivers, and OS Security

8.6.1 Kernel

A kernel is the main component of most computer operating systems; it is a bridge between applications and the actual data processing done at the hardware level. Figure 8.12 shows a diagram of a kernel in a computer system. The kernel's responsibilities include managing the system's resources (hardware, software, and the communication them). Usually as a basic component of an operating system, a

Fig. 8.12 Kernel is a bridge
between hardware and the
applications

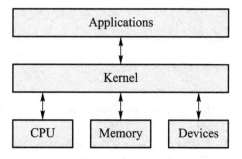

kernel can provide the lowest-level abstraction layer for the resources (especially
processors and I/O devices) that application software must control to perform
its function. It typically makes these facilities available to application processes
through inter-process communication mechanisms and system calls.

Operating system tasks are done differently by different kernels, depending on
their design and implementation. While monolithic kernels execute all the operating
system code in the same address space to increase the performance of the system,
micro-kernels run most of the operating system services in user space as servers,
aiming to improve maintainability and modularity of the operating system. A range
of possibilities exists between these two extremes.

The kernel's primary function is to manage the computer's resources and allow
other programs to run and use these resources. Typically, the resources consist of:

- The Central processing unit.
- The computer's memory.
- Any I/O devices present in the computer, such as keyboard, mouse, disk drives,
  printers, displays, etc.

8.6.2   BIOS

The System BIOS or ROM BIOS is a de facto standard defining a firmware interface.
BIOS software is stored on a non-volatile ROM chip on the motherboard. It is
specifically designed to work with each particular model of computer, interfacing
with various devices that make up the complementary chipset of the system. In
modern computer systems, the BIOS chip's contents can be rewritten without
removing it from the motherboard, allowing BIOS software to be upgraded in place.
The author of this book invented this non-volatile ROM as early as 1985.

The BIOS software is built into the PC and is the first code run by a PC when
powered on ("boot firmware"). When the PC starts up, the first job for the BIOS
is the power-on self-test, which initializes and identifies system devices such as the
video display card, keyboard and mouse, hard disk drive, optical disc drive, and
other hardware. The BIOS then locates boot loader software held on a peripheral

device (designated as a "boot device"), such as a hard disk or a CD/DVD, and loads and executes that software, giving it control of the PC. This process is known as booting, or booting up, which is short for bootstrapping.

A BIOS has a user interface (UI), typically a menu system accessed by pressing a certain key on the keyboard when the PC starts. In the BIOS UI, a user can:

- Configure hardware.
- Set the system clock.
- Enable or disable system components.
- Select which devices are eligible to be a potential boot device.
- Set various password prompts, such as a password for securing access to the BIOS UI functions itself and preventing malicious users from booting the system from unauthorized peripheral devices.

The BIOS provides a small library of basic input/output functions used to operate and control the peripherals such as the keyboard, text display functions, and so forth, and these software library functions are callable by external software. From around 2010 the BIOS firmware of PCs started to be replaced by a unified extensible firmware interface (UEFI).

8.6.3   Boot Loader

BIOS is a boot loader (bootstrap loader). This small program's only job is to load other data and programs which are then executed from RAM. Often, multiple-stage boot loaders are used, during which several programs of increasing complexity load one after the other in a process of chain loading.

The boot process can be considered complete when the computer is ready to interact with the user, or the operating system is capable of running system programs or application programs. Typical modern personal computers boot in about 1 min, of which about 15 s are taken by a power-on self-test (POST) and a preliminary boot loader, and the rest by loading the operating system and other software. Time spent after the operating system loading can be considerably shortened to as little as 3 s by bringing the system up with all cores at once, as with coreboot. Large servers may take several minutes to boot and start all their services.

Many embedded systems must boot immediately. For example, waiting a minute for a digital television or GPS satellites to start is generally unacceptable. Therefore such devices have software systems in ROM or flash memory, so the device can begin functioning immediately. For these types of embedded system, little or no loading is necessary, since the loading can be precomputed and stored on the ROM when the device is made.

Most computers are also capable of booting over a computer network. In this scenario, the operating system is stored on the disk of a server, and certain parts of it are transferred to the client using a simple protocol such as the Trivial File Transfer

Protocol. After these parts have been transferred, the operating system then takes over control of the booting process.

Once the BIOS has found a bootable device, it loads the boot sector to linear address 0x7C00 and transfers execution to the boot code. In the case of a hard disk, this is referred to as the master boot record (MBR) and is often not operating system specific. The conventional MBR code checks the MBR's partition table for a partition set as bootable. If an active partition is found, the MBR code loads the boot sector code from that partition and executes it. The main function is to load and execute the operating system kernel, which continues startup.

8.6.4   Device Drivers

A device driver or software driver is a computer program allowing higher-level computer programs to interact with a hardware device. Figure 8.13 shows a device driver diagram. A driver typically communicates with the device through the computer bus or communications subsystem to which the hardware connects. When a calling program invokes a routine in the driver, the driver issues commands to the device. Once the device sends data back to the driver, the driver may invoke routines in the original calling program. Drivers are hardware-dependent and operating-system-specific. They usually provide the interrupt handling required for any necessary asynchronous time-dependent hardware interface.

Writing a device driver requires an in-depth understanding of how the hardware and the software of a given platform function. Drivers operate in a highly privileged environment and can cause disaster if they get things wrong. In contrast, most user-level software on modern operating systems can be stopped without greatly affecting the rest of the system. Even drivers executing in user mode can crash a system if

Fig. 8.13 Device driver diagram

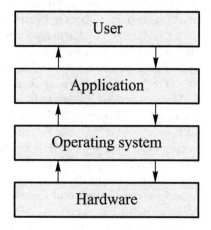

the device is erroneously programmed. These factors make it more difficult and dangerous to diagnose problems.

Device drivers can run in kernel mode or in user mode. The primary benefit of running a driver in user mode is improved stability, since a poorly written user mode device driver cannot crash the system by overwriting kernel memory. On the other hand, user/kernel mode transitions usually impose a considerable performance overhead, thereby prohibiting user mode drivers for low latency and high-throughput requirements.

Because of the diversity of modern hardware and operating systems, drivers operate in many different environments. Drivers may interface with:

- Printers.
- Video adapters.
- Network cards.
- Sound cards.
- Local buses of various sorts—in particular, for bus mastering on modern systems.
- Low-bandwidth I/O buses of various sorts (for pointing devices such as mouse, keyboards, USB, etc.).
- Computer storage devices such as hard disk, CD-ROM, and floppy disk buses (ATA, SATA, SCSI).
- Implementing support for different file systems.
- Image scanners.
- Digital cameras.

An application programming interface (API) is a source code-based specification intended to be used as an interface by software components to communicate with each other. An API may include specifications for routines, data structures, object classes, and variables.

An API specification can take many forms, including an International Standard or vendor documentation such as the Microsoft Windows API or the libraries of a programming language (Wang et al. 2008), e.g., Standard Template Library in C++ or Java API.

8.7 Windows, Linux, and Mac OS

8.7.1 Windows OS and Security

Windows is a graphical operating system replaced MS-DOS in 1985. Later versions include Windows 3.1, Windows 95, Windows NT, Windows XP, Windows 7, and now Windows 10. The server family includes Windows 2003, Windows 2012, Windows 2016, and now Windows 2019.

The graphical user interface makes it easy to use for everybody including non-computer professionals.

Before Windows Server 2003, all services and associated ports were open after installation. This cause security problems as a guest user can easily access a Windows server and upload/download files via port 25, a non-secured FTP service. Starting Windows 2008 R2, Windows has improved security significantly but incidents of system breach are still common.

A zero-day attack happens once a flaw, or software/hardware vulnerability, is exploited and attackers release malware before a developer has an opportunity to create a patch to fix the vulnerability. On the other hand, it could be a government agency discovered the exploits and decided not to publish the vulnerability so it can later be used as cyber weapon to attack the adversaries. The latter may have adverse consequences if the adversaries know the exploit. External Blue is one of the examples.

8.7.2   Linux, Mac OS, and Security

Linux is an open source operating system that is similar to Unix, a command-line based operating system. Earlier Linux versions were mostly command-line based. The newer distributions such as Ubuntu, Debian, and Fedora can add desktops such as KDE and GNOME, so they look and function much similar to Windows.

Classical Mac OS used operating systems developed for the Macintosh family by Apple Computers. There is little compatibility with other major operating systems. The evolution of Max OS X transitioned the CPU from G5 to Intel processors. Users can choose to run native OS X (a version of Linux) or Windows if he deems to do so.

The user and file permissions and non-root access are among many advantages in Linux security. The open source nature makes it a perfect choice for many household, industrial, and IoT applications.

Like Unix, Linux is a multi-user OS by default. Unlike Windows non-server editions that only allow one user to access, Linux allows multiple users to operate simultaneously.

8.7.3   Kali Linux

Kali Linux is a variation of Debian operating system that is designed for cybersecurity-related talks such as vulnerability assessment, penetration testing, and digital forensics. There are about 600 pre-installed cybersecurity tools on Kali Linux.

Kali can run on a standard computer. It also comes with virtual appliances that can be loaded directly on virtual machines, such as Virtual Box and VMWare. A smaller ARM package can run on a Raspberry Pi computer.

8.8   Mobile OS

Apple iOS and Google Android are the most common mobile operating systems. BlackBerry OS was one of the most favorite OS years ago. It faded away due to the fact that some analysts say the pretty good policy (PGP)-based end-to-end encryption is so secure that governments couldn't monitor the traffic.

8.8.1   iOS

iOS is a mobile OS for Apple running on iPhones or iPads. Apple designed the iOS platform with security at its core with an entirely new architecture. As a result, iOS is a major leap forward in security for mobile devices. Every iOS device combines software, hardware, and services designed to work together for maximum security and a transparent user experience. iOS protects not only the device and its data at rest, but the entire ecosystem, including everything users do locally, on networks, and with key Internet services. iOS and iOS devices provide advanced security features, and yet they're also easy to use.

For iOS devices, encryptions are not configurable, so users are unable to disable them by mistake. Other features, such as Face ID, enhance the user experience by making it simpler and more intuitive to secure the device.

The iOS security is organized into the following topic areas:

- System security   The integrated and secure software and hardware that are the platform for iPhone, iPad, and iPod touch.
- Encryption and data protection   The architecture and design that protects user data if the device is lost or stolen or if an unauthorized person attempts to use or modify it.
- App security   The systems that enable apps to run securely and without compromising platform integrity.
- Network security   Industry-standard networking protocols that provide secure authentication and encryption of data in transmission.
- Apple Pay   Apple's implementation of secure payments.
- Internet services   Apple's network-based infrastructure for messaging, syncing, and backup.
- User password management   Password restrictions and access to passwords from other authorized sources.
- Device controls   Methods that allow management of iOS devices, prevent unauthorized use, and enable remote wipe if a device is lost or stolen.
- Privacy controls   Capabilities of iOS that can be used to control access to Location Services and user data.

8.8.2 *Android*

Android is an open source OS that is built on the Linux® kernel and provides an environment for multiple apps to run simultaneously.

With Android, multiple layers of security support the diverse use cases of an open platform while also enabling sufficient safeguards to protect user and corporate data. Additionally, Android platform security keeps devices, data, and apps safe through tools like app sandboxing, exploit mitigation, and device encryption. A broad range of management APIs gives IT departments the tools to help prevent data leakage and enforce compliance in a variety of scenarios. The work profile enables enterprises to create a separate, secure container on users' devices where apps and critical company data are kept secure and separate from personal information.

8.9 Network OS

Early network operating systems provided just the basics in terms of network services, such as file and printer sharing. Today's network operating systems offer a far broader range of network services, some of these services are used in almost every network environment, and others are used in only a few.

Despite the complexity of operating systems, the basic function and purpose of a network operating system is straightforward: to provide services to the network. Network operating systems provide several services to the client systems on the network. The following are some of the most common of these services:

- Authentication services.
- File and print services.
- Web server services.
- Firewall and proxy services.
- Dynamic host configuration protocol (DHCP) and domain name system (DNS) services.

8.10 Software Reverse Engineering

Software reverse engineering (SRE) is the practice of extracting design and implementation information of a software system. In other words, SRE is related to reveal the source code from the binary executable.

Reverse engineering can be used to detect and neutralize viruses and malware, as well as to protect or steal intellectual property. SRE falls into one of two categories, software development-related and security-related.

8.10.1 Debug Tools (IDA and Ghidra)

Interactive DisAssembler (IDA) is one of the most common disassemblers used by cybersecurity professionals. It is a cross-platform tool written in C++.

Ghidra is a software reverse engineering framework created and maintained by the National Security Agency Research Directorate (Ghidra 2019). This framework includes a suite of full-featured, high-end software analysis tools that enable users to analyze compiled code on a variety of platforms including Windows, Mac OS, and Linux. Capabilities include disassembly, assembly, decompilation, graphing, and scripting, along with hundreds of other features. Ghidra supports a wide variety of processor instruction sets and executable formats and can be run in both user-interactive and automated modes. Users may also develop their own Ghidra plug-in components and/or scripts using Java or Python. The source was published on Github.

Ghidra's existence was originally revealed to the public via WikiLeaks in March 2017, but the software itself remained unavailable until its declassification and official release 2 years later.

8.10.2 Discovering APIs and DLLs

There are needs to reverse engineering APIs and DLLs, one reason might be to identify flaws and security vulnerabilities of software.

For a web-related API, setting up a web proxy server is a common way to use it as a middleman to harvest data. A proxy server can monitor and eavesdrop on HTTP network traffic. It can also hide the public IP address and filter or redirect requests. There are several free web proxy tools such as Postman, Fiddler, and Burp.

8.10.3 Decompilation and Disassembly

Software decompilation and disassembly are the process to exposure binary code to find secrets such as passwords, connection strings, and encryption keys. Adversaries may use the tool for intellectual proprietary and software piracy or add backdoors to original code for later exploit.

8.11 Summary

Assembly language is the lowest level computer language that can be easily remembered and understood. Instructions written in assembly languages can be executed by processors directly.

Instructions are formatted in opcode + operands format. An opcode specifies the type of command for an instruction. The operands are arguments or numbers to be used during the operations. Some operands are immediate or direct, which stored in registers. Some operands are stored in memory that the operands are pointers (or offset) pointing to the data location in memory.

Stack is a very important data structure in computer science. The BOTTOM is fixed or in other words cannot be accessed; data can only be accessed from the TOP by following the LIFO rule. Stack can be used in I/O interfaces to connect the low speed I/O devices to the high-speed processors. Procedures can use stack to save the current execution location and return from the subroutine when finish.

Due to the limited capacity, a stack may overflow if push data to the stack once the stack is full or a stack may underflow if pop data on the stack is empty. If the stack overflow (or underflow) is caused by an attack, then the computer could be compromised and the data rested on the computer may be in danger.

Using non-executable memory for stack is one method to reduce the stack buffer overflow exploitation.

Queue is another important data structure. It has two ends: a FRONT and a BACK. Data always move into the queue from back and leave queue from front (FIFO). The single-server queuing model (M/M/1) has widely applications in many areas. The arrivals rate λ should be less than the service rate μ with traffic intensity $\rho = \lambda/\mu < 1$. The number of customers in the system is $\rho/(1 - \rho)$ and the average time spent in waiting is $\rho/(\mu - \lambda)$.

Computer architecture (no matter it is a quad-core or a pipeline) cannot function itself well without the support of the operating system. A kernel is the center of operating systems working directly with the hardware and the resources. The BIOS is a boot firmware (bootstrap loader) in personal computers that is stored on a non-violate memory. BIOS is first executed followed by the kernel after a cool start.

Device drivers are programs that on one side to communicate directly with the specific device and on the other side to provide interface to high-level computer programs. Application program interface (API) is a software interface to let other programs to call the functions inside the software. A complied software application without API can hardly be modified or expended.

Windows and Linux are two main operating systems. Security has improved over the years, but it is still a challenge in today's cyberspace.

Mobile devices are no longer being used just for making phone call and listening music. The new generations of mobile processors and the use of computational power from the cloud make them an everyday use for almost everything by many people.

Software reverse engineering (SRE) is the practice of extracting design and implementation information of a software system. In other words, SRE is related to reveal the source code from the binary executable.

Reverse engineering can be used to detect and neutralize viruses and malware, as well as to protect or steal intellectual property. SRE falls into one of two categories, software development-related and security-related.

Projects

8.1 Buffer overflow attack

A buffer overflow is a situation where a running program attempts to write data outside the memory buffer which is not intended to store this data. When this happens, we are talking about a buffer overflow or buffer overrun situation. A memory buffer is an area in the computer's memory (RAM) meant for temporarily storing data. This kind of buffers can be found in all programs and are used to store data for input, output, and processing.

Use Kali Linux to demonstrate a buffer overflow attack.

8.2 Malware analysis with Ghidra

Like IDA pro, Ghidra is a software reverse engineering (SRE) suite of tools developed by NSA's research directorate in support of the cybersecurity mission. Install Ghidra on your computer and run a tutorial.

Exercises

8.1 Today most programs are written either in C and Java. Is there any benefit to write an assembly language program?

8.2 Addition is to add two numbers together. Explain how to do addition using instructions with one operand.

8.3 A PC (=FE17) points to the top of the stack. The bottom of the stack is at address FFFF. After execute instructions: PUSH, PUSH, and POP, what is the value in the PC?

8.4 Read Sect. 8.5.2 and answer the question: how to modify the program and to prevent the buffer overflow problem.

8.5 A queue has two pointers FRONT and BACK. Write two functions,

(1) Enqueue ()—move data into queue.
(2) Dequeue ()—move data out of queue.

8.6 A cell phone service provider has the capacity of connecting 1000 people per second. Due to an emergency, the incoming requests reach to 999 people per second. Calculate the number of people waiting in line to be served. Explain why the result shows almost nobody is served?

8.7 There are researches to develop driver-free devices. One way is to store the driver into the device. When a device is connected, the driver is loaded automatically. Find an example of this device and explain how it works.

8.8 A programmer wants to add features to a software application developed by another company. Unfortunately, there is no source code he can revise. What he should do to finish his job?

8.9 Compare Linux shell and Windows command-line shell/Power Shell. What are the similarities and differences?

8.10 You forgot password on your computer and decided to use Kali Linux to reset the password. What type of tools you will use in Kali Linux? List at least two of them.

References

Assembly language. (2012). *Wikipedia*. Retrieved February 2, 2012.
Dumas, J. D. (2006). *Computer architecture: Fundamentals and principles of computer design*. Oxford: Taylor & Francis.
Ghidra. (2019). *National security agency*. Retrieved October 29, 2019.
Hwang, K. (1993). *Advanced computer architecture: Parallelism, scalability, programmability*. New York: McGraw-Hill, Inc.
Shiva, S. G. (2000). *Computer design and architecture* (3rd ed.). New York: Marcel Dekker, Inc.
Wang, S., Dong, Z., Chen, J., & Ledley, R. (2008). PPL—A whole image processing language. *Computer Language, System and Structures, 34*(1), 18–24.

Chapter 9
Communication, TCP/IP, and Internet

Data communication is the fundamental for network communications. It sits at the physical layer of ISO OSI architecture. In data communication field, we take an abstract view of the network naming computer and servers as notes and networks as links.

TCP/IP is one of the most important prototypes in modern communications and is the foundation of the Internet. Routers, switches, gateways, and other key equipment on a network mostly follow TCP/IP prototypes. Wireless communication networks provide the flexibility of easy Internet connection anywhere, anyplace, and at any time. IoT devices supported by the IoT architecture use SoC or microprocessors therefore more vulnerable to attacks. Network security is a very broad topic. VPN and VPC are used in applications to protect the remote access of applications and data.

9.1 Data Communications

Data communication is to study the transmission of digital messages to devices besides the message source. The devices or channels are generally thought of as being independently powered circuitry that exists beyond the chassis of a computer or other digital message source. In general, the maximum permissible transmission rate of a message is directly proportional to signal power and inversely proportional to channel noise. It is the aim of any communication systems to provide the highest possible transmission rate at the lowest possible power and with the least possible noise.

For instance, there are many government and state agencies that rely on the Internet to function. The US Department of Homeland Security is an example of an agency that rely on the Internet to communicate and share critical mission-related information with sub-units in the field and with other outside agencies important to the completion of its mission. Thus, part of its mission is dependent on the efficiency, power, and effectiveness of the Internet, which likewise is dependent on the efficient flow of data communications. So, the importance of development of a computer network protocol to maintain this efficiency cannot be ignored.

The goal of data communication is to provide a means of reliable and efficient data communication between two end nodes or hosts. Communications between these entities are in the form of messages composed and received by senders and receivers. This concept may appear quite simple on the surface; however, it actually involves unique protocol models that are keys to ensuring the success of the transmission of the message. There are various models that can be used to facilitate this process. One model in particular is the transmission control protocol/Internet protocol (TCP/IP), which is a universal suite that offers reliable software that facilitates communications between diverse vendor equipment and which is now the basis for the operation of the Internet.

9.1.1 Signal, Data, and Channels

Electromagnetic signals, which are capable of propagation on a variety of transmission media, can be used to convey data. We use the term data to represent something meaningful. We use the term signal to stand for physical transmission of data along various mediums. In real world, we have two types of signals, analog signal and digital signal. The word channel refers either to a physical transmission medium such as a wire or to a logical connection such as a radio channel. A channel has a certain capacity for transmitting information, often measured by its bandwidth in Hz or its data rate in bits per second (b/s).

An analog signal is a format of representing data with continuously varying electromagnetic wave. An old telephone system transmits analog signals from the source to the destination. A digital signal is a format of representing data with sequence of voltage pulses. Nowadays most network signals are all digital signals. Most IP phones also transmit digital signals. Figure 9.1 shows an analog signal and a digital signal.

Digital communication has the advantages of cost-effective, data integrity, large capacity, security and privacy, and easy integration. Digital data, voice, and video can be easily integrated and transmitted through a single communication channel.

Fig. 9.1 Analog signal and digital signal

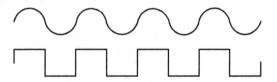

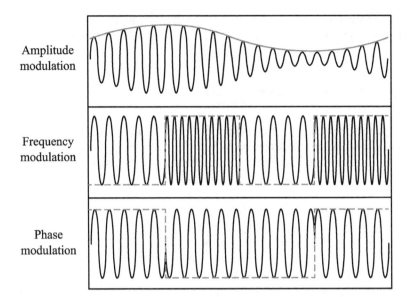

Fig. 9.2 AM, FM, and PM signals

9.1.2   Signal Encoding and Modulation

Analog data are often encoded and modulated during transmission. The amplitude modulation (AM) is used by many radio stations to broadcast news information. The frequency modulation (FM) is often used by radio stations to broadcast music, since FM can have better voice quality comparing with AM. There is another modulation method that modulates phase of the signal (PM). Figure 9.2 shows the AM, FM, and PM signals.

In telecommunications, a carrier is a waveform (usually sinusoidal) that is modulated with an input signal for the purpose of conveying information. This carrier wave is usually a much higher frequency than the input signal. The purpose of the carrier is usually either to transmit the information through space as an electromagnetic wave (as in radio communication) or to allow several carriers at different frequencies to share a common physical transmission medium by frequency division multiplexing.

An example of this is the telephone system where many people can talk through one cable. Since human voices fall between 20 Hz and 20 kHz, there is no way to transmit multiple voice signals over one cable without modulation. The carrier helps to modulate the voice signals to different consecutive frequencies, so there is no overlap between any voice signals. At the destination, the modulated signal is de-modulated to restore the signal to the original (audible) signal.

Digital signals can also be encoded to reduce errors during transmission. An analog/digital (A/D) converter is used to encode the analog signal to digital signal.

9.1.3 Shannon Theorem

The Nyquist-Shannon sampling theorem is a fundamental result in the field of information theory, in particular telecommunications and signal processing. Sampling is the process of converting a signal (e.g., a function of continuous time or space) into a numeric sequence (a function of discrete time or space). Shannon's version of the theorem states:

If a function $x(t)$ contains no frequencies higher than B hertz, it is completely determined by giving its ordinates at a series of points spaced $1/(2B)$ seconds apart. If the highest frequency B in the original signal is known, the theorem gives the lower bound on the sampling frequency for which perfect reconstruction can be assured. This lower bound to the sampling frequency, $2B$, is called the Nyquist rate.

In summary, the Shannon theorem states: if the original signal has the highest frequency B, the sample rate should be $2B$ in order to reconstruct the original signal lossless.

For CDs, the sample rate is 44,100 Hz. The reason to choose this sample rate is because the human hearing range is roughly 20 Hz–20,000 Hz. According the Shannon' sample theorem, the sample rate should be no less than twice of the highest frequency, or 40,000 Hz. In addition to this, signals must be low-pass filtered (LPF), and LPF is hardly perfect, so we keep a transition band 2000 Hz. As a result, it requires additional 4 kHz sampling. The extra 100 Hz is added to comply with the video recording methods. For NTSC, 245 lines × 60 frames × 3 samples = 44,100 samples per second. For PAL, 294 lines × 50 frames × 3 samples = 44,100 samples per second. The new high-definition TV standards have much more lines per frame. A 4k TV or monitor supports 3840 × 2160 pixels.

9.2 TCP/IP

The TCP/IP architecture originated during the 1970s, as a result of the US Defense Department's need for a wide-area communication system, covering the United States and allowing the interconnection of heterogeneous hardware and software systems. It is a result of protocol research and development conducted on the experimental packet-switched network, ARPANET, funded by the Defense Advanced Research Projects Agency (DARPA), and is generally referred to as the TCP/IP suite. Although it was at first used to facilitate consistent communications with governments, military, and educational sites together, commercial companies were eventually allowed to access this realm. Eventually, this protocol would become the foundation of the Internet.

9.2.1 Network Topology

There is a concept of using layer to describe Internet protocols. There are no physical layers in the protocol, the layer is logical concept, or in other words, it is virtual. The common five-layer model contains application, transport, network, data link, and physical. The ISO model contains seven layers, application, presentation, session, transport, network, data link, and physical. An easy way to remember OSI model is "All People Seem To Need Data Processing." Figure 9.3 shows the TCP/IP network topology.

TCP/IP revolutionized and greatly improved the transmission of digitized information throughout the Internet. It is used as a tool to transmit data in the form of a message or file through the Internet and consists of several levels of functionality. TCP/IP has become the most common suite for telecommunications as the Internet was originally created around it, and the access to the Internet would not be

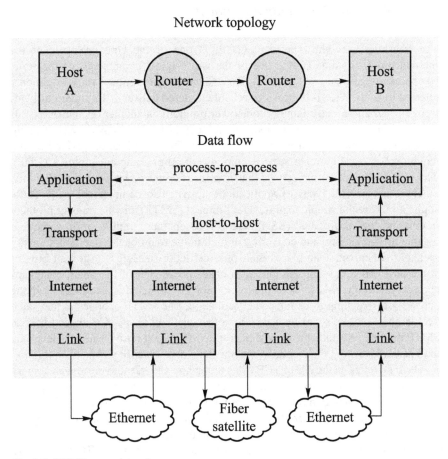

Fig. 9.3 TCP/IP network topology

possible without it. The communication layers associated with TCP/IP consist of the application layer, host-to-host or transport layer, Internet layer, network access layer, and physical layer. The most commonly used protocol at the transport layer is the transmission control protocol (TCP). TCP provides a reliable stream delivery and virtual connection service to applications through the use of sequenced acknowledgment with retransmission of packets when necessary. Since many network applications may be running on the same machine with one single IP address, computers need something to make sure that the correct software application on the destination computer gets the data packets from the source machine and the replies get routed back to the correct application on the source computer, and this is accomplished through the use of the TCP "port numbers" and the combination of IP address of a network station, and its port number is known as a "socket" or an "endpoint."

9.2.2   Transmission Control Protocol

The transmission control protocol (TCP) is one of the core protocols of the Internet protocol suite. TCP is one of the two original components of the suite, complementing the Internet protocol (IP), and therefore the entire suite is commonly referred to as TCP/IP. TCP provides reliable, ordered delivery of a stream of bytes from a program on one computer to another program on another computer. TCP is the protocol that major Internet applications such as the World Wide Web, E-mail, remote administration, and file transfer rely on. Other applications, which do not require reliable data stream service, may use the user datagram protocol (UDP), which provides a datagram service that emphasizes reduced latency over reliability.

There are several types of applications designed to complement TCP. These applications are the simple mail transfer protocol (SMTP), the file transfer protocol (FTP), and the secure shell (SSH). The SMTP operates similar to the gathering, organizing, packaging, and delivering of mail in the traditional sense. Traditionally speaking, when someone places their physical letter (message) in a mail box, or at the post office, a mailroom employee takes possession of that mail, completes necessary action consistent with mailroom protocol procedures, and places it in the queue for dispatching to its intended destination. The SMTP operates in that same vein in an electronic sense by accepting a message and using TCP to send it to an SMTP module on another host, and then the SMTP makes use of a local electronic mail package to store the incoming message in a user's mailbox.

The FTP relies on the use of TCP when uploading and transferring text and binary files that are to and from multiple host systems on the Internet, and the SSH is actually what its name implies, a secure method of logging on to a systems, i.e., a terminal or other computerized device, with the ability to encrypt data ensuring that no one is able to contaminate, taint, or corrupt that data.

There are other protocol suites that serve the same purposes as TCP/IP, such as the open systems interconnection (OSI) reference model. However, TCP has led the way in effortless communications and the exchange of data across the Internet spectrum. OSI was developed by the International Organization for Standardization (ISO) as a model for a computer protocol architecture and as a framework for developing protocol standards. OSI was also based on the use of layering with each layer performing a related subset of the functions required to communicate with another system. It was anticipated that the OSI model would bypass other known communication suites; however, this system came up short, and the TCP/IP is still the leading architecture in this area of technology.

9.2.3 User Datagram Protocol

The user datagram protocol (UDP) is one of the core members of the Internet protocol suite, the set of network protocols used for the Internet. With UDP, computer applications can send messages, in this case referred to as datagrams, to other hosts on an Internet protocol (IP) network without requiring prior communications to set up special transmission channels or data paths.

UDP uses a simple transmission model without implicit handshaking dialogues for providing reliability, ordering, or data integrity. Thus, UDP provides an unreliable service, and datagrams may arrive out of order, appear duplicated, or go missing without notice. UDP assumes that error checking and correction is either not necessary or performed in the application, avoiding the overhead of such processing at the network interface level. Time-sensitive applications often use UDP because dropping packets is preferable to waiting for delayed packets, which may not be an option in a real-time system. If error correction facilities are needed at the network interface level, an application may use the TCP which is designed for this purpose.

UDP's stateless nature is also useful for servers answering small queries from huge numbers of clients. Unlike TCP, UDP supports packet broadcast (sending to all on local network) and multicasting (send to all subscribers).

Common network applications that use UDP include the domain name system (DNS), streaming media applications such as IPTV, voice/video over IP (VoIP), trivial file transfer protocol (TFTP), IP tunneling protocols, and many online games.

9.2.4 Internet Protocol

The Internet protocol (IP) is another layer critical piece in the successful transmission of data. It is designed to handle the address part of a packet so that it gets to the right destination. It is used at the Internet layer to provide routing function across multiple networks, implemented not only in the end systems but also in routers. Routers are essential to the entire process of effecting efficient communications in that they are used to connect multiple networks and send disseminate information from network to network on various routes on the Internet from the sender to the receiver. The network layer involves the routing of data to its specified location, and the physical layer pertains to the actual hardware that is used to physically generate the data that is to be routed.

TCP/IP communication protocol is a prime example of the cutting-edge technology that has evolved since the development of the Internet. It is considered one of the most powerful tools to have evolved during the era of computer technology, and its development has essentially revolutionized the speed, clarity, and authenticity of data communications like never before. Since its conception, the efficiency of computer networking has grown by leaps and bounds. As the world continues to seek methods of increasing efficiency of data communications, and as new applications are defined, there is no doubt that TCP/IP will continue to be one of the leading protocol suites ensuring enhanced Internet connectivity and easy communications between people in the inter-networking realm of cyberspace.

9.3   Network Switches

A network switch is a computer networking device that connects network segments. There are basically two types of switches, unmanaged and managed.

An unmanaged switch works right out of the box. It's not designed to be configured, so you don't have to worry about installing or setting it up correctly. Unmanaged switches have less network capacity than managed switches. You'll usually find unmanaged switches in home networking equipment.

Managed switches create a network. Routers connect networks. A router links computers to the Internet, so users can share the connection. A router acts as a dispatcher, choosing the best path for information to travel so it's received quickly.

Switches and routers are the building blocks for all business communications, from data to voice and video to wireless access. Switches are able to connect different types of networks, including Ethernet, Fibre Channel, ATM, ITU-T G.hn, and 802.11. Figure 9.4 shows a switched network topology.

9.3.1   Layer 1 Hubs

A network hub, or repeater, is a simple network device. Hubs do not manage any of the traffic that comes through them. Any packet entering a port is broadcast out or "repeated" on every other port, except for the port of entry. Since every packet is repeated on every other port, packet collisions affect the entire network, limiting its capacity.

There are specialized applications where a hub can be useful, such as copying traffic to multiple network sensors. High-end switches have a feature which does the same thing called port mirroring. The throughput of a hub is very limited. For

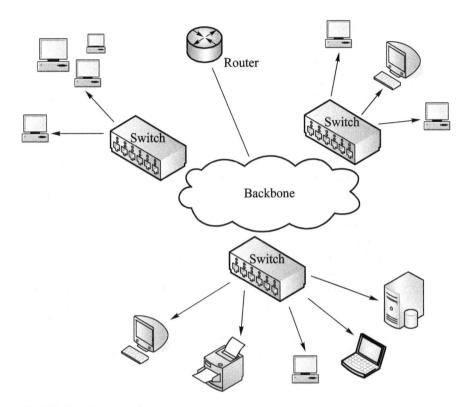

Fig. 9.4 Switched network topology

example, an 8-port hub connects to 100 Mb/s network using the uplink connector. Then each port can only have the maximum speed of 100 Mb/s/8 = 12.5 Mb/s.

Hubs and switches appear very much alike. Both also serve the same basic function, to provide a centralized connection for local networks and other network equipment. In fact, hubs and switches operate quite differently. Replacing a hub with a switch is definitely worthwhile.

A network hub is essentially a "dumb" device that has no knowledge of what devices are plugged into it, where data is coming from, or where it's going. Therefore, when Computer A sends data to Computer B through a hub, the hub simply retransmits, or "repeats," the data to each and every port in a process called a "broadcast." Each device connected to the hub then checks to see if the data, known as a frame, is addressed to it in order to determine whether to accept or ignore it.

The problem is that the hub's "send everything to everyone" approach is that it generates lots of unnecessary network traffic, which in turn causes network congestion and seriously limits performance. Since all devices connected to a hub must take turns sending or receiving data, they spend lots of time waiting for network access or retransmitting data that was stepped on by another transmission. The lights on a hub indicate such "collisions."

9.3.2   Ethernet Switch

A network switch is an intelligent device that can actively manage the data going through it. Unlike a hub, a switch knows which computers are connected to each of its ports as well as the source and destination address of each data frame it encounters. The switch identifies each computer by its unique MAC address.

When Computer A sends data to Computer B over a switch, the switch sends only the data to the port Computer B is connected to. This limits unnecessary traffic, provides better performance, and leaves other devices connected to the switch free to simultaneously communicate via their respective ports. So even while Computer A and Computer B are exchanging data, Computer C and Computer D (and may be others) can still transmit and receive data.

In addition, a hub is a shared-bandwidth device. It provides 10 Mb/s or 100 Mb/s of total data throughput that's shared among all of its ports. Each port on a switch gets portion of the 10 Mb/s or 100 Mb/s of bandwidth.

Switches were considerably more expensive than hubs, so the hub was commonly used in situations where cost was as important a consideration as performance. Nowadays, switches have become quite inexpensive and common. A basic 16 port 10/100 Mb/s switch can be had for as little as $60. While faster gigabit (1000 Mb/s) switches and those that provide more advanced features such as data prioritization or network management do cost more, they're still relatively inexpensive.

9.3.3   Virtual Switches

Virtual switches enable network components, such as virtual machines, to communicate with each other. Additionally, a virtual machine and its associated virtualized network adapter are connected to a switch. This requires creating virtual switches with a hypervisor, which hosts multiple virtual machines on a single piece of computer hardware. They are also similar to physical switches in being isolated, which thwarts virtual machines from sharing resources with each other. Additionally, virtual switches can help with the migration of virtual machines across physical hosts by eliminating the need to reconfigure each virtual machine. They can also enhance operational efficiency, improve communications, and scale system bandwidth capacity.

9.4   Routers

Routers are one of the most critical components involved in the success of the Internet. They allow for packets to flow from source to destination with little delay. The process used is packet switching, which builds a virtual circuit between two connection points. While other protocols, standards, and technologies are a major part of the Internet that we enjoy today, the router has to be credited with the Internet's existence. The device allows network engineers to break large networks into smaller logical sub-networks. Then these routing devices are able to communicate with each other to ensure that packets can traverse the Internet and reach their ultimate destination. The Internet has truly made the world a smaller place and has allowed efficient communications between any two locations in the world. On the other hand, routers are vulnerable to all kinds of intruders. The solution to security on the Internet is often attributed to firewalls and anti-virus programs. Perhaps the routers themselves can also play a critical role in network security.

A router is a device that forwards data packets between computer networks, creating an overlay inter-network. A router is connected to two or more data links from different networks. When a data packet comes in from one of the links, the router reads the address information in the packet to determine its ultimate destination. Then, using information in its routing table or routing policy, it directs the packet to the next network on its journey. Routers perform the "traffic directing" functions on the Internet. A data packet is typically forwarded from one router to another through the networks that constitute the inter-networking until it gets to its destination node.

The most familiar type of routers are home and small office routers that simply pass data, such as web pages and E-mail, between the home computers and the owner's cable or fiber-optic modem, which connects to the Internet (ISP). However more sophisticated routers range from enterprise routers which connect large business or ISP networks up to the powerful core routers that forward data at high speed along the optical fiber lines of the Internet backbone.

9.4.1 History of Routers

Much of the credit for the invention of the router is unfairly given solely to Cisco systems, but it is important to also credit William Yeager. He was a researcher at Leland Stanford Junior University when in 1980 his boss assigned him the task of connecting the computer science department, medical center, and the department of electrical engineering. His first router operated on a 3-megabit Ethernet. He later updated his routing system to function with the Internet protocol (IP).

Shortly after Yeager created his routing configuration, Len Bosak and Sandy Lerner started a company called Cisco. They also worked with Yeager and were provided access to his code and improved upon it. They released the first commercially available router product, and Hewlett-Packard was their first customer. Cisco went on to become the largest distributor of routing products.

9.4.2   Architecture

Routers range in size from small home devices to large rack mounted units. The larger units are extremely costly, but can handle a high rate of traffic. Cisco CRS-1 is capable of routing 40 gigabits per slot and has a capability of housing 16 slots. The CRS series of router can even be run in a multi-rack configuration with a total routing capability of up to 92 terabits per second. Obviously, this type of router is intended for a location that is processing tremendous traffic.

Figure 9.5 shows the system architecture of Cisco CRS-1 router. There are mainly three components inside the router: router processors, multi-stage switch fabric, and 40 Gb/s link cards.

A line card consists of interface module and modular services card (MSC). The interface module provides the physical connections to the network. The module services card is a high-performance layer 3 forwarding engine. Each MSC is equipped with two high-performance Cisco Silicon Packet Processors (SPP). The SPP is a sophisticated ASIC consisting of 188 32-bit RISC processors per chip with 40 Gb/s processing power.

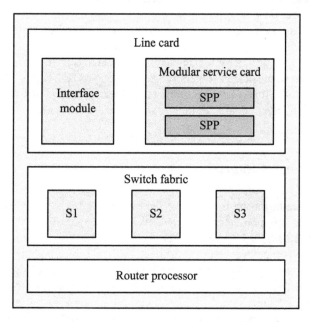

Fig. 9.5 Cisco CRS-1 architecture

The switch fabric provides the communications path between line cards and is a three-stage, self-routed architecture with 1296 × 1296 buffering. The three stages of switching are as follows:

- S1 is connected to the ingress link card.
- S2 supports multicast replication.
- S3 connected to the egress line card.

The route processor is available to execute algorithms such as Border Gateway Protocol (BGP) and supports up to 4 GB DRAM, 40 GB hard drive (HDD), and 2×|32 GB solid-state drive (SSD). The system software is built on memory-protected software architecture.

Most office routers are nothing more than a specialized computer that is optimized for the function of routing traffic at a highly efficient rate. A router generally contains seven major internal components: CPU, RAM, NVRAM, flash memory, ROM, console, and interfaces. The router itself can have one or more different types of interfaces such as fiber optic, coaxial, and Ethernet. The Ethernet connection is one of the most common types of interfaces.

The smaller home routers are better suited for handling a few computers, but still offer many advanced features. A Linksys E-series router has integrated switch ports. In some models these ports are as fast as 1000 megabits per second. This unit is also capable of connecting to both wired and wireless devices. This is because a wireless access point (WAP) is built inside.

In order to allow for inter-networking, routers have to accomplish a few fundamental tasks. Stallings lists the following essential functions:

- Connect or link multiple networks.
- Route and deliver data between the end systems attached to the networks.
- Not require modification of architecture of the attached networks in order to accomplish these tasks.

Routers are fundamentally different from other networking devices such as hubs, switches, and bridges. This is because routers provide the inter-networking capabilities, while these other devices are used to segment a single network. Figure 9.6 shows a diagram of a simple inter-networking that includes a switch. The router is the device that is connecting the two networks and creating an Inter-network between them.

9.4.3 Internet Protocol Version 4

At the core of a router is a simple process. When a packet arrives at an input port, the processor makes a decision on where the packet is to be directed and sets the switch to direct the packet to the correct output port. In order to be able to make these routing decisions, a router must function on protocols. If it were not for standardized protocols, the Internet would not be where it is today. These protocols

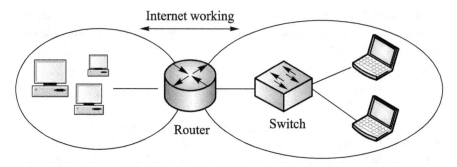

Fig. 9.6 Inter-networking diagram

allow devices from different vendors to transmit data with confidence to another device knowing that the other device will be able to understand the message and reply. There are many different protocols, but the following are some of the most important to understand.

The Internet protocol version 4 (IPv4) is an open systems interconnection (OSI) layer 3 addressing protocol that uses 32-bits to identify a device. All packets sent on the network contain a header for layer 3 addressing. The address is similar to an address for a house, and the packet is like a letter that is being mailed by the postal system. Routers use this addressing to determine which network the packet belongs to. This is because the packet is split into two different portions, the network bits and the host bits. To identify which portion is network and which is host, a number called a subnet mask is configured on the computer or router. There is a one-to-one correlation between the bits in the IPv4 address and the subnet mask. All address bits that correspond with a binary 1 in the subnet-mask are part of the network. All bits that line up with a 0 are the host bits.

Routers use IP addresses to send packets to other routers. Routing protocols help the router make the decision on the best path to take. IPv4 itself does have built-in security. Therefore, the network administrator can configure the router to use access control lists (ACL) to block or allow specific addresses. This can allow an administrator to segment their network into different layers. One suggested method is to divide a network into a public, application, and data layer. Then servers can be placed in one of the three layers based on which systems will be able to reach the server. In some cases, this access control measure is only slightly protective, because an attacker can spoof an IP address and pretend to be an authorized machine.

A better method of providing security with IPv4 is through the use of IP security (IPSec), which allows for both authentication and confidentiality. When IPSec is implemented in a firewall or a router, it provides strong security that can be applied to all traffic crossing the perimeter. IPSec allows, with the use of authentication headers (AH), for two hosts to prove their authenticity. This provides assurance that the device on the other end is the intended recipient. IPSec also allows, with the use of encapsulating security payload (ESP), for the IP packet's data to be encrypted. This ensures that only the intended recipient can view the traffic. IPSec is an excellent choice to use when traffic over an unsecure network of routers is necessary. IPSec is a technology that came about to solve the need for security and is not being currently used by most home users and many enterprise users.

9.4.4   Internet Protocol Version 6

Due to IPv4 only using 32-bit for addressing, there are not enough unique addresses to assign to every public device on the Internet. $2^{32} \approx 2^2 \times (2^{10})^3$ is roughly four billion (4×10^9). Many have been able to stretch the life of IPv4 by using technologies such as network address translation (NAT) along with private IPv4 addresses, but this is not a permanent solution to the problem. The real solution is to use a larger address space. IPv6 solves this problem by using 128-bit for an address ($2^{128} \approx 3.4 \times 10^{38}$) theoretically. In addition to solving the issue of the number of addresses, IPv6 is also including IPSec as part of the protocol's standard. This will ensure that IPv6 traffic through a router is secure from sniffing attacks.

More and more modern routers are being made with IPv6 capabilities built in, but many older devices are not ready for the IPv6 transition. It is important to upgrade older routers to support IPv6 in order to take advantage of these new capabilities. It may be advantageous to upgrade older routers because newer routers include advanced security features.

9.4.5   Open Shortest Path First

Another dynamic routing protocol that is used by routers is open shortest path first (OSPF), which uses the Dijkstra algorithm. This protocol will calculate the shortest path first and then create the routing table, which will result in the best path for network traffic.

The Dijkstra algorithm involves the process of checking the difference between every link in search of the quickest route. This process is repeated on each link or series of links until a table is built that identifies the cost associated with each path. The router can use this table to find the best route for each packet that it processes. OSPF takes advantage of the Dijkstra algorithm in order to ensure that traffic can travel on the quickest router to its final destination. It is important for a router to have a clear and correct routing table so that it can maintain a fast processing rate.

In Fig. 9.7, for example, to find the shortest path from vertex $n1$ to vertex $n7$, the Dijkstra algorithm provides a way by just looking one step ahead to find the

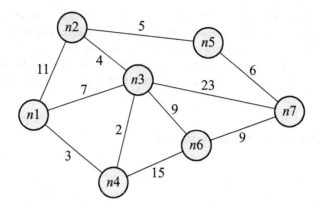

Fig. 9.7 The shortest path algorithm

solution. This is particular useful for writing a program running on computers. The conceptual algorithm is as follows:

```
1   function Dijkstra (Graph, Source):
2       for each vertex v in Graph:
                            // Initializations
3           dist [v] := infinity;
            // Unknown distance function from source to v
4           previous [v] := undefined:
                // Previous node in optimal path from
                source
5       end for;

6       dist [source] := 0;
                // Distance from source to source
7       Q := the set of all nodes in Graph;
                // All nodes in the graph are unoptimized

8       while Q is not empty:      // The main loop
9           u := vertex in Q with smallest distance in
            dist[];
10          if dist [u] = infinity:
11              break; // inaccessible from source
12              end if ;
13              remove u from Q ;

14              for each neighbor v of u:
            // where v has not yet been removed from Q.
15                  alt := dist [u] + dist_between (u, v);
16                  if alt < dist [v]:  // Relax (u,v,a)
17                      dist [v] := alt ;
```

(continued)

```
18                         previous [v] := u;
19                         decrease-key v in Q;
                              // Reorder v in the Queue
20               end if;
21            end for;
22         end while;
23      return dist [];
24 end Dijkstra.|
```

When the program runs, it checks the neighbor (v) of the current vertex (u) to see whether distance from the current vertex (u) plus the distance between u and the neighbor (v) is the smallest. If neighbor (v) has another path which is greater than the sum of the distance u plus the distance between u and v, then the distance for the neighbor (v) is updated with the small value.

```
for each neighbor v of u:
    alt := dist [u] + dist_between (u, v);
    if alt < dist [v];
        dist [v] := alt ;|
    end if;
end for;
```

Using Dijkstra's shortest path algorithm, the shortest path from $n1$ to $n7$ can be obtained as follows:

Starting from $n1$, initially the shortest path from $n1$ to $n2$, $n3$, and $n4$ is 11, 7, and 3, respectively. This is shown in Fig. 9.8a. However, there is another path $n1 \rightarrow n4 \rightarrow n3$; its cost is less than $n1 \rightarrow n3$ directly. So, we take the better one (3+2) shown in Fig. 9.8b. Next, we found out that $n3 \rightarrow n2$ is better than $n1 \rightarrow n2$. So, we take the new value of 9, shown in Fig. 9.8c. Continuing the loop statement, we got the shortest path from $n1$ to $n7$ is 20 ($n1 \rightarrow n4 \rightarrow n3 \rightarrow n2 \rightarrow n5 \rightarrow n7$) shown in Fig. 9.8d.

9.4.6 Throughput and Delay

The two most important factors for a router are to find the best route and to have highest throughput. The Dijkstra algorithm answers the first question. To increase the throughput, we need to look at how to reduce the delay while a packet at a router. We will use the M/M/1 model that we discussed in Chap. 8 to look into the problem. Figure 8.10 shows a single queue single server system.

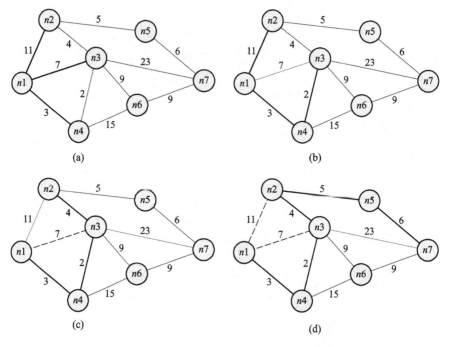

Fig. 9.8 Dijkstra's shortest path algorithm. (**a**) initial value. (**b**) update $n1 \rightarrow n3$. (**c**) update $n1 \rightarrow n2$. (**d**) final

Here we define traffic intensity

$$\rho = \frac{\lambda}{\mu}(<1) \qquad (9.1)$$

The expected number of users N in the queue is given by

$$N = \frac{\rho}{1-\rho} \qquad (9.2)$$

The total expected waiting time (include queue and servers) is

$$T = \frac{1}{\mu - \lambda} \qquad (9.3)$$

To verify the equations are correct, first look at Eq. (9.2). When the arrival rate λ is approaching to the processing rate μ, then the traffic intensity is approaching to the limit $\rho \rightarrow 1$. When ρ is approaching to 1, the number of users in the queue N is approaching to infinity. This means that more and more packets will wait in the queue not being processed. For Eq. (9.3), when the arrival rate λ is approaching to the processing rate μ, then the waiting time T is approaching to infinity. This means packets will stay in the queue forever. Ideally the arrival rate λ should be less than the processing rate μ. In practice ρ should be no keep no more than 80% to get the best performance. If traffic intensity reaches 90% or higher, then the waiting time will increase dramatically.

9.5 Gateways

In a communications network, gateway is a network node that is used for interfacing with another network that uses different protocols. A gateway may contain devices such as protocol translators, impedance matching devices, rate converters, fault isolators, or signal translators as necessary to provide system interoperability. It also requires the establishment of mutually acceptable administrative procedures between both networks. A protocol translation/mapping gateway interconnects networks with different network protocol technologies by performing the required protocol conversions. Gateways, also called protocol converters, can operate at any network layer. The activities of a gateway are more complex than that of the router or switch as it communicates using more than one protocol.

For the TCP/IP network, a gateway is a node that serves as an access point to another network. A default gateway on a network is a node that routes traffic from a workstation to another network segment. The default gateway commonly connects the internal networks and the outside network. Sometime the gateway node could also act as a proxy server and a firewall. The gateway is also associated with both a router, which uses headers and forwarding table to determine where packers are sent, and a switch, which provides the actual path to the packet in and out of the gateway. In other words, a default gateway provides an entry point and an exit point in a network.

9.6 Wireless Networks and Network Address Translation

Wireless network by its name is a computer network without using any cables. Data are transmitted and received through radio signals in the air. It is easy to set up and cost less money than Ethernet networks.

Wireless local area network is the technology that is rapidly improving and quickly being adopted by IT industries and professionals. The study of wireless LAN includes definitions, history, architecture, protocols, war driving, and security issues. The study on network address translation (NAT) includes configurations, administration, and security issues.

The modern IT industry needs professionals with understanding of the IT communications, structural design, computer hardware, software, networking, new concepts, and tools. Some of the notions were most significant and considerable to the growing IT industry. The use of wireless networks extended in a way that it has become part of our life. It is essential to the IT professionals to understand the basics of wireless networking.

9.6.1 Wireless Networks

A typical wireless local area network is a network, which is connecting multiple devices or computers with no wires. It uses spread-spectrum technology which is radio waves to connect among devices in a limited region. It became popular because of the portability and simplicity of installation. Businesses like McDonald's, Starbucks, and shopping malls have begun to offer wireless access to their customers.

Wireless LAN (WLAN) connects multiple computers or devices in short distance. It connects to the Internet through a router or access point. The spread-spectrum technologies give portability to devices while remaining connected to the network. 802.11 comes with several flavors of 802.11a and transmits at 5 GHz and may increase up to 54 megabits of data/sec. WLAN uses orthogonal frequency-division multiplexing or OFDM technology. Table 9.1 compares different wireless networks.

Wireless personal area network (WPAN) connects multiple devices in comparatively shorter area (Fig. 9.9). For instance, many of us use Bluetooth headset which uses invisible Infrared light to connect to your phone or computer. WPAN equipped devices becoming more popular nowadays because of the size and price of the device.

Wireless metropolitan area network (WMAN) connects numerous wireless networks (Fig. 9.10). For instance, WiMax which is a WMAN established by IEEE 802.16 standards.

Wireless wide area network (WWAN) covers huge areas, long distances like from cities, states, and countries. These types of networks use point to point microwave links using parabolic dishes on the 2.4 GHz band where MAN and WAN uses antennas. A WWAN include base station gateways, access points, and wireless

Table 9.1 Different wireless networks

	PAN	LAN	MAN	WAN
Standards	Bluetooth	801.11 HiperLan2	802.11 WiMAX(.16)	GSM, GRPS CDMA, 3G/4G/5G
Speeds	<1 Mb/s	11~54 Mb/s	11~100+ Mb/s	10 ~ 384 Kb/s 1.8/3.6~7.2 M
Range	Short	Medium	Medium-Long	Long
Application	Peer-to-Peer Device-Device	Enterprise Networks	E1 replacement Last mile	Mobile Phones Cellular data

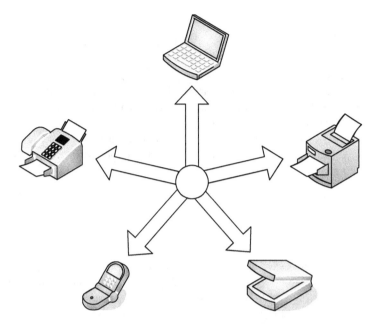

Fig. 9.9 Wireless personal area networks

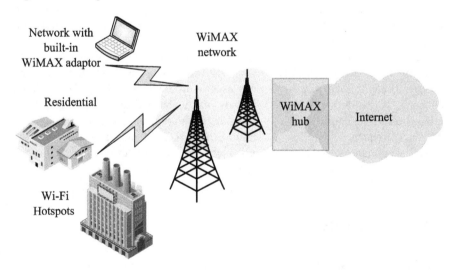

Fig. 9.10 Wireless metropolitan area network

bridging relays, for example, cellular networks GSM, GPRS, 3G, 4G, 4G LTE, and 5G.

Wireless mesh networks are created by radio nodes and structured by a mesh topology. Every node can send messages on behalf of other nodes. If the power is lost it has the capability to re-route to another node.

Cell phone networks:

- Personal communications service (PCS) uses a radio band that can be used by mobile phones in North America and South Asia. For example, Sprint first established a PCS network.
- Digital advanced mobile phone service (D-AMPS) is an upgraded version of AMPS and is being phased out due to advancement in technology. The newer GSM networks are replacing the older system.
- Global system mobile (GSM) is divided in to three parts such as switching, base station and operation support systems. It is a common standard for most cell phone companies.

9.6.2 Bluetooth

Bluetooth is a radio wave technology designed for communicating over short distances less than about 10 m or 30 ft.[1] Typically, to download photos from a digital camera to a PC, to hook up a wireless mouse to a laptop, to link a hands-free headset to your cellphone so you can talk and drive safely at the same time, and so on. Generally, Bluetooth devices fall into one of three classes: class 1 are the most powerful and can operate up to 100 m (330 ft), class 2 (the most common kind) operate up to 10 m (33 ft), and class 3 are the least powerful and don't go much beyond 1m (3.3 ft).

Bluetooth devices automatically detect and connect to one another, and up to eight of them can communicate at any one time. They don't interfere with one another because each pair of devices uses a different one of the 79 available channels. If two devices want to talk, they pick a channel randomly and, if that's already taken, randomly switch to one of the others (a technique known as spread-spectrum frequency hopping). To minimize the risks of interference from other electrical appliances (and also to improve security), pairs of devices constantly shift the frequency they are using—thousands of times a second.

9.6.3 Wireless Protocols

IEEE 802.11 is a set of standards for implementing wireless local area network (WLAN) computer communication. IEEE 802.11 is a subset of IEEE 802 which is the standard for LAN and MAN. The 802.11 standard (Table 9.2) provides the foundation for wireless network products using the Wi-Fi band.

---

[1] ☉ 1 ft=0.3048 m.

Table 9.2 Different 802.11 standards

Protocol	Release date	Op. Frequency	Date rate (Typical)	Date rate (Max)	Range (Indoor)
802.11 Legacy	1997	2.4~2.5 GHz	1 Mb/s	2 Mb/s	
802.11b	1999	2.4-2.5 GHz	6.5 Mb/s	11 Mb/s	~ 50 m (~ 150 ft)
802.11g	2003	2.4~2.5 GHz	11 Mb/s	54 Mb/s	~ 30 m (~100 ft)
802.11n	2009	2.4 GHz or 5 GHz	200 Mb/s	540 Mb/s	~50 m (~150 ft)
802.11ad	2012	60 GHz	5 Gb/s	6.7 Gb/s	33 ft

- 802.11 legacy   It is now obsolete. It is the original version of the standard IEEE 802.11 first invented in 1997. It can transfer data up to 2 Mb/s. It has three physical layer technologies:

  – Diffuse infrared operating at 1 Mb/s.
  – Frequency-hopping spread spectrum up to 2 Mb/s.
  – Direct-sequence spread spectrum up to 2 Mb/s.

- 802.11b   The highest data transfer rate is 11 Mb/s. It uses the media access method which is the same as the original standard and direct extension of the modulation technique. It first came into the market at 2000. This technology is widely accepted in the market because of its lower price and has an increased throughput compared to the original standard, but it has interference issues with other products operating in the 2.4 GHz band such as microwave ovens, Bluetooth devices, baby monitors, and cordless telephones.
- 802.11g   802.11g first came out at 2003 and has less interference issues with 2.4 GHz band products like the 802.11b has. It uses the same OFDM method like 802.11a. It has a maximum speed of 54 Mb/s at physical layer. 802.11g has an average throughput of 22 Mb/s, and it is backward compatible with 802.11b. 802.11g standard was widely accepted by customers because of the cost and faster data transfer rate. End of 2003, the majority of dual-band 802.11a/b products become dual-band/tri-mode which means a NIC card or router will support all 802.11a, 802.11b, and 802.11g.
- 802.11a   It uses data link layer protocol. 802.11 is a protocol which can transmit at 5 GHz to 54 Mb/s of data. It applies orthogonal frequency-division multiplexing (OFDM), which splits that radio signal into numerous sub-signals before they reach a receiver. The range of 802.11a is less than 802.11b/g. 802.11a signal is absorbed more by buildings and solid objects in their way to smaller wavelength.
- 802.11n   In 2009, 802.11n came out with better performance than the previous versions of a, b, and g. It has new multiple-input multiple-output antennas (MIMO) which previous versions did not have. 802.11n are able to works with 2.4 GHz band product with lesser interference.
- 802.11ad   The 802.11ad specification operates in the 60 GHz frequency band, as opposed to earlier 802.11 specifications such as 802.11ac, which operates in the

5 GHz range, and 802.11n, which operates in both the 5 GHz and 2.4 GHz ranges. It is also designed to offer much higher transfer rates than previous 802.11 specs, with a theoretical maximum transfer rate of up to 6.7 Gb/s but with much shorter distance (10 m).

9.6.4   WLAN Handshaking, War Driving, and WLAN Security

Below is the handshaking process when browsing the web using WLAN:

- Wireless NIC card sends out a radio signal to search for local router.
- When the router is found, then router takes the instruction and sends it to a gateway server using WAP.
- Then the gateway server regains the data using HTTP.
- The gateway server encodes the HTTP data as WML.
- The WML-encoded data is sent back to the client computer.
- Then the page is ready to be viewed.

The WLANs became popular because of convenience, cost efficiency, portability, and simplicity of incorporation with other network devices and access points. Mostly newly computer comes with WLAN adapters. Some of the benefits include:

- Portability   Users can easily move around with the laptops or smartphones. Users can access the Internet even when they are outside of the home networks. Many restaurants, hotels, and shopping malls offer free Wi-Fi connections. A user can buy a 4G air card from cellular carriers and enjoy high-speed Internet almost anywhere.
- Pricing   The cost of wireless products is little bit higher than wired products. The Wi-Fi devices price is continuously decreasing.
- Productivity   It is to be seen that in Starbucks, McDonald's, Wendy's, and Taco Bell, employees use wireless headsets to take customers with faster than traditional speed.
- Installation   To set up a wireless network requires setting up wireless routers, switches, and antennas. But wired networks are hard to install, and many times it is hard to take connections from one building to others.
- Expandability   The network admin can easily increase connections using the existing equipment. But in wired network, new employees will require extra cabling.

Years ago, two people drove around the city with laptop computers. They went to different areas where wireless networks were detected and started capturing packets using their pre-configured laptop. They used the software named NetStumbler 0.4.0, and they captured 802.11b/g packets using Link Ferret 3.10 software. They had found roughly 50% of the wireless traffic is not encrypted. Among the 50% encrypted wireless networks, some are encrypted with WEP. The 104-bit WEP key can be easily cracked by using Aircrack 2.1 software or many others that can be downloaded free from the Internet.

Wireless gateway attacks and rogue access point installation are among some common attacks on wireless networks. A hacker may set a proxy server in between the wireless client and gateway. When a user tries to connect to the Internet using wireless NIC card, it will connect to the proxy instead. The proxy will establish a secure socket layer (SSL) connection. Next, the proxy will create an SSL connection to the wireless gateway. The hacker will see the wireless gateway and authenticate to it without the owner's knowledge.

DoS attacks and session hijacking are other types of attacks. The hackers can insert traffic into the radio network without login into a wireless router. The 802.11 MAC is designed to allow multiple networks to share the same space and radio channels. DoS attacks can be done to WLANs to overwhelm networks.

In MAC spoofing attack, the hacker is able to change the MAC or Ethernet address of a wireless NIC card, by using software such as MAC Makeup.

In address resolution protocol (ARP) poisoning, that can be done using Cain and Abel software, an attacker can exploit the ARP cache and intercept network traffic between two computers in the network.

9.6.5 Security Measures to Reduce Wireless Attacks

Here are some security measures recommended to reduce being a victim of wireless attacks:

- Use WPA with TKIP/AES and use the CCMP with AES in future.
- Turn off the SSID broadcast.
- Change default SSID.
- Change default IP address.
- Change default login/password.
- Use MAC filtering in AP level or in RADIUS server.
- Position and shield the antenna to direct the radio waves to a limited space.
- Use limited DHCP clients to control the number of users that may connect to the WLAN.
- Use firewall between AP and the wired LAN to secure the wired LAN from further intrusion.
- Enable the accounting and logging to locate and trace.
- Use good intrusion detection software to monitor the network activity.
- Use VPN, IPSec, and secure tunneling.
- Use honey pots or fake APs in the regular network to confuse the hacker.
- Use biometric authentication such as fingerprinting.
- Update drivers and firmware of the routers.
- Use strong passwords

Fig. 9.11 An example of
MiFi device

9.6.6   The Future of Wireless Network

The future of WLAN will change because of the success of wireless air-cards or portable hotspots which use 3G, 4G, WiMAX, or 5G cellular networks. Telecoms are rapidly improving the speeds of their networks with fourth-generation technology. Some people claim that MiFi, a device that can support up to five users to access Internet through cellular network (Fig. 9.11), could eventually replace wired broadband subscriptions in the same way that Americans are canceling home phone lines in favor of cell phones.

The future wireless networks are expected to be a meeting of different kinds of wireless technologies, such as cellular technologies, wireless local area networks, wireless metropolitan area networks, wireless sensor networks, and traditional wired networks.

Although users will be oblivious to the specific underlying network being used by their applications, the networks should be able to provide the resource (bandwidth) with guaranteed quality of service (QoS). Users should be able to move seamlessly among different networking technologies, e.g., among Ethernet, WLANs, WiMAX, and 2G/3G/4G/LTE/5G, with stringent QoS requirements.

- Mobility   The existing Internet which is built for stationary end-hosts does not handle mobility easily within the Internet architecture. The issue of mobility relates to handling changes in location and underlying network connectivity of mobile end-systems at each protocol layer.
- Multi-homing   In the past, most hosts/nodes or computers had only one networking interface. Hosts stayed within one network with one egress path. However, multi-homed hosts or devices having multiple networking interfaces are becoming more common.
- Routing scalability   A common solution for IP network sites to allow changing their service providers is to use Provider-independent (PI) addresses. However, these addresses are not aggregatable and lead to an exponential increase in size of the routing table.
- Deploy ability   To deploy new system from the scratch can be hectic. Many times companies lack an appropriate and realistic deployment plan.

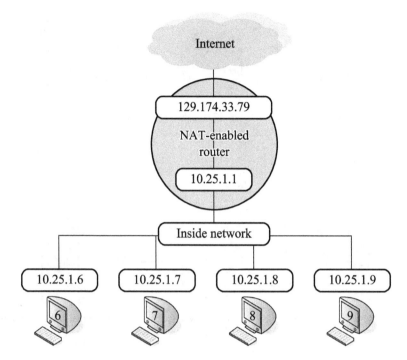

Fig. 9.12 A wireless router with NAT

9.6.7 Network Address Translation

Network address translation (NAT) used a set IP addresses for internal and external traffic. NAT acts as a mediator between the Internet and LAN. It uses only one IP address for an entire LAN (Fig. 9.12). It is a solution to the shortage of IP addresses also. NAT has three functionalities:

- It hides the internal IP and act as a firewall.
- It organizes the use of internal IP and removes IP conflict with other networks.
- It can join numerous ISDN connections to a single Internet connection.

The router in Fig. 9.12 uses the IP 10.25.1.1 for the inside and 129.174. 33.79 for outside network. When users try to connect to the Internet from any of these computers, the NAT will convert the 10.25.1.x to 129.174.33.79.

Static NAT changes an unregistered IP address to registered IP. It is useful when someone from outside is trying to access inside network. Dynamic NAT changes a registered IP address to an unregistered IP. Figure 9.13 shows the static (a) and dynamic (b) address translation.

Dynamic NAT acts as a firewall between a client computer and the Internet. Outside users can only connect to the inside computer by using NAT. NAT prevents

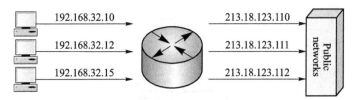

(a) Using static NAT, 192.168.32.12 will always translate to 213.18.123.111

213.18.123.112 | 192.168.32.12
213.18.123.113 | 192.168.32.31
213.18.123.114 | 192.168.32. 7
213.18.123.115 | 192.168.32.11
213.18.123.116 | 192.168.32.10

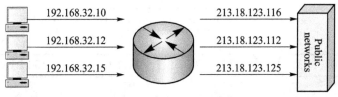

(b) Using a dynamic NAT, 192.168.32.15 will translate to the first available address in the range from 213.18.123.100 to 213.18.123.150

Fig. 9.13   NAT address translations

outside users to access inside computers directly but let inside computers connect to the Internet.

Static NAT allows external devices to initiate connections to computers on the stub domain. It allows a host in stub domain to keep a specific IP address when connecting to the Internet.

9.6.8   *Environmental and Health Concerns Using Cellular and Wireless Devices*

There have been increased concerns about the safety of wireless communication. National Cancer Institute (NCI) at the National Institute of Health (NIH) has the following statements regarding the cell phone with cancer risk:

- Cell phones emit radio-frequency energy, a form of non-ionizing electromagnetic radiation, which can be absorbed by tissues closest to where the phone is held.
- The amount of radio-frequency energy a cell phone user is exposed to depends on the technology of the phone, the distance between the phone's antenna and the user, the extent and type of use, and the user's distance from cell phone towers.

- Studies thus far have not shown a consistent link between cell phone use and cancers of the brain, nerves, or other tissues of the head or neck. More research is needed because cell phone technology and how people use cell phones have been changing rapidly.

A team of 31 scientists from 14 countries, including the United States, made the decision after reviewing peer-reviewed studies on cell phone safety. The team found enough evidence to categorize personal exposure as "possibly carcinogenic to humans." The type of radiation coming out of a cell phone is called non-ionizing. It is not like an X-ray, but more like a very low-powered microwave oven.

What microwave radiation does in most simplistic terms is similar to what happens to food in microwaves, essentially cooking the brain. So, in addition to leading to a development of cancer and tumors, there could be a whole host of other effects like cognitive memory function, since the memory temporal lobes are where we hold our cell phones.

The European Environmental Agency has pushed for more studies, saying cell phones could be as big a public health risk as smoking, asbestos, and leaded gasoline. The head of a prominent Cancer Research Institute at the University of Pittsburgh sent a memo to all employees urging them to limit cell phone use because of a possible risk of cancer.

"When you look at cancer development—particularly brain cancer—it takes a long time to develop. I think it is a good idea to give the public some sort of warning that long-term exposure to radiation from your cell phone could possibly cause cancer." A statement from a professor who has studied radiation for more than 30 years.

Results from the largest international study on cell phones and cancer were released in 2010. It showed participants in the study who used a cell phone for 10 years or more had doubled the rate of brain glioma, a type of tumor. Children's skulls and scalps are thinner. So, the radiation can penetrate deeper into the brain of children and young adults. Their cells are at a dividing faster rate, so the impact of radiation can be much larger.

The Apple iPhone safety manual says users' radiation exposure should not exceed FCC guidelines: "When using iPhone near your body for voice calls or for wireless data transmission over a cellular network, keep iPhone at least 15 mm (5/8 in^2) away from the body."

Former BlackBerry Bold advises users to "keep the BlackBerry device at least 0.98 in (25 mm) from your body when the BlackBerry device is transmitting."

The logic behind such recommendations is that the further the phone is from the body, the less radiation is absorbed. Users can also use the speakerphone function or a wired earpiece to gain some distance. Users can text instead of talk if they want to keep the phone away from their faces.

---

[2] ① 1 in=25.4 mm.

9.7   Mobile Networks

Mobile networks are commonly referred to cellular networks that a physical device can be taken anywhere. Mobile networks consist of mobile systems and devices, mobile operating systems, mobile computing, cellular 3G, 4G, LTE, 5G networks, and mobile device management.

9.7.1   Modern Wireless and Mobile Networks

The first-generation (1G) mobile communications technologies are analog-based voice only service. They had limited capacity, serving only niche markets for the military, certain government agencies, and users in special industries. In the 1960s and 1970s, this service was geographically limited, and the mobile device was too large, so it was usually mounted in cars or trucks, and the smallest was a briefcase model. This form of mobile communications was certainly not ready for mass development, because of (I) the limited capacity to service the general population, (II) the limited technology capability to cover large areas, (III) the large size of the mobile device, and (IV) the high prices of mobile devices.

The second-generation (2G) digital network improved voice quality and increased capacity. The two widely deployed 2G systems are global system for mobile communication (GSM) and code-division multiple access (CDMA). While the 1G market was becoming saturated, the main technological problem was the limited capacity in 1G mobile communications systems. To solve this problem, we needed new technologies that allow multiple users to share a frequency channel at the same time. There were various such technologies available including time division multiple access (TDMA), frequency division multiple access (FDMA), and CDMA. These digital technologies made it possible to provide multiple access within a frequency band.

The third-generation (3G) networks enhance voice and data services. The 2G was focused on delivering ubiquitous voice communications though GSM did have simple data delivery via short message service (SMS). With the 3G, ubiquitous communications had to encompass all media—voice, data, and video. The enabling technological advances such as Internet infrastructure, IP, and high-performance integrated circuit (IC) were making the 3G possible.

The fourth-generation (4G) technology allows wireless carriers to take advantage of greater download and upload speed. The 4G wireless networks aim at supporting various multiservice applications over IP architectures that satisfy enhanced users' demands through innovative services of increased quality of service (QoS). QoS can be assured through independent optimal design of network components or by optimizing interoperability. The supported services impose their classification into IP network service models and their specifications description. The integration of different wireless access technologies into the 4G network architecture leads to a heterogeneous network environment.

The long-term evolution (LTE) standard comes with increased performance. Today, mobile tools, such as smartphones and tablets, have become primary computing devices for many users. One mobile tool to satisfy this is the 4G network technology LTE-Advanced (LTE-A). LTE-A supports wider bandwidth (up to 120 MHz) than the bandwidth supported by LTE.

The fifth-generation (5G) mobile technology enables very high data rates, up to 10 Gb/s, with low latency. The coming generation, 5G, is aiming at the wider concept of the Internet of things (IoT). Fifth-generation cellular communication networks are going to revolutionize current life styles by providing ubiquitous and reliable communication. Thus, 5G platform can be defined as a cellular platform, which provides a ubiquitous, reliable, low-power, and high data rate mobile communication network between smarter devices.

9.7.2 3GPP Initiatives

The 3rd-generation partnership project (3GPP) unites telecommunications standard development organizations and produce the reports and specifications that define cellular telecommunications technologies, including radio access, core network, and service capabilities, which provide a complete system description for mobile telecommunications.

There are three technical specification groups (TSG) in 3GPP. They are:

- Radio access network (RAN).
- Services and systems aspects (SA).
- Core network and terminals (CT).

9.7.3 Long-Time Evolution

The long-time evolution (LTE) is the project name given to development of a high-performance air interface for cellular mobile communication systems. It is the final step toward the 4th-generation (4G) of radio technologies designed to increase the capacity and speed of mobile telephone networks. While the former generation of mobile telecommunication networks are collectively known as 2G or 3G, LTE is marketed as 4G.

According to 3GPP, the following set of advanced requirements was identified:

- Reduced cost per bit.
- Increased service provisioning—more services at lower cost with better user experience.
- Flexibility in terms using existing and new frequency band.

- Simplified architecture, open interface.
- Reasonable terminal power consumption.

LTE features a simplified network architecture, higher performance, and lower cost per bit. With the rapid dispatch of LTE deployments and the upgraded mobile user experience that it delivers, LTE is clearly emerging as a successful technology for mobile communications.

The uplink peak rate can reach over 50 Mb/s, and the downlink peak rate can be over 100 Mb/s. In order for high data link speed, LTE adapts new technologies that are new to 3G network such as orthogonal frequency division multiplexing (OFDM) and multiple-input multiple-output (MIMO). MIMO allows the use of more than one antenna at the transmitter and receiver for higher data transmission. The LTE bandwidth can be scalable from 1.25 to 20 MHz, satisfying the need of different network operators that may have different bandwidth allocations for services, based on its managed spectrum.

The universal terrestrial radio access network (UTRAN) is a core protocol for mobile networks that connects mobile handsets to the Internet. It connects the base stations, which are called Node B and radio network controllers (RNC). The evolved UTRAN (E-UTRAN) architecture has been improved dramatically from the 3G radio access network. The evolved base station eNB includes not only the NodeB but also the RNC.

LTE-Advanced is the real 4G standard and is a response to the rapidly growing traffic generated by the widespread adoption of smartphone devices. The new standards aim to achieve a higher level of system performance while maintaining backward compatibility. LTE comes with enhanced security using token-based authentication and strong data encryption.

9.7.4 Mobile 5G

The 5th-generation cellular communication networks are going to revolutionize communication by providing ubiquitous and more reliable communication. Internet of things (IoT) concept and tactile Internet are the major drivers for 5G communications and its use cases. Thus, 5G platform can be defined as a cellular platform that provides a ubiquitous, reliable, low-power and high data rate mobile communication network between smarter devices.

5G networks present the opportunity for the operators to launch new services efficiently and cost-effectively, which will create an ecosystem for technical and business innovation. Moreover, the 5G infrastructure provides customized network solutions to support vertical markets such as automotive, energy, food and agriculture, and healthcare. In addition, the higher efficiency of such 5G networks is essential to accelerate the delivery of services to all the involved stakeholders. Compared to the evolution of earlier generations of mobile networks, 5G networks require not only improved networking solutions but also involves sophisticated integration of massive computing and storage infrastructures.

Here is a list of high-level key performance indicators (KPI's) that are proposed for 5G:

- Providing 1000 times higher wireless area capacity and more varied service capabilities compared to current platforms.
- Saving up to 90% of energy per service provided.
- Reducing the average service creation time cycle from 90 h to 90 min.
- Creating a secure, reliable, and dependable Internet with a "zero perceived" downtime for services provision.
- Facilitating highly dense deployments of wireless communication links to connect over 7 trillion wireless devices serving over 7 billion people.
- Enabling advanced user-controlled privacy.

Some companies such as AT&T and Verizon have announced earlier launch of 5G network in 2020 with the peak data rate of 10 Gb/s, cell edge data rate 100 Mb/s, and latency less than 1 ms.

9.7.5 Security and Privacy

Network virtualization solutions address three important aspects: (I) access control, (II) path isolation, and (III) services edge. Access control provides secure and customized access for individuals and groups to protect the enterprise LAN from external cyber threats. The access control features usually include port authentication using standards such as IEEE 802.1x for strong connections between authorized users and VPNs and network admission control (NAC) to minimize security risks by removing harmful traffic. Path isolation maps validate users or devices to the correct secure set of available resources (virtual private network-VPN). Services edge provides access to services for legitimate sets of users and devices by using centralized policy enforcement.

Software-defined networking (SDN) is an umbrella term encompassing several kinds of network technologies aimed at making the network as agile and flexible as the virtualized server and storage infrastructure of the modern data center. The goal of SDN is to allow network engineers and administrators to respond quickly to changing business requirements. In a software-defined network, a network administrator can shape traffic from a centralized control console without using individual switches. In addition, it can deliver services to wherever they are needed in the network regardless of whether specific devices, servers, and other hardware components are connected. The key technologies for SDN implementation are functional separation, network virtualization, and automation through programmability.

Most cloud services provide IoT devices management and application program interface (API) support. The Amazon AWS IoT Device SDK helps to easily and quickly connect hardware device or mobile application to AWS IoT Core. The

AWS IoT Device SDK enables devices to connect, authenticate, and exchange messages with AWS IoT Core using the MQTT, HTTP, or WebSockets protocols. The AWS IoT Device SDK supports C, JavaScript, and Arduino and includes client libraries, developer guide, and porting guide for manufacturers. The AWS CloudWatch provides a centralized monitoring services for all devices and network usage.

9.8   Network Security

As Internet use has expanded over the decade with an overwhelming number of users. The crimes and ethical issues related to computing and its use have also become an issue. Organizations and Internet users implement different mechanisms to protect their information or data over the network from malicious users. Firewall technology is no doubt the widely used network equipment to detect and prevent attacks. Networks are inherently insecure. Therefore, strong security measures must be taken independently of the network to protect the components of the network as well as the data flowing through the network.

Since the frequency of attacks on networks have increased, denial of services (DoS) and IP spoofing are very common. DoS and distributed denial of services (DDoS) are major problems because they are very hard to be detected (Wang and Ledley 2013, 2007, 2006; Wang and Kelly 2017, 2015).

The prompt growth of computer networks has transformed the prospect of network security. An easy availability causes computer networks to be vulnerable against various and possibly devastating threats from hackers. Researchers have developed intrusion detection systems (IDS) capable of discovering attacks in numerous available environments. Intrusion prevention systems (IPS) evolved to resolve uncertainties in passive network monitoring by assigning detection systems on the line of attack. IDS and IPS are capable of providing prevention commands to firewalls and access control changes to routers. They can also make access control assessments based on application content, rather than IP address or ports as traditional firewalls do. The next advancement is the blend of IDS and IPS known as intrusion detection and prevention systems (IDPS) capable of identifying and averting attacks from happening.

9.8.1   Introduction

Internet has already become an essential part of our lives. It is where we work, shop, enjoy, or communicate with one another. It is where we access our banking records, credit card statements, tax returns, and other highly sensitive personal information. Regardless of the business, an increasing number of users on private networks are demanding access to Internet services. In addition, corporations want to offer websites for public access on the Internet. Moreover, its purpose and use are growing quickly and exponentially, and the need for security has also increased substantially over the years.

9.8.1.1 Network Security Basics

As the number of computer users all over the world has increased dramatically over the years, the numbers of malicious users and attackers have also increased. And that security has become one of the primary concerns when an individual or organization connects its computer or private network to the Internet. Network administrators, responsible for maintaining system efficiency and security, have an increasing concern about the security of their network when they expose private data and networking infrastructure to Internet malicious users. Thus, to provide the required level of protection, an organization needs a security policy to prevent unauthorized users from accessing resources on the private network and to protect against the unauthorized export of private information. Even if an organization is not connected to the Internet, it may still want to establish an Internal security policy to manage user access to portions of the network and protect sensitive or secret information.

A firewall is anything, whether hardware or software (or a combination of hardware and software), that can filter the transmission of packets of digital information as they attempt to pass through a boundary of a network. Figure 9.14 shows a diagram of firewall and network.

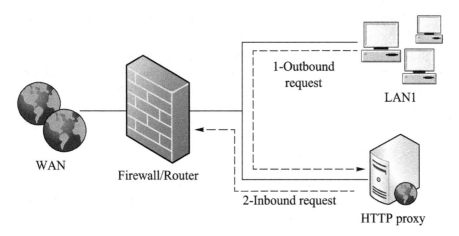

Fig. 9.14 Firewall and network

9.8.1.2 Information Hacking

It is difficult to describe a typical hacker attack because intruders have different levels of technical expertise and many different motivations. Some hackers are intrigued by the thrill or challenge involved, others just want to make life more difficult for others, and still others are out to steal sensitive data for profit or self-financial gains. Moreover, there are many sites which can teach how to hack, trace IP addresses, and port scanning and that the concern of security has increased. There are different categories of hackers:

- Neophyte hackers are a set of people who is full of stuff and enthusiasm but low on experience, usually hack for thrill.
- Script kiddy hackers are group of people who uses existing and frequently well-known and easy-to-find techniques and programs or scripts to search for and exploit weaknesses in other computers on the Internet—often randomly and with little regard or perhaps even understanding of the potentially harmful consequences.
- White hat hackers refer to an ethical hacker or a computer security expert, who specializes in penetration testing and in other testing methodologies to ensure the security of an organization's information systems.
- Gray hat hackers sometimes arguably act illegally, though in good will, or to how they disclose vulnerabilities. They usually do not hack for personal gain or have malicious intentions, but may be prepared to technically commit crimes during the course of their technological exploits in order to achieve better security.
- Blue hat hackers refer to outside computer security consulting firms that are employed to bug test a system prior to its launch, looking for exploits so they can be closed.
- Black hat hackers refer to hacker who breaks into a computer system or network with malicious intent or for self-financial gain.

System administrators and developers adopt different network security standards and mechanisms to prevent their network from different hackers and malicious users. One of the mechanisms used to protect private network from outside Internet network is Internet firewall.

9.8.1.3 Benefits of Using Firewalls

Firewalls are helping protect intrusions and provide a secure and reliable environment from unauthorized users. In addition, here are some of the benefits of having a firewall from security point of view:

- Monitor and record the access information to a network.
- Firewalls are used to secure and filter email viruses and malware attacks.
- Firewalls are used to give role-based access to different parts of a network and hence manage use of the resources on the network.

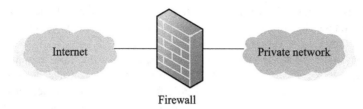

Fig. 9.15 Firewall in a network

- Firewalls allow calculate usage of the Internet, mainly to check individual users and performance effects.
- Allows manage and enforce computing ethics issues for an organization.

9.8.1.4 Firewall and Firewall Technologies

An Internet firewall is a system or group of systems that enforces a security policy between an organization's network and the Internet. The firewall determines which inside services may be accessed from the outside, which outsiders are permitted access to the permitted inside services, and which outside services may be accessed by insiders (see Fig. 9.15). It inspects all incoming traffic when it passes through it. The firewall must permit only authorized traffic to pass, and the firewall itself must be immune to penetration. Unfortunately, a firewall system cannot offer any protection once an attacker has gotten through or around the firewall. Firewalls offer a convenient point where Internet security can be monitored and alarms generated. It should be noted that for organizations that have connections to the Internet, the question is not whether but when attacks will occur.

Several types of firewall technologies are available. And their capabilities are also different based on the TCP/IP layer that each is able to examine. Firewalls can inspect application traffic and use it as the basis for policy. Basic firewalls operate on one or a few layers—typically the lower layers (Network layer and transport layer)—while more advanced firewalls examine all of the layers. Those firewalls that examine more layers can perform more granular and thorough examinations. Firewalls that understand the application layer can potentially accommodate advanced applications and protocols and provide services that are user-oriented. For example, a firewall that only handles lower layers cannot usually identify specific users, but a firewall with application layer capabilities can enforce user authentication and log events to specific users.

Firewalls are often placed at the perimeter of a network. Such a firewall can be said to have an external and internal interface, with the external interface being the one on the outside of the network. These two interfaces are sometimes referred to as unprotected and protected, respectively. Firewalls are often combined with other technologies as most notably routing. Many firewalls also include content filtering features to enforce organization policies not directly related to security.

Some firewalls include intrusion prevention system (IPS) technologies, which can react to attacks that they detect to prevent damage to systems protected by the firewall.

Firewall devices at the edge of a network are also sometimes required to do more than block unwanted traffic. A common requirement for these firewalls is to encrypt and decrypt specific network traffic flows between the protected network and external networks. This nearly always involves virtual private networks (VPN), which use additional protocols to encrypt traffic and provide user authentication and integrity checking. VPNs are most often used to provide secure network communications across not trusted networks.

9.8.2 Firewall Architecture

A firewall quality is measured by the components integrated inside it. A typical firewall is composed of one or more of the following building blocks in addition to the software enabling it:

- Packet filtering routers.
- Application level gateways or proxy server.
- Circuit-level gateway.

9.8.2.1 Packet Filtering Routers

A packet filtering router in firewalls make a permit or deny decision for each packet that it receives. The router examines every packet's header information to determine whether it matches one of its packet-filtering rules. The header information consists of the IP source address, the IP destination address, the encapsulated protocol (TCP, UDP, ICMP, or IP Tunnel), the TCP/UDP port source port, the TCP/UDP destination port, the ICMP message type, and the incoming interface of the packet. If a match is found and the rule permits the packet, the packet is forwarded according to the information in the routing table. If a match is found and the rule denies the packet, the packet is discarded. If there is no matching rule, a user-configurable default parameter determines whether the packet is forward or discarded. There are two types of packet filtering:

- Service-dependent filtering   The packet-filtering rules allow a router to permit or deny traffic based on a specific service, since most service listeners reside on well-known TCP/UDP port number. For example, a Telnet server listens for remote connections on port 23 an SMTP listens to port 25. Some typical filtering rules include:

   - Permit incoming Telnet sessions only to a specific list of internal hosts.
   - Permit incoming FTP sessions only to specific internal hosts
   - Deny all incoming traffic from specific external networks, etc.

- Service-independent filtering   These are used to filter attacks that are difficult to identify using basic packet header information because the attacks are service independent. Routers can be configured to protect these types of attacks, and they are difficult to specify. Some of these types of attacks include:
  - Source IP address spoofing attack.
  - Source routing attacks.
  - Tiny fragment attacks.

9.8.2.2   Application Level Gateways

Application level gateways are often referred to as a "bastion host" which is designated system that is specifically armored and protected against attacks. Application level gateways allow information to flow between systems but do not allow the direct exchange of packets, unlike packet filtering.

9.8.2.3   Circuit Level Gateways

A circuit level gateway is a specialized function that can be performed by an application level gateway. A circuit level gateway simply relays TCP connections without performing any additional packet processing or filtering.
  Here are some practical examples of firewalls:

- Packet-filtering router firewall   The most common Internet firewall system consists of a packet-filtering router deployed between a private network and the Internet (Fig. 9.16).
- Screened host firewall   Firewalls which employ both a packet-filtering router and an application level gateway (bastion host) (Fig. 9.17).
- Demilitarized zone (DMZ) or screened-subnet firewall   These kinds of firewalls employ two packet-filtering routers and an application level gateway (bastions hosts). Figure 9.18 shows a DMZ and the network.

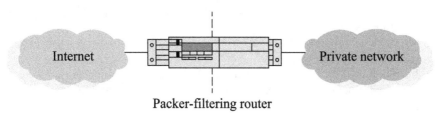

Fig. 9.16 Packet filtering router firewall

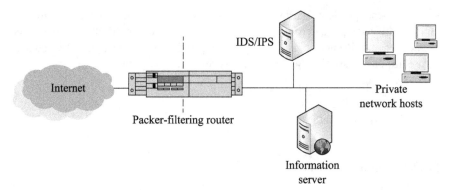

Fig. 9.17 Screened host firewall (Color)

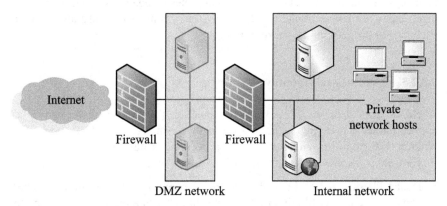

Fig. 9.18 Screened subnet firewall (Color)

9.8.3 Constraint and Limitations of Firewall

Below are some constraints and limitations of firewalls.

- Firewalls cannot protect against attacks that do not go through the firewall.
- Internet firewalls cannot protect against the type of threats posed by traitors or unwitting users.
- Firewalls do not prohibit traitors or corporate spies from copying sensitive data and remove from the building.
- Internet firewalls cannot protect against the transfer of virus-infected software or files. Concerned organizations should deploy anti-virus software at each desktop to protect.
- Internet firewalls cannot protect against data-driven attacks that occur when seemingly harmless data is mailed or copied to an internal host and is executed to launch an attack.

A firewall management program can be designed one of two basic ways:

- A default-deny policy. The firewall administrator lists all the allowable network services, and everything else is denied.
- A default-allow policy. The firewall administrator lists network services which are prohibited, and everything else is accepted.

A default-deny approach to firewall security is the most secure, but many networks use the default-allow approach instead.

9.8.4 Enterprise Firewalls

There are various types of enterprise firewalls of network security devices that help optimize IT operational and financial risk management to maximize IT performance for business. Here are a few examples of the most popular versions:

- Cisco Firewall Cisco is a manufacturer of a widespread range of computer security and networking products. They offer routers for joining public and private IP networks for mobile, data, voice, and video including switches, IP phones, access points, and servers. They also provide services for application networking and network security products including firewall, intrusion detection prevention, virtual private network (VPN), and E-mail security products.
- Barracuda Firewall Contain security products such as spam and virus firewall, storage, and data protection. Barracuda Networks products are easy to use and deploy. There is no software installation or network modifications are required. It also features web filtering and web application firewall products; network access control and application delivery are managed through a simple to use interface which can help secure networks from E-mail, web, and Internet messaging threats.
- Checkpoint Firewall This option provides top-tier firewall software for enterprise security. It features a stateful packet inspection, VPNs, and content filtering and also employs all the standard features expected from a commercial grade firewall. Checkpoint's enterprise-wide firewall management interface is a first-rate choice for companies needing to manage a geographically scattered network from remote locations.
- Juniper Networks NetScreen A maker of routers, switching equipment, firewall, networking security hardware, and security systems that integrates firewall, VPN, traffic management, denial of service (DoS), and distributed DoS security intended for large enterprise, carrier, and data center networks.
- Windows ISA Server Microsoft Internet Security and Acceleration Server (ISA) is multi-layered firewall network security that employs both stateful packet inspection and application-layer filtering to deliver Internet security.
- SonicWall Provides intrusion prevention, malware protection, and application control and is a producer of comprehensive network security solutions providing

appliances for E-mail security, remote access, and data security to meet enterprise network management requirements for a total firewall solution which includes VPN, anti-virus, and spyware protection.

Firewall plays the key role in traditional security architecture, since it controls most of the incoming and outgoing traffic of an enterprise. Essentially the firewall is almost a must-have in each enterprise. To review the challenges for the traditional architecture, undoubtedly it is necessary to address on the limitation of traditional firewalls.

9.8.5 *Intrusion Detection and Prevention*

Intrusion detection is the process of monitoring the events occurring in a computer system or network and analyzing them for signs of possible incidents, which are violations or imminent threats of violation of computer security policies, acceptable use policies, or standard security practices. Intrusion prevention is the process of performing intrusion detection and attempting to stop detected possible incidents. Intrusion detection and prevention systems (IDPS) are primarily focused on identifying possible incidents, logging information about them, attempting to stop them, and reporting them to security administrators. In addition, organizations use IDPSs for other purposes, such as identifying problems with security policies, documenting existing threats, and deterring individuals from violating security policies. IDPSs have become a necessary addition to the security infrastructure of nearly every organization.

IDPSs typically record information related to observed events, notify security administrators of important observed events, and produce reports. Many IDPSs can also respond to a detected threat by attempting to prevent it from succeeding. They use several response techniques, which involve the IDPS stopping the attack itself, changing the security environment (e.g., reconfiguring a firewall), or changing the attack's content.

Below are common types of IDPS technologies:

- Network-based, which monitors network traffic for particular network segments or devices and analyzes the network and application protocol activity to identify suspicious activity.
- Wireless, which monitors wireless network traffic and analyzes it to identify suspicious activity involving the wireless networking protocols themselves.
- Network behavior analysis (NBA), which examines network traffic to identify threats that generate unusual traffic flows, such as distributed denial of service (DDoS) attacks, certain forms of malware, and policy violations (e.g., a client system providing network services to other systems).
- Host-based, which monitors the characteristics of a single host and the events occurring within that host for suspicious activity.

9.8.6   Security Logs and Log Analysis

Web log file is log file automatically created and maintained by a web server. Every "hit" to the website, including each view of a HTML document, Image, or other object, is logged. The raw web log file format is essentially one line of text for each hit to the website. This contains information about who was visiting the site, where they came from, and exactly what they were doing on the website.

Log analysis is the term used for analysis of computer-generated records for helping organizations, businesses, or networks in proactively and reactively mitigating different risks. Most organizations and businesses are required to do data logging and log analysis as part of their security and compliance regulations. Log analysis helps in reducing problem diagnosis, in resolution time, and in effective management of applications and infrastructure.

Splunk is one of the log analysis software packages to collect, analyze, and act upon the untapped value of the big data generated by technology infrastructure, security systems, and business applications—giving users the insights to drive operational performance and business results.

Machine learning can assist the threat analysis from the log and other source of server data. The book website lists one example with Python source code.

9.9   IoT Architecture

The Internet of things (IoT) connects home appliances, sensors, traffic, vehicles, medical aids, smart grids, and industrial automation. The heterogeneous collection of microcontrollers, sensors, data interfaces, and networks make it difficult to set up a SCADA network and to design a database schema for storing the collected data (Wang et al. 2015). The study of IoT and SCADA architecture involves how to integrate different technologies and how to interconnect the heterogeneous set of subsystems and sensors, whether centralized or distributed (Wang and Zhang 2014; Wan and Kelly 2014, 2015; Wilder et al. 2019).

An example of one of these systems in smart cities is IoT traffic monitoring and control systems, which can let authorities adjust traffic based on the congestion. In addition, drivers are able to receive a real-time traffic updates that allow them to re-route the trip when necessary. Unlike the classic "the shortest path algorithm" that uses a static network map, the IoT enables traffic systems to use dynamic network maps, which update continuously based on the information gathered from sensors at intersections, along the road, or on the smart cars.

9.9.1   IoT Reference Model

The Internet of things (IoT) reference model (see Fig. 9.19) contains seven layers.

Collaboration & Processes
  People and Business Process
Application
  Report, Analytics, Control
Data Abstraction
  Aggregation and Access
Data Accumulation
  Storage
Edge Computing
  Data Element Analysis
Connectivity
  Communication & Processing
Devices and Controllers
  The "Things" in IoT

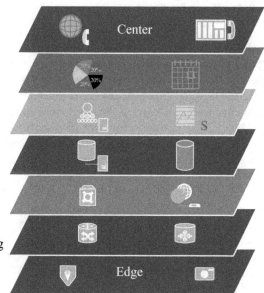

Fig. 9.19 Internet of things reference model (Color)

9.9.2 Paired Firewall Architecture

SCADA networks and corporate networks should be segregated to enhance security. Using a two-port firewall between the corporate and SCADA networks, security can be improved on condition that the firewall is properly configured.

Setting up a DMZ between the corporate and SCADA networks shields the networks from outside world. Creating a DMZ requires that the firewall offer three or more Interfaces: one is connected to the corporate network, the second to the SCADA network, and the third to the shared or insecure servers or wireless access points on the DMZ network.

The paired firewall architecture (Wang 2016) uses a pair of firewalls positioned between the corporate and SCADA networks. Data servers are placed in the DMZ. The advantage of this architecture is that the first firewall blocks the arbitrary packets coming to the SCADA network or servers in the DMZ. The second firewall prevents unwanted traffic from a compromised device from entering into the SCADA network. It also prevents SCADA network traffic from impacting the shared servers in the DMZ.

The new architecture we proposed uses paired firewalls. It has three zones and contains a DMZ. It is a more secure, manageable, and segregation architecture for SCADA systems (Fig. 1.9).

Though the paired firewall architecture increased cost and management complexity, it has strong advantages by increasing the security.

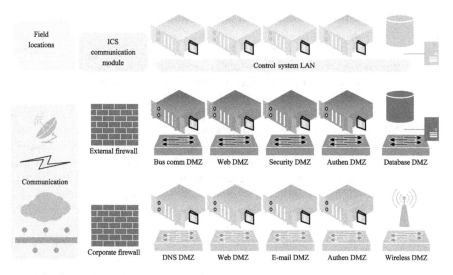

Fig. 9.20 Defense-in-depth architecture (Color)

9.9.3 Defense-in-Depth SCADA Architecture

Using firewalls alone cannot adequately protect SCADA networks. A multiple layer architecture involving two or more security mechanisms is a better approach. This is a technique commonly known as defense-in-depth where the impact of a failure in one measure cannot cause failure of the whole system thus minimizing the business services to be interrupted. Defense-in-depth includes the use of two or more firewalls, the creation of DMZs, and the employments of IDS/IPS devices along with effective security policies and business operations.

Our defense-in-depth strategy includes firewalls, the use of demilitarized zones (DMZ), and intrusion detection capabilities throughout the SCADA architecture. The use of several DMZs provides the added security to separate functionalities and access privileges and has proved to be effective in protecting large architectures from being comprised (Fig. 9.20).

9.9.4 IoTCP-Trusted Computing Protocol for IoT

Trusted computing is to build digital identities and increase assurance of trust among devices that are connected to the network. It adds a level of security on top of what is provided by the operating systems and hardware. Trusted computing base adds a hardware device, which has non-volatile storage and cryptographic execution engines on each device.

Trusted platform modules (TPM) and hardware security modules (HSM) are cryptographic hardware that improve the overall security of a system. TPM is usually embedded into a device. For a device that does not come with a TPM, an HSM can be added.

Message queue telemetry transport (MQTT) is a device-to-device IoT connectivity protocol. It has the advantages of small code footprint, low network bandwidth requirement, and lightweight therefore a good candidate especially for IoT/CPS systems.

A blockchain is a distributed ledger. For IoT/IoBT/CPS systems, it records all actions and operations. Each block contains the data and a hash of a previous block. If any of the previous block is tempered with, it will affect the hash of the current block. The temper-proof property makes it a perfect candidate to guarantee packages authenticity for over the air updates. Guin et al. recently proposed to integrate blockchain technology to authenticate resource-constrained, low-cost edge devices. SRAM-based physically unclonable functions (PUFs) were used to generate a unique "digital fingerprints" to identify edge devices (Wang et al. 2018).

IoTCP is a trusted computing protocol that employs discrete trusted platform modules and hardware security modules for key management, a blockchain-based package verification algorithm for over-the-air security, and a secure authentication mechanism (Hufstetler et al. 2017) for data communication. The IoT-based trusted computing protocol implements integrated hardware security, strong cryptographic hash functions, and peer-based blockchain trust management.

9.10   VPN and VPC

A virtual private network (VPN) is a virtual network built on top of existing networks that can provide a secure communications mechanism for data and IP information transmitted between networks. It is commonly used to connect corporate networks from remote places as though one is within the corporate premise. In addition, VPN can be used to hide browsing activity from local network and ISP, bypass Internet censorship, and access or download files.

The virtual private cloud (VPC) enables users to launch cloud resources into a virtual network that have previously defined. This virtual network closely resembles a traditional network that a corporate operates in its own data center, with the benefits of using the scalable infrastructure of the cloud.

It is beneficial for corporations to use a VPC inside a public cloud comparing directly putting all resources especially human resource and marketing data in a public cloud.

9.11   Summary

Data communication is at the physical level of TCP/IP. It is to study the transmission of data over various channels or networks. The goals for data communication are high throughput, fast speed, error-free, and reliable. In order to let many signals to share a common communication channel, signal encoding and modulation are needed. Shannon theorem states that in order to restore the original signal at destination lossless, signal must be sampled at double the frequency of the highest frequency of the original signal.

The transmission control protocol and Internet protocol (TCP/IP) is the foundation of modern computer network. Computer networks are logically divided into layers. There are four-layer, five-layer, and seven-layer models. The seven-layer model is the international standard named OSI.

TCP provides reliable stream delivery and virtual connection service to applications. It is connection-based, so there are some overhead or in order word delay. UDP is connection-less and the overhead is little, so the speed is faster. Unlike TCP, UDP does not guarantee the packet delivery, so there may be packet loss. For file transfer, we need to guarantee there is no any error; otherwise the file would not be open again. In this case TCP is the perfect choice. For voice/video over IP (VoIP) such as IP phone, a millisecond error would not be realized as long as the voice is synchronized with the speaker. So UDP is definitely the perfect choice.

Network switches are the basic devices to set up networks and connect network segments. A gateway serves as a bridge to interface with different protocols. Besides, it also connects the internal networks and the outside networks.

Routers find the shortest paths from source to destination and guarantee with least delay. It is a piece of key equipment to set up virtual circuits between sources and destinations. Usually people use graph theory to study network. Dijkstra algorithm is a very useful program to find the shortest paths between sources and destinations. The queue theory is another important tool to analyze the throughput of a router and therefore to reduce the delay packets that stay in the queue.

Wireless networks have many advantages over the Ethernet networks. Even though the speed generally cannot match the broadband Internet, it can satisfy the need for most occasions and it getting better. WLAN provides flexibility to enable people and different kinds of devices to be connected anywhere at any time. Because radio frequencies are spread in the air, enhancing the security is an important task for most users.

NAT lets several users to share one IP and separate an internal network from outside networks. It is a technology commonly seen in home and office wireless networks.

Network security involves securing information, data, and network equipment from all kinds of attacks and intruders. Firewall, IDS, and IPS are common technologies to secure networks and devices.

To enhance the network security, organizations usually use white hat hackers (or in other word ethical hacker) to find the vulnerabilities of an IT system. On the other hand, there are many black hat hackers on the Internet that constantly trying to break into a computer system or network to steal data.

A firewall provides a single point of defense between two networks—it protects one network from the other. Usually, a firewall protects the company's private network from the public or shared networks to which it is connected.

The 5th-generation cellular communication networks are going to revolutionize communication by providing ubiquitous and more reliable communication. Internet of things (IoT) concept and tactile Internet are the major drivers for 5G communications and its use cases. Thus, 5G platform can be defined as a cellular platform that provides a ubiquitous, reliable, low-power, and high data rate mobile communication network between smarter devices.

IoT connects home appliances, sensors, traffic, vehicles, medical aids, smart grids, and industrial automation with a heterogeneous collection of microcontrollers, sensors, data interfaces, and networks.

VPN gives online privacy and anonymity by creating a private network on top of a public Internet connection. The strong encryption makes it un-exploitable on local networks.

Projects

9.1 Router simulator
    Conduct research on network simulators to simulate a router.
9.2 Virtual cyber-security laboratory
    As we know, distant learning provides flexible learning environment where people can learn from books and other reference material, from instructors if a distance education class is formed, and from each other by collaborations. On the other hand, distant learning lacks tools and environment for people to participate in lab activities and gain hand-on experiences. Common labs are cyber ranges, hosted cyber labs, and standalone cyber labs. Conduct study and write a 300–400 words report to recommend the type of lab you recommend. Testing data and screenshots are recommended.

Exercises

9.1 What are the difference between signals, channels, data, and information?
9.2 Why most music radio station uses FM instead of AM?
9.3 The voice of an opera singer contains the highest frequency component of 20 Hz. In order to re-play on a high-fidelity (Hi-Fi) amplifier with the best quality, what is the sample rate to consider? If the voice is travel through a telephone, what does the sound quality (bandwidth) would be?
9.4 Describe the functions of each layer for the five-layer TCP/IP.
9.5 Some people say TCP is better since it is connection-based which means it can correct errors. Some people say UDP is better because it is faster. What is your opinion on this?
9.6 With regard to the throughput, what is the difference between Ethernet switches and hubs?

9.7 What are the most important factors for a router?

9.8 Use the Dijkstra algorithm and the graph below to find the shortest path from $n6$ to $n1$.

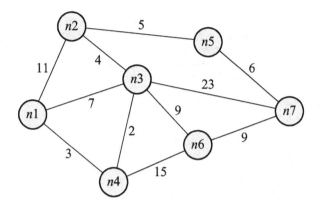

9.9 A single queue single server router has the capacity of processing 1000 Mb/s. When the packet arrival rate is 500 Mb/s, find out the number of packets in the router waiting to be process and the average waiting time (ms). When the packet arrival rate reaches to 990 Mb/s, what will happen?

9.10 For Internet access, most families have only one public IP. However each family may have many devices, computers, smartphones, pads, printers, etc. How to handle multiple devices over one public IP?

9.11 Amazon, Visa, and many other websites have suffered DDoS attacks. Find the most recent incident of DoS or DDoS attack and describe how to stop them.

9.12 For CISSP certification, the study of information security is divided into ten domains. List the ten domains in information security.

9.13 Most companies have security policies in place. False positive means there was an attack trigger and action was taken but actually it was not an attack. False negative means there was an attack but was not detected. Provide examples why sometime false positive is good and sometime it is not.

9.14 Describe how VPN works and why it is considered a secure connection.

9.15 Why paired firewalls can improve security on both IoT control network and corporate network?

References

Hufstetler, W., Ramos, M., & Wang, P. (2017). NFC Unlock: Secure Two-Factor Computer Authentication Using NFC. In *IEEE 14th International Conference on Mobile Ad Hoc and Sensor Systems (MASS 2017)* (pp. 507–510).

Wang, P., Ali, A., Guin, U., & Skjellum, A. (2018). IoTCP: A novel trusted computing protocol for IoT. *Journal of Colloquium for Information System Security Education (CISSE), 6*(1), 165–180.

Wang, S., & Robert, S. L. (2013). *Computer Architecture and Security*. New York: Wiley.

Wang, S., & Robert, L. (2007). *Modified Neumann architecture with Micro-OS for security* (pp. 303–310). CIICT.

Wang, S., & Ledley, R. S. (2006). Connputer—A Framework of Intrusion-Free Secure Computer Architecture. In *Proceedings of the 2006 International Conference on Security & Management, SAM 2006* (pp. 220–225).

Wang, S., & Kelly, W. (2017). Smart cities architecture and security in cybersecurity education. In *The Colloquium of Information Systems Security Education (CISSE) (2017)* (2).

Wang, P., & Kelly, W. (2015). A novel threat analysis and risk mitigation approach to prevent cyber intrusions. *Colloquium for Information System Security Education (CISSE), 3*(1), 157–174.

Wang, S. (2016). Dual-Data Defense in Depth Improves SCADA Security. *Signal, 2016*(10), 42–44.

Wang, S., & Zhang, J. (2014). A video data search engine for cyber-physical traffic and security monitoring systems. In *IEEE/ACM Fourth International Conference on Cyber-Physical Systems* (pp. 225–226).

Wang, S., Ali, A., & Kelly, W. (2015). Data security and threat modeling for smart city infrastructure. In *IEEE Cyber Security of Smart Cities, Industrial Control System and Communications* (Vol. 2015, pp. 1–6).

Wang, S., & Kelly, W. (2014). In *Video-A novel big data analytics tool for video data analytics*. IEEE/NIST IT Pro Conference (pp. 1–19).

Wilder, V., Gao, Y., Wang, S., & Perez, A. (2019). Multi-factor stateful authentication using NFC and mobile phones. In *Proceeding of IEEE SoutheastCon*

Chapter 10
Cryptography and Architecture Security

Almost all modern computers have crypto processors embedded into the systems. Crypto processors are specialized processors that execute cryptographic algorithms within hardware. Functions include accelerating encryption algorithms, enhanced tamper, and intrusion detection, enhanced data, key protection, and security enhanced memory access and I/O.

A crypto processor offers several distinct advantages, such as strong encryption and crypto key protection, and exploits prevention. They can be integrated into SoCs or FPGAs or integrated using a hybrid approach, such as a computer with a trusted platform module.

10.1 Zimmermann Telegram

Using encryption to protect sensitive data has been well established over 100 years or even longer. One example is a telegram that led the United States into WWI.

In January 1917, British cryptographers deciphered a telegram from German Foreign Minister Arthur Zimmermann to the German Minister to Mexico, von Eckhardt, offering US territory to Mexico in return for joining the German cause. This message helped draw the United States into the war and thus changed the course of history.

The Zimmermann Telegram (Fig. 10.1) had such an impact on American opinion that, "No other single cryptanalysis has had such enormous consequences." It is the opinion that never before or since has so much turned upon the solution of a secret message.

© The Author(s), under exclusive license to Springer Nature Singapore Pte Ltd. 2021   293
S. P. Wang, *Computer Architecture and Organization*,
https://doi.org/10.1007/978-981-16-5662-0_10

Fig. 10.1 Zimmermann
Telegram

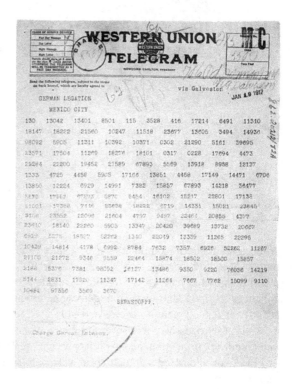

10.2   Substitution Cipher

The mono-alphabetic substitution cipher (commonly named as the simple substitution cipher) is to substitute every plaintext character with a different character. Caesar cipher is a special case of substitution cipher where each letter is shifted with a same distance.

10.2.1   Simple Substitution Cipher

Caesar cipher is a special case of the substitution cipher where the key is the number of letters shifted. Text for the simple substitution cipher usually consist of 26 letters with random order. Here is an example key:

```
plain alphabet : abcdefghijklmnopqrstuvwxyz
cipher alphabet: phqgiumeaylnofdxjkrcvstzwb
```

To encrypt a message, one replaces each letter in the plaintext with the corresponding ciphertext from the key. For example:

```
plaintext : defend the east wall of the castle
ciphertext: giuifg cei iprc tpnn du cei qprcni
```

Keep in mind that the spaces in ciphertext are usually removed. So, the ciphertext is usually in all capital letters. For the example above, the ciphertext is

```
ciphertext: GIUIFGCEIIPRCTPNNDUCEIGPRCNI
```

Sometime, people divide the ciphertext into segments (e.g., a group of five) for easy reading. So, the above ciphertext is commonly seen as:

```
ciphertext: GIUIF GCEII PRCTP NNDUC EIGPR CNI
```

Again, when you see ciphertexts, you should not assume the space as the real space between words. It may be just separators.

Substitution cipher was considered strong during WWII but was later cracked by British scientist Alan Turing, one of the greatest cryptologists and computer scientists.

10.2.2 Cryptologic Analysis of Substitution Cipher

There are many ways to crack the simple substitution cipher. English letter frequency analysis is one of them. Others include hill climbing and word patterns.

10.2.2.1 English Letter Frequency

Cornell counted 40,000 sample words. The result English letter frequency table is:

Letter	E	T	A	O	I	N	S	R	H	D	L	U	C
Frequency	12.02	9.10	8.12	7.68	7.31	6.95	6.28	6.02	5.92	4.32	3.98	2.88	2.71
Letter	M	F	Y	W	G	P	B	V	K	X	Q	J	Z
Frequency	2.61	2.30	2.11	2.09	2.03	1.82	1.49	1.11	0.69	0.17	0.11	0.10	0.07

For each letter in the ciphertext, you count how many times each letter appears and then sort the list. According the English letter frequency table, a letter appears the most would be E, the second would be T, the third would be A, and so on. After replacing all letters, the ciphertext would be changed back to the plaintext.

English letter frequency method would be accurate if the ciphertext is very long. For short ciphertext, it may not follow the statistical rule; therefore the cracked text may not be accurate or would not be accurate at all.

10.2.2.2 Hill-Climbing Algorithm

We need to find a way to determine how close/similar a piece of text is to English text, in other words, the "fitness" of the text. Here is an example to calculate fitness for "ATTACK." The quadgrams are ATTA, TTAC, and TACK. The total probability is:

```
p(ATTACK) = p(ATTA) * p(TTAC) * p(TACK),
where,
p(TTAC) = count(TTAC)/N,
count is the number of times the particular quadgram
occurred, N is the total number of quadgrams in the
training sample.
```

To avoid underflow for multiplying many very small probabilities, we take the logarithm (to "amply" the number).

```
log(p(ATTACK)) = log(p(ATTA)) + log(p(TTAC)) + log(p(TACK))
```

The piece of text will get a high score (fitness) if it is very similar to English. We rank different decryption keys. Below is the algorithm:

I. Generate a random key, called the "parent"; decipher the ciphertext using this key. Rate the fitness of the deciphered text; store the result.
II. Change the key slightly (swap two characters in the key at random); measure the fitness of the deciphered text using the new key.
III. If the fitness is higher with the modified key, discard our old parent and store the modified key as the new parent.
IV. Go back to II, unless no improvement in fitness occurred in the last 1000 iterations.

As the cycle proceeds, the deciphered text gets fitter. The key either becomes better to a solution or the solution is not found. This means it is stuck in a "local maximum." This method would have trouble breaking short ciphertext (e.g., less than 100 characters in length).

10.2.2.3   Word Patterns

Create a word pattern with a set of numbers with periods in between the numbers that tell the pattern of letters for a word, in either ciphertext or plaintext. A plaintext word has the same word patterns as its cipher word, no matter which simple substitution key was used to do the encryption. For example:

- The word pattern for "cat" is 0.1.2.
- The word pattern for "catty" is 0.1.2.2.3.
- The word pattern for "roofer" is 0.1.1.2.3.0.
- The word pattern for "blimp" is 0.1.2.3.4.
- The word pattern for "classification" is 0.1.2.3.3.4.5.4.0.2.6.4.7.8.

Using a dictionary, we can do a cipher letter mapping; we then get the deciphered text that is close to the plaintext. The only problem for this one is that it needs the space (encrypted or not).

10.3 Symmetric Key Algorithms

Symmetric key encryptions use one fixed key to encrypt and another key to decrypt. When the encryption function satisfies "⊕—exclusive OR," then both encryption and decryption can be one key. That is why many literatures describe symmetric key encryptions using one key to encrypt and decrypt.

Common symmetric key algorithms include DES, 3DES, and AES. Currently only AES is considered strong.

10.3.1 DES, 3DES and AES

The original data encryption standard (DES) block cipher algorithm was developed by IBM in the early 1970s and published as a standard by the US National Institute of Standards and Technology (NIST) in 1977, quickly becoming a de facto international standard.

By the 1990s, the 56-bit (plus 8 parity bits) key length became insufficient against brute-force attacks. Thus Triple-DES was introduced in 1998, using a bundle of three keys, giving a nominal strength of 168 bits, but at the price of slow performance. Triple-DES, due to its security concern and poor performance, was replaced by advanced encryption standard (AES).

Following a competition run by the NIST, advanced encryption standard was introduced in 2001 to replace DES; it is now commonly known as the AES algorithm, featuring a block size of 128 bits and three key length options: 128, 192, or 256 bits. The number of rounds varies with key length.

AES is the symmetric algorithm-of-choice for most applications today and is very widely used, mostly with 128- or 256-bit keys, with the latter key length even considered strong enough to protect military *Top Secret* data. Note that, assuming there are no known weaknesses in an algorithm, a single 128-bit key will take billions of years to brute force using any classical computing technology today or in the foreseeable future.

There may be a possibility that the asymmetric algorithms predominantly used today can be effectively broken by future quantum computers. Fortunately, the impact on symmetric algorithms appears to be less severe—Grover's algorithm has the effect of halving the key length; thus AES-128 has an effective strength equivalent to a 64-bit key, and AES-256 is reduced to the strength of a 128-bit key. This means that AES-256 can still be confidently used in the face of quantum computing.

10.3.2   Key Generation and Management

Symmetric key algorithms use the same (secret) key to both apply cryptographic protection to information and to remove or verify the protection. Keys used with symmetric key algorithms must be known by only the entities authorized to apply, remove, or verify the protection and are commonly known as secret keys. A secret key is often known by multiple entities that are said to share or own the secret key, although it is not uncommon for a key to be generated, owned, and used by a single entity (e.g., for secure storage).

Symmetric keys that are to be directly generated from the output of a random bit generator (RBG) shall be generated with desired security strength following NIST SP 800-133.

10.4   Public Key Encryption

Public key cryptography involves a pair of keys known as a public key and a private key where public key is published and the corresponding private key is kept secret.

Public key cryptography is asymmetric encryption. It allows two communicating parties to encrypt data that they send to each other. The sender encrypts the data before sending it. The receiver decrypts the data after receiving it. While in transit, the encrypted data is not understood by an intruder. Public key encryption also guarantees non-repudiation, which prevents the sender of the data from claiming, at a later date, that the data was never sent or the data from being altered.

The most commonly used implementations of public key cryptography (also known as asymmetric encryption) are based on algorithms developed by Rivest-Shamir-Adleman (RSA).

10.4.1   RSA

RSA is one of the most famous public key cryptosystems which is named after its three developers Ron Rivest, Adi Shamir, and Leonard Adleman. At the time of the algorithm's development (1977), the three were researchers at the MIT Laboratory for Computer Science. Their algorithm was first announced in Martin Gardner's "Mathematical Games" column in the August, 1977, *Scientific American*. Their formal paper "A method for obtaining digital signatures and public-key cryptosystems" was published in 1978 in the communications of the Association for Computing Machinery.

The idea of RSA is based on the fact that it is difficult to factorize a large integer. The public key consists of two numbers where one number is multiplication of two large prime numbers. And private key is also derived from the same two prime numbers. So, if somebody can factorize the large number, the private key is compromised. Therefore, encryption strength totally lies on the key size and if we double or triple the key size, the strength of encryption increases exponentially. RSA keys can be typically 1024 or 2048 bits long, but experts believe that 1024-bit keys could be broken in the near future. But till now it seems to be an infeasible task.

RSA algorithm can be explained in the following steps:

```
1. Let p and q be the two large prime numbers
2. Let N = pq be the modulus
3. Choose e relatively prime to (p-1)(q-1)
4. Find d such that ed = 1 (mod (p-1)(q-1))
5. Public key is (N, e)
6. Private key is d
```

To encrypt a message, a sender first converts the message into a numerical form (M) and computes

$$C = M^e (\bmod N)$$

To decrypt a message, a receiver computes

$$M = C^d (\bmod N)$$

Below is a simple example using the RSA algorithm to encrypt and decrypt.

```
1. Select two "large" primes p = 11, q = 3
2. N = pq = 33 and (p-1)(q-1) = 20
3. Choose e = 3 (relatively prime to 20)
4. Find d such that ed = 1 mod 20, then d =7 works
5. Public key is (33, 3)
6. Private key is 7
```

Suppose message $M = 8$, cybertext

$$C = M^e (\bmod N) = 8^3 \bmod 33 = 17 \bmod 33$$

Decrypt the ciphertext C to recover the message

$$M = C^d (\bmod N) = 17^7 \bmod 33 = 12434505 \times 33 + 8 = 8 \bmod 33$$

Currently, RSA is the golden standard in cryptography. It may become vulnerable when practical quantum computers are available (probably another decade), as quantum algorithms (such as Shor's algorithm) can improve the factoring speed from exponential to polynormal (Monz et al. 2016; Patrick et al. 2018; Shor 1994; Vandersypen et al. 2001; Wang and Sakk 2021; Wang et al. 2020).

10.4.2   Certificate Authority

A certificate authority (CA) is a trusted third party entity that issues digital certificates and manages the public keys and credentials for data encryption for the end users. The responsibility of a CA is to ensure that a company or user receives a unique certificate for an efficient identity authentication.

As part of a public key infrastructure (PKI), a CA checks with a qualified information source (QIS) to verify the data supplied by the applicant, before issuing the digital certificate.

Normally, the CAs have partnerships with financial organizations like the credit reporting agencies to help them with the process of business and identity authentication of the applicants. CAs are a critical component in the field of data security and e-commerce as they guarantee identities of both parties to each other.

There is a debate about the pros and cons of CA. CA is a critical component for PKI. It provides the identity and non-repudiation. On the other hand, some people question adding a third party for two-party communication. For example, two high rank military officials want to communicate; the so-called "trusted" third party could listen to the conversation. This apparently is a vulnerability. For most people, using the certificates issued from the trusted CA who uses strong encryption is considered secure.

10.4.3   Secure Socket Layer

The secure sockets layer (SSL) is the standard technology for keeping an Internet connection secure and safeguarding any sensitive data that is being sent between two systems, preventing criminals from reading and modifying any information transferred, including potential personal identifiable data. The two systems can be a server and a client or server to server.

SSL makes sure that any data transferred between users and sites or between two systems remain impossible to read. It uses strong encryption algorithms to scramble data in transit, preventing hackers from reading it as it is sent over the connection.

Transport layer security (TLS) is just an updated and more secure version of SSL. When you buy SSL certificates, you are most likely getting the up-to-date TLS certificates with the option of ECC, RSA, or DSA encryption.

Hypertext transfer protocol secure (HTTPS) is actually HTTP over SSL. It appears in the URL when a website is secured by an SSL certificate. The details of the certificate, including the issuing authority and the corporate name of the website owner, can be viewed by clicking on the lock symbol on the browser bar.

10.5   Hash vs. Encryption

In security domain, hash is referred as crypto hash where the hash function is based on cryptographic algorithms vs. regular hash that may use direct mapping.

Like crypto hash, encryptions use cryptographic algorithms to protect data. The big difference is that hash is one-way function (encryption only) but encryption is two-way function (encryption-decryption).

10.5.1   Hash Functions

A common crypto hash function is MD5. It produces a hash digest of 16 bytes. Due to the collision issue, it is not considered secure to use.

SHA-1 produces a hash digest of 20 bytes. Collision has been found, so it is considered broken.

SHA-2 was designed by NSA. It consists of two main streams: SHA 256 and SHA 512. SHA512 produces a hash digest of 64 bytes. It is preferable to SHA 256 as it is more secure and faster.

SHA-3, also called Keccak, provides the same output sizes as SHA-2. It is an alternative implementation of SHA-2.

10.5.2   HMAC

Hash-based message authentication codes (or HMACs) are a tool for calculating message authentication codes using a cryptographic hash function coupled with a secret key. You can use an HMAC to verify both the integrity and authenticity of a message.

HMAC algorithm is a result of work done on developing a MAC derived from cryptographic hash functions. HMAC is a great resistant toward cryptanalysis attacks as it uses the Hashing concept twice. HMAC consists of twin benefits of Hashing and MAC and thus is more secure than any other authentication codes. RFC 2104 has issued HMAC, and HMAC has been made compulsory to implement in IP security. The FIPS 198 NIST standard has also issued HMAC.

The working of HMAC starts with taking a message M containing blocks of length b bits. An input signature is padded to the left of the message, and the whole is given as input to a hash function which gives us a temporary message digest MD'. MD' again is appended to an output signature, and the whole is applied a hash function again; the result is our final message digest MD.

10.5.3   Random Numbers

Deterministic random bit generator (DRBG) is a random bit generator (RBG) that includes a DRBG mechanism and has access to a randomness source. The DRBG produces a sequence of bits from a secret initial value called a seed, along with other possible inputs. A DRBG is often called a pseudorandom number (or bit) generator. Contrast with non-deterministic RBG (NRBG).

Quantum random number generators have the advantage over conventional randomness sources of being invulnerable to environmental perturbations and of allowing live status verification. The operation is continuously monitored, and if a failure is detected, the random bit stream is immediately disabled. In addition, quantum true random number generator (TRNG) provides full entropy (randomness) instantaneously from the very first photon (bit).

10.6   Strong Encryptions

Encryption algorithms have constantly updated over the years. Among a number of encryption algorithms, AES, RSA, and PGP are considered strong encryptions.

10.6.1   Pretty Good Privacy

Pretty good privacy (PGP) is a digital data encryption program created by Phil Zimmermann, a special director of Computer Professionals for Social Responsibility (CPSR) from 1997 to 2000. He created PGP to promote awareness of the privacy issue in a digital age.

As we know symmetric encryption has the advantage of being fast but hard for key exchange. Asymmetric encryption is good for its easy key exchange but it is much slower than symmetric encryption. PGP integrates the advantages of both symmetric and asymmetric encryptions making easy for key exchange while running fast. It also adds hash to improve the identity. So, PGP is a good candidate for end-to-end encryptions.

For encryption:

```
1. Alice generates a random key.
2. Alice uses the random key to encrypt message.
3. Alice encrypts the random key with Bob's public key
using RSA algorithm.
4. Alice sends the encrypted message along with the
encrypted key to Bob.
```

For decryption:

```
1. Bob decrypts the encrypted key using his private key
using RSA algorithm.
2. Bob uses the deciphered key to decrypt the encrypted
data which he received.
3. Bob reads the original message Alice sent to him.
```

For added security and identity, Alice can add hash to the encrypted message and send the hash value to Bob. When Bob receives the whole package, he decrypts the message and computes the hash value himself. If the hash values match, then it passes the integrity check. A detailed description with illustrations of PGP algorithm can be found in book author's blog (Wang 2021).

10.6.2 Transport Layer Security

The transport layer security (TLS) is a widely adopted security protocol designed to facilitate privacy and data security for communications over the Internet. A primary use case of TLS is encrypting the communication between web applications and servers, such as web browsers loading a website. TLS can also be used to encrypt other communications such as E-mail, messaging, and voice over IP (VOIP). In this section we focus on the role of TLS in web application security.

TLS was proposed by the Internet engineering task force (IETF), an international standards organization, and the first version of the protocol was published in 1999. The most recent version is TLS 1.3, which was published in 2018.

TLS evolved from a previous encryption protocol called secure socket layer (SSL), which was developed by Netscape. TLS version 1.0 actually began development as SSL version 3.1, but the name of the protocol was changed before publication in order to indicate that it was no longer associated with Netscape. Because of this history, the terms TLS and SSL are sometimes used interchangeably.

TLS can be used on top of a transport-layer security protocol like TCP. There are three main components to TLS, encryption, authentication, and integrity.

- Encryption hides the data being transferred from third parties.
- Authentication ensures that the parties exchanging information are who they claim to be.
- Integrity verifies that the data has not been forged or tampered with.

10.6.3 Elliptic Curve Cryptography

The elliptic curve cryptography (ECC) is a public key cryptography method, which evolved from Diffie-Hellman.

The Diffie-Hellman key exchange protocol, and the digital signature algorithm (DSA) which is based on it, is an asymmetric cryptographic system in general use today. It was discovered by Whitfield Diffie and Martin Hellman in 1976 and uses a problem known as the discrete logarithm problem (DLP) as its asymmetric operation. The DLP concerns finding a logarithm of a number within a finite field arithmetic system.

Since the discovery of RSA, their ability to withstand attacks has meant that these two cryptographic systems have become widespread in use. They are being used every day for both authentication purposes and encryption/decryption. Both systems cover the current security standards—so why invent a new system? Even though ECC is relatively new, the use of elliptic curves as a base for a cryptographic system was independently proposed by Victor Miller and Neal Koblitz. What makes it stand apart from RSA is its ability to be more efficient. The reason why this is important is the developments in handheld, mobile devices, sensor networks, etc. Somehow, there must be a way to secure communications generated by these devices; however their computing power and memory are not nearly as abundant as on their desktop and laptop counterparts. A contemporary desktop or laptop system has no problems working with 2048-bit keys and higher, but these small embedded devices do since we do not want to spend a lot of their resources and bandwidth securing traffic.

It is worth mentioning that a 160-bit ECC key and a 1024-bit RSA key offer a similar level of security. To reach the same level of security with 15,360-bit RSA key, one only needs 512-bit ECC key.

10.7   Authentication

Authentication is the process of determining a claim about someone or something's identity using a secret or piece of evidence called a "factor." Authentication is followed by authorization. For example, once your E-mail login is authenticated, the mail server authorizes you to access your E-mail or may be more resources if a single sign-on service is used.

10.7.1   Access Control

Access controls are security features that control how users and system communicate and interact with other systems and resources. Access is the follow of information between a subject and resource (object). A subject is an active entity that requests access to resources. An object is a resource that contains the information. Access controls give organization the ability to control, restrict, monitor, and protect resource confidentiality, integrity, and availability.

There are three variations of access control. They are discretionary access control (DAC), mandatory access control (MAC), and role-based access control (RBAC).

1. Discretionary access control

   Discretionary access control (DAC) is a type of access control system that holds the business owner responsible for deciding which people are allowed in a specific location, physically or digitally. DAC is the least restrictive compared to the other systems, as it essentially allows an individual complete control over any objects they own, as well as the programs associated with those objects. The drawback to discretionary access control is the fact that it gives the end user complete control to set security level settings for other users and the permissions given to the end user are inherited into other programs they use which could potentially lead to malware being executed without the end user being aware of it.

2. Mandatory access control

   Mandatory access control (MAC) is more commonly utilized in organizations that require an elevated emphasis on the confidentiality and classification of data (i.e., military institutions). MAC doesn't permit owners to have a say in the entities having access in a unit or facility, instead, only the owner and custodian have the management of the access controls. MAC will typically classify all end users and provide them with labels which permit them to gain access through security with established security guidelines.

3. Role-based access control

   Also known as rule-based access control (RBAC), RBAC is the most demanded in regard to access control systems. Not only is it in high demand among households, RBAC has also become highly sought after in the business world. In RBAC systems, access is assigned by the system administrator and is stringently based on the subject's role within the household or organization, and most privileges are based on the limitations defined by their job responsibilities. So, rather than assigning an individual as a security manager, the security manager position already has access control permissions assigned to it. RBAC makes life much easier because rather than assigning multiple individuals particular access, the system administrator only has to assign access to specific job titles.

10.7.2 Username and Password

Authentication is about something you know, something you have, and something you are.

Username and password belong to "something you know." It is the most common and least secure authentication method. The reason most users use it is because it is free.

10.7.3 Biometrics

Biometrics includes fingerprints, facial recognition, iris recognition, retina scan, voice, DNA data, etc.

Common biometric authentication method uses fingerprints and iris recognition. Facial recognition is becoming common in mobile payments.

10.7.4 Multifactor Authentication

Multifactor authentication uses two or more factors to authenticate a user, for example, a username (something you know), a text message (something you have), and fingerprints (something you are). Multifactor authentication is essential to improve authentication security.

10.7.5 Security Models

Security models of control are used to determine how security will be implemented, what subjects can access the system, and what objects they will have access to. Simply stated, they are a way to formalize security policy. Security models of control are typically implemented by enforcing integrity or confidentiality.

1. Confidentiality
   Although integrity is an important concept, confidentiality was actually the first to be addressed in a formal model. This is because the department of defense (DoD) was concerned about the confidentiality of information. The DoD divides information into categories, to ease the burden of managing who has access to what levels of information. DoD information classifications include confidential, secret, and top secret.

   The Bell-LaPadula model was actually the first formal model developed to protect confidentiality. This is a state machine that enforces confidentiality. A state machine is a conceptual model that monitors the status of the system to prevent it from slipping into an insecure state. Systems that support the state machine model must have all their possible states examined to verify that all processes are controlled. The Bell-LaPadula model uses mandatory access control to enforce the DoD multilevel security policy. For a subject to access information, he must have a clear "need to know" and meet or exceed the information's classification level.

2. Integrity
   Integrity is a good thing. It is one of the basic elements of the security triad, along with confidentiality and availability. Integrity plays an important role in security because it can verify that unauthorized users are not modifying data,

that authorized users don't make unauthorized changes, and that data remains internally and externally consistent. Two security models of control that address integrity include Biba and Clark-Wilson.

Biba addresses integrity only, not availability or confidentiality. It also assumes that internal threats are being protected by good coding practices and, therefore, focuses on external threats.

The Clark-Wilson model was created in 1987. It differs from previous models because it was developed with the intention to be used for commercial activities. This model dictates that the separation of duties must be enforced, subjects must access data through an application, and auditing is required. It also differs from the Biba model in that subjects are restricted. This means a subject at one level of access can read one set of data, whereas a subject at another level of access has access to a different set of data.

10.8 Cryptographic Hardware*

Cryptographic operations can be very expensive when performed in software. These operations can be performed by a hardware accelerator to improve performance. Cryptographic hardware acceleration is the use of hardware to perform cryptographic operations faster than they can be performed in software. Hardware accelerators are designed for computationally intensive software code.

Using hardware accelerators to perform RSA operations allows a system to perform up to several thousand RSA operations per second, a great increase compared to software RSA operations.

10.8.1 PCI Cryptographic Coprocessor

IBM PCI cryptographic coprocessor (PCICC) uses dedicated hardware to process cryptographic keys, certificates, and bulk data. These cryptographic functions are performed within a tamper-resistant module that is designed to meet the FIPS PUB 140-1 specification for detecting attacks through temperature, radiation, voltage, and physical penetration.

10.8.2 AES-NI

AES-NI stands for the Intel Advanced Encryption Standard New Instructions. It was the first major implementation with an extension to the x86 instruction set architecture for microprocessors from Intel and AMD.

AES-NI is a fast way for the processor to execute the calculations of AES. Normally the computer has to calculate every single step of the AES key schedule and the rounds as a single instruction: substitute it with the S-boxes, shift the rows, mix the columns, and XOR the round key. This is called a software implementation. Every instruction has to be done in software from the program.

Using the AES instruction set, the program can do a whole round in a single instruction. There are several different instructions to do this. The instructions will be executed on hardware level, in the transistors of the processor. Without doing other tasks, a processor normally does execute the encryption and decryption much more efficient. This is called a hardware implementation. As we know, every block cipher is more efficient in hardware than in software.

10.9   Privacy and Anonymity

The ability for individuals to interact online without sacrificing their personal privacy is a vital part of the Internet's value and is intimately related to its trustworthiness.

Privacy is about retaining the ability to disclose data consensually and with expectations about the context and scope of sharing. Identifiability, likability of data, and the mining of vast quantities of aggregated information all erode the individual's ability to manage disclosure, context, and scope. Networks depend on the use of unique (and often identifying) numbers and facilitate the instant global dissemination of information; increasingly, devices and applications gather and use geolocation data that builds up into a unique "track" for each user. A growing commercial ecosystem based on targeted and behavioral advertising results in an inexorable financial pressure for service providers to exploit personal data. The privacy implications of the current Internet represent a significant and growing concern.

One of the most important concepts in the EU general data protection regulation (GDPR) is transparency. Individuals own their personal data. As a company that's involved in processing that personal data, you must disclose everything that you do with it. This is why having a privacy policy is so important.

A privacy policy is mandatory under many privacy laws. And under the GDPR, it's one of the most important documents your company has. It's the only way to demonstrate to your customers, and to the authorities, that you take data protection seriously.

A GDPR privacy policy is sometimes called a GDPR privacy statement or a GDPR privacy notice.

TOR is an open source project that is claimed to defend against tracking and surveillance to make people anonymous online. The name is derived from an acronym for the original software project name "The Onion Router." Dark web or dark net refers to access online content using untraditional browsers and methods, such as TOR.

People usually use VPN to access the dark net. The VPN provides a fake IP address that makes the trace leads to somewhere else but not the user. Some VPN keeps no logs, accepts Bitcoin as payment, has a kill switch for DNS leaks, and is compatible with TOR.

It is "advised" never send cryptocurrency directly from your exchange account (where you buy the coins). Instead, send coins to a wallet and then from the wallet to the dark web. It is also "advised" not to change the TOR window size and turn off JavaScript, disconnect mic, and webcam and never use real name, photos, E-mail (hushmail), or password that you've used before. There is a comprehensive guide on how to stay "safe" in the deep web.

Organizations should have policies in using TOR and external encrypted emails at workplace. Balancing security and privacy have been constantly a battle and don't expect to get a good solution soon.

10.9.1 RSA Key Splitter

Key splitter is related with key recovery and key escrow. One of the problems with any type of encryption system—public key or secret key—is key management. One solution is to ask a "trusted third party" to maintain a copy of the key.

Another solution is to split the key into two or more parts and ask a different third party to store each part. The purpose of a laboratory exercise is to explore a method for doing this. The method is based on a famous mathematical theorem called the Chinese remainder theorem. To make things easy, the lab uses three-digit keys.

This is also the basic idea behind the various "key-escrow" proposals from the US government. All keys would be split into two or more parts, with each part entrusted to a different public or private agency. The idea is that the police could recover the key without the individual's knowledge by obtaining warrants against each of the escrowing agencies. This would permit the police to "listen in" on encrypted communications or to read encrypted files without the key holder's knowledge.

The book's website contains an exercise of RSA key splitter. Due to key splitting, one could read an experimental RSA encrypted message without the privacy key! This should never happen from security perspective. But it may be a reality.

10.9.2 Blockchain

Blockchain is the backbone technology of digital cryptocurrency. The blockchain is a distributed database of records of all transactions or digital event that have been executed and shared among participating parties. Each transaction is verified by the majority of participants of the system. It contains every single record of each transaction. Bitcoin is the most popular cryptocurrency example of the blockchain. Blockchain technology first came to light when a person or group of individuals name "Satoshi Nakamoto" published a white paper on *Bitcoin: A peer to peer electronic cash system* in 2008. Blockchain technology records transaction in digital ledger which is distributed over the network, thus making it incorruptible. Anything of value like land assets, cars, etc. can be recorded on blockchain as a transaction.

Blockchain builds trust through the following five attributes.

- Distributed   The distributed ledger is shared and updated with every incoming transaction among the nodes connected to the Blockchain. All this is done in real-time as there is no central server controlling the data.
- Secure   There is no unauthorized access to blockchain made possible through permissions and cryptography.
- Transparent   Because every node or participant in blockchain has a copy of the blockchain data, they have access to all transaction data. They themselves can verify the identities without the need for mediators.
- Consensus-based   All relevant network participants must agree that a transaction is valid. This is achieved through the use of consensus algorithms.
- Flexible   Smart contracts which are executed based on certain conditions can be written into the platform. Blockchain network can evolve in pace with business processes.

A blockchain contains the following functions:

- Blocks.
- Transactions.
- Timestamps.
- Proof of work.
- Network for collecting new transactions, finding proof of work of its block, broadcasting new blocks to all nodes after finding proof of work, accepting blocks, and validating blocks.
- Incentive mechanism.

10.9.3   Cryptocurrency

Cryptocurrency is a digital currency that uses encryption (cryptography) to generate money and to verify transactions. Transactions are added to a public ledger—also called a transaction block chain—and new coins are created through a process known as mining.

As of 2019, Bitcoin is the most commonly known and used cryptocurrency. Meanwhile, other coins including Ethereum (ETH), Ripple (XRP), Litecoin (LTC), and more are notable mentions.

1. Public Ledgers
   All confirmed transactions from the start of a cryptocurrency's creation are stored in a public ledger. The identities of the coin owners are encrypted, and the system uses other cryptographic techniques to ensure the legitimacy of record keeping.

The ledger ensures that corresponding "digital wallets" can calculate an accurate spendable balance. Also, new transactions can be checked to ensure that each transaction uses only coins currently owned by the spender. Bitcoin calls this public ledger a "transaction block chain."

2. Transactions

A transfer of funds between two digital wallets is called a transaction. That transaction gets submitted to a public ledger and awaits confirmation. Wallets use an encrypted electronic signature when a transaction is made. The signature is an encrypted piece of data called a cryptographic signature, and it provides a mathematical proof that the transaction came from the owner of the wallet. The confirmation process takes a bit of time (10 min for Bitcoin), while "miners" mine. Mining confirms the transactions and adds them to the public ledger.

3. Mining

Mining is the process of confirming transactions and adding them to a public ledger. To add a transaction to the ledger, the "miner" must solve an Increasingly complex computational problem (like a mathematical puzzle). Mining is open source so that anyone can confirm the transaction. The first "miner" to solve the puzzle adds a "block" of transactions to the ledger. The way in which transactions, blocks, and the public blockchain ledger work together ensure that no one individual can easily add or change a block at will. Once a block is added to the ledger, all correlating transactions are permanent, and they add a small transaction fee to the miner's wallet (along with newly created coins). The mining process is what gives value to the coins and is known as a proof-of-work system.

4. Proof-of-Work

Most cryptocurrencies use a proof-of-work system. A proof-of-work scheme uses a hard-to-compute but easy-to-verify computational puzzle to limit exploitation of cryptocurrency mining. Essentially, it's similar to a difficult to solve "captcha" that requires lots of computing power. NOTE: Other systems like proof-of-work (such as proof-of-stake) are also used.

10.9.4 Smart Contracts

A smart contract is a computer protocol intended to digitally facilitate, verify, or enforce the negotiation or performance of a contract. Smart contracts allow the performance of credible transactions without third parties.

Smart contracts provide a dynamic element to otherwise static blockchain systems that would require centralized oversight. A regular paper contract dictates the legal agreement between two recognized parties on the ground of legal enforcement. A smart contract, on the other hand, is an automated piece of software that allows two or more parties to fulfill agreements without the need for federal enforcement. As smart contracts can potentially replace standard legal agreements in less intensive peer-to-peer conduct, their security is of great concern. With the primary purpose of blockchain systems which is to manage and record transactions, the software behind automating these exchanges would need to be functionally secure.

Due to the autonomy of smart contracts, there is a necessity for adequate security mechanisms and practices to be in place to prevent exploitation. However, as it stands, smart contracts are not sufficiently regulated nor audited for existing vulnerabilities. Different platforms, languages, and implementations create roadblocks for widespread solutions. The goal of this project is to optimize the process of assurance in smart contracts by documenting known bugs and providing a baseline categorization by which smart contracts can be compared, analyzed, and improved.

10.10   Quantum Cryptography

Quantum cryptography offers the possibility of a significant increase to the security of communications, at a time when electronic communications are already of vital importance and only becoming more and more critical to a wide variety of industries and government functions. Experimental hardware is constantly under development, but the cost of custom cutting-edge optical equipment, satellites, and other equipment makes performing tests prohibitively expensive in many cases (Artur 1991; Bennett and Brassard 1984; Dagmar et al. 2007). While physical experiments will always be necessary, simulations based on robust models can provide the opportunity to study many different communications protocols and hardware configurations, leading to new methods of implementing quantum cryptography and suggesting the most promising paths to pursue in the development of new hardware.

10.10.1   Cryptographic Key Distribution

Today's computer systems and networks have vulnerabilities that provide a playground for hackers. Cache and pipelines improve the performance of computer systems but vulnerable to side channel attacks that could lead to leaking data among the supposed to be "isolated" virtual machines. Strong public encryptions provide convenience for key exchanges and "unbreakable" complexity to digital computers. However prime numbers are under attack by quantum computers that quantum algorithms can run considerable faster to make the impossible possible. Quantum Internet uses quantum communication satellites to entangle particles that exhibit "spooky action at a distance." Quantum key distribution provides a more secure way of key exchanges that immune to man-in-the-middle and other exploits. Quantum communication enables quantum networks transfer entangled quantum states directly between nodes without actually transmitting a single physical qubit, thus further improving the security (Chip et al. 2005).

A qubit is a fundamental unit of quantum gates that exist two aspects of quantum mechanics, superposition and entanglement. Mathematically a qubit can be

represented as a two-dimensional system using the ket-notation. The superposition
sate can be represented as

$$|\psi\rangle = \alpha|0\rangle + \beta|1\rangle$$

The two energy levels $|0\rangle$ and $|1\rangle$ can be represented as

$$|0\rangle = \begin{bmatrix} 1 \\ 0 \end{bmatrix} \quad |1\rangle = \begin{bmatrix} 0 \\ 1 \end{bmatrix}$$

where $|\alpha|^2 + |\beta|^2 = 1$.

A qubit or a system of qubits changes its state by going through a series of unitary
transformations. A unitary transformation is described by a matrix U with complex
entries. The matrix U is unitary if

$$U \cdot U^\dagger = U^\dagger \cdot U = I$$

A quantum algorithm can call a classical subroutine only if it is compiled into a
sequence of reversible logical gates such as CNOT or Toffoli gate (in particular, the
number of input and output wires in each gate must be the same).

A quantum algorithm can be thought of as three steps:

I. Encoding of the data, which could be classical or quantum, into the state of a
set of input qubits.
II. A sequence of quantum gates applied to this set of input qubits, and finally.
III. Measurements of one or more of the qubits at the end to obtain a classically
interpretable result.

Quantum algorithms are often classified into different categories: number theory-
based, oracle-based, quantum simulation algorithms, etc. Quantum Fourier transform is one of the number theory-based quantum algorithms that we will study in
this book.

Due to the high cost and availability of the quantum computing devices, most
people use simulations (e.g., ibmq_qsim_simulator) to test and develop quantum
algorithms. When running properly, algorithms are put onto real quantum backends, such as ibmq_5_yorktown (5 qubits) or ibmq_16_melbourne (14 qubits),
ibmq_manhattan (65 qbuts), etc. Computer simulation is also very beneficial in
quantum cryptography where people can simulate quantum crypto protocols such
as BB84.

Quantum algorithms can outperform the classical ones when adding the superposition of qubits in entangled states. Geometrically, quantum state transformations
on n qubits are rotations of 2^n dimensional complex state space.

An important insight made in 1973 by our IBM colleague Charles Bennett is that
any classical computation can be transformed into a reversible form. Figure 10.2
shows a reversible classical circuit.

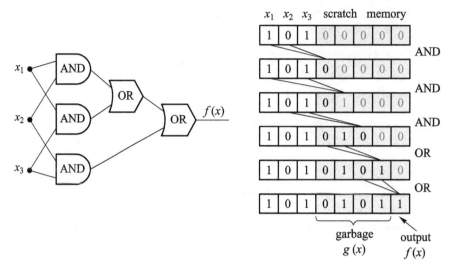

Fig. 10.2 Reversible classical circuit

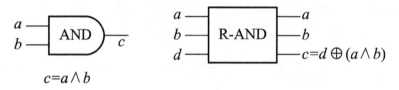

Fig. 10.3 Logic AND gate and its reversible circuit

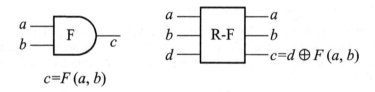

Fig. 10.4 Converting general logic circuit to reversible circuit

For individual circuit, the reversible circuit can be obtained by adding all inputs to the output and adding an additional input. Figure 10.3 shows an "AND" gate and its corresponding reversible circuit.

In general, for $c = F(a, b)$, its reversible function R-F can be done by adding $c = d \oplus F(a, b)$, such as Fig. 10.4.

Given input $N(= p \times q)$, the Shor's algorithm consists of three steps:

I. period finding based on number theory,
II. QFT speed up, and
III. calculate the factors based on the "period."

10.10.2   Shor's Algorithm

Shor's algorithm can factor integers with significant improvement in speed on quantum computers.

I. Randomly choose an integer a such that $0 < a < N$. Use the Euclidean algorithm to determine whether a and N are relatively prime.

II. If not prime, use quantum parallelism to compute $f(x) = a^x \bmod N$ for $x \in [0, 2^n - 1]$, choose

$$T = 2^n, N^2 \leq T \leq 2N^2$$

Initialize two register of qubits, first use an argument register with t qubits and second a function register with $n = \lceil \log_2 N \rceil$ bits. These registers start in the initial state

$$|\psi_0\rangle = |0\rangle |0\rangle$$

III. Apply a Hadamard gate on each of the qubits in the argument register to yield an equally weighted superposition of all integers from 0 to $T - 1$

$$|\psi_1\rangle = \frac{1}{\sqrt{T}} \sum_{0}^{T-1} |a\rangle |0\rangle$$

IV. Implement the modular exponentiation (Archimedes and Gizopoulos 2014; Markov and Saeedi 2012) function $x^a \bmod N$ on the function register, giving the state

$$|\psi_2\rangle = \frac{1}{\sqrt{T}} \sum_{a=0}^{T-1} |a\rangle |x^a \bmod N\rangle$$

V. Perform a quantum Fourier transform on the argument register, resulting in the state:

$$|\psi_3\rangle = \frac{1}{\sqrt{T}} \sum_{a=0}^{T-1} \sum_{z=0}^{T-1} e^{(2\pi i)(\frac{aZ}{T})} |z\rangle |x^a \bmod N\rangle$$

VI. Measure. With the high probability, a value v close to a multiple of $2^n/r$

$$v = \frac{T}{r} = \frac{2^n}{r}$$

will be obtained, where q ranges from 0 to $r - 1$.

VII. Find r using Euclid's algorithm. With the measured v, the period can be calculated with

$$r = \frac{T}{v} = \frac{2^n}{v}$$

Example $N = 21$, then $N^2 \leq T = 2^9 \leq 882(2N^2)$. We take $n = 9$. Since $\lceil \log_2 N \rceil = 5$, the second register requires five qubits. Suppose random select $a = 11$ and the measure of the second of the superposition produces $u = 8$. Suppose that measurement of the state returns $v = 427$. Continue fraction to obtain a guess q for the period. Finally, we got $q = 6$.

Since 6 is even, $a^{6/2} - 1 = 11^3 - 1 = 1330$ and $a^{6/2} + 1 = 11^3 + 1 = 1332$. We compute gcd $(21, 1330) = 7$ and gcd $(21, 1332) = 3$. As a result of the integer factorization, we got $N = 7 \times 3$.

10.10.3   Quantum Error Correction

The main problems in quantum computing are environmental noise, which is due to incomplete isolation of the system from the rest of the world, and control errors, which are caused by calibration errors and random fluctuations in control parameters. Attempts to reduce the effects of these errors are confronted by the conflicting needs of being able to control and reliably measure the quantum systems. These needs require strong interactions with control devices and systems that are sufficiently well isolated to maintain coherence, the subtle relationship between the phases in a quantum superposition. The fact that quantum effects rarely persist on macroscopic scales suggests that meeting these needs requires considerable outside intervention.

When considering the problem of limiting the effects of errors in information processing, the first task is to establish the properties of the physical systems that are available for representing and computing with information. Thus, it is necessary to learn the following: the physical system to be used, in particular the structure of its state space; the available means for controlling this system; the type of information to be processed; and the nature of the errors, that is, the error model. With this information, the approaches used to correct errors in the three examples provided in the previous section involve the following:

- Determine a code, which is a subspace of the physical system, that can represent the information to be processed.
- Identify a decoding procedure that can restore the information represented in the code after any one of the most likely errors occurred or determine a pair of syndrome and information-carrying subsystems such that the code corresponds to a "base" state of the syndrome subsystem and the primary errors act only on the syndrome.
- Analyze the error behavior of the code and subsystem.

10.10.4   Post Quantum Cryptography

Post-quantum cryptography refers to cryptographic algorithms (usually public key algorithms) that are thought to be secure against an attack by a quantum computer. Post-quantum cryptography is all about preparing for the era of quantum computing by updating existing mathematical-based algorithms and standards.

The security of most standard algorithms today relies on very difficult-to-solve mathematical problems. That means today's public key encryption protocols, like secure socket layer (SSL) and transport layer security (TLS), are sufficient for defending against most modern technology. But quantum computers running Shor's algorithm will be able to break those math-based systems in moments.

10.11   Summary

In this chapter, we discussed classical cryptography and basic cytological analysis to "attack" simple substitution cipher.

Symmetric key algorithm can use one key for encryption and decryption if the encryption function satisfies exclusive OR. AES is one of the frequently used asymmetric encryptions nowadays.

Public key encryption belongs to asymmetric encryption. Each party has a key pair known as public key and private key. RSA is one of the most famous public key cryptosystems. The idea behind the RSA is it is hard to factor a large integer.

SSL secures data in motion.

Though with similarities, crypto hash and encryption are different. Hash in one-way function, while encryption is two-way function.

PGP is a strong encryption and is good for end-to-end encryption. It has the advantage of symmetric encryption, which is fast, and the advantage of asymmetric encryption, which is easy for key exchange.

Access control is to decide who can access the systems and usually involves multifactor authentication.

Cryptographic hardware not only makes the encryption/decryption fast; it also improves the security as the crypto computation is independent to the main computer.

Internet privacy is a challenge nowadays as surveillance is anywhere. GDPR is an important privacy law that not only applies to business in Europe; it also applies all entities that do business with Europe. So it is considered an international regulation.

Blockchain is a distributed ledger that usually contains blocks, transactions, timestamps, proof of work, network, and incentive mechanism. Bitcoin is the most famous cryptocurrency based on the blockchain technology. Other applications include smart contracts and banking system as well.

Quantum computing shows the possibility to break the current crypto system. QKD is to use quantum mechanics to distribute keys to prevent crypto keys being intercepted or observed (Al-Khateeb et al. 2013; QKD Simulator 2019).

Projects

10.1 NSA job tweet

Write a program to crack the mono-alphabetic (simple) substitution cipher. You can do it manually or write a program (strongly recommended) to solve it.

```
TPFCCDLFDTTE PCACCPLIRCDT DKLPCFRP?QEIQ LHPQLIPQ EODF
GPWAFOPWPRTI IZXNDKIQPKII KRIRRIFCAPNC DXKDCIQCAFMD
VKFPCADF.
```

If you do not understand the deciphered message, how to improve the decryption accuracy?

10.2 NFC-based multifactor authentication

Follow directions from the book's website; develop a NFC-based multifactor authentication application. Upload your code to GitHub and create a one page poster.

Exercises

10.1 For Zimmermann telegram, what do you consider the best technique to decipher the code?

10.2 Assume we have discovered the random key for simple substitution cipher is

```
phqgiumeaylnofdxjkrcvstzwb.
```

Decipher the following message:

```
JVPFCVO QDOXVCAFM REDTR CEI XDRRAHANACW
CD HKIPL CEI QVKKIFC QKWXCD RWRCIO.
```

What is the accuracy of your decipher for Exercise 10.2? How to improve it?

10.3 Suppose two "large" prime numbers are 3 and 7 and the message $M = 9$. Follow the RSA algorithm described in the book to find the ciphertext and then decipher the ciphertext.

10.4 Which layer/layers does SSL reside on the 7-layer OSI model?

10.5 Crypto hash uses different crypto algorithm than encryption algorithms. (T/F)

10.6 MD5 is commonly seen on downloading websites. This means it is for sure the downloads are not altered if the hash value of the downloading software matches the published one. (T/F)

10.7 True random numbers can be generated by software using random bit generator. (T/F)

10.8 MD5, AES, RSA, and PGP are all considered strong encryption. (T/F)

10.9 PGP is a combination of symmetric, asymmetric, and hash algorithms. (T/F)

10.10 TLS is an updated version of SSL, and it is more secure. (T/F)

10.11 Blackberry was a favorite type of phone that has good security. Conduct some study and identify what encryption was used on Blackberry phones?

10.12 Username and password authentication is the weakest in term of security. Why people still use it?

10.13 What are the main components for a blockchain?

10.14 Why quantum key distribution (QkD) is more secure than traditional key distribution methods, such as RSA?

10.15 What are the considerations for post quantum cryptography, knowing that the current public key algorithm could be broken by future quantum computers?

References

Al-Khateeb, W., Al-Khateeb, K., Ahmad, N. E., & Salleh, S. N. M. (2013). Practical Considerations on Quantum Key Distribution (QKD). In *International Conference on Advanced Computer Science Applications and Technologies* (pp. 278–283).

Archimedes, P., & Gizopoulos, D. (2014). Fast quantum modular exponentiation architecture for Shor's factoring algorithm. *Quantum Information and Computation, 14*(7&8), 0649–0682.

Artur, K. E. (1991). Quantum cryptography based on Bell's Theorem. *Physical Review Letters, 67*(6), 661–663.

Bennett, C. H., & Brassard, G. (1984) Quantum cryptography: Public key distribution and coin tossing. In *Proceedings of IEEE International Conference on Computers, Systems and Signal Processing* (Vol. 175, pp. 175–179).

Chip, E., Colvin, A., Pearson, D., et al. (2005). Current status of the DARPA Quantum network. In *Proceedings of the Quantum Information and Computation* (Vol. 5815, pp.12).

Dagmar, B., Erdélyi, G., Meyer, T., et al. (2007). Quantum cryptography: A survey. *ACM Computer Surveys, 39*(2), Article 6 (July 2007). p27.

Marcin N., & Pach, A. R. (2012). The measure of security in Quantum Cryptography. In *2012 IEEE Global Communications Conference (GLOBECOM)* (pp. 967–972).

Markov, I. L., & Saeedi, M. (2012). Constant-optimized quantum circuits for modular multiplication and exponentiation. *Quantum Information and Computation, 12*(5–6), 361–394.

Monz, T., et al. (2016). Realization of a scalable Shor algorithm. *Science, 351*, 1068–1070.

Patrick, J. C., et. al. (2018). Quantum algorithm implementations for beginners. In *Los Alamos National Laboratory*, pp. 1–18.

QKD Simulator. (2019). Arash Atashpendar. Retrieved September 22, 2019.

Shor, P. W. (1994). Polynomial-time Algorithms for Prime Factorization and Discrete Logarithms on a Quantum Computer. In *Proceeding of IEEE the 35th Annual Symposium on Foundations of Computer* (pp. 124–134).

Vandersypen, L. M. K., et al. (2001). Experimental realization of Shor's Quantum factoring algorithm using nuclear magnetic resonance. *Nature, 414*(6866), 883–887.

Wang, S. (2021). PGP Encryption. pNeumann Security https://pneumannsecurity.blogspot.com/2020/09/pgp-encryption.html. Last accessed: November 1, 2021.

Wang, S. P., & Sakk, E. (2021). Quantum algorithms: Overviews, foundations, and speedups. In *The 5th IEEE International Conference on Cryptography, Security and Privacy* (pp. 17–21).

Wang, S., Rohde, M., & Ali, A. (2020). Quantum cryptography and simulation: Tools and techniques. *ACM Proceedings of International Conference of Cryptography, Security and Privacy (ICCSP)* (pp. 36–41).

Appendix A
Design and Implementation: Modifying Neumann Architecture

In this chapter, we discuss the design and implementation of an invention of a new type of computer architecture that is capable of preventing data stored on computers from being stolen.[1]

Modified Neumann architecture has shown promising in solving computer security problems. The architecture separates the network communication component from the other parts of computer system with a separate system bus. Data exchange between the two system buses can only be performed through the bus controller via a command issued by the computer operator. A secured micro-operating system is used to guarantee the integrity of communications.

The micro-OS that runs on a microprocessor resides in the "red" zone. It uses a firmware image that automatically loads to the microprocessor memory during booting process. A watchdog monitors the system and reset the system whenever a preset threshold is met. In addition, memory protection and virtualization techniques are used to enhance runtime security and prevent code injection.

The invention has been prototyped and tested; it was awarded a national high-tech grant.

A.1 Data Security in Computer Systems

Computers nowadays are very easy to be intruded via network especially through the Internet. Therefore, information stored on a computer such as SSN, credit cards, bank accounts, personal privacy information, etc. is vulnerable to computer hackers.

---

[1] The chapter was based on a patent application the book authored files in 2005. The invention received high recognition by then US Senator Orrin Hatch, a renowned Harvard professor, a national medal of technology awardee and National Academy of Science member, and top companies in the private sector.

© The Author(s), under exclusive license to Springer Nature Singapore Pte Ltd. 2021   321
S. P. Wang, *Computer Architecture and Organization*,
https://doi.org/10.1007/978-981-16-5662-0

Firewalls in some extends can prevent information stored on a computer be stolen. However, it can only effective in a certain period of time. Some firewalls are mere software; some others even though use "hardware" to set up a "wall" between the computer and the outside world; the core components are based on algorithms or in other word software. On the other hand, a firewall is not designed to be used on personal computers or handheld devices. So, it cannot guarantee that the information stored on a computer will never be stolen.

A.1.1   Computer Security

Computer security is to study and to enhance the confidentiality, integrity, and availability of computer systems (Bishop 2019). Certified information systems security professionals (CISSP) classifies computer and information security into ten domains* (Gregg 2019):

- Access control.
- Application development security.
- Business continuity and disaster recovery planning.
- Cryptography.
- Information security governance and risk management.
- Legal, regulation, investigations, and compliance.
- Operations security.
- Physical security.
- Security architecture and design.
- Telecommunications and network security.[2]

Computer security also can be classified into physical security and technological security (ISC[2] 2010). Technological security can be divided into five aspects: application security, operating system security, network security, architecture security, and data security.

However, if the applications running on the web server are not properly designed to prevent attacks, then hackers may be able to break into the database server from the web server. One of such attacks is called SQL injection attack.

We are all tired of installing security updates on our computers. This is an example of operating system security. An operating system (no matter it is Windows, Mac iOS, or Linux) contains hundreds of millions of lines of source code. It is very likely that there are bugs and other vulnerabilities. If an attacker has

---

[2] Since 2015, the CISSP has changed to 8 domains. They include: Introduction to Security and Risk Management, Asset Security, Security Architecture and Engineering, Communication and Network Security, Identity and Access Management (IAM), Security Assessment and Testing, Security Operations, and Software Development Security.

very good knowledge about the operating system and discovered the vulnerabilities, security bleach would happen.

Data security is to guarantee the safety of data stored on a computer system (Daswani et al. 2007). There are all kind of data on computers, from web browsing data (cookies, history, etc.) to sensitive data such as passwords, banking information, or even SSN. Identity theft would happen if those data are not properly protected (Merkow and Breithaupt 2005).

A.1.2   Data Security and Data Bleaches

Privacy is one of the biggest concerns nowadays. Some employers use centralized monitoring software to monitor employee's E-mails and other private information. Google operates under a streamlined privacy policy that enables the Internet's most powerful company to dig even deeper into the lives of its more than 1 billion users. Google will share their users' data across Gmail, Google Plus, YouTube, and other products.

Identity theft is a more serious problem which draws attentions recently by the Congress. Nearly 10 million people were victimized by identity theft in 1 year, according to Time magazine, the lost reached 5 billion. In early March 2005, the nation's largest data miner ChoicePoint with 19 billion data files including driver's license, SSN, credit history, birth certificate, real estate deed, and even thumbprint and DNA was broken into and some 145,000 people's data was extracted. In Senator Charles Schumer's words, "Our system of protecting people's identity is virtually nonexistent in this country." His staff was able to download personal information on the likes of Dick Cheney and Brad Pitt from a ChoicePoint rival, Westlaw.

In a letter former US Senator Orrin Hatch wrote to the book author in responding the invention in computer security, Senator Hatch said, "Identity theft is a serious problem that has drawn much attention recently in Congress. As we know, the damage caused can go beyond money and privacy and become a real threat to our national security."

So far, many current researches or inventions may have some impacts to reduce the risk of information theft in one way or another. However, those solutions have not solved the information security problems thoroughly due to the limitation of the computer architecture they used. There is a problem that exists in John von Neumann computer architecture model—the foundation of computer architecture. If this problem is not solved, information stored on a computer will hardly be secure.

The main goal for the invention is to propose a new type of secure computer system with a microprocessor-based hardware-assist and a micro-OS that can not only monitor the system security but also enable computers to prevent intruders from getting data stored in the computer system. In a pending patent, the book author proposed a new computer architecture model—modified Neumann model. Based on this new model, the network communication component is separated from the other parts of a computer system with a separate system bus. All components in a computer system (except network) reside on another system bus. Data exchange between those two system buses can only be performed through the bus controller via a command issued by the computer operator. So, data stored in this computer (main storage) can only be accessed by the computer operator. In other words, user data is isolated from outside networks and therefore cannot be accessed even if the computer is compromised or taken over from outside networks.

In addition to preventing information theft, the system contains a security agent that can monitor and report any security-related events. The recorded security events can be transmitted to or viewed by the central monitoring system in real time.

A test bed has been developed, and experiments show that the system is very promising. The major technology breakthrough is that it can prevent unauthorized access of any information in a protected computer system. Security is guaranteed as the system is implemented using the patent pending secure computer architecture (hardware).

The theme of the research is stated as following:

- Study the widely used John Neumann computer architecture model.
- Modify the Neumann model and proposed a new secure architecture model.
- Complete the technical details and the implementation.

An add-on security board is constructed by using a coprocessor, FPGA, and other digital circuits together with kernel software. A multiport I/O and a dual-port memory interface circuits are designed in combing with the add-on circuit board. The dual-bus system can be switched over one another through another add-on circuit names bus controller. A micro-OS manages the add-on operations and monitors the system security. In the following sections, each of the new designs will be discussed in detail.

A.1.3   Researches in Architecture Security

There are many researches related to the secure computer architecture area. Largman et al. (2004) proposed "automatically create multiple sequentially or concurrently and intermittently isolated and/or restricted computing environments method to prevent viruses, malicious, or even computer or device corruption and failure." According to this method, untrusted content is only exposed in the user processor logic environment in a temporary storage. The question that remains for this method is how to determine which content is trusted and which is not. There might be a pre-determination process.

Anderson put "removable trusted (hardware) gateway devices" between each of the inputs/outputs and the bus to secure the file transmission. As described, the approval of access the data is dependent on a so-called LOCK. Once the lock is stolen, intercepted, or hacked, sensitive data is then open to those hackers.

Hewlett-Packard (HP-Compaq 2002) has been working on a new type of secure platform architecture (SPA). It is a set of software interfaces built on top of HP's

Itanium-based product line. SPA will enable operating systems and device drivers to run as unprivileged tasks and will allow services to be authenticated and identified. The problem that exists in the SPA is that, as the company described, it uses a set of software interfaces to authenticate and identify the tasks. Once the system is compromised, SPA will not be able to function well.

Sean Smith and Steve Weingart (1999) developed a prototype using a high-performance, programmable secure coprocessor. It is a type of software, Hardware, and cryptographic architecture (Suh et al. 2005). This architecture addressed some issues especially how to secure programs running on coprocessors and system recovery. In term of secure information and data, there are lots of works that need to be done.

Recently, MIT researchers proposed secure processors that enable new applications by ensuring private and authentic program execution even in the face of physical attack.

So far, many current researches may have some impacts to reduce the risk of information theft in one way or another. However, those solutions have not solved the information security problems thoroughly due to the limitation of the computer architecture they used. We have found that there is a problem that exists in John von Neumann computer architecture model—the foundation of computer architecture. If this problem is not solved, information stored on a computer will hardly be secure.

A.2   Single-Bus View of Neumann Architecture

Neumann architecture is the foundation of modern computer systems. It is a single bus, stored program computer architecture that consists of a CPU, memory, I/O, and storage. The CPU is composed of a control unit (CU) and arithmetic logical unit (ALU) (von Neumann 1945). Almost all modern computers are Neumann computers which are characterized as a single system bus (control, data, address) with all circuits attached to it.

A.2.1   *John von Neumann Computer Architecture*

John von Neumann wrote *First Draft of a Report on the EDVAC* in which he outlined the architecture of a stored-program computer. He proposed a concept that has characterized mainstream computer architecture since 1945. Figure A.1 shows the Neumann model.

A "system bus" representation of the Neumann model is shown in Fig. A.2. This is just another view of the Neumann model, with the introduction of the concept of direct memory access (DMA).

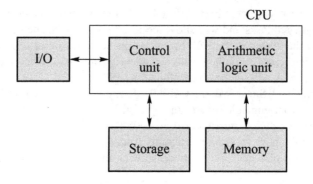

Fig. A.1 Block diagram of John von Neumann's computer architecture model

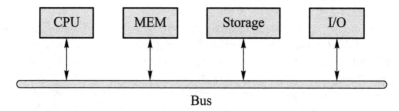

Fig. A.2 A "system bus" representation of the Neumann model. It is equivalent to Fig. A.1 with the introduction of DMA

A.2.2   Modified Neumann Computer Architecture

Since the 1990s, computer networks especially the Internet has been widespread around the world. Computers are no longer only being used to compute as a standalone machine. The feature of information exchange through network is a vital component in today's computers. Unfortunately, John von Neumann was not able to foresee this change. One can argue that we can consider network as part of input/output device which is already included in the Neumann model. However, the network interface is so important that it is not appropriate to classify it as in the general I/O device category. Furthermore, an I/O device in Neumann model refers to those devices such as a keyboard, a display, a printer, etc. which are used for direct interact with the computers. Now, the way people use a computer is quite different than that of 70 years ago. So, a modification of Neumann's computer architecture model is necessary to reflect this change. Figure A.3 shows the modified Neumann model. In Fig. A.3, a network unit (interface) is added to the computer system bus so that the I/O unit only deals with input and output devices such as keyboard, mouse, display, etc. Separating network unit from the general I/O offers great advantages.

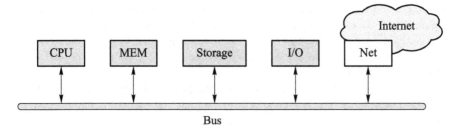

Fig. A.3 Modified Neumann computer architecture model. Here network interface is added to the Neumann model and is separated from the general input and output devices

A.2.3   Problems Exist in the Neumann Model

As we all know, Newton's three law and theory of gravitation make essentially identical predictions as long as the strength of the gravitational field is weak, which is our usual experience. It was so dominant that no one would dare doubt until Einstein predicts that the direction of light propagation should be changed in a gravitational field. This discovery modified the Newton's law and made the modern theory of gravitation possible.

The Neumann model is so dominant that no one dare to challenge it since its birth in 1945. However, if we look into the Neumann model from security perspective, we could find out that it does have some drawbacks.

In the Neumann model, CPUs, memory, I/O, external storage, and network interface are all connected to one single system bus which includes control bus, data bus, and address bus. Once intruders break into the system from any network locations, they can totally take over the computer system and do whatever they want.

For the Neumann model, the concept of CPU is a centralized control and arithmetic unit. Even though nowadays a computer with multiprocessors is very common, however those processors are merely coordinated together by software to perform one task or a series of tasks. In other words, they share the same system bus. Intruders can take over the whole system once they break into the system from any network ports.

A.3   A Dual-Bus Solution

The main idea for this invention was to propose a new computer architecture that enables computers to prevent intruders from getting data stored in the computer system. Based on the modified Neumann model, the network communication component is separated from the other parts of a computer system with a separate system bus. All components in the computer system (except network) are run on another system bus. Data exchange between those two system buses can only be performed through the bus controller via a command issued by the computer operator. So, data stored on this computer (main storage) can only be accessed by the computer operator. In other words, user data is isolated from outside networks and therefore cannot be accessed even if the computer is compromised or taken over from outside network.

A computer platform constructed in accordance with the principles of the present invention is intrusion-free, information and data secure computer system. It comprises:

- Two zones (red zone and green zone) with two separated system buses.
- The network interface is only attached on one bus in red zone.
- Each bus has its own CPU and private memory.
- Main (protected) external storage is attached only on one bus in green zone.
- One cache storage (temporary external storage or dual-port external storage) is connected to both internal system buses via a bus controller.
- A bus controller connects two internal system buses between the red zone and green zone.
- Input and output devices such as keyboard, mouse, display, etc.

In Fig. A.3, a network interface is added to the Neumann model. Even though a network interface can be considered as an input/output device, adding this interface to the system bus and separating it from other parts (even the general I/O port) has many advantages. The modification made it possible for this invention to isolate network from other parts within a computer system, while data can still be transmitted through the network.

Figure A.4 depicts a functional block diagram of such intrusion-free, information and data secure computer system architecture (Wang 2005). Normally the computer is in the state of green zone where all computation works are performed. In green zone, network is disabled. When data transmission is needed, the bus controller (BC) switches to red zone where another CPU is taken over the job. In red zone,

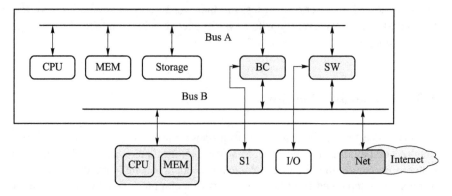

Fig. A.4 Block diagram of intrusion-free computer architecture. User data is stored on the main storage which will never expose to the network (Color)

there is no external storage, all data is stored on cache storage via the bus controller. The bus controller is managed by the computer operator or delegates (programs) assigned by the computer operator. A switch (SW) is used to switch I/O devices to the active bus.

Looking from network side (outside), this intrusion-free, information, and data secure computer has one or more CPUs, internal memory, input/output devices such as a keyboard and a mouse, network ports (Ethernet or wireless), and cache storage. Because the red zone only deals with the network communication, suppose a hacker break into the system from the Internet, what the hacker will see is just the temporary data on the cache storage and maybe some of the system data. It is impossible for the intruder to see data on the main (protected) storage.

A.4   Bus Controller

Figure A.5 is the block diagram of the bus controller. Bus A in green zone can access the cache storage only if the EN 1 signal is enabled. Similarly, the bus B from the red zone can access the cache storage only if the EN 2 signal is enabled. Notice that EN 1 and EN 2 are controlled by the computer operator. Intruders cannot make any enable actions without directly operating the computer.

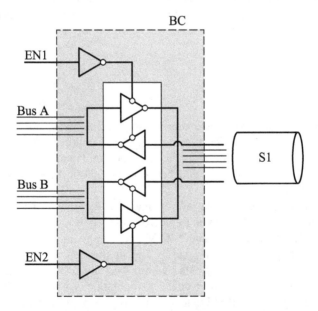

Fig. A.5 Block diagram of bus controller that connects two buses and a cache (dual-port) storage device for data exchange between the red zone and green zone

A.4.1   Working Mechanism of the Bus Controller

Computer operators can automatically enable the data access to the cache storage. To automatically enable the data access to the cache storage, an operator set default to bus A (green zone) so that data can be accessed directly from/to the cache storage. When network communication is needed such as launching an Internet explorer, the EN 2 is automatically enabled so that bus B is connected and bus A is disconnected from the system so that main storage is isolated from the system.

A multiport interface is used to switch the keyboard/mouse and display devices between those two buses either automatically. For automatic switching, the switching process is synchronized with the bus controller.

Combining the cache storage or temporary external storage with the bus controller forms the dual-port storage which can be accessed by two computer system buses. It is different from so-called dual-port external storage devices which, for example, have one USB port and one FireWare port. In that case you can only attach one port at a time. Attaching two ports simultaneously would damage the system.

When the cache storage is attached onto bus A in green zone, the files are displayed, and then the trusted files are ready to be copied to the main storage. After the operation, the cache storage is erased (Wang and Ledley 2006). User data can then be copied to the cache storage if network transmission is further required. When the cache storage is switched to the bus B in red zone, the data is displayed and is ready to be transmitted. Data download from network or Internet can then be stored on the cache storage. All data have to pass through the bus controller which is controlled by the computer operator.

A.4.2   Coprocessor Board

The coprocessor board contains a coprocessor, an field programmable gate array (FPGA), flash memory, multiport memory interface, multiport I/O interface, a bus controller, and kernel program that enable the add-on board. The kernel program also coordinates the communication between the add-on board and the current computer system.

FPGA solutions from Lattice deliver unique features, high performance, and excellent value for FPGA designs. LatticeXP FPGA devices utilize a combination of non-volatile FLASH cells and SRAM technology to deliver a single-chip solution supporting "instant-on" startup and infinite re-configurability. A non-volatile FLASH cell array distributed within the LatticeXP FPGA device stores the device configuration. At power-up the configuration is transferred from FLASH memory to configuration SRAM in less than 1 ms providing an instant-on FPGA. In addition, LatticeXP FPGA devices provide security by eliminating the need for an external configuration bit-stream and by providing non-volatile security features. Non-volatile, reprogrammable FPGAs are well suited for implementing system logic for this project.

The LatticeXP architecture contains an array of logic blocks surrounded by programmable I/O cells (PIC). Interspersed between the rows of logic blocks are rows of sysMEM ^{TM} embedded block RAM (EBR).

On the left and right sides of the PFU array, there are non-volatile memory blocks. In configuration mode, this nonvolatile memory is programmed via the IEEE 1149.1 TAP port or the sysCONFIG ^{TM} peripheral port. On power up, the configuration data is transferred from the non-volatile memory blocks to the configuration SRAM. With this technology, expensive external configuration memories are not required, and designs are secured from unauthorized read-back. This transfer of data from non-volatile memory to configuration SRAM via wide busses happens in microseconds, providing an "instant-on" capability that allows easy interfacing in many applications.

There are two kinds of logic blocks, the programmable functional unit (PFU) and programmable functional unit without RAM/ROM (PFF). The PFU contains the building blocks for logic, arithmetic, RAM, ROM, and register functions. The PFF block contains building blocks for logic, arithmetic, and ROM functions. Both PFU and PFF blocks are optimized for flexibility, allowing complex designs to be implemented quickly and efficiently. Logic blocks are arranged in a two-dimensional array. Only one type of block is used per row. The PFU blocks are used on the outside rows. The rest of the core consists of rows of PFF blocks interspersed with rows of PFU blocks. For every three rows of PFF blocks there is a row of PFU blocks.

Each PIC block encompasses two PIOs (PIO pairs) with their respective sysIO interfaces. PIO pairs on the left and right edges of the device can be configured as LVDS transmit/receive pairs. sysMEM EBRs are large dedicated fast memory blocks. They can be configured as RAM or ROM. The PFU, PFF, PIC, and EBR blocks are arranged in a two-dimensional grid with rows and columns. The blocks are connected with many vertical and horizontal routing channel resources. The place and route software tool automatically allocate these routing resources.

At the end of the rows containing the sysMEM blocks are the sysCLOCK phase locked loop (PLL) blocks. These PLLs have multiply, divide, and phase shifting capability, they are used to manage the phase relationship of the clocks. The LatticeXP architecture provides up to four PLLs per device.

Every device in the family has a JTAG port with internal logic analyzer (ispTRACY) capability. The sysCONFIG port allows for serial or parallel device configuration. The LatticeXP devices are available for operation from 3.3 V, 2.5 V, 1.8 V, and 1.2 V power supplies, providing easy integration into the overall system.

- PFU and PFF blocks   The core of the LatticeXP devices consists of PFU and PFF blocks. The PFUs can be programmed to perform logic, arithmetic, distributed RAM, and distributed ROM functions. PFF blocks can be programmed to perform logic, arithmetic, and ROM functions. Except where necessary, the remainder of the data sheet will use the term PFU to refer to both PFU and PFF blocks. Each PFU block consists of four interconnected slices, numbered 0–3 as

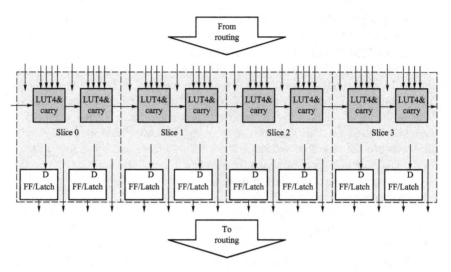

Fig. A.6 PFU diagram

shown in Fig. A.6. All the interconnections to and from PFU blocks are from routing. There are 53 inputs and 25 outputs associated with each PFU block.

- Slice Each slice contains two LUT4 lookup tables feeding two registers (programmed to be in FF or Latch mode) and some associated logic that allows the LUTs to be combined to perform functions such as LUT5, LUT6, LUT7, and LUT8. There is control logic to perform set/reset functions (programmable as synchronous/asynchronous), clock select, chip-select, and wider RAM/ROM functions. Figure A.7 shows an overview of the internal logic of the slice. The registers in the slice can be configured for positive/negative and edge/level clocks.

There are 14 input signals, 13 signals from routing, and 1 from the carry-chain (from adjacent slice or PFU). There are seven outputs, six to routing, and one to carry-chain (to adjacent PFU).

A.5   Dual-Port Storage

Computer memory and storage are mostly single-port. This means that they can only be attached to one processor. Dual-port storage is a type of external memory which can be accessed by two processors simultaneously without worrying about the read/write conflicts.

Motorola's MPC 8260 is a chip that contains a 64-bit PowerPC microprocessor and a versatile communications processor module (CPM). The MPC 8260 is used in a wide array of applications, especially those in the communications and networking

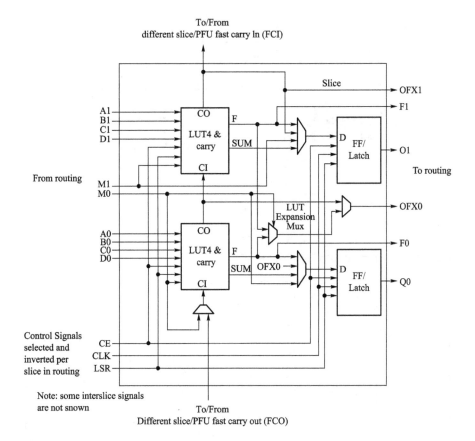

Fig. A.7 Slice diagram

markets. Examples include remote access servers, regional office routers, cellular base stations, and SONET transmission controllers.

A Lattice's ispGDX2 ^{TM} generic digital crosspoint switch is used as a multiport interface. The ispGDX2 device can interface the MPC 8260 with an external master and a number of slaves including SDRAM and FLASH. The control logic for the SDRAM and FLASH is built in a CPLD which is used to interface the MPC 8260 to the ispGDX2 device and to control the read/write to the memory. This function can be implemented in Lattice CPLDs.

The PowerPC core of the 8260 (the PowerPC 603e) can be replaced by other processors or ASIC. The memory controller within the MPC 8260 is utilized in this design. Figure A.8 shows the diagram using MPC 8260 with the multiport interface.

Figure A.9 shows in detail the function, internal logic, and cross-connections that the ispGDX2 performs in the design. This section includes the signal list and descriptions of all signals used in this design and also provide a functional description of the design.

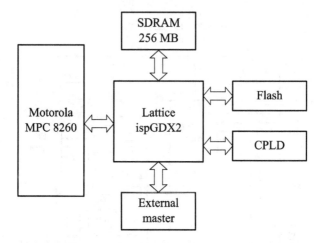

Fig. A.8 Diagram of ispGDX2 multiport interface

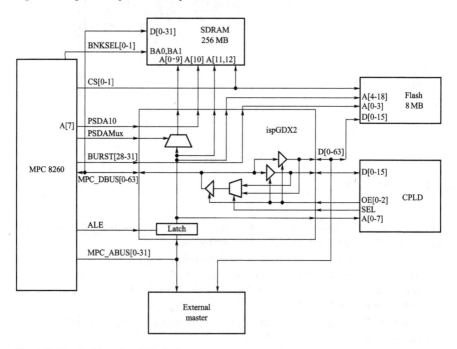

Fig. A.9 Detailed functional block diagram

A.6 Micro-Operating System

Software design involves with controlling and monitoring the communication between two zones. A micro-operating system is designed. It runs on a micro-processor that resides in the "red" zone. The micro-OS uses a firmware image that automatically loads to the microprocessor memory during booting process. A watchdog monitors the system and reset the system whenever a preset threshold is met. In addition, memory protection and virtualization techniques are used to enhance runtime security and prevent code injection.

A.7   Putting Together

A prototype computer based on the newly proposed secure computer architecture has been built (Fig. A.10). Preliminary tests show that it meets the design goals. The Windows firewall was intentionally removed, and all security updates were declined in order to test the data security on this computer system. Several intrusion tools have been used to the tests including Key Loggers, Spyware, Spyware cookies, Trojans, Worms, Virus, etc. The system has also undergone a series of tests by senior security professionals and "white hat" attackers. So far, no data bleaches have been found. The initial experiments prove that the proposed secure computer architecture model can enhance the computer security. And hopefully it can be adopted to modern personal computers.

Further research may result in the possibility of extending the scope of this architecture from personal computers to server systems. In order to make the system to be widely used in the market, software developing and hardware improvements

Fig. A.10 Prototype of a computer system based on the modified Neumann architecture

are needed to make the system not only prevent intruder from getting information but also monitor the system security and capture and report any security-related events.

A.8   Summary

In this chapter, we discussed a design of a secure computer architecture. A prototype computer was built based on this architecture. Experiments show that it meets the design goals to guarantee the data security even by turning off the Windows firewall and removing and all security updates. The prototype was tested under several intrusion and exploitation tools. There has been no incident to indicate that it had been compromised by hacking into the system using tools such as Key Loggers, Spyware, Spyware cookies, Trojans, Worms, etc. The system was also tested by inviting some senior security personnel (white-hat attackers) to "attack" the system remotely. The results proved that the proposed secure architecture machine can enhance the computer security and therefore can be easily adopted to modern personal computers.

Further research will improve the architecture and find the possibility to extend its scope from personal computers to server systems. In order to make the system to be widely used in the market, the research team is developing software that can make the system not only prevent intruder from getting information but also monitor the system security and capture and report any security-related events.

Exercises

A.1 What are the similarities and differences between the study of computer security, information security, data security, and network security?

A.2 What are the eight domains for information system security defined by CISSP?

A.3 An attacker breaks into an information system by modifying data through the web application. What type of the attack is?

A.4 Modern computers have many buses such as ISA, EISA, PCI, AGP, USB, SATA, SCSI, etc. Why we still consider these computers as single-bus computers?

A.5 Many people consider network interface is essentially an I/O device. Explain why to separate the network interface from the general I/O devices is better in studying computer security?

A.6 The dual-bus computer discussed in this chapter use two (main) buses. What will happen if those two buses want to access the CPU or memory at the same time? How to prevent it from happening?

A.7   A dual-port memory is defined such that two processors can be attached to the memory together. A control bit is used to enable one processor to access the memory while disabling the other. Draw a diagram of such implementation.

References

Bishop, M. (2019). *Computer security: Art and science* (2nd ed.). Boston: Addison-Wesley.

Daswani, N., Kern, C., & Kesavan, A. (2007). *Foundations of security: What every programmer needs to know*. New York: Springer.

Gregg, M. (2019). *CISSP exam cram* (4th ed.). San Antonio: Pearson.

HP-Compaq Sets Platform Security (2002). *eWeek*.

ISC^2 (2010). *Fundamentals of information systems security*. Bolingbrook: Jones and Bartlett Learning LLC.

Largman, K., More, A. B., & Blair, J. (2004). *Computer system architecture and method providing operating-system independent virus-, hacker-, and cyber-terror-immune processing environments*. U.S. patent: US 2004-0236874, USPTO.

Merkow, M., & Breithaupt, J. (2005). *Information security: Principles and practices*. San Antonio: Pearson Education Inc.

Smith, S. W., & Weingart, S. (1999). Building a high-performance, programmable secure coprocessor. *Computer Networks, 31*, 831–860.

Suh, G. E., O'Donnell, C. W., Sachdev, I., & Devadas, S. (2005). Design and implementation of the AEGIS single-chip secure processor using physical random functions. In *Proceedings of 32nd International Symposium on Computer Architecture (ISCA'05)* (pp. 25–36).

von Neumann, J. (1945). *First Draft of a Report on the EDVAC*. Philadelphia: Moore School of Electrical Engineering, University of Pennsylvania.

Wang, S. (2005). *Intrusion-free secure computer architecture for information and data security*. U.S. patent application.

Wang S., & Ledley, R. S. (2006). Connputer-a framework of intrusion-free secure computer architecture. In *WORLDCOMP International Conference on Security and Management (SAM'06)*.